THE SILENT LANGUAGE OF
PSYCHOTHERAPY

Modern Applications in Psychology

under the editorship of

Joseph D. Matarazzo

UNIVERSITY OF OREGON MEDICAL SCHOOL

Judson S. Brown

UNIVERSITY OF IOWA

ERNST G. BEIER

University of Utah

THE SILENT LANGUAGE OF

PSYCHOTHERAPY

Social Reinforcement of Unconscious Processes

ALDINE PUBLISHING COMPANY

Chicago

773300

First published 1966 by
Aldine Publishing Company
529 South Wabash Avenue
Chicago, Illinois 60605

Designed by Bernard Schleifer

Library of Congress Catalog Card Number 66-15196
ISBN 202-26009-7 cloth; 202-26061-5 paper
Printed in the United States of America

Second Printing, 1968
First Paperbound Edition, 1971
Fourth Printing, 1973
Fifth Printing, 1974
Sixth printing, 1976
Seventh printing, 1977 ·

To Mrs. Howard Mumford Jones

Ernst G. Beier, formerly Head of the Mental Hygiene Clinic in Syracuse, New York, is presently Professor of Psychology and Director of the Clinical Training Program at the University of Utah, Assistant Clinical Professor of Psychiatry in the college of Medicine at that University, and Consultant to the Veterans' Administration. Author of many articles on psychotherapy and clinical psychology, and with eighteen years of experience as teacher and practitioner, Dr. Beier is an eminent and respected authority in this field.

ACKNOWLEDGMENT

The friendly cooperation of many colleagues, students, and friends is gratefully acknowledged. Miss Barbara Brown has been of much help with the typing of the many drafts. Particularly Mr. Don Miller has most generously given of his time. Dr. Mark Graeber, Mrs. Marilyn Buckwalter, Dr. Russell Neale, Dr. Robert Card, Dr. George Larimer, Dr. Martin Capell, Dr. Paul Porter and my wife, Dr. Frances Beier, have greatly contributed with their stimulating discussions and their aid with the manuscript.

RECENTLY *a newspaper reported that a young man went into a grocery store, pulled out a gun and told the elderly woman who was at the cashier's desk to "stick 'em up and hand over the money." The woman smiled at the bandit and said kindly, "How much do you really need, son?" The man dropped his gun and said meekly, "Two dollars, ma'am." He took the two dollars handed him, and left in a hurry. What went wrong? Why did the woman's response change the bandit's intentions? The bandit's original purpose certainly was frustrated—what happened? How did this occur?*

TALLEYRAND *once remarked that man used words to conceal and disguise inner thoughts and feelings. It appears that in the above exchange certain attitudes and expectations were indeed concealed behind the words, but that the words themselves were not the only relevant information exchanged. One might suggest that the two individuals not only exchanged some obvious, manifest information, but at the same time affected each other with cues, which one may call covert or hidden. One way to approach the problem of understanding the change of behavior in the young man would be to analyze the information he obtained from the covert or hidden cues of the woman's response. This book will be devoted to just such an analysis of the communication process. It is hoped that the student of psychotherapy will obtain both theoretical and practical information that will help him to effect behavioral change within the psychotherapeutic process.*

CONTENTS

FIVE/THE COMMUNICATION PROCESS IN PSYCHOTHERAPY

The Social Reinforcement
of Unconscious Processes

PART ONE

CHAPTER I

INTRODUCTION AND OVERVIEW

The Therapeutic Model

MANY theorists have attempted to explain how therapeutic changes occur. Often these investigators talk about "therapeutic gains" or "therapeutic changes" as if these occurred only in the unique setting of the therapeutic hour. But there is evidence that therapeutic changes occur in many places, and among animals as well as humans. A theory that attempts to explain therapeutic changes should be based on principles that apply not only to those changes occurring during the hour, but also to those observed in the educational process, in interpersonal relations, and in the social milieu, as well as with animals. It would be desirable to discover principles broad enough to provide a deeper understanding of therapeutic change in this wide variety of situations.

Actually, it is not so difficult to reach this goal as it may seem. Experienced therapists appear to be very similar in what they are doing, although they may disagree as to why they do it. In spite of the arguments about theoretical formulations, it can be observed that during an hour with a patient many psychotherapists may not follow their own theories too well. There probably is some relevance in a comparison of psychotherapy with a concept formation test: the subject gives the correct answers but is unable to state why he did so or what principles he followed in making his choices. The therapist, too, may help a patient but he is often uncertain as to "why" and "how." It is very likely that the effective principles in therapeutic work rest on processes that are more general than the specific principles advanced by different schools.

Psychotherapy is essentially a situation where two or more individuals behave together and affect each other through a mutual exchange of information. The contact hopefully results in a situation

4 : The Social Reinforcement of Unconscious Processes

where the patient can give up old behavior patterns and assume new and more appropriate ones which lead to greater happiness and more effective functioning. In explanation of this process much confusion has resulted from the fact that "change" and "change for the better" have been treated as one. It is probable that more accurate explanations can be advanced when the processes of change of behavior and those of mental health goals (adjustment) are separated. Ideally, one should be able to describe separately both *how* changes of behavior take place, and *under what circumstances* these changes are directed toward better adjustment.

In the following an attempt will be made to analyze *what sort of information* effects change in a patient's attitude and behavior, with the focus on the *process of change,* rather than on possible goals of such change.

Among humans the exchange of information involved in the therapeutic hour is based largely on verbal cues. It is the fashion to think of verbal behavior as essential in the therapeutic process, but the chances are that its role is not quite so significant. A general theory, particularly one ambitious enough to include unconscious processes, must explain changes where other sources of information are utilized. The necessity for other, broader sources of information requires observation of both verbal and nonverbal behaviors. Thus, a person is seen as providing information by merely behaving; whether or not he verbalizes is not an essential feature of exchange.

It is believed that if reinforcement theory can be integrated in a meaningful way into a behavior therapy (Grossberg, 1964), one must consider the individual's state of awareness. We do know that humans can countermand conditioning efforts at will (at least sufficiently to give conflicting results), if they are aware of such efforts and if they desire to do so. To consider psychotherapeutic efforts as one form of reinforcing behavior is likely to be a stale effort if one does not consider the patient's state of awareness.

Certain information that is conveyed by the individual's behavior, then, is of special interest to a general theory of psychotherapeutic change; and that is the information which is not under the direct conscious control of the individual. This covert information, given without awareness, has definite consequences for both the sender and respondent. Most messages, next to their manifest meaning, also convey information which is not easily recognized: ambiguous information, which serves primarily to create an emotional climate in the respondent. These two categories, *manifest* and *covert informa-*

tion, and how they are used to effect a given respondent, form the basis for the model of psychotherapy contained in this book.

The effort, then, is to look at communication processes and study each message and its response. The aim, broadly speaking, is a marriage between Skinner and Freud, an attempt to discover reinforcement principles that are sophisticated enough to take account of unaware states and human complexities.

Toward a More Sophisticated Reinforcement Model

That reinforcement, i.e., repeated reward (or punishment) of a desired behavior, provides behavior changes is a widely accepted theorem. Psychologists differ as to the reasons why reinforcement should work, particularly with regard to the quality of the reward (or punishment) which is most effective and the scheduling program which is most meaningful. In particular, Skinner's model of a scheduled learning has been widely used, both in rigorous research efforts as well as in somewhat hasty applications to clinical practice. A schizophrenic patient who talked very little was trained to talk more by reward of chewing gum for talking (Isaacs et al., 1960); a decerebrate individual was trained to raise his arm when hungry (Fuller, 1949); homosexual patients were supposedly trained to respond favorably to women through the influence of drugs (Barker, 1965; Feldman and MacCulloch, 1964); children were trained at a very early age to learn how to typewrite or master languages (Haas, 1964); and a whole industry (teaching machines) (Schramm, 1964) came into existence utilizing these ideas of programming instruction through scheduled reinforcement. In fact, we are familiar with some five families in the United States who have adopted scheduled reinforcement methods in the raising of their children. Even very young children were monetarily rewarded for behaviors the parents desired, while the children had to pay for those parental behaviors they wanted. The justification for using such direct schedules in the home has been that "as parents we reinforce anyway, so we may as well do it in a planned scheduled way."

While it is too early to evaluate the application of scheduled reinforcement in clinical settings, the general criticism of clinicians is that these direct applications of reinforcement oversimplify human behavior and do not take into account the complexity of stimuli to which humans are exposed. For example, if parents reward a child's getting up on time with a monetary reward, the child is learning not only that "it pays" to get up early, but also that this selected item of behavior is significant to the parents and that he can make his parents anxious (or raise the pay?) by failing to comply. In one family the child had to pay for his meals. He was supposed to learn that he must give in order to receive. But what if the mother cooked the meal and the child did not wish to pay? If the mother is "unhappy" or "concerned," will the trade have to be reversed so that the mother now has to pay the child? How often are the feelings of parents unscheduled reinforcements? Even if desirable, would it be possible to schedule such "feeling tone" reinforcement (parents being angry or happy) in view of the observation that people are not always ready to admit to a given feeling even though their behavior seems to indicate to others that it nevertheless exists?

It is particularly this last observation—that awareness plays a role in the reinforcement schedule—that makes a marriage of Freud and Skinner desirable when reinforcement principles are applied to human behavior. Conditioning procedures in humans seem to proceed most effectively with naive subjects, i.e., individuals who are not aware of the intent of the method and cannot counteract it, though this controversy is far from being resolved. Work on nonverbal operant conditioning shows not only that individuals properly reinforced with "Hm, hm" (Greenspoon, 1962) will produce more of the reinforced words (such as nouns); but also that if the length of time of the therapist's comments is controlled, the average length of time of the patient's response becomes predictable (Matarazzo *et al.*, 1965). But what would happen if the experimenter did not use a "naive" subject but one who was aware of the experimental procedure? It can be anticipated that under such circumstances certain individuals would comply while others would "not play along." Again, awareness plays a role in the effect of the methods.

Reinforcement
in Behavior Therapy

It would be most unreasonable to assume that people have learned to create displeasure for themselves, unless this "displeasure" which they often so actively complain about (collecting injustices) also has a rewarding function. This rewarding function is likely to be unconscious, i.e., it stands in the service of solving some problem; it serves the psychological economy of the patient by giving him some meaning and sense of existence. The person who attempts suicide may say that he did so because he felt cornered by the many demands made on him, but we would also assume that he has learned to obtain reward from the fact that he can imagine guilt over rejection or lack of love in another significant person. The attempt of suicide in these terms becomes a communication, a cry for help, which is the basic assumption around which suicide prevention centers are organized.

A person may have learned that threatening others with his own suffering can be a meaningful behavior. A suicidal patient, for example, said in his second interview: "I was not happy here last week. You did not talk enough; you did not talk about my deeper problem. I felt quite without hope when I left," and the therapist responded, "Why don't you tell me about your mother. Did you say you had a dream about her?" What are the subtle reinforcement patterns in this exchange? One hypothesis about the patient would be that with this message he is "setting up" the therapist to give a specific response, to talk about "deep things." One may reason that this patient has been very successful in this subtle blackmail behavior, forcing another person to do his bidding by threatening "hopelessness." Reinforced by the response of the therapist who begins to talk about "deep things" (dream about mother), the patient is actually trained to use such eminently successful behavior again. Had the therapist responded here with "Hm, hm," simply notifying the patient that he was listening, he would not have reinforced the response expectations of the patient. We note that the therapist reinforced them without much awareness, as would many of the people around the patient, having also been "set up" by the patient for the desired response. The therapist, however, failed the patient in this response precisely because he was caught in the social role.

The patient does not know what he is doing in this message. If asked, he may say that he is complaining about the therapist's effectiveness. He would hardly be aware that he is trying to blackmail the respondent, using his own unhappiness (and a threat) as levers. He is unaware that he selects out of his universe of experiences those which lend themselves toward this particular gratification, and he would be likely to reject such hypotheses if they were stated to him. Nevertheless, he has learned to create for himself these situations in which he can complain but also get some sense of reward, a sense of existence, by controlling the other person. If one learns to disregard the manifest meaning of the message but begins to understand the unconscious expectations inherent in it, one will have the tool to help the patient unlearn previous associations and possibly be open for new ones. It will be our task to show how reinforcement principles and unconscious motivation are related in the maintenance of maladjusted behavior, and how the analysis of communication can modify behavior.

In psychotherapy, there are the historical-oriented schools which claim that therapeutic gain comes through re-experiencing of one's traumatic moments of the past; the insight schools which attempt to produce an awareness of inner dynamics; and the relationship schools which, through love, warmth and understanding, attempt to re-create a sense of human closeness. Many of their efforts have contributed greatly to a clearer understanding of the psychotherapeutic process, but psychotherapists have chosen one school over another more often because of their temperament than because of the actual consequences of a given model on their behavior in the hour.

Here we shall present a communication model of behavior therapy, precisely because it is the most general model. We assume that the psychotherapeutic intervention makes the patient uncertain of his automatic behavior and gives him freedom to explore the unknown. The patient can permit himself to experience feelings and think thoughts which he previously had shut out from his life.

To engage in experiences long shunned may be both a painful and hopeful endeavor because the patient has to leave his previous "libidinal position" for a promise of new gratification. To make the patient uncertain about his present behavior is not enough. Uncertainty can end up in psychological deficit. Therefore the practice of psychotherapy has, perhaps empirically, found a way of providing "beneficial" uncertainty. The "beneficial" aspect comes from essentially two sources: the sense of concern which the therapist communicates to the patient, and the relative freedom from judgmental processes.[1] These two features are of the essence. The therapist's concern communicates an existential meaning to the patient: "Another person is with me, he is listening to me even though my usual social skills are of little value here. I am meaningful to him." Freedom from being judged by the therapist implies an equally important meaning to the patient: "I am responsible here—I need not blame the environment for my misfortune. Another person can tolerate me; I

1. From the patient's point of view it is very undesirable that psychotherapy ordinarily last a long time. He wishes he could change and be happier as soon as possible. But from the point of view of society, the very fact that "personality" is a relatively stable variable has many desirable consequences. Imagine a society where change could be brought about overnight! We would not only have a very unstable society, but also be subject to the whims and control of manipulators. Our increasing understanding of the processes of change may indeed involve such dangers.

need not give all my energy to defending myself." The presence of concern and the freedom from having judgment imposed permit the patient to interpret the responses to his messages as beneficial rather than threatening. The messages of the therapist are, in a true sense, persuasion; they are designed to give the patient both hope and courage to dare into the unknown.

Ethical Considerations

When psychotherapy is simply seen as a facilitating device whereby the patient discovers his own values, ethical considerations have to deal only with the occasional violation when a given therapist inculcates a patient with values of his own. When, however, the therapeutic process is seen as one in which value judgments are transmitted, though often without awareness, we are facing a different problem altogether.

Although the therapist may not consciously wish to direct the patient's behavior, he nevertheless instills his own value system through the subtle force of nonverbal communication. Furthermore, under a behavior therapy model a patient need not be a volunteer for therapy but can be affected just by the fact that he is present, and the ethical question of what values the therapist is transmitting, and to whom, becomes a very significant problem. It becomes important to know which choices a given therapist, through subtle or not-so-subtle information, reinforces in a given patient. It is quite possible that all reputable therapists reinforce specific choices in the patient (Rogers, 1960); and this would be an even more urgent reason to discover both the nature and processes of such value transmittal.

We have professed for a great many years that we are only playing the "midwife," as Socrates put it so curtly, and that the patient must help himself. Now that many of us recognize that we do more than that, we can no longer disregard the ethical questions involved. That the mental health professions represent a danger to a free society has been claimed for political purposes in some quarters. While such claims are based on a total (and often vicious) misunderstanding of the goals, methods, and purposes of these professions, we must try to spell out specifically limited conditions wherein we are justified for an "invasion of privacy of the individual," be it in psychodiagnosis or treatment processes.

CHAPTER II

THE ANATOMY OF A MESSAGE

The Persuasive Message

WE can distinguish two different types of messages, one persuasive and the other evoking. This differentiation helps us analyze the communication process in the therapeutic hour. First we will discuss the "Persuasive Message," the elements of which contain both contextual and nonverbal (paralinguistic) cues. In the persuasive message the sender codes his message in full *awareness* of what he is doing. The purpose of his message is to create in the respondent an emotional climate favorable to the sender's intent. For this purpose to be achieved properly, the respondent must not have any awareness of the sender's intent. He must be made to feel, not to think.

THE PERSUASIVE MESSAGE:

Sender	*Message*	*Respondent*
		choice made on basis
	contextual and	of emotional climate,
conscious coding →	nonverbal cues →	not awareness

The persuasive message can be illustrated with examples from advertising, though this is only one of its many uses. A sender wants to sell soap. In order to persuade the prospective buyer to purchase it, he tries to create a favorable emotional climate. He finds that he sells more soap by packaging it in yellow paper; this works only so long as he keeps his manipulation hidden. Once aware of the device, the respondent (the buyer) at least has a choice, and may use criteria other than package color to make up his mind.

We use this type of message frequently in daily exchange. It is surprisingly effective. A lover sends flowers to his beloved, a student slips the proverbial apple to the teacher—these are behaviors designed to gain the ends of the sender by arousing favorable emotional climates in the respondent.

The goal of a persuasive message can be stated as follows: to impose a condition on the respondent under which he behaves as the sender wishes without becoming aware that he has been led to that particular choice with a certain message. The respondent should be persuaded to (1) make the choice desired by the sender and (2) believe that he made the choice on his own judgment. Once a sender is successful in achieving these two ends he is a "persuader." With the persuasive message the sender increases the probability of the occurrence of a specific response by constricting the respondent's response activity. The persuader literally does not permit the respondent to use his head.

Persuasion is also used for the purpose of producing an emotional response where no particular action (such as purchasing soap) is required. An existentialist type of play such as *Waiting for Godot,* by Samuel Beckett (1954), is made up of persuasive messages. The overt component of the message does not make any sense—the plot is without meaning—but the covert component achieves a strong emotional impact. These covert cues cause the respondent to emote and, just as dream symbols make him feel uncomfortable, he does not quite know why he feels the way he does. It is not clear whether or not the author wrote with an awareness of what emotions he wanted to elicit, but his highly skillful use of covert cues to elicit an emotional response in the absence of an identifiable source is worth mentioning. When the play was banned in Spain, the author could say "what silliness," as he had not commited himself to any purpose.

The persuasive message is often used as a "testing" device, precisely because it evokes responses without accountability. A boy "accidentally" touches the hand of his beloved and fearfully waits for the desired response—always ready to defend the "accidental" nature of his forwardness if challenged.

The persuasive message is also put to use in the educational process: the young child is manipulated into beliefs and attitudes by planned covert cues, which he will prehend rather than comprehend (Sullivan, 1953). Family and religious practices often include such planned covert communication. The little boy asks a question about sex and his mother changes the topic. The child is affected by the response. He may be "reinforced" in feeling that sex is something to avoid, without ever knowing why he feels this way. Or the child hits his sister and the parent diverts him by offering to play with him. The child here is persuaded to avoid aggression by the new emotional climate set up for him. Repeated persuasive messages will create certain value systems in the child without his ever becoming aware of where he learned these values. This is an emotional part of the process of *introjection*.

In the therapeutic process, too, the therapist uses persuasion to help the patient discover new choices. The "Hm, hm" and many other responses act as powerful tools to emphasize and reinforce certain values. Psychotherapy can be seen as an act of counterpersuasion. (See Chapter XVI, "The Ethical Problems of Control of Behavior.")

The Evoking Message

An important variation of a persuasive message is the "Evoking Message." The difference occurs in the state of awareness of the sender. The sender of the persuasive message knows what he wants from the respondent and gets it through the use of subtle cues which reduce the respondent's awareness that he has been "set up" or persuaded. The sender of the evoking message has no awareness of his wish to persuade. He codes information without awareness and consequently obtains responses for which he cannot account, even though he himself evoked them.

THE EVOKING MESSAGE:

Sender	Message	Respondent
unconscious coding →	contextual and nonverbal cues →	choice made on basis of emotional climate, not awareness

As an illustration of the evoking message we can consider an individual who thinks of himself as lonely and without any friends. In a careful analysis of his messages, we discover the coding of very subtle cues that are likely to create an emotional climate in the people he addresses, resulting in negative and angry feelings. The sender evokes this negative response but is nevertheless able to see himself as the victim of circumstances. As he was not aware that he coded this information, he does not have a feeling of responsibility for the response he obtained. Indeed, the evoking message seems to be the type of communication which maintains the patient's present state of adjustment. With this message he helps to create those responses in his environment which confirm his view of the world. Through the responses he elicits, he constantly obtains proof that the world is exactly the place he thinks it is!

One can see the therapeutic process as one in which the therapist refuses to reinforce the patient's present state of adjustment by refusing to make the response the patient forcefully evokes in him. The patient makes an ambiguous statement which in his experience has the effect of making the respondent feel uncomfortable. The therapist, however, responds with an asocial response (such as "Hm, hm") rather than confirming the patient's expectations; this gives the patient a sense of uncertainty—and the possibility for new choices. Historically, the therapist has learned to respond to the social expectations of the patient's message empirically, rather than through a theoretical stratagem. The most frequent responses found in psychotherapy (such as "Hm, hm," "Go on," etc.) are simple, asocial responses.[2]

The evoking message is probably one of the basic tools used by individuals to maintain their consistency of personality. With this message an individual can elicit responses without being aware that he is responsible for doing so. To a certain extent he can create his environment without feeling that he is accountable for the responses which come his way. If a given individual does not have overwhelming problems, we call the fact that he creates a peculiar, idiosyncratic environment for himself his "character" or his "eccentric" behavior. The person with emotional conflict, however, creates a world in which he typically feels victimized by others, in which he experiences great unhappiness, though he has little awareness that he is often the creator of this world.

The evoking message gives us clues to characteristic differences among people. Once we understand the kind of response an individual repeatedly evokes in his environment, we can gain a beginning understanding of his psychological dynamics. A businessman evokes fear in his employees by means of such cues as *setting, words,* and *gestures,* but he is surprised that he is not loved for all the good he does for them. He gives us some tentative information about the nature of his

2. Dr. Arnold Bernstein in New York reported to us that he placed conventional responses such as "Hm, hm" and "Go on" on a tape and had an experimental volunteer patient alone in a room turn a switch which activated a tape recorder, whenever she wanted the therapist to respond. She was given the understanding that the therapist would be sitting next door. After six hours the patient was asked to describe the therapist and she said that she thought of him as "most understanding, warm, and considerate."

conflict. We could speculate that while he thinks of himself as a person who is sacrificing himself for his men, he acts as if he should be feared by them. Message by message he elicits a different emotion than he thinks he elicits, reinforcing in himself a feeling that his "true nature" is understood.

Another example is the dentist who gives his patients the message that he is unconcerned about their pain by many subtle hints at their being "sissies." He may not be aware of this behavior and is surprised that his practice does not flourish. Message by message, perhaps with the *conscious* intent of helping them, he creates an emotional climate in which he makes the patients ashamed of their expressions. He is surprised to learn that instead of returning, the patients reject him. Observing that he does not learn from the feedback (rejection), we can speculate that perhaps this dentist has a conflict about being in the profession of dentistry.

This is not to say that all environmental responses are elicited, but a great many are, and when one is concerned with the prediction of behavior, a careful analysis of the evoking message is often accurate and helpful in prediction. People live in a fairly consistent world because, to some extent, it is a world of their own creation even if they do not consciously want it that way. The responses people obtain through the use of the evoking message are likely to be rewarding and meaningful to them within their total psychological economy; consciously, though, they may reject such an implication. They may not always want to pay the price of their unaware "manipulation," but they nevertheless use all their skill to maintain their present state of adjustment.

Reason and Emotion

The *manifest* cues of the message contain information which the sender consciously wants to give and for which he assumes responsibility. "Give me this book" manifestly means that the sender wants the respondent to act in a certain way and that he is willing to be held accountable for his manifestly expressed wish. With the *covert* component, on the other hand, the sender may convey information for which he does not want to be held accountable. Though his effort is not always successful, the covert cues of a message are coded to leave the respondent without recognition of the covert message but still subject to an emotional impact. We shall introduce another illustration of the relationship between reason and emotion. An unkempt juvenile says to a stranded motorist: "Can I give you a hand with your car?" The overt cues of the message are clear; the conventional meaning of the statement is one of solicitude. But the boy's unkempt appearance and perhaps his intonation keep the motorist in doubt; the emotional impact may be "danger," and so he responds, "No, thanks." The answer may perhaps be quite against his immediate interests and given with only the general rationale: "I wonder what this boy really wants from me."

When one considers the sender of the message, the unkempt juvenile, it appears that there is some dissonance between the overt and covert cues he conveys to the motorist. Disregarding whether the boy is in fact honest or dishonest, it can be inferred that he wants to be recognized for offering help (overt) and most likely does not wish to be recognized as a doubtful or criminal character. Even if he had dishonorable intentions, it would not be plausible to assume that he wants to alert the motorist to that fact. Assuming for the moment that the boy has again and again had the experience of creating doubts in respondents and having his friendly gestures of help rejected, it is quite likely that he has some conflict about his identity. He maintains behaviors which permit him to hold on to the opinion that he is a helpful person, but that the *world* is hostile and rejects even his worthwhile efforts.

One could speculate that the boy's psychological economy requires the maintenance of his discordant messages: he elicits and obtains the type of response that he has found to be an acceptable compromise between various needs. The conflict seems to be his need to see himself as both helpful (overt) and threatening (covert) at the same time; it is expressed in such a manner that the response (rejection) is typically elicited and serves to reinforce not only his use of such a message, but also his feeling that he lives in a world filled with injustice. After all, his good efforts are not recognized or rewarded. It is quite possible that this sense of living in an unjust world also gives this boy an alibi, a sense of freedom to engage in retaliatory acts. With the discordant message he can maintain his psychological adjustment.

To generalize, through the covert component of his message a person may code his information in a way that impedes another person's recognition of certain of his needs. Yet though he does not want to be recognized or held accountable for expressing these needs, he does want to have an emotional impact on other people, an impact that elicits a specific constricted response from them.

A person may want to impede recognition of certain of his needs because he wants to avoid having a respondent bring judgmental processes to bear on the message. The person who is trying to avoid being fully understood in what he says is possibly afraid that if he were understood he would then obtain responses which do not fit his self-image, responses with which he feels he cannot cope.

On the other hand, to use a message for an emotional impact allows a person to obtain a response which is at least partially determined by the emotional climate he has created, with which he can cope precisely because he has succeeded in impeding recognition of *some* of his wishes. There seems to be a negative relationship between "recognition" and "emotional impact." Information that creates an emotional impact seems to constrict recognition in the respondent. This suggests that the stronger the emotions in which a person becomes engaged, the less active are his cognitive processes. A respondent facing direct aggression such as a fist in his face is likely to react to the source of the aggression and then fight back, talk, run, or whatever else he does as his typical reaction to aggression. It is unlikely, however, that he has the time or the inclination to try to understand and recognize the full context and meaning of the aggressive act. It is also unlikely that he can use his best judgment to fight it. (Japanese soldiers learn how to yell during an attack for this reason.)

The emotional impact of a strong gesture is likely to deprive one of the use of cognitive processes: the emotion occurs at the cost of one's judgmental processes. The loss of adeqate judgment becomes even more obvious in a case of covert aggression in which the respondent has no awareness that he has been aggressed against. He cannot find the object and merely feels discomfort. Since he cannot identify the source of his discomfort, he is thus deprived of an object he can fight. The use of covert cues has created an emotional impact which effects and controls the respondent's behavior precisely because his recognition, his discriminative cognitive process, and his judgmental powers are constricted. We may say that, for purposes of communication, the modes "to know" and "to feel" are separate and, to some extent, mutually exclusive states. That is not to say that these two modes of behaving *must* be mutually exclusive, but merely that one can be used to the exclusion of the other. It is our suspicion that a persuasive message that uses covert cues to create an emotional impact in a given respondent is probably more effective in reaching this goal than a message that tries to persuade by the power of reason. The use of emotions constricts the choices. The use of reason, however, gives the individual freedom to make his own choice and so is not likely to have an equal degree of persuasive power.

Some field researchers would support this conjecture. Some social scientists (Watson, 1947) placed some "Jewish-looking" persons in such a manner that they blocked the sidewalk. Pedestrians who had to detour into the street to pass by made various comments about the Jews. The social scientists, camouflaged as pedestrians, engaged these people in conversation and used, among others, rational and irrational methods of approach. To give an example of the rational comments, people who made a negative comment were approached with: "How do you know they are Jews?" or "You should not call all Jews names when you find some annoying." One of the emotional comments was: "This is a very un-American thing to say." The report stated that the emotional-impact statements created more uncertainty in the respondents than statements of any other category. It appears that emotional-impact statements constrict the respondent's response activity and are persuasive, while rational-impact statements are more easily disregarded.

A message designed to arouse an emotional impact must be based on redundancies, i.e., cues which have been overlearned by the respondent. These cues have to convey emotional meaning without benefit of thought. The words or gestures used for such a purpose must, in addition, be transmitted in the right setting and with some concern for timing.

To call a person "a Communist" at a Communist gathering is ordinarily not threatening and may even have a favorable meaning ("comrade"). However, it can be threatening when it is done in a different setting, such as at a meeting of the House Committee on Un-American Activities. A redundant cue designed to create an emotional experience in the respondent must be overlearned before it is effective. It will often include three different sources of information in its coding: words, adjuvant cues (tone of voice, choice of words, sequence of thoughts, pauses, timing), and setting cues. The stick-up man, in order to arouse the designed response in the bank teller, may need a determined voice, the supporting gesture of a threatening pistol, and the ability to convey the information that he is serious about his task. A father, in order to impress others with his authority, may raise his voice and, as Machotka (1966) pointed out, he may also raise his head!

These subtle cues are important elements of the message, often determining the nature of the response in a more significant way than the manifest component of the message. By shifting the emphasis from one component to the other, a person can choose to what extent he wants to constrict the response activity of the respondent or to what extent he wants to allow judgmental processes to enter in the choice of a response. The above distinctions are made to remind us of the great lability in human communication and the large number of possible connotations a person can code into his message.

We have been looking at the message from one particular viewpoint, its consequences on the respondent. We distinguished between the manifest or lexical component and the covert or hidden component. We found that with a different emphasis on each of the message components, a sender can determine the degree of restriction he wishes to impose on the response activity of a given respondent. This task is accomplished through the creation of an emotional climate (engagement) in the respondent which produces responses favorable to some of the wishes of the sender. We distinguished the persuasive message, in which manipulation is conscious, from the evoking message, in which the manipulation occurs without awareness. We believe that in the evoking message we have found the means by which a person is able to maintain consistency of behavior as well as his state of maladjustment. We believe that our analysis of the message in terms of the consequences on the respondent will help us in the understanding of the psychotherapeutic process.

CHAPTER III

LEARNING TO USE COVERT CUES

Learning to Select Responses from His Environment

THE rather subtle use an adult makes of covert cues can be appreciated more completely when one understands how he has learned these skills. How is a child exposed to this type of information and how does he learn to utilize it? It is likely that the child learns to respond to the covert cues of the significant adults around him very early in life (Sullivan, 1953). In fact, even prenatal stress appears to be transmitted (Abramson et al., 1961). In his first few weeks of life the child probably has only generalized feelings of comfort or discomfort, and his communications are so highly personalized that they are not easily understood and often appear unrelated to his needs In fact, some investigators hold to the view that the child simply makes movements, cries, and behaves in certain ways; only later does he learn the meaning of his behaviors from the reaction of the people around him. A child may cry without any observable or measurable motivation; they believe his early cry may be nothing but a survival mechanism, i.e., inflating the lungs to obtain air. We have some doubts about such claims and cannot believe that the child identifies crying with discomfort only because people react to him as if he were uncomfortable.

Rank (1929) believed that the newborn infant has an instinctual need to maintain the feeling of omnipotence he experienced in the womb. According to this belief, the birth cry is fundamentally a meaningful behavior expressing a feeling of woe. Freud went along with Rank in thinking that this expression of woe was specific, signifying a wish to return to the womb.

It is certainly not clear whether the infant actually has organized his needs and behaviors sufficiently so that his needs are related to and can be inferred from his earliest behavior. It is widely accepted, however, that the developing child constantly learns to replace personalized behaviors with some which have interpersonal significance (Snygg and Combs, 1949).

At the very early stages of development, mothers—if not scientists —seem nevertheless to distinguish between two communications. A baby's crying is typically interpreted as a reflection of discomfort. Gurgling, furtive attempts to smile, etc., are interpreted as reflections of a state of comfort. These states of feeling are not only communicated, but mothers typically choose different responses to react to them. To comfort a crying child, the different behaviors the mother might try are holding the child, feeding him, or rocking him. Very soon, however, his needs seem to become more highly differentiated. Feeding no longer satisfies the child when he is cold; rocking no longer serves when he is hungry. Along with the differentiation of needs, we assume that the child experiences the necessity to communicate, to differentiate pertinent messages from each other. He must now invent ways of coding information. Such early inventions of the child may be reflected in almost imperceptible changes in those previous behaviors which the child had identified as eliciting responses, i.e., communication behaviors. For example, he would now cry differently for each different want. The first thing the child seems to learn is a personal idiosyncratic language which only his mother can understand. As the need arises to communicate ever more differentiated detail, a search for more highly differentiated signs becomes necessary and the signs become less and less personalized: they are reinforced only when they are correctly understood by a respondent. The search for a language begins.

The child learns very early that he can reliably expect a certain response when he gives certain information. He progressively learns to distinguish successful from unsuccessful messages by the reinforcement he obtains for various attempts to communicate. Eventually a child learns to associate certain of his messages with specific responses. Moreover, through differences in the "percentage" of partial reinforcements he obtains for his messages, he learns that his messages differ in the *degree of probability* with which he can expect a specific response.

The need to create order and security in life by being accurate in predicting and controlling events has been elaborated by Kelly (1955). By learning how to predict responses accurately, the child learns to control or even "select" his own environment. He uses cer·

tain information with which to elicit responses; he can now seek out certain responses and avoid others. He learns the use of language to create a reasonably consistent environment for himself. Language becomes his most prized possession because it has become his tool for ordering his world.

The use of this tool is enhanced when the child learns that in those instances where he cannot determine the behavior of others by direct overt messages, he can sometimes succeed in having an impact on a significant adult if he uses indirect subtle means of communication. When he begins to realize that nonverbal behaviors such as "being sick," "having an accident," or "sulking" have emotional impact on the adult, he is discovering that subtle cues will often get him a response when overt cues will not. The advantages of the covert cue must become obvious to the child at an early age. The power lies in his discovery that he can now determine the certainty with which a desired response will occur. He can use the arousal of an emotional climate to constrict the respondent, and with the help of this tool he can frequently elicit the responses he wants. He has learned that when people are emotionally engaged they have fewer choices than when they are not. In other words, he has learned the game of manipulation.

For example, he learns that, instead of asking for candy, he can get it more easily by using emotional impact behavior such as "flattery" or by arousing guilt feelings. He can now become a self-fulfilling prophet by predicting the occurrence of certain events and indeed doing his share to ensure their occurrence. He can do all this without taking the responsibility for seeming to have desired the behaviors in the first place. When the child eventually learns that even just *desiring* certain things will bring him rejection and pain, this discovery will stand him in good stead. He is now in the possession of a tool which is very useful with behaviors that he feels he needs to hide.

Vulnerability

While very severe trauma may effect a child's interest in his total environment, less destructive frustrations are likely to create the wish to be extra cautious in the area in which the child experienced his hurt. He may not only avoid the area, but he may even wish to deny having any desires within it. For example, a child very much wanted his father to teach him to ride a bicycle. Though he had asked him many times, his father always seemed to be too busy to teach him. This child had emotionally invested in the thought that if his father were to teach him to ride a bicycle, this desired behavior would prove that his father loved him. Therefore, he insisted that he wanted his *father* to teach him to ride the bicycle, and no one else would serve the purpose. His wish was not fulfilled, and one day the child declared that he no longer wanted to learn to ride the bicycle. He no longer asked his father to help him and he avoided showing any desire to learn the task. Apparently, in terms of our conjectures, he had come to the conclusion that his father did not love him and there was no sense in asking for love.

But the observer noted that the boy was now "talking bicycle" all the time, particularly when his father was near, and even placed himself near bicycles when they were in the yard. The father, who was surprised by the boy's sudden let-up in pressure, actually asked the boy if he still wanted to learn to ride the bicycle. The boy answered "No." There was an apparent discordance in the way he declared that he did not care for bicycles and the way he acted around them and talked about them. This discordance or ambivalence was the boy's way of finding a compromise between his wish to avoid the unpleasant area (father's rejection) and his wish, his hope, to still succeed (Father will love me yet!). His compromise involved subtle ambiguous cues ("talking bicycle" and being around bicycles) designed to tell his father that he was in fact still interested in learning to ride the bicycle, or, more precisely, in obtaining a show of love. While his verbal declaration that he was no longer interested could be seen as a way to discourage his father from teaching him, it was actually a test, a demand for his father to take the initiative and convince the boy that he should learn to ride the bicycle. The rejected lover always seems to need this extra effort in order to be convinced; ordinary effort is no longer sufficient. This is probably due to the rejected lover's awareness that he is forcing a response; he wants to make doubly sure that the desired response, when it finally occurs, comes from the other person's initiative, "from the heart."

And yet, while the boy did not take the chance of being recognized for the wish (to be loved by his father), which made him feel vulnerable, he did let his father know that he was hurting (his "bicycle talk"). He apparently was successful in arousing his father's guilt feelings—after all, he made father come to him. The child's advantage in using covert cues, therefore, is that he can safely communicate his hidden wish and obtain a response (guilt), which indicates at least some concern, rather than indifference. The manipulation is not fully successful (the child creates guilt and not love) but it is better than total indifference. The child successfully constricted the response activities of his father through the emotional climate he created for the purpose of achieving a specific response.

On Being Misunderstood

If control through covert cues were characteristic of only the maladjusted, mental testers could relax and patients could easily be distinguished from "normals." This, of course, is not so: *all* children learn the use of covert cues to control the behavior of others. The difference between patient and nonpatient does not lie in the fact that one uses covert information to affect others, but in the importance of the need to control others through subtle methods. The patient seems to be extremely concerned about his ability to control others and, in addition, seems exceedingly sensitive about his successes; the nonpatient seems to take defeat with greater ease. The patient seems to get a special pleasure from the use of covert messages to engage another person, both because he can control him to some extent and because he can expose his vulnerable wish safely—just enough to sense pleasure but not enough to experience retaliation. He gets his pleasure from being successfully misunderstood. The pleasure we speak of is neither a reportable pleasure in the sense that the child would say "I am happy," nor is it a feeling of comfort. It can best be described as an experience that one "exists," that one is involved in an important matter in life, that one is battling on an important battlefront and for high stakes. The game becomes even more important than the success: Even when the boy has his father at the point he wanted him all along, where his father offers assistance, this success does not stop the game. The stakes have become higher than just riding a bicycle—father must beg him now, prove his love beyond doubt.

Our reason for calling the boy's manipulations a gratifying behavior (provided he is successful in his task) is that we can observe that the father's response of guilt seems to reinforce the behavior. It seems to be a "reward" which is sought again and again. After all, to be misunderstood is quite a game; the boy goes through the challenging experience of approaching a risky task. There is an odd chance that his hidden wish (to be loved by his father) will be exposed—or even fulfilled. The father's guilt response promises such a possible reward.

Learning to Code
the Components of the Message

The child wants something which he feels would involve too great a risk to himself and acts in the best tradition of men to get around this unpleasant feeling. He denies any responsibility for expressing the wish, but at the same time gets what he can—and hopes for the best. To achieve this compromise he must discover ways to control his environment without his wish to control being recognized; he must subtly test his vulnerable wish without exposing it fully. He wants both to express the vulnerable wish (ever so lightly) and to protect against the trauma experience. Both sources become components for the resulting discordant message. Here we shall illustrate such an analysis in more detail with the boy's message: Talking bicycle talk near father after having declared that he is no longer interested in learning how to ride the bike. This behavior is observed *after* the boy made a great effort over a long period of time to involve his father in teaching him to ride the bike.

The covert component of the message is contained in the setting, which includes the history of the event: the fact that the boy was talking bicycle talk within hearing distance of his father. The meaning of these covert cues is ordinarily not easily recognized by the respondent because they are designed to arouse an emotional climate in him. In this case these cues aroused enough guilt in the father that he offered assistance to the child, *after* the boy had stopped asking for it. (We do not presume that this alone is enough evidence to speak of a guilt response, but use it merely as an illustration).

Trauma, pain, and the resulting feeling of vulnerability which the failure experience (rejection) had given the child determines the coding of the *manifest* component of the message: the bicycle talk. Both components of the discordant message must be coordinated in order to achieve a favorable compromise solution between expressing the wish and avoiding recognition and trauma. The act of coordination and the coding of the resulting message takes great skill, which most children will learn at an early age.

The resulting message is essentially one that gives ambiguous information: the covert component sets off an emotional response in the respondent ("I should have taught the boy"), while the manifest meaning does not support this emotional response (the father may ask: "Why is he talking about bicycles? He just mentioned that he is no longer interested"). There is a feeling of distortion between the private and public meanings of the message, as the boy wants to punish his father by arousing guilt—or to be loved, but does not want father to know it. To the father the meaning becomes ambiguous, as he does not know what is expected of him—he can't tell what the child "really" wants. He may feel uncomfortable but does not quite know why.

It can also be assumed that the more desperate the child's attempts to constrict the response of the significant person, the greater must be his feeling of vulnerability. For example, if he commits covert acts which have a high probability of constricting his father's feeling to intense anger, one could speculate that the child must be very concerned with obtaining *this* response and not another one. Also, the very intensity of his impact behavior tells us that the child desperately needs to prevent recognition of what he truly desires. His message is likely to be designed to camouflage deeply vulnerable feelings.

This line of thinking leads to a rather startling conclusion. If one assumes that covert information is used to control the behavior of others, it would follow that children who are exposed to much trauma or who have an unfriendly environment must be far more skillful in exercising this control than children who live in a friendly environment. In other words, children living in an environment that they feel is threatening will have a great need to control their environment through covert cues, in order to survive. They will use covert messages to control the dangerous adult, developing great skill in these efforts. Because they cannot leave the responses of others to chance without feeling insecure and threatened, they will strive to determine the outcome; by scanning, they will thoroughly familiarize themselves with the cues that affect other persons. So in this sense, the insecure and deeply threatened child develops far greater skills in the transmission of subtle and covert information than the more secure child.

This very important point has often been overlooked, primarily because a person with mental problems often appears so inefficient in the ways he handles his life. This appearance, however, is most deceptive and is primarily due to the fact that he is judged in terms of public values. By these judgments he obviously falls below the mean. But if judgments were made of how skillfully he achieves his set of private values, he would probably rank high both in skill and perseverance. Having highly effective skills and using them to gain his private values is, in fact, the characteristic of this maladjusted individual.

Learning to Maintain a State
of Adjustment

It can also be postulated that the more discord between the meanings of the covert cues and the manifest expression, the more vulnerable the child feels in the area of his message. With increasing discord it becomes increasingly difficult for the respondent to "read" the message, though the response activity is more constricted. The manifest behavior appears truly irrelevant to the covert cues, so that the respondent, in the face of extremely discordant ambiguity, becomes confused, reacting strongly within a limited range of responses. The schizophrenic child often creates such confusion. The respondent is at a loss to understand what the child wants and so often reacts strongly by turning away from the child, leaving him to his own devices and calling him "crazy." One might speculate that some children identify this predictable behavior as "rewarding."

Once the child has learned to use the discordant message, it will serve him in more than just the ordering of his environment. Using it to constrict the response activity of the respondent, the child not only reduces his feeling of vulnerability but also gains the feeling that there is still a possibility of his wishes being fulfilled. Since the child will be *unaware* of the fact that he is using this subtle tool in human communication, he will maintain with it his present state of adjustment. We shall offer an illustration:

A mother showed preference for the younger brother of Joan, a four-year old. Joan had had a rewarding relationship with her mother. When she wanted love she simply reached out and her mother was available. When she cried her mother showed concern and took care of her. When we first saw this case, the younger brother was getting all the love and attention. Joan had tried to tell her mother that she needed her but her mother did not notice. Joan cried but the mother still did not respond; to her, Joan was then an object of indifference. Mother was not only busy, but preferred the boy for reasons of her own. She justified her indifference to Joan's advances with the conviction that the boy needed her now—all of her.

Joan soon recognized that the wish itself—to be loved by mother —made her vulnerable. She could not dare to express it directly for fear of being repulsed and having the feeling she did not count. So she hid this vulnerability. She then had to find a way of coding her wish to be loved by her mother that would still not let her mother know that she wanted it. Joan had to learn to "deceive," to be misunderstood, but at the same time, to gain a little satisfaction from the way she was misunderstood.

The particular type of discordant message Joan would send was likely to be determined by earlier experiences, by cues which had predictable consequences. Because she was using such overlearned responses from the past, Joan's behavior may have appeared regressive. She began wetting her bed, having tantrums, behaving aggressively, alternating these behaviors with sulking and withdrawal. Previously, these behaviors had all been successful in obtaining her mother's involvement; they were again reinstated to elicit an emotional response, while at the same time preventing her from recognizing Joan's wish to be loved. Joan would accept the punishment for her "misbehavior" because she was bargaining for a sense of existence, for not being alone, for her share of her mother—regardless of the emotional quality of this share.

It may appear that Joan had actually given up her wish to be loved by her mother and had settled for an arousal of anger, but we do not believe this to be true. Joan's new message (she had at the time chosen to pull down the curtains) was successful in involving her mother. Although mother punished her for this act, she was closer to Joan than she had been before; she was no longer indifferent. Although many people see the feelings of love and hate as opposites, clinical observation indicates that the more significant opposites are indifference vs. love or hate. People seem to prefer being hated to being treated with indifference. Thus, Joan's discordant communication was rewarded with a sense of excitement. She felt gratified that she could force her mother to take cognizance of her existence. Through her devices, Joan could still feel that she was battling for her rights to her mother. When asked why she was such a bad girl she would say, probably honestly, "I don't know." She was unaware of her gambit and could not explain why she persevered in her "bad" behavior against all better judgment. The gratification from her compromise was probably not so rewarding as the full gratification of her original wish to be loved, but it was all the pleasure she could get at the moment. Joan's current adjustment was probably the best possible compromise she could achieve, though she did not find it fully graifying.

Psychotherapy capitalizes on the half-awareness that life could be more gratifying than it is. An individual has learned to give information to others which will leave his vulnerable wishes properly misunderstood and yet give him some semblance of satisfaction. He is motivated to maintain, through his compromise, his present state of adjustment. At the same time, he seems to wish to transcend it. The individual has learned to express his compromise in his discordant messages, but the results are not fully gratifying He holds on to what he has, but does so at the cost of not reaching out for new experience. While he clings to his compromise solutions, they also give him a feeling of constriction, of hopelessness, of missing out on life. He now seeks help, but he truly does not know where he "hurts." It is through the careful analysis of his discordant messages and their effect on others that his "hurt" can be discovered.

Therapeutic Reinforcement
of Unconscious Processes

PART TWO

CHAPTER IV

THE INFORMATION-GATHERING PROCESS IN PSYCHOTHERAPY

Where Does the Patient Hurt?

THE therapist wants to help the patient to be open for new choices in his life. In order to do so, he has to understand where the patient "hurts." This discovery is not as easy to accomplish as it sounds. There are many difficulties in obtaining an understanding of where the patient hurts. Most patients simply do not know. They may come to the hour with an idea, with a story, with the description of some symptoms. Some patients come armed with psychological jargon to describe their "hurts" in precise detail. However, listening to the manifest content of such descriptions gives the therapist very little information indeed. It tells the therapist where the patient thinks he hurts, and perhaps it represents the recurring behavior in which the patient is engaged.

A patient may state that he is depressed, that he suffers from a loss of motivation, that nothing seems worthwhile anymore. But is his depression his hurt? We assume here that depression is the state to which the patient has assigned the term "hurt," but that it is in fact a behavior being used to alleviate the hurt. The patient sees himself as depressed because this state permits him to act out some rewarding behaviors which he cannot accept in himself. The source of his hurt is most efficiently discovered not by listening to the description of the symptom but by analyzing the consequences of his depression. This analysis of the communicative aspects of his symptom will give us the information we need about what the symptom does for the patient.

The therapist should be trained to disengage from his usual social role. He must not be "caught" in the social, manifest meaning of the message. Instead, he must attempt to discover the consequences of the patient's symptom behavior. The therapist is more likely to find the patient's hurt in what the patient unawarely "demands" from him than in analysis of the history of the symptom. The statement (or the gesture) "I am depressed" communicates information which is bound to affect a given respondent in a specific way. Every patient has learned that his symptom behavior constricts the respondent's response activity and eliminates certain responses altogether (i.e., no respondent is likely to tell a depressed patient "I am happy to hear that you are feeling so good"). The therapist can ask himself the question: "What does this symptom do for the patient?" or, more specifically, "What does the patient expect of me with this behavior?" "Why is it important for the patient that I feel sorry, hopeful, or whatever the case may be?" While the therapist, with this question, has not yet achieved an hypothesis as to where the patient hurts, he is at least looking at evidence that may present him with good data.

In terms of the model presented here, the therapist can assume that the patient introduces cues in social intercourse with him that are very much like the cues the patient has successfully used previously with others. In other words, the therapist can assume that the patient attempts to create in the therapeutic hour the emotional climate that has been useful to him on other occasions. This assumption permits inferences as to the source of the "hurt." The inferences will become more accurate as they are based on more adequate information, but useful inferences can be made from even one simple message. A good therapist will make inferences from minimal information, but will revise them as more data become available.

One depressed patient gives as his reason for depression an "unnatural sexual sin" he had committed in his past. The therapist asks himself: "Where does this patient hurt? What does his depression do for him?" The answer to this question based on this minimal information can only be tentative. However, one possible convention of depression is a demand to feel sorry for the person suffering; another lead comes from the preoccupation with the sexual sin. One inference as to where the patient hurts is that he makes others sympathize with him while thinking of prohibited love. If such an inference is true, one can speculate that the patient has learned that certain love objects can only be approached (in fantasy or reality) with the consent or sympathy of a significant person and that he must get this consent by means of his own suffering. The inference may be wrong but it serves to bring order into the therapeutic process. As more information becomes available, it can be corrected.

Although the patient perhaps hurts in more than one area, the therapist cannot deal with all the hurts at the same time. The hierarchy of symptoms of which Horney speaks is probably due more to the observer than to the bearer of the symptoms. The therapist does well to isolate one hurt at a time; after he has verified it (see Chapter V) he has to set a given therapeutic objective (see Chapter VI) for the hour, which has as its objective to reduce the "hurt."

The Therapist Uses Himself as an Instrument

The message of the patient, with its manifest and covert components, has an impact on the therapist. An analysis of the covert component will give the therapist some information as to where the patient hurts. It should be remembered that the patient codes his message in such a way that most people, including the therapist, will become emotionally engaged. This attempt to engage another person in a specific emotional climate serves to protect one's vulnerability by hiding information. But the therapist must learn to be emotionally disengaged in order to recognize the motive for hiding. He will obtain some evidence for the meaning of the covert component of the message by looking into his own emotional involvement in it; to do so he will, as it were, make the careful understanding of his own feeling tone the object of his analysis.

In order to understand the patient properly, he must look at himself first. He will have to become aware of whether the patient's message creates feelings of anger, seduction, friendliness, helpfulness, ineffectuality, or whatever in him; and he must discover what specific cues have created these feeling tones in him. Even the well-experienced therapist will often enough "feel" without awareness (i.e., socially engage in the patient's demands) for he, too, is a child of our culture. His therapeutic skill, however, consists of his ability to disengage from the demand of the message and recognize the patient's unconscious manipulations. The therapist, rather than the patient, has to have the "insight" to understand the patient's unconscious bid for involvement, and he should be trained for this understanding by learning to observe the evidence from covert information.

To what extent can the therapist ascribe his own "feeling tone" to the message of the sender? Perhaps he had too little sleep the night before and reacts with irritation to even the most harmless message of the sender. Under these circumstances, how can he use his own feeling tone as the sounding board for a deeper understanding of the patient?

The therapist's predispositions for certain feeling tones do present a problem. The patient, to be successful in his demand to engage another person, must discover these possible predispositions; he cannot create feeling tones but only elicit those of which a given respondent is capable. The patient knows that to involve another person he must send messages that are meaningful to the respondent's repertoire of responses. However, the therapist is also capable of responding to stimuli that are quite independent of the patient's message. These do not give information about the patient, and responses to them are very likely to interfere with the decoding process. The therapist in these cases may distort the meaning of the patient's message.

Misinterpretations occur frequently enough in interpersonal relations, and the information obtained can obviously be only as good as the instrument providing it. In using the recognition of his own emotional responsiveness as evidence for the covert meaning of the patient's message, the therapist must be quite certain what he is responding to. Only to the extent that he can "read" himself can he be an accurate instrument. It is this quality of recognizing his own contributions to the interpretation of a given message that differentiates a good therapist from a poor one.

To obtain accurate information, the therapist must not only know his own contribution, but must also develop the capability to disengage from the emotional climate the patient has prepared for him and look at the patient's message from the outside—from a different viewpoint altogether. For example, when a patient arouses an emotional climate of threat in the therapist, he may feel like responding with a defensive statement. As long as he is dominated by the feelings of discomfort and threat, he is in no position to recognize the evidence presented to him. He is reacting to covert, ambiguous symbols in the socially demanded way; he is caught in the social expectation of the patient's covert message. Only after he has disengaged himself from his feelings of discomfort and threat can he recognize that he has been put on the defensive and begin to ask himself why the patient sent this message in the first place. A therapist can give a disengaged therapeutic response only after he has withdrawn from the emotional climate which the patient imposed on him.

The therapist must be trained to recognize the emotional climate that a given message promotes. From the recognition of his own feeling tone he will draw information that will help him toward a deeper knowledge of the patient. After he has experienced the meaning of certain messages from a given patient, he will be able to simplify the decoding process. He will learn the symbols and signs this patient uses to arouse certain feeling tones and then he will learn to react to these signs alone. It is probably unavoidable for the therapist to learn about the patient first by reacting to him emotionally, before disengaging and recognizing the covert meaning of the messages. The difficulty involved in discovering the covert meaning of a message by actually experiencing it is probably one of the reasons why therapy takes such a long time. Not all messages will cause such reactions; with many, the therapist will know from experience what involvements and demands they contain. Every patient has special skills, developed to involve another person, to constrict this other person's response activity, and to maintain in this manner his present state of adjustment.

The therapist is the instrument of disengagement. To paraphrase Reik (1948) he has three ears: one to understand the manifest meaning, one to store information, and one to sense the covert meaning.

Interpersonal Repression as a Source of Information

Why therapeutic responses are unique is a puzzling question. Why should they be reserved largely to the therapeutic hour and occur only occasionally on the "outside"? The answer clearly has to do with the everyday skill of the patient. He consistently formulates his information with a high probability of obtaining a constricted response. As skillfully as he can, the patient forces the ordinary respondent into responses with which he can deal. He makes his psychological living by exercising control over the respondent's response activity. Yet, he himself is not aware of his skill because he is unable or unwilling to take responsibility for the consequences of expressing his feelings, done so subtly through his covert cues. The patient has "repressed" his own awareness of certain of his cues; and in order to reach his goal of control, he must also prevent the respondent from recognizing his motivations. "Repression," then, is a concept that can be used fruitfully not only in the understanding of individual dynamics, but also in the understanding of social process.

Freud's theory of repression is, of course, central to psychoanalytic theory. In brief, the theory states that the ideational representation of an instinct can be repressed before it ever enters consciousness (primary repression) or that a thought process can be "expulsed" from consciousness after it has entered (secondary repression). But repression is not mere forgetting. Wishes, no longer conscious, still affect behavior. Also both primary and secondary repression require energy from the ego: one might say that the person constantly has to "pay" to keep certain ideation out of actual awareness, and that when a "repressed" idea begins to reach consciousness, anxiety occurs.

Repression is a useful concept in the present discussion, although there is more interest in the behavior associated with it than in the process. An early prohibited wish, which has been meaningful in childhood and then forgotten, but which later makes an individual feel "vulnerable," is reminiscent of "repression"; the wish has not merely been forgotten, but has had definite consequences in the individual's behavior. The facility of humans for "forgetting" a wish and yet devoting much effort to gratifying it is characteristic of much of our behavior generally, and of our use of language specifically.

The nature of this inquiry requires conclusions which go beyond Freud's conceptualization. Freud was principally interested in explaining the dynamics of individual behavior and did not overly concern himself with the social relevance of his concepts. The communication process, of course, is principally a social phenomenon, and the social aspects are of prime importance.

The patient has developed the skill to communicate in a complicated manner, whereby he expresses a wish but hides it from being recognized by either himself or the respondent because he wants to avoid taking the responsibility for certain consequences of his message. Although the consequences may fit into his psychological economy, he does not want to be seen nor to see himself as having elicited them. The covert expression of his wishes makes it possible for him to keep on living in a semblance of peace; he can express wishes without being held accountable for them. In the process of coding the message, lack of awareness within himself as well as the lack of awareness of the receiver is an important goal: the individual wants to be only partially understood. A desired emotional impact that expresses the wish and engages and involves the respondent must be created, but the intent must not be recognized.

The individual's hidden wish to be only partially understood is central to the understanding of maladjusted behavior. A successfully working message is an exciting event for the patient. With it he acts out the dangerous, prohibited wish, he renews his battle, he has an experience in prediction and control, and he can handle the constricted responses successfully. He promotes the course of events, and he forces the responses which he has learned to accept in lieu of fulfillment of his wish. He plays with fire and knows that he will not get burned. Although he never gains full satisfaction, he retains the feeling that he is still in the fight, that he exists.

The reason that a therapeutic response occurs so rarely on the "outside," then, is the patient's skill in being misunderstood through the use of covert, ambiguous cues. Most individuals around the patient will be easily engaged in these gambits because they have neither the inclination nor the skill to properly decode the difficult messages. In the therapeutic hour, though, the therapist has learned to disengage from the social demands of the patient's message and, by analyzing it for the meaning it is supposed to hide, to gain significant information about the patient.

We once worked with a beginning therapist who saw a patient in a hospital setting and reported in his supervisory hour that he could no longer work with his patient, who got him "too angry." The young therapist was not himself so impulse-ridden that he was unable to control himself, and so we discerned that his strong feeling may have been a response to this very demand on the part of the patient. On the basis of this hypothesis we formulated that the patient "hurts" in that he must elicit anger and rejection from his respondents, the very anger and rejection which he had so skillfully elicited in the therapist. In accordance with this hypothesis, the patient was making a bid to reinforce his present adjustment by obtaining another rejection and consequently maintaining his view (and with it his peculiar satisfaction) that he is a "rejected" person.

The therapist through his own experience can analyze the patient's impact on him and attempt to differentiate the cues which may have been used by the patient to elicit anger. The therapist cannot afford to be caught in the "social role" and actually be angry, for this very act would severely retard the patient's progress. If this particular therapist had, in fact, discontinued the patient because of his anger, he certainly would have reinforced the patient's current state of adjustment. The patient would then have learned that his skill to engage another person in his customary way was successful even with a therapist; such a discovery would then convince the patient that there is no "special hope" in the relationship.

Disengaging from skillful social demand is certainly easier said than done. Yet, a linguist going to a movie to study inflections is not likely to get too involved in the plot of the story; he is centering his attention on other events. The therapist's responses are unique precisely because he must make the effort to disengage from the social demands of the message in order to understand the covert demands and provide the patient with a nonreinforcing response on the basis of this knowledge.

Information through Scanning

How does the patient arrive at his coding? He cannot use "canned" or absolute coding and be effective because cues which are hidden for some individuals may be quite manifest to others. To be most effective, the patient must "cue in" on the respondent, must sense how particular cues would affect a specific individual. He must learn where the respondent himself is vulnerable, where he can most readily be predicted and controlled. This process of "cuing in" on the respondent is here called "scanning." One may note in passing that the process of resistance in the therapeutic hour is often based on the use of information gained by scanning. The patient scans the therapist for vulnerabilities so that he can throw him "off base" at critical times, protect his own vulnerabilities, and maintain his present "libidinal" position. He must know where the therapist is most vulnerable and where he blocks, so that he can build toward the times when he will need this control as a safeguard.

Scanning appears to be largely an unconscious mechanism for sensing another individual's emotional attitudes. It is probably an ability that dates back to early infancy. A young child, for example, often appears upset when his mother is nervous, and feels at ease when she is composed. Communication at this age seems to take place on the basis of prehending rather than comprehending (Sullivan, 1953). With information gained unconsciously by scanning, a husband can arouse the love or hate of his wife with certain well-selected messages at a given time; the pupil can tease the teacher where it hurts most.

Nor are these observations restricted to the human being. One is reminded of the observation that a horse seems to be able to sense the attitude of the man approaching; it often responds to fearfulness with aggression. The barking dog will accept some approaching strangers, but not others. So animals, too, seem to scan the outsider for emotional attitudes.

Scanning appears to play a major role in an encounter with a stranger. Frequently an individual does not know whether the stranger is friendly or unfriendly, and his first impression is formed on the basis of highly undifferentiated cues. Hamlet's demand of the ghost, "Where wilt though lead me? Speak, I'll go no further," and his request for the ghost to tell him if he is "a spirit of health or goblin damn'd" is typical of first encounters, including therapeutic interviews. The patient often judges the therapist in terms of how the therapist feels in his presence. He scans the attitudes and value system of the therapist in terms of the therapist's reaction to him, not unlike a bat sounding out its environment. The patient's strategy of approach throughout therapy is likely to be based on information he gains through this scanning. The patient will know from cues (the source of which he cannot determine) whether he should talk fast or slow, and whether he should try to impress, exaggerate his problems, or look depressed. These behaviors may not all be in the repertoire of the patient, and it is not assumed that an individual can produce them all at will. But there is certainly some choice, and the sender typically scans the receiver for cues from which to learn which behaviors will be most efficient with this particular person. When danger is present, scanning is an invaluable aid in determining areas of safety. The sender can also use scanning to determine the most effective ways in which to combat the danger: he senses whether he should seduce, pacify, aggress, or flatter. As in chess, half the game is sensing the approach of the opponent—whether he is going to play a daring or a conservative game, likes to make surprise moves, or is given to feelings of overconfidence. Consequently the therapist, by observing the patient's attempt to engage him, can learn not only about the patient but also about himself. Patients who typically flatter the therapist not only let him know about their own needs, but should also give the therapist some insight about himself, i.e., his apparent susceptibility to flattery. It is precisely because of the selective responses that the patient gives upon scanning the therapist that therapy is also a "growth experience" for the therapist. Neither the patient nor the therapist himself is spared the mirror.

Scanning occurs most often without awareness. The patient can rarely report the cues he obtains by scanning, although one may infer that he has differentiated them. His consequent messages indicate that he has integrated them in his behavior. It may be that the information he gains through scanning "triggers" certain feeling tones in him, and that he reacts to these feeling tones even before he can label them. The information he gains has been not cognitively, but emotionally, effective; and the consequent message is then specifically formulated by his own emotions, aroused by scanning. Although speculative, this assumption explains how scanning information helps the individual to avoid noxious responses.

Scanning appears to lean heavily on such information as is gained by observation of posture, facial expression, gestures, way of speaking, choice of words, etc. Before the patient codes his message, he is likely to scan the respondent for the possible repertoire of responses, and he makes his estimate of such a repertoire on the basis of these nonverbal cues. If his motivation is to predict and to control the therapist's response, he must estimate in advance what responses are possible, and to which cues the respondent is most likely to respond in the desired way.

Some of the processes which have been described under the term "scanning" have been under investigation. Therapists have learned that even nodding one's head at selective stimuli (Greenspoon, 1962) gives information and encourages the client to produce certain types of themes while discouraging others. Apparently the patient is alert to (though not necessarily conscious of) the therapist's covert cues, and codes his messages in terms of these reinforcements.

The ability to scan seems to be related to states of adjustment. Most nonpatients use scanning primarily for information that will help them relate adequately with other people. For the patient, scanning is a more limited and desperate ability, keeping him out of "danger" by helping him to predict and control others. The cues he selects through scanning are precisely those which give him a sense of power in his vulnerable areas. From this selectivity, however, a curious discrepancy arises. On the one hand, many patients are extremely sensitive in scanning for particular cues; they are so perceptive in some areas that others are actually afraid of their sharp observations. (It is well known, for example, that some hospital patients are quite aware of their fellow patient's difficulties.) On the other hand, the patient is often indifferent to the point of deficiency in sensing other cues. Because he is sensitive only to specific cues, his understanding of other persons is often highly distorted and accounts for his inability to "get along" socially.

This ability to scan another individual and sense his emotional attitudes is a necessary condition not only for interpersonal repression, but for communication in complex messages. A complex message could not fulfill its mission and create the proper impact without the sender's being sensitive to the respondent. It is because of these abilities of the patient that he can perpetuate his problems with most people. He studies them and "deceives" them, both to get the pleasure of control and to protect himself from a feeling of vulnerability. The uniqueness of the therapeutic hour is determined by the fact that the therapist has learned to handle some of his own vulnerabilities. He is aware of his areas of vulnerability and he can afford to have the patient both know and use them. Anticipating this skill of the patient is of great value in the therapeutic hour.

Evidences Used for Formulation
of a Therapeutic Hypothesis

Many writers have written psychological essays in praise of a scientific attitude in interpersonal relations (Kelly, 1955; Freud, 1953), but it is likely that these hopes are more enthusiastic than sensible. In the communicative process many messages are—and must be— received without an attempt at verification, lest communication be slowed to a stand-still. Automatic acceptance of certain information, i.e., acceptance without demanding further evidence, is a measure to make communication more efficient, even at the price of some error. This fact has often been overlooked in psychological literature, where rigidity, or responding automatically, is defined as being synonymous with psychological deficit. Yet man has to accept unverified information if he wishes to free his time for any endeavors other than the most essential ones. Closing questions in one area permits him to raise new questions elsewhere.

Although an individual in ordinary social intercourse cannot constantly ask questions or verify information, it is precisely this alertness, the attempt to differentiate many possible meanings in the patient's message, which is the special endeavor of the therapist. He must investigate many possible meanings of the message; he must be able to understand the evidence for these meanings and differentiate their various sources. The task is indeed a difficult one. He must discover the favorite hiding places of the patient, recognize the cues that are the sources of his information, and respond to them in such a way that the patient cannot maintain his automatic behaviors. While in ordinary social intercourse an individual may simply feel annoyed and turn his back on the person annoying him, the therapist does not have this liberty. He is likely to be affected by the social information causing annoyance, but he must use this information for the benefit of the patient—to annoy people may be exactly the behavior which the patient has chosen to perpetuate his problem. The therapist must disengage from the demand of the annoying message and then ask himself: "Just what did the patient do to annoy me?" In this manner he can get at the process by which the patient perpetuates his problem.

Thus, the foremost and perhaps the only source of information is the therapist himself. He is the sounding board, the instrument, the judge. He must have the ability both to understand the social demand of the message and to disengage from it, to read and differentiate the cues designed to have an impact on him, yet withstand the impact. He has to be the programmer, the computer, and the memory. He must select the pertinent information from the many verbal and nonverbal cues and from the cues coming from the setting and context. He must interpret this information for meaning, judge how certain he is of his interpretation, and finally evaluate what sort of response would contribute to the desired goal of helping the patient. To understand the meanings of the patient's messages, he has to be on the alert for many cues: choice of words, use of emotional words, gestures, facial expressions, body movements. In addition, he must understand and draw meaning from dreams and associations, and remember the reported "monuments" of the patient's life. Most of all, he has to know what cues he, as a person, is producing himself. Moreover, beyond all these methods of gathering information, the therapist has to be a "genuine," honest, and concerned person.

Let us assume that a therapist possesses all this demanding equipment. How does he use it? How does he become "more certain" that his understanding is accurate? In other words, what is the nature of such evidence? Let us assume that the therapist interprets a given message as one connoting "anger." He obviously cannot simply ask the patient, "Are you angry?" for he cannot evaluate from the answer if the patient was in fact angry. He can, however, use "recurrence" as support for his hypothesis, provided this recurrence of response has not been provoked by the therapist himself. The therapist is dealing with covert, well-hidden cues. He must be "tuned in" to observe the specific recurrence, and yet not "tuned in" in the sense that he will become a self-fulfilling prophet and create the response. Recurrence of a given feeling tone appears to be a basic tool for obtaining evidence.

"Consistency of personality" is another and broader concept which helps to establish the meaning. Consistency is a concept that demands *recurrence* of significant behavior. If an observed significant behavior does not recur, evidence for its presence as an important motivational state is very slim indeed. But another issue has to be considered with regard to the problem of evidence. The therapist has to make a judgment not only on the meaning of a behavior ("the patient is angry"), but also on the degree of certainty which he has about his own interpretation. This is important, as the degree of certainty he has will determine the quantity and quality of the supporting information he seeks. If the therapist is indeed very uncertain that a given patient is angry, he needs more convincing evidence before responding to the message than if he were quite certain. The therapist is both the judge of the meaning of a message and the respondent, and consequently his attitude toward evidence is most important. On one hand, he has to give a response to the patient; he cannot constantly ask himself, "Do I understand the patient correctly?" as such uncertainty would, in essence, not permit him to respond at all. On the other, he has to be aware that most of his responses are based on tentative judgments, with the result that he must constantly be on the alert for new cues and new information which may force him to conclusions different from his earlier ones. This we call the *necessary scientific attitude of the therapist*. He must act on limited information, but be open for new information. It is as though the therapist has to ask himself what kind of information a given patient would have to offer to support or reject a given hypothesis. Without such thought, the therapist would too easily define, rather than observe, the patient's state.

To summarize, the therapist is the only instrument in the therapeutic hour. His measurements are his sensitivity to covert cues and his skill in disengaging from the social involvement which the patient tries out with him. When he asks himself "Where does the patient hurt?" he can find the answer only by half-listening to the plot, or content, of the patient's talk. His major attention must be given to the subtle manners of the patient, which can only be inferred from subtle covert cues, and which are designed to evoke an emotional climate in the respondent.

The therapist must learn to become aware of the emotional climate created for him and to evaluate to what extent he can treat himself as an instrument.

The therapist then will learn where the patient has his problem, his "hurt." He has experienced the effect of the unaware component of the message which the patient directs toward him. For example, in our previously mentioned case, the therapist received covert messages which produced anger in him. After disengaging from the emotional climate evoked in him, the therapist recognized the meaning of the covert cues and formed the hypothesis that "the patient hurts" by making people angry in these specific ways and thus driving them away. The therapist now may reason that obtaining an angry reaction probably gives the patient satisfaction.

The information-gathering process is directly related to the sensitivity, insight, and experience of the therapist, and the information gained will be contingent upon his capabilities in using himself as an instrument.

CHAPTER V

THE USE OF CONVENTIONS

CONVENTION refers to practices that have been established by general consent and sanction. In terms of communication theory, conventional practices may be seen as behavior to which responses can be predicted with high probability. By common usage certain behaviors almost automatically elicit rather specific responses; in this sense we can say that a person is using conventions to constrict another person's response activity. Conventions are often used by a sender to hide the meaning of the covert component of a message from the respondent. They are useful for hiding certain information just because they customarily elicit automatic responses that the respondent ordinarily does not consciously control.

Conventions as a Hiding Place

It is common knowledge that a person can hide behind well-established conventions. If an individual does use conventions consciously, he knows that he frequently invests his communications with meaning beyond their lexical meaning. For example, the greeting of "good morning" implies a wholesome wish for another person. The conventional usage of the exchange implies that a friendly set is established in the respondent; the sender "sets him up" to respond in a conventional manner to a conventional symbol. In some cases, though, the greeting is uttered so gruffly that "good morning" does not mean a friendly wish at all. Here the person consciously hides his ill feelings behind a conventional cue. He apparently wants the respondent to know that he does not feel well or that he bears ill feeling toward him. In this way a convention can be consciously misused by the introduction of paralinguistic or adjuvant cues. (An example of an adjuvant cue is raising one's voice.) With adjuvant cues an individual is permitted safe expression of a feeling for which he cannot immediately be held responsible. Using a conventionally friendly cue for an unfriendly meaning, he escapes responsibility by hiding behind the ambiguity. If taken to task, he can escape with a retort, "I didn't mean it that way."

He can also hide behind the convention without knowing it. Here the individual is not aware of his grouchy intonation: he will be surprised with the respondent's response. He will not understand why he does not obtain the friendly return greeting he expects. Again the convention has been used to cover up meaning to avoid full responsibility, but this time the sender neither admits nor recognizes the process. Both the knowledgeable and unknowledgeable sender use ambiguous information because they do not desire or are unable to communicate the underlying feeling more directly. By using a message which conventionally means "friendliness" to express ill feelings, an individual can confuse the respondent and so avoid direct exposure of his feelings. Were he able to express his feelings directly at the time, he would not have to code the information ambiguously. But by "hiding" under conventions, he can express feelings without having to face the consequences immediately.

This same process undoubtedly takes place in many subtle ways in the interaction of most people. By using certain conventions, an individual first creates a set in the respondent that limits his response activity, and then introduces stimuli that represent the sender's hidden purpose. Advertising men, political campaigners, religious speakers, and educators have all utilized this process of constricting response activity in order to promote specific emotional attitudes along with their product in prospective buyers (Packard, 1957). It is interesting to note that the emotional impact of hidden cues on the respondent will often create very strong, durable attitudes which become quite inaccessible to reason. In other words, once a person is made to feel strongly about something through a use of conventions, he is not likely to let facts confuse him. Typically the victim of a confidence man who has established himself under the conventions of a "friend" or honest businessman will not believe the police officer's assertion that the man is a criminal.

The convention may be nonverbal but not covert. The underlying meaning which goes along with the use of a convention can only be understood if the convention itself is understood. One must always know the context of a particular use of a convention in order to understand accurately the expectations invested in it. A speaker may hold out his hand for greater emphasis but does not want a gift. The beggar, conversely, holds out his hand in a similar conventional position to create a set of need.

The same act can be interpreted differently in different contexts, and the conventional formal meaning of a sign cannot be fully understood by itself. However, the conventional meaning of a sign is usually understood by both sender and respondent because they both have learned to take the context as part of the meaning. A child learns to raise his fist to communicate that he is angry, and his knowledge that the sign can be understood by others permits him to use it as a convention. The child would be disappointed if his anger were not taken seriously and the respondent burst out laughing, particularly if the context did not permit jocular interpretation.

Blind Spots for
the Use of Conventions

In trying to understand maladjustment it is important to discover how the patient hides his meaning through the use of conventions. Without being aware of it, the patient uses conventions to promote response activity and set up emotional climates favorable to his needs. Very often the respondent is also unaware that he has been "engaged" in a limited response activity and that he is consequently missing the underlying meaning of the message. The following example is illustrative:

A young lady who sees herself as quite a charmer, and a rather "liberated" charmer at that, always seems to have several young men around her. Her style, in which she first appears as charming but shy, permits her to attract particularly "unliberated" and prudish fellows. On one occasion, the young lady was with a returned missionary of a strict religious sect and used the term "getting laid," a phrase which predictably shocked the young man severely. She rationalized her behavior as an act to help put the young man more at ease. The missionary was reacting to the convention used in this setting and was unaware that the girl's underlying purpose in using it was to force him to reject her without her taking the responsibility for breaking off the relationship. The girl could now add the missionary to her collection of "good men who will have nothing to do with me," under the banner of rejection. She might rationalize: "I am trying very hard to find a man whom mother would want for me, but these men do not want *me*." In this manner she could express covert aggression to her mother and also remain, in her own mind, innocent of such aggressive feelings. Whenever rejection occurs, she is heartbroken and cannot understand where her efforts have failed her—she had only the very best intentions. And yet even this young lady knows the social meaning of the slang she used when she encounters it in other people. In her own case, however, she explained that all her relationships with young men end so quickly because she is misunderstood.

This inability to apply one's understanding of conventional meanings to one's own use of conventions should be noted because it is a *modus operandi* found in many maladjusted persons. The maladjusted individual has learned the meaning of certain conventions and there is evidence that he knows them; his behavior is *not* due simply to a lack of information. Still, he seems to be blind to his own behavior, and thus blind also to the reason for perpetuating his particular state of maladjustment.

In some cases a patient may become aware of his "misuse" of convention but be unable to do anything about it. Knowing that this misuse exists clearly is not the answer, as the misuse itself stands in the service of certain important goals of the individual. The "blind spots" in the case of the girl had to do with her dependence on, and hostility toward, her mother, both of which feelings had to be acted out covertly. Rejection, though painful to her, is the punishment she inflicts on herself for her goal of both depending upon and aggressing against her mother. Even if the girl could recognize the fact that she wants to be rejected, she probably would continue to promote this specific response activity until she found courage to withdraw from the emotional involvement with her mother or, in other words, found a new "libidinal" position.

The above formulation not only permits the identification of the "misused" convention (the girl's "liberated" language) that promotes the response (rejection) but also gives the therapist a firm answer to the question of "where the patient hurts." He can reason now that the patient needs a "desirable" suitor's rejection for her psychological economy. He can now advance the deductive hypothesis that the patient wants to tell someone that she is trying to find the "right" suitor but is not successful. The therapeutic objective is to discover (1) what psychological advantage she has by staying in the conflict, and (2) what experience she needs in the therapeutic hour to allow her to find a "libidinal" position of her own choice.

Unusual Conventions

Sometimes the individual attempts simultaneously to express and to cover up strong feelings, but his feelings are so powerful that there is danger they will be recognized even when coupled with the safest of conventions. Unable to hide under safe conventions, the sender then re-creates his own personalized and probably regressive language, which again permits him to express his feelings but greatly minimizes the danger of being understood correctly. The resulting messages again contain both the prohibited wish and the defense against the feeling of vulnerability, but in such a manner that the responsibility for being recognized as having such feelings is greatly reduced. An illustration is a schizophrenic patient's statement that he is "followed by a plane." The patient's feelings of vulnerability have become so severe that he does not wish to let the other person know what is bothering him, what he is feeling at the moment. Nevertheless, his message does communicate to others his feeling that *something* bothers him. He does not communicate in ordinary conventional terms but still uses *some* conventions, even though unusual ones. In other words, he still permits a small degree of understanding, just as some very highly personalized poetry can have an emotional impact on the reader even though it comes through a rather unconventional use of language. The patient's unusual statement that he is being followed by a plane probably evokes for the respondent a picture of danger as well as a response to the inappropriateness of the statement. It is quite possible that the patient has learned to find some sense of existence and control in promoting just these feelings of danger and unreality in the respondent.

It is well known that some mental patients promote feelings of anger in most of those dealing with them. Others promote pity, erotic feelings, or feelings of strangeness and bewilderment. Such patients promote these feelings fairly consistently; they are also skilled in selecting individuals who are somewhat predisposed to have strong feelings in the patient's area of skill. The mental patient, through his use of unusual language and conventions, has actually acquired great skill in promoting certain specific feelings in the respondent. In the extreme case, even by babbling nonsense syllables, a patient can restrict the response activity of the other person, remain safe in his hidden wish, and yet feel power in predicting some very general response activity (bewilderment or rejection) in the other person. From the proposition that the person *wants* to create these feelings in the respondent, it can be argued that the patient will feel "successful" once he obtains his response and that the predicted response therefore serves to reinforce his state of adjustment. The term "success" is based on the theory that with his manipulation of such broad conventions as being "unresponsive" or "crazy," the patient (1) can evoke responses in others, (2) is still "safe" (his vulnerability is not recognized), and (3) is still in the battle for fulfillment of vulnerable wishes.

Conventions in Therapy

The increasingly closer contact among men in modern civilization, which brings so many previously isolated subcultures into contact with each other, creates a need for each individual to have a greatly expanded knowledge of conventions. The child has the ever-increasing task of mastering the conventions of his age. He has to know what these conventions mean in order to grow up successfully in this society. Without this knowledge he cannot successfully predict, control, or even respond to behaviors of others. The use and misuse of conventions is in fact one of the keys for understanding psychological deficit. The maladjusted person who has developed blind spots for conventional information and who uses conventions under which to hide is necessarily socially ineffective (even though he may have great skills in a limited area). He is unable to take advantage of the time-saving factors which conventions allow. It is through his messages that he reinforces himself in his maladjustment, continually proving to himself that he can remain safe and obtain some gratification from engaging others.

To understand the conventions used by a particular patient, the therapist uses himself as an instrument. When he receives certain information, he can get at the meaning of the convention by asking himself what sort of response the information demands. The information "you-son-of-a-bitch" can ordinarily be assumed to arouse anger or fear in the respondent. The experienced therapist, however, will neither be angry nor fearful for long, but will ask himself why it is important for the patient to arouse fear or anger in him. The therapist will try to understand the meaning of the convention and then ask what response it was designed to elicit. Once he has an answer to these two questions, he can "disengage" from the emotional climate created for him and refuse to reinforce the present state of adjustment of the patient.

CHAPTER VI

INTERVENTIONS IN PSYCHOTHERAPY

Therapeutic Objective

WHEN the therapist has formulated a hypothesis to answer the question "Where does the patient hurt?" he is in a position to formulate a tentative therapeutic objective. The therapeutic objective should then determine the nature of his interventions.

Many systems of psychotherapy have developed only very general therapeutic objectives, as those implied in terms such as "adjustment," "well-being," and "mature." These objectives are certainly useful, but they do not give the therapist any guidance in facing the immediate problem. In effect, much of the therapeutic hour is often aimless and "free-floating." Good reasons are often advanced about why the hour should be "nondirective"—it will give the patient the chance to express thoughts and ideas he had not preplanned, and will permit him to take the initiative in looking at his problem and finding solutions.

When we speak of a specific therapeutic objective, we do not want to do away with the searching attitude of the patient. On the contrary, we want to follow up on a given theme that the patient himself has introduced. The therapeutic objective should not be seen as contradictory to a searching attitude on the part of the patient, but rather as a way of helping the patient find an answer to his own question.

We should note that the therapist is often unable to formulate a specific objective for the patient, simply because he has not yet been able to properly understand what the patient is saying. Therapists have learned to deal with situations in which they lack such understanding.

They have learned to encourage the patient to give more information. The simplest device to achieve this end is to assume a listening attitude and give short responses that communicate to the patient that the therapist is attentive. This response will be referred to as a "delay response" as it provides the therapist with both more information and more time to formulate a meaningful hypothesis. Delay responses such as "Hm, hm," "Go on," "Tell me more about that," however, are not only listening devices but also the prototype of *asocial* responses which fail to reinforce the patient's expectation. An example might be:

Patient: "I hate you."
Therapist: "Go on."

When the patient's expectations are not met, he will become uncertain about them. Such responses give the therapist time for a deeper understanding of where the patient "hurts," and for a formulation of a useful response.

The setting of a therapeutic objective is a useful tool in the therapeutic process. It is designed to help the patient within a specific problem area. In communication analysis it has these two goals:

(1) Through an analysis of the communication process, the patient will experience how he, himself, creates a share of his problem.

(2) The patient will experience that his covert or unaware communication, with which he creates problems, stands in the service of certain needs that can be more effectively dealt with in alternate ways.

Perhaps it is best to explain the formulation of a therapeutic objective with some case material.

A young woman patient came to the sixth hour with the statement: "You did it! You made me accept this job [secretary instead of typist], And I feel totally inadequate. I constantly make a fool of myself. You are incompetent not to know what I can and cannot do. How dare you set yourself up as a therapist when you don't know what you are doing?"

The therapist was reasonably certain that he had not given any such advice. While listening to the patient he experienced a wish to defend himself, but checked this wish and responded with delay statements like "Hm, hm, tell me more about it." This statement first provided the patient with the experience that the therapist would not accept responsibility for her change of job; but more than that, she obtained the information that her communications did not arouse defensive behavior or guilt in the respondent.

The therapist then formulated the hypothesis, on the basis of this and other similar behavior, that the patient "hurts" in that she has to arouse guilt in an authority figure to justify her advancement. She apparently is incapable of accepting responsibility for her striving to "get ahead" and needs to blame someone else. Why can this idea of "getting ahead" be so dangerous to her? He may answer tentatively that staying in an inferior position is perhaps desirable for this girl. A number of phrases used by this girl came to his mind: "Mother always wants me to be in there slugging." "I am their [parents'] only hope, they want me to support them." "Girls who are too far ahead in the game never find a husband."

He then formulated the hypothesis that this girl had "libidinized" her inferior position, that it was to her a way of arousing guilt in the parents (who pushed her too hard).

This hypothesis may have been wrong, and an erroneous selection of events may have been made by the therapist. Correcting a hypothesis with new evidence is a constant procedure. However, this hypothesis did give him an operating basis. He tied in the experience he had with the patient (guilt arousal) with a meaningful behavior of the patient (maintaining the inferior position). He could then formulate the therapeutic objectives: (1) to have the patient learn by experience what her messages mean to another person (she learns how she perpetuates her problem), and (2) to help with the discovery of other more adequate ways of maintaining her integrity with her mother or other authority figures.

Once the therapist has identified a therapeutic objective, he will work on this objective by developing a sensitivity to the behavior he has identified. Here, for example, he became sensitive to patient messages designed to evoke guilt in him; and message by message, he responded to the patient's subtle manipulation, providing her with the experience that this behavior no longer created the desired emotional climate. His responses were designed to guide her into a feeling of uncertainty about her message. His aim was for her to open up the closed question and inspect whether her guilt arousal mechanism was the most adequate behavior to get to her goal of integrity.

While the nature of the disengaging message will be discussed elsewhere, the above illustration will be completed here. The patient had just blamed the therapist for advising her to take the better job He responded with:

Therapist: "I am a quack, an ignoramus. How could I have advised you toward such a miserable goal?"

The therapist at this point was using a paradigmatic approach (Nelson, 1962) which is intended to "join the patient's resistance" rather than fighting it, and force the patient to use her ego strength rather than her defenses. This response, sailing with the wind, as it were, shifted the responsibility back to the patient, who could no longer use a "hostile" environment as an alibi. With this response the therapist created some uncertainty within her as to the righteousness of her case. We note that the therapist did not defend himself, even though he believed he was not to blame.

Patient: "You sure are a quack. I don't think I should come to see you again."

The patient had not given up her guilt arousal scheme and was still determined to win her point. Or perhaps she was really testing the therapist with this message to ascertain if he was really disengaged.

Therapist: "To seek help from an ignorant man like myself, this is crazy."

The therapist exaggerated the guilt arousal mechanism in the best paradigmatic tradition, at the same time giving the patient information that her guilt arousal had not created the emotional climate she desired. But it also told the patient the therapist was not angry—that he would stay with her.

Patient: "Well, I guess I could have said 'no' to the boss, but you must never do that to me again."

The patient then acted from the experience that the changing of her job was, after all, her responsibility, and added the last sentence as a face-saving device.

Therapist: "But you are stuck with being a full-fledged secretary rather than a typist. You are in there slugging now, as your mother wants you to be."

The therapist wanted to tie in the fear of advancement with the fear of being ruled by mother. On the surface, this sounds like a comment directed toward a greater insight. In this particular context it was, however, a truly disengaging statement. The therapist provided the patient with the experience that the guilt arousal behavior was unnecessary; the real problem had not been solved but was still around.

Patient: "Maybe Mother was right after all."

This statement was probably said in irony, a ploy to test the therapist for his interest in this area. The statement also implied that on this playful level the patient was considering a new exploration: how to deal with mother.

The formulation of a therapeutic objective was based on information available to the therapist. He accumulated information from various sources: the content of the message, its covert component, and his own response to her messages. Certainly, he can err. His most convincing quality is to be aware of this fact.

We speak specifically of "experiencing" rather than of "having insight," because these two objectives can be most successfully realized when the patient is alerted to his own, immediate behavior as it occurs (when he is caught in the act of behaving, as it were) and not when it is discussed with him in the abstract. This condition is essential, as the patient is more likely to re-code when his expectations are unfulfilled and he is in a state of uncertainty. One can compare this process to the learning of a new serve in tennis. The player will become uncertain if one points out to him how he holds his racquet; provided he is motivated, he can better learn to restyle his game when the faults of his poor game are pointed out to him on the spot.

The analogy is only a crude approximation to the therapy hour, and the key phrase "provided he is motivated" gives us the greatest difficulty in therapy. We know that the patient is often as much motivated to maintain his "libidinal" position as he is to get well. That is precisely the reason why the first therapeutic objective—alerting the patient to the fact that he perpetuates his problem through communication—is not sufficient in and of itself.

The patient says: "Yes, I see now how I always arouse the anger of my wife by telling her the very things I know will make her mad, but I cannot help myself." Translated into psychological language, the patient says: "Part of me needs to create the anger in her." An understanding of how he does so is clearly not enough. The patient must also be brought to experience that the anger he arouses in his wife, contrary to his beliefs, gives him some gratification and perhaps some sense of freedom. Only when he experiences that, ever so subtly, he is seeking to *anger* her, can he learn that his behavior is not simply "part of me" but has purpose.

In other words, the patient learns to accept responsibility for communications that he made unknowingly, because they have been recognized by the therapist. The therapist, not the patient, had the insight! The patient experiences that his subtle communications no longer hide his intent, and he needs to recode. Besides being alerted to just how he is coding his anger, he is also alerted to the fact that his behavior (such as angering his wife) has meaning, within his psychological economy.

Once a patient learns that he can take responsibility for being the agent who *wants* to anger his wife, a host of new questions are open to him (all previously shut off) and he can now explore for himself whether there are more adequate ways of dealing with the problems which he had previously solved automatically, without success. He must experience uncertainty before undertaking this new exploration.

We realize that this formulation almost sounds like Ellis' Rational Therapy (1964) but there is a difference. Ellis argues the patient into behaving rationally, while we propose to provide the patient with responses that give him the experience of beneficial uncertainty about his previous expectations. We propose that with the proper, disengaged response by a therapist, the patient is placed in a position where he can make more adequate choices. The therapist is not representing rational behavior to the patient, but rather a unique relationship which permits him to accept his transitory state of uncertainty without having to defend himself. The uniqueness probably comes from the "representative" nature of the relationship, the unrealness of it, and its temporary sanctuary from the world of judgments.

Disengagement and Beneficial Uncertainty

The therapeutic hour gives the patient the unique opportunity to explore himself. People apparently cannot look at their behavior objectively when they feel defensive, threatened, or judged. Empirically, the nature of the therapist's behavior has become one of "acceptance" and "understanding." He is trained to listen and not enter into the evaluating decisions, even though he may have a general therapeutic objective, such as broadening the patient's choices. In our analysis of the communication process it became clear that the permissive atmosphere which the therapist has to create to allow the patient new explorations is a necessary but not sufficient condition for therapeutic change. The purpose of this permissive condition is to give the patient freedom to inspect his previous automatic behavior, to open new questions he thought were answered, and to try out new behaviors. For a patient to explore his life in this manner, he first must become "uncertain" of his previous behavior. This experience of "uncertainty" is a luxury which most people cannot afford in ordinary living.

A sense of uncertainty is experienced by individuals who permit their vulnerability to be exposed. If a person feels vulnerable in his masculine adequacy, he will generally hide this vulnerability from recognition by others, and often even from himself. When he gives information to others that he is uncertain in this area, he takes a chance of being hurt. Clearly, the patient resists expressing feelings of uncertainty—or when he does so, he more often than not misleads the respondent in order to defend himself.

However, there are various methods of making a person feel "uncertain." These methods create uncertainty in order to influence a person's behavior. The deodorant scare and the accident insurance scare are examples, though they actually are only very temporary scare-arousal systems. The psychology graduate student who uses a "psychological line" with his girl friend is a familiar example of the use of uncertainty arousal in every day living. So is the demagogue reaching for votes. The arousal of uncertainty by breaking down defenses can also have unfortunate consequences. The movie gambit of a husband driving his wife insane by making everything she does seem wrong, until she stops doing things and retreats into a world of her own, is probably exaggerated, but it still serves as an illustration of how uncertainty arousal can produce constricted responses rather than exploratory behaviors.

Uncertainty aroused in a hostile atmosphere, such as the use of ridicule among schoolboys, is likely to produce anything but exploratory behavior in the ridiculed person. It is most likely to result in withdrawal and constrictive responses. The victim is made uncertain of himself and feels compelled to defend himself against such vulnerability in the future.

Yet the feeling of uncertainty is also the basic experience which permits modification of behavior in the direction of better functioning. Creating merely a permissive atmosphere is not enough, as the patient may enjoy this unique experience without making new exploratory efforts.

The patient, within the experience of a permissive atmosphere, has to be challenged to experience and tolerate uncertainty; but as such a challenge does occur within the framework of a permissive atmosphere, the sense of uncertainty experienced by the patient is likely to be beneficial—one which leads to an exploration rather than defense.

While on first inspection, this challenge—to experience and tolerate uncertainty in a beneficial emotional climate—may sound somewhat contradictory, the behaviors involved are not. The permissive climate is created by the therapist's responses, which do not question the patient's right to think or feel in any way he wants. Listening, following the patient production with care, giving responses which communicate to the patient that he is understood and not judged, all give the patient a feeling that the therapist has concern for him, that he is of some importance to another person, and that in this climate he can test out his fears and hopes. However, these behaviors of the therapist also contain a very real challenge to the patient because of the asocial character of the responses he is using.

The response "Hm, hm" given when the patient speaks of killing himself, for example, is essentially an asocial one as it does not follow the general social convention of either reprimand or sympathy. The challenge consists in making the patient—within the permissive atmosphere—uncertain of the expectations which he has associated to *his* messages. The asocial response of the therapist necessarily creates a feeling of uncertainty in the patient; he can no longer properly predict the outcome of his behavior in this setting. The uncertainty which the patient gradually learns to tolerate becomes the very basis for new hope about his life.

Asocial Responses:
General Disengagement Responses

There are two categories of asocial responses, both of which serve the therapist in disengaging from the expectations of the patient. The first category contains the empirically evolved responses that are often given in the absence of real understanding of what the patient is saying. The "Hm, hm," "Go on" type of response is often used when the therapist is still unable to respond more specifically. With this response, he provides the patient with the information that he is listening but that the relationship is an asocial one in that none of the socially expected responses are given. Thus even these responses arouse uncertainty, and it is not surprising that they have been reasonably effective with certain patients, even when used alone.[3]

A second category of asocial responses is not as general in its aim. These responses aim at specific disengagements and are in the nature of counterpersuasive responses.

Asocial Responses:
Specific Disengagement Responses

The labels *Interpretation, Reflection,* and *Probing* have been given to responses that guide the patient through a state of uncertainty to act in specific behaviors. However, these responses are also counterpersuasive, in that they make the therapist's value system relatable to the patient. The therapist translates the patient's message into his own dynamic language, not only teaching the patient to think in the new language, but also providing him with a means of obtaining freedom from the ordinary consequence of his own language; that is, he acquaints the patient with his own value system. Korzybski (1941) recognized this process and emphasized the aspect of re-teaching language, making the error, perhaps, of thinking that this new language should be "more precise." It seems more likely that the new language the patient learns simply serves to break up earlier associations and suggest new ones. These responses of the therapist are grounded in comprehensive theories which prescribe rather definite consequences through new semantic ordering. By teaching the patient a new language, the therapist becomes both the persuader and the one who arouses "beneficial uncertainty." We shall illustrate "specific disengagement" responses and both their asocial character and their persuasiveness. A female patient says:

Patient: "Dad told me I could not go out with the boy."

The therapist gives an interpretation:

Therapist: "He wants you for himself."

This interpretation is first of all asocial, in that it does not follow the social expectation of the message such as: "Go anyway, and be a person in your own right" or "Father probably has your welfare in mind." The therapist trains the woman to think: "Whenever my

---

3. It is conceivable that such responses may be machine programmed, particularly if the mood of the patient's language can be ascertained from a frequency spectrum. This is one aspect of the work currently being done at the Langley Porter Clinic (Hargreaves and Starkweather, 1965).

father does not like my dates, he is competing for me." Of course, this represents the therapist's language and way of looking at things. He believes that learning the new language will help the patient discontinue her usual associations and eventually aid her in exploring other alternatives of behavior than those in which she had customarily engaged in relationship to her father.

A "reflection of feeling" is also an asocial counterpersuasive response. Another therapist may respond differently to our female patient's statement: "Dad told me I could not go out with the boy."

Therapist$_2$: "You feel angry at your Dad for this interference."

This type of reflection is again asocial, as it does not correspond to the social expectation. It is persuasive in that it trains the patient to think of her own emotional response rather than her father's actions. Again, this asocial, persuasive response is thought to be helpful for the patient because she learns a new language and, with it, new ways of looking at things. Although these responses are effective, often the therapist is not really aware that he is, in fact, persuading the patient. It is likely that the therapist would be more effective if he were to recognize the communicative meaning of his action.

Probing, also, can be counter-persuasive. A third therapist might respond in yet a different way to the same statement:

Therapist$_3$: "Did your mother mind?"

As previously, the asocial nature is clear, though the question appears to minimize the impact of the asocial character of the response. (Questions are conventionally allowed to interrupt the social expectation of a message.) The statement is clearly counterpersuasive because it teaches the patient that she should be concerned with the family triangle as an interrelated part of her father's actions.

These responses have not been described to point out their inadequacy but rather to dissect them into the type of information they present to the patient. It has been shown here that responses can serve specific and useful therapeutic objectives. The therapist should not delude himself into thinking that he is merely a midwife; he also fathers the child. He should plan his responses to arouse beneficial uncertainty in the patient and use them to teach a given therapeutic objective. His responses are his tool.

The Paradigmatic Response

One class of response, recently developed by Nelson (1964), is somewhat reminiscent of Potter's "oneupmanship," but is nevertheless both effective and theoretically sound. The emotional character of a paradigmatic response is that it "travels with the resistance" rather than analyzing it. When a patient brings to the hour disguised information that serves to maintain his libidinal position or, in simpler terms, to prevent his exploration of new alternatives, many therapists have responded to this information as the patient's wish to resist change. This was done with the expectation that the patient needs to know where he is resisting, and that such knowledge will help him to "work through" his resistance. In the paradigmatic response the therapist desires to help the patient to overcome resistance not by description, but by confrontation through the patient's own resources. To accomplish this feat, the paradigmatic therapist will exaggerate or dramatize the patient's way of behaving and thereby take the "wind out of the sails" of this behavior, with the hope that the respondent can behave more genuinely.

A patient may complain to a therapist:

Patient: "You only see me for the money anyway."

The therapist may respond paradigmatically:

Therapist: "Why would anyone want to see a fellow like you for anything but money?"

This response is counter-persuasive. It calls the patient's bluff, but it also brings his worst fears about himself into the open, and in that way trains him to face, not camouflage, those real fears.

With this response the patient is taken aback and made to feel uncertain. When said within a positive emotional climate, it is likely to arouse a beneficial uncertainty.

The therapist may have used the paradigmatic responses for the following therapeutic objective: He wants to change the patient strategy ("I must attack a person in order to involve him") into "Must I attack a person in order to involve him?" and eventually into "I am not that bad. People may even like to be involved with me." The paradigmatic response, often used throughout a whole hour, is a dramatic form of disengagement by role-playing a social engagement. It is played with the strongly implied suggestion to the patient: "Must you really use your social skills in this manner? Is it really necessary to engage me in this way? You can face these fearful thoughts without anticipated danger coming true."

There are of course, dangers in the use of the paradigmatic response, and they lie in failing to properly estimate the beneficiality of the emotional climate. If the patient feels that the therapist is not playing a role paradigmatically, but in fact means what he says, the response can bring a severe sense of threat into the hour. However, even when the patient misunderstands and distorts the meaning of a paradigmatic response as a real feeling of the therapist, the experienced therapist will be able to deal with such distortion.

A patient who claims she had been raped says:

Patient: "I like you very much, I even dream of you."

The therapist responds paradigmatically:

Therapist: "You want me to lie with you on the couch?"

This response was designed to explain the mildly implied sexual wish in this message, with the therapeutic objective of giving the patient the experience that her own suggestive sexual demands may have something to do with the rape complaint. The response verbalizes that which was supposed to remain hidden. This dangerous exchange can only be successfully accomplished by the therapist who is actually free from "countertransference," i.e., from desire for his patient. In a case where he is, in fact, engaged and is too fond of the patient, he would be totally unable to use such an exchange for the benefit of the patient. He would threaten rather than help her. Only the disengaged therapist can continue.

Patient: "Yes, why don't you come?"
Therapist: "Tell me what we would do were I to come."
Patient: "Hell, you weren't born yesterday."
Therapist: "What would you want me to do?"
Patient: "Embrace me, sleep with me—but you are just hedging. Why don't you come?"
Therapist: "You are really challenging me to come?"
Patient: "I sure am."
Therapist: "What would you do if I really were to come over?"
Patient: "Yell."
Therapist: "Because you really were only teasing. You would have again had the experience that a doctor raped you."

This daring exchange gives the patient an immediate experience for her share in the rape of which she complains. The responses also contain the suggestion: "Must you really deny responsibility for your sexual wishes?" Surely the paradigmatic response stresses the ability of the therapist to maintain his role. The patient may not always come through with giving up the social expectation of the messages, as she did when she responded with "yell"! The therapist must know when to clarify the class of meaning and withdraw from the social role he has been playing. The therapeutic impact of a well-handled paradigmatic exchange, however, is as rewarding as Nelson's monograph points out.

The paradigmatic response fits well into our theoretical basis of behavior. It is asocial by being too loudly social in its nature. It is so social, indeed, that it forces the patient to deal with his own social behavior as if it were projected into an oversized convex mirror. This view forces the patient to explore new alternatives in his behavior.

Verbalizing the Impact

Felder (Ellis, et al., 1963) demonstrated another technique which could be called paradigmatic, but which was concerned with a different aspect of the message. When the patient extended unaware expectations to the therapist, the therapist played the role by verbalizing these expectations out loud.

The patient touched the therapist's foot with her own, then quickly moved it away.

Patient: "Sorry."

The therapist sensed that the touching was not accidental.

Therapist: "I liked it when you touched my foot."

He tried to verbalize her unaware expectation in the message, believing that she wanted him to be pleased. In our terms, the therapist attempted to alert the patient to the consequences of her unaware coding of information, and to give her the experience that these feelings do not have to stay hidden—that even though they were recognized, no "hurt" actually had occurred.

Rational Therapy

Even Ellis (1964) can be said to use paradigmatic responses, though he gives a different explanation for them.

Patient: "I cannot marry this boy. It would hurt mother."

Ellis perhaps would respond:

"*Not hurt her? She is the tyrant who hurts you by having trained you not to hurt her. The worst kind of tyranny, because you cannot even fight her outright.*"

This response also exaggerates the social expectations of the message. "It would hurt mother" is a nice considerate statement that demands social endorsement. Ellis does not give endorsement but instead attacks the convention. He admits that his responses are persuasive, though he believes they are persuasive in that they help people engage in clear rational thinking. Ellis's responses probably work because they interrupt the patient's social expectation in a beneficial climate.

The paradigmatic response is a way of playing at social involvement; even though the exaggeration makes it asocial in nature, it sounds like a social response. Some therapists feel uneasy about it. It seems to bring a half-honest, manipulatory note into the therapeutic relationship. On closer analysis, the serious, searching therapist and the therapist more ready to use a smile or a game are both deeply concerned, within their approach, with effecting a beneficial change in their patient. They play the role most comfortable for them, and it would be difficult to state that one method is superior to the other.

Hypnosis

Hypnosis in the psychotherapeutic hour has been most often used to (1) recover particular memories which are difficult to locate, (2) assist in symptom removal, and (3) help the patient relax.

We should be aware that there is no physiological indicator, independent of testimonials and judgment, to show that a hypnotic trance is really present in a given person. We should also be aware that the literature on hypnosis is controversial in many of its findings. The reports of lasting changes in personality characteristics, state of adjustment, state of concentration, effective learning, etc. can be seriously questioned in the light of numerous contradictory findings.

Using hypnosis to discover early memories is a doubtful enterprise. Orne (1961) pointed out in his discussion of hypnosis as used during World War II that an informant under hypnosis will produce information but, unfortunately, not reliable information. Consequently, it is very doubtful that the "early memories" produced under hypnosis result, in fact, from anything more than the subject's wish to please the therapist.

Although both hypnosis and waking state devices can be used to induce relaxation, hypnosis is probably inefficient in symptom removal. There are, however, some more modern ways in which hypnosis can be used to *initiate* symptom removal. Some particular disorders (such as stuttering) can often be temporarily affected by a suggestion not to stutter while under hypnosis (Kroger, 1963). A person may thus learn that he has the ability not to stutter. This experience produces a sense of "uncertainty" for him, which may result in a wish to discover why he would "want" to stutter. Such a temporary demonstration then motivates him to search for new alternatives. Occasionally, of course, a symptom can be directly removed by hypnotic suggestion. That should not surprise us too much, as a few people can even be talked out of their symptom (such as smoking) or can give it up after reading scientific reports.

Nevertheless, from a communicative point of view hypnosis is quite useful. Conventionally, it stands for a "shift of responsibility" from the subjet to the hypnotist, a shift readily believed in by both the public and many practitioners. There is a widespread belief that a hypnotic subject in a trance "cannot help himself" and *follows* suggestion, with the hypnotist in control. While this may not be true, we have here a media of communication which, conventionally speaking, does leave the patient free from responsibility for his thoughts and behaviors. This medium for shifting responsibility to the therapist is an exceedingly useful tool for intervention in therapy. This is particularly true in cases where the patient needs to hide, where he is scared of responsibility, where he needs to find a sanctuary. Hypnosis may be particularly useful in cases where somatic symptoms are found. A patient's symptom can be viewed as a communication to the effect that he does not wish to be held responsible for his behavior. In hypnotic treatment what the patient says is not important, but it is necessary for him to discover whether talking itself is dangerous. This seems to be useful in hypnotherapy: through the medium of a hypnotic trance the patient can allow himself to discover which message he can express without fear of retaliation.

Another use of hypnosis in psychotherapy has been hypnotic role-playing. Parmelee reported to us that he used hypnosis in order to obtain this characteristic "shift of responsibility"; he ordered the patient to live through the most feared episodes of his life. A man afraid of sexual relations with his wife would be told, under hypnosis, to imagine that he was approaching his wife, had made a pass at her, etc. A patient afraid of talking back to his boss would role-play his assertive role under the command of the therapist. This method makes use of the "shift syndrome." The therapist openly accepts responsibility for bringing the patient face to face with his fears, in order to train the patient to explore himself in relation to the feared acts.

Tougas once told us that a rat, which had never voluntarily chosen a certain pathway after once receiving a shock there, was forcefully pushed across this dangerous pathway—and from then on, it used it freely! Hypnotic role-playing is such a method of pushing a person into his feared behavior in a beneficial setting. There have been reports of group hypnosis (Illovsky, 1962) used with schizophrenics where the patients imagined some encounters with people or feared events. It was successful with several of the patients.

Role-playing

Ever since Moreno (1946) first popularized this form of therapy, role-playing has been one of the possible interventions in psychotherapy. In role-playing, as in hypnosis, the overriding principle is that an individual is only "play acting," that is, he is not fully responsible for what he is doing. It is a trial situation to discover one's freedom of action. Anyone who has used this type of intervention is struck by the fact that most individuals cannot follow instructions when role-playing; they come through with their automatic, consistent behavior. However, even role-playing can be a severe threat to some individuals and they may refuse to act out certain modes of behavior, even though there can be no retaliation.

A young man once was supposed to tell his father, played by another patient, the harmless-sounding phrase, "Thanks, Dad," but he could not bring himself to do it. Of course, it is not important whether or not the "Thanks, Dad" was really said. The young man experienced his difficulty in the open and this was enough to arouse uncertainty. There have been many uses of the role-playing device. A hospital patient government group once decided to role-play one patient's symptom at each of their meetings. One woman wailed loudly every few minutes, and so the patients decided to break into a loud wailing chorus whenever she wailed. The woman continued to wail during the hour. Later, when she heard a recorded playback of the behavior, she said, "No wonder they threw me out of my house." She attempted never to wail again. This is not to say that all these episodes came out beneficially or that they were examples of successful one-trial learning. But some of these efforts did work, and we attribute their success to the forceful asocial response in a beneficial setting. Failures are possibly due to an inability to perceive the beneficiality of the setting.

In some cases the patient perceived the imitation of their symptom as an affront, and it is quite possible that the group intent in such cases was not just beneficial; they may also have wished to punish the patient.

At the Utah State Hospital another role-playing device was an agreement among patients to compete for a prize to be awarded to the one who could prove he had suffered most. This cruel-sounding device, suggested by a patient, was adopted; patients gave speeches extolling their suffering, and the most dramatic sufferer obtained the prize. The structure of this competition set a new counterpersuasive convention for "suffering" as something "put on," something under one's control, and something slightly ridiculous. These performances seemed to help the patients to take their own self-suffering less seriously. This asocial competition in a beneficial setting (without malice) was a powerful tool to force patients to become slightly uncertain about their previously automatic self-indulgence in suffering.

The role-playing device has also been used in our work with delinquent groups, where some of the children took the role of teachers or parents—not so much to learn directly how the adults see the situation, but (using our term) to produce pseudosocial responses in a beneficial situation. Conversely, an individual patient may role-play himself in a situation where he can behave as he feels he would like to behave, and in this process learn his own resistances. As a tool, role-playing has some very real advantages in providing a patient with a sanctuary-type of atmosphere. However, in suggesting this method the therapist is also suggesting that, in his opinion, such an artificial climate is needed; that is, the patient is not yet able to assume responsibility. As the therapist's evaluation of the patient is of greatest importance, this method must be, at best, used only as a temporary tool because of its covert meaning. In the final analysis the therapist who wants to help his patient must communicate to him that he can hold him responsible for his behavior.

CHAPTER VII

LABELING THE THERAPIST'S ACTIVITY

In going through hundreds of recordings and transcripts, an attempt was made to find classes of responses which could be clearly distinguished on the basis of their impact on the respondent. This attempt to categorize by description is consistent with the hypothesis that information is passed on with all behaviors. In previous chapters attention was given to the meaning of the patient's messages, and especially to the differentiation between manifest and covert cues. This sequence was necessary to show that the patient, beyond symbolically representing his problems, also "acts out" his maladaptive behaviors by specific operations in the therapeutic hour. Therapeutic gain was directly linked to what can be called a "sophisticated reinforcement" model, which involves a beneficial interference with the patient's "acting out" sequences at the time they occur. While the patient tries to engage the therapist, the therapist seeks to break up the automatic message-response association of the patient by an asocial response and disengagement from his demands. To do so effectively, the therapist must not only carefully analyze the patient's communication, but also be aware of his own behaviors and the information he gives the patient.

Specific techniques, such as reflection of feelings or interpretations, are manifest ways of showing concern, but we know that the same words can be varied in meaning by the covert codings. The therapist still must know what sort of information he conveys to the patient via such media, and which behaviors he is likely to reinforce consequently. For example, a technically correct reflection of feeling accompanied by covert cues that communicate "I am bored with this hour" will not have a beneficial effect, for the covert component when perceived by the patient will have non-beneficial reinforcement value.

Customarily, psychotherapeutic responses are classified by the intent of the therapist. "Reflecting of feeling," "probing," and "interpretation" are all labels describing what the therapist wants to do. In the following section we shall categorize the therapist's activities in terms of what he is doing rather than what he wants to do. This shift of emphasis permits us to look at the covert information that the therapist conveys, and how it is perceived by the patient. It calls to our attention the reinforcement values of the more subtle behaviors of the therapist, the meaning of which to the patient can be all too easily overlooked.

The very facts that a statement has been made and a response is expected may convey covert information that goes far beyond the manifest content of the statement. The therapist's construction of his statement, such as: "Tell me more about this childhood memory," gives different covert information to the patient than a question about a specific association, even if one disregards the content altogether. A particular statement creates a certain set-expectancy in the respondent; classification of responses is made here, on the basis of major sets of expectancies which have been identified by communication analysis. Thus certain activities of the therapist may be grouped simply because they are likely to arouse a similar set-expectancy in the patient.

**Therapist's Activity
prior to Therapy**

Most experienced therapists in hospitals, educational institutions, or private practice want to be certain that they are treating a psychological or psychiatric deficit and that the patient's complaints are not based on a physical illness. Many therapists insist that their patients be referred to them by a physician or that they have a medical examination before they enter treatment. The set-expectancy created by this activity prior to the therapeutic contact is important to the treatment process because the patient learns from the start that the therapist himself does not deal with his physical illness; he may have certain feelings about this limitation. The very structure of this setting permits him to use the term "physical illness" as a symbol of withdrawal ("I must see another doctor") or as a defense against accepting psychological treatment. The therapist should be aware that he may have helped to promote the use of these responses and should understand their covert meaning.

The patient will sometimes use statements about physical illness as covert aggression toward the therapist who does not have a medical degree. The psychiatrist, who often neither diagnoses nor treats the physical aspects of his patient's illness, may have similar experiences.

In other cases, where the referral comes from a court or a dean's office, much covert information is also transmitted prior to the first hour. For example, a student may be told that he is suspended from school until the therapist gives him a "green light." This setting will intensify certain patient responses to the disadvantage of others, and unless the therapist can recognize the covert cues created by the setting, he may overlook critical information needed to properly decode the patient's statements.

Prior psychological testing also plays a role. Some therapists seek such diagnostic information because they feel it will help them to understand the patient more quickly; others avoid it because they feel it biases their views or places them in a situation where they may be expected to render expert decisions rather than helping the patient to "help himself." Prior diagnostic information is probably helpful in many ways, particularly when the therapist is alert to the covert meaning that the testing experience possesses for the patient. For example, the use of prior testing information may promote certain set-expectancies in the patient, such as increased dependency or fear of the therapist, "who knows more about me than I want him to know." If he is on the alert for such feelings, the therapist can use them for therapeutic gain.

The physical setting of the therapist's office may also be of significance and may create feelings and expectancies which can be anticipated. A therapist who practices in his home with noisy children next door or in his university office with students or colleagues periodically disregarding the "do not disturb" sign may do well to consider what feelings this setting creates in the patient. Any other peculiarity of the physical setting, be it size of office, distance from town, or adequacy of seating facility (for example, whether or not a couch is in the room), must be considered and then taken into consideration when information is to be decoded.

Therapist Activity in the Therapeutic Hour: Request for Descriptive Information

In the early hours of therapy, some therapists attempt to obtain a description of the patient's problem, and in addition a detailed personal history and memories of important childhood events. The quest for descriptive information also occurs in later hours. Questions such as "What is your brother's name?" "Tell me precisely what you did yesterday after you went to bed," "Elaborate on what the boss said to you," all represent demands for descriptive information.

In this type of exchange the patient is given certain covert cues by the nature of the total setting. The very fact that such a question is asked tells him that the therapist grants some significance to the answer. The therapist determines the direction of the discussion and implies that the answer will advance therapy. When asking a question, he assumes a "directive" role to a certain degree. The question itself is never so important as the covert information that goes along with it. For example, should a request for descriptive information typically come after a discussion which deals with embarrassing or "banal" problems or after a pause, the patient will learn to expect the therapist to take the reins at such times. The therapist strengthens the idea in the patient that certain cues will shift the reins to the therapist.

Under certain circumstances some questions are more leading than others. A patient may say, "I had a feeling of fright when I saw all these people coming toward me," and the therapist responds, "Do you recall if these people were predominately male?" This question not only tries to elicit broad information but forces a more specific commitment. The therapist gives a hint as to what he suspects to be significant. The leading question not only suggests the answer in a rather specific way, but also tells the patient that the therapist is taking some direct responsibility for the exchange; he is taking the initiative away from the patient. The covert information inherent in the very fact that a leading question has been asked teaches the patient that the therapist has taken the lead and seems to know where he is going.

The therapist must then be prepared to understand consequent information in light of feelings aroused by the expectancies he himself has created. He not only reinforces but also persuades the patient to talk about themes he is interested in.

There are also the unfortunate times when the therapist gives covert information that clearly shows his inadequacies to the patient. For example, a patient talked about a certain "Fred" and the therapist asked him, "Who is Fred?" thinking that he was simply requesting further information. However, the patient had just explained who Fred was, and knew from this response that the therapist had not paid attention to him. The alert therapist could, of course, learn from the patient's next response what covert cues he had transmitted, but then it is not usually the alert therapist who commits such a *faux pas* in the first place.

Is the psychotherapeutic process advanced by the use of descriptive information? Many therapists believe that they need this information to understand more precisely what the patient is talking about. In order to understand the covert cues the patient produces, the manifest cues must be understood first. Thus the request for descriptive information is principally an attempt to identify more closely the manifest meaning of the discussion. Some therapists ask for more descriptive information than others, and a few insist on asking such questions consistently. Apparently they feel more comfortable in a leading role. On the other hand, some schools have "outlawed" questions altogether just because the covert information (the directive role) inherent in asking them does not fit in with their goals. However, if understanding the covert cues of the patient is the goal, there is certainly a place for ascertaining the manifest meaning of the discussion, providing the therapist is aware of the fact that with his questions he conveys more information than meets the ear.

Request for Dynamic Information

On occasion the therapist encourages the patient to give information, not to identify the manifest meaning of a statement, but to understand the thought processes underlying certain activities and to get at the covert cues themselves. One technique for gaining such information is the encouragement of associations, dreams, or elaborations. The way the therapist structures his comments informs the patient that the request is for dynamics rather than for content.

The therapist can do his job adequately only when he can decode the covert information given him by the patient. Associations, dreams, and elaborations are some of the raw material for covert cues. From a large number of possible ideas the patient selects some and states a few in sequence. The contiguity of thought processes can be analyzed from this raw material, which represents information the patient cannot easily give in any other way. The therapist knows that information which the patient can only give covertly is likely to represent areas where he feels vulnerable; it is valuable information pertaining to the automatic behaviors that promote the patient's problems. Dynamic information can thus be an important source of knowledge about the operations the patient goes through to perpetuate his problems.

However, a request for dynamic information also gives covert information to the patient, information which is strikingly different from that involved in a request for descriptive facts. With the request for dynamic information the therapist asks the patient to depend on him and to give up significant information which only he and not the patient can decode. The therapist becomes truly indispensable; he not only leads, but he subtly asks the patient to place his fate into his hands. A request for information transmits such covert information easily, and the therapist must be on the alert for the feelings created by it.

By glancing through the records one also discovers that the request for information often becomes a vehicle for the therapist to communicate to the patient that both of them are now engaged in a sort of "detective work." Sometimes the two can even go into cahoots to discover a particularly "interesting" dynamic, as if they were putting a picture puzzle together. For example, a therapist may say, "Go ahead, you are on the right track." This type of comment promotes the idea that both are looking for something rather specific and that the patient will be rewarded when he helps in the discovery. The patient may now seek to please the therapist and much covert information can thereby be lost.

Silences also transmit covert cues. For example, the interruption of a rhythmic exchange with a "Hm, hm" is often interpreted by the patient as an invitation to elaborate, to give novel and more dynamic information. Again, to understand the succeeding productions of the patient, the therapist must recognize that he has given him this covert information.

It is interesting to note in passing how client-centered therapy (before its latest change) used the "Hm, hm" technique, which gives much covert information and was quite contrary to its claim to be nondirective. By and large, client-centered therapists object to any request for dynamic information on the grounds that any "lead" interferes with the patient's own productions and thereby offends his integrity. The patient, they argue, thus receives the information that his own productions are not good enough, that he cannot be trusted to handle his problems by himself and in his own way, and that he needs the therapist. They regard such requests as establishing an unwholesome dependency relationship by reinforcing the idea that the therapist is in authority and that it is he who determines the course of events. This argument is based on the recognition that simply asking this sort of question conveys certain covert cues. It is true that where the intent is to minimize the authority relationship, this type of inquiry indeed seems out of place. However, where the intent is to obtain knowledge of covert cues, it can be most useful, provided the therapist is aware that through his very act of questioning he does arouse certain feelings in the patient. With this awareness he can utilize the emotional state of the patient to therapeutic advantage.

The client-centered therapist used to see himself as a person who enters into a warm understanding relationship with the client involving none, or at least few of his own values. It is our thesis that the therapist is more human and therefore more fallible than this, that he cannot keep his personality out of the treatment hours, and that the patient will, as Rogers has also recognized of late, skillfully involve and engage him. The therapist's strength is not in remaining uninvolved but in being able to disengage from involvement in a beneficial way. Beneficial disengagement from the patient's covert expectancies is here seen as essential in the process of therapeutic gain. The therapist is much less concerned with the question of the patient's equality than he is with a very thorough understanding of the covert cues which the patient uses to perpetuate his problems.

Delay

One behavior that can be clearly distinguished from others in the therapist's repertoire is his reluctance to commit himself at any given time. This behavior delays the patient's expectation of a response. Delay generally is used when the patient "demands" that the therapist commit himself by either a specific emotional involvement or a statement of values. Although the therapist fails to identify this demand, he feels that there is something he does not understand, and he tries to avoid getting caught in an ineffectual or detrimental response by passing the lead back to the patient. He makes a noncommittal remark which encourages the patient to explore further, to give more information.

A delay response is often needed in the therapeutic process because the patient has learned that his own security lies in hiding information, and there are many occasions when the therapist simply does not understand what the patient is saying. He gives a delay response because he wants to know more before he commits himself. Such responses are particularly useful when the patient is skillful in scanning the therapist for his vulnerabilities. For example, the patient may discover that the therapist wants to be seen as a "nice guy." He will use this information to render the therapist ineffectual. Another patient may discover that the therapist becomes upset when talking about sexual matters; this information will also provide the patient with weapons to ineffectuate the therapist. The therapist, on the other hand, can use delay responses both to minimize giving this sort of information, and to avoid "engagements." Delay responses are legitimate methods of communication to indicate that the therapist is listening and wants to hear more, but that he is not yet ready to respond with more detail.

When the patient covertly promotes an emotional set in the therapist, the latter may make a delay response. Sometimes delay responses can be misunderstood. Here is an illustration of a rather subtle demand:

Patient: "*I went to the store today and exchanged a pair of trousers. I just told them I did not want them. A year ago [before therapy] I never could have done this.*"

Therapist: "*You are getting better.*"

To the extent that the therapist really believes his own statement, he has responded "engaged" to the demand of the patient. The patient has asked for praise and the therapist has given it. However, if the therapist is not caught in the patient's demand for agreement that he is getting better, these very same words can be adequately used as a delay statement. The response can be a reflection of feeling rather than a statement of belief. Perhaps Rogers' earlier recommendation that the statement should be "*You feel you are getting better*" is a safer way of responding to this particular message, because it reminds both patient and therapist that no value judgment is involved. To the extent that the therapist's response does not communicate his beliefs, he will be able to deal with the patient's possible misinterpretations as they appear in later statements.

Delay is the method used to avoid giving value statements and beliefs and to withhold a more meaningful response until the therapist adequately understands the covert cues of a patient's statement. Typical delay responses are: "Hm, hm" (I heard you), or "Tell me more about it" (I don't understand as yet, elaborate), silence (Go on), or simple reflections of content or feeling. Gestures, sounds, breaking the rhythm of exchange—all can serve to tell the patient that he is expected to go on or to elaborate.

Delay often advances the relationship, and it may prevent the therapist from commiting a serious error. With a delay response the therapist may admit to himself and the patient that he has not caught the meaning of the patient's statement; or, he indicates that he is not emotionally involved in the patient's expectations of him. Since such situations are bound to occur frequently in the hour, a delay statement has a definite place and purpose.

One characteristic of the inexperienced therapist is to phrase and time a delay message so that it arouses anger in a patient, instead of encouraging him to go on. This is probably due to the fact that the therapist cannot as yet tolerate being ignorant of the meaning of a given statement. Although he feels the need to delay, he is unhappy about his ignorance, and consequently his delay statement becomes aggressive. Here is an example:

Patient: "So I left her. I could not stand her anymore. Wouldn't you have done the same thing?"
Therapist: "Go on."

One might speculate on the process which produced the harsh response: The therapist realized that the direct question put him in danger of commiting himself to a value judgment. He has learned to avoid judgmental responses but his anger (or anxiety) at being placed in a judgmental role makes him aggressive. His "go on" actually tells the patient, "I can't answer that. You have caught me." The words "go on" do not convey such meaning but the adjuvant cues (such as tone of voice) may do so.

The very fact that a patient asks questions of this kind often means that something has gone wrong. He may have sensed that the therapist cannot deal with direct questions adequately, and so uses this method whenever he wants a feeling of control. In this case the therapist's response achieved precisely what it was designed to avoid, namely, the introduction of a value judgment into the hour. Because the response punishes the patient for his question, the therapist is caught in the very trap to which he was alerted, and loses his opportunity to disengage.

Sometimes, of course, the patient calls the therapist on a delay statement even if it is to the point. He gets impatient with delays. To a proper delay, such as a reflection of content—"You wonder how I would have acted"—the patient may reply, "Yes, I wonder how you would have acted. Won't you tell me?" Now the therapist must ask himself why the patient is pressing the point. By repeating, the patient gives information that he is no longer interested in his original question, but is joining the battle. Should the therapist now answer the question he would miss an issue which apparently is of real significance to the patient, that is, the issue of the "fight" between them.

Repetitions by the patient are often very obvious in conveying meaning to the therapist, and such meaning can be used for a beneficial experience. For example, he could respond to the repeated question, "You feel that I am unwilling to give you a straightforward answer." The patient may still insist with, "Yes, why don't you?" In this case the therapist, provided he has evidence that such meaning is important to the patient, might say, "You really don't know how helpful this is going to be, since I seem to refuse to answer your question." More often than not, however, the patient will not drive on to the "existence" question (Should I be in this relationship?) unless he is really deeply dissatisfied with the progress of his contact. And if that is so, it should be discussed.

Delay statements cannot be given indefinitely. Somewhere along the line the therapist must understand and disengage, or even the best delay statement becomes a communication of ineffectuality. For example, the therapist may delay with the statement, "You wonder how I would have acted?" and the patient's response is, "Yes, how would you have acted?" It becomes apparent that a further delay statement would only prolong the fight. The therapist cannot effectively repeat a delay statement, but must now concern himself with the emotions which promote the fight. There are times when delay becomes a hindrance to the therapeutic experience; it cannot be used indiscriminately.

Teaching

Many therapists believe that the therapy hour can be characterized as a process of facilitation. The patient is motivated to seek help, and the therapist helps him to "help himself" and to discover new ways of behaving. Some systems (characterized by Ellis, 1964) hold an opposite view and claim that the therapist must help the patient more directly by showing him which of his behaviors are inefficient and suggesting more appropriate ways of behaving. When the therapist follows this method of "teaching," he communicates to the patient two particulars: (1) that he expects him to be able to follow the suggestions, and (2) that he would not be in trouble if he used his head in the first place.

The viewpoint that direct teaching is not an effective tool for people with psychological problems is based on the observation that the patient cannot really utilize directions and advice because he needs his problems for his psychological economy. They serve a purpose and are not simply noxious as he wishes to believe. In fact, it can be reasoned that to live and maintain his problem gives the patient a direct feeling of control and a sense of accomplishment. The psychological symptom is a compromise solution for a patient's hopes and fears. He appears to cling to this compromise solution even though he says that he wants to overcome his problems, because by giving up his problems he would not only give up his discomfort but also his hopes. Advice has little impact because, for the patient, it means "giving up" some gratification. But in the therapeutic hour the patient may have the experience that his compromise solutions are not the only way of obtaining gratification, and through the experience of uncertainty he can now explore new choices.

Views akin to these have been widely accepted, yet many therapists who hold them often advise, guide, or direct the patient anyway, though most do so subtly and without awareness. Through covert cues, and in spite of theory, an effort is made to teach the patient more "efficient" solutions.

Some covert forms of therapeutic behavior communicate very indirectly to the patient that he really should pull himself together, use his head, and adopt better ways of acting. One of these forms can be labeled "contradiction," and is illustrated in the following excerpt from a therapy session with a woman who has marital problems.

Therapist: "You tell me that you know that it infuriates your husband if you cut your nails in the living room, yet you tell me you do it again in spite of the fact that you also tell me you want to get along with your husband."

The therapist defended this statement on the grounds of his intent to make the patient aware of her ambivalence about her husband. Why a patient should give up her maneuvers because she is told that she is foolish is not explained. The truly obvious communication in this statement is the challenge to behave rationally, not in a confused manner; it is therefore a "teaching" statement, whether it was given with this intent or not.

Sometimes the patient may misinterpret a comment as a leading statement; and the true intention of the therapist comes through in the way he handles the consequences of his "misunderstood" statement. In the above example, the patient may respond to what the therapist said with the following:

Patient: "But I can't see anything wrong in cutting my nails! After all, it's my home and I hate to have to control every one of my behaviors in my own house."

At this point one can discover whether or not the therapist can deal with the effects of his own statement. The patient here clearly tells him that he criticized her and that she chooses to defend herself. Should the therapist respond with "You feel you should have these rights in your own home," his statement is reasonably neutral, and he appears to have disengaged from the leading implication. It would be called a "delay" statement. On the other hand, if the teaching intention was really present, one may expect the therapist to respond with "You should quit it." With this response he shows her the ill effects her behavior has. One might suspect that the therapist's leading behavior derives from too close identification with the patient's "abused" husband. In any event, the comment is likely to achieve the opposite of what is intended; the patient must now defend her apparent stupidity. She may become angry, either with her husband or the therapist, and say, "Yes, quit it if it annoys him." Or she may just become angry with herself and respond, "I just don't know what to do." Or she may just plead, "I can't always give in."

A more adequate response after a patient misinterprets a statement as teaching behavior would be to reflect on the misperception:

Therapist: "*You tell me that you know that it infuriates him if you cut your nails in the living room, yet you do it in spite of the fact that you tell me you want to get along with him.*"

Patient: "*But I can't see anything wrong in cutting my nails. After all, it's my home and I hate to have to control every one of my behaviors in my own home.*"

Therapist: "*You don't like me giving you a lecture.*"

This response suggests to the patient that the therapist has understood the meaning of her response, but is not caught in the consequences. He shows he has understood the meaning by using the following reasoning: "I realize that you have to defend yourself against what you interpreted as criticism. I understand that you are angry at me, but I am not really critical of you."

The patient replies: "*I love him. I do love him. I must be an awful problem to him.*"

The patient's response in this particular sequence may be interpreted to mean that she had an intense experience, one which may be described in these words, "I do not need to attack my husband all the time. You [therapist] seem to like me even if I do get angry. My anger is a problem to me and to my husband." The therapist's response made possible a therapeutic experience, because he could recognize the possible teaching implication of his own statement and communicate this recognition to the patient.

An intention to teach does not appear only in pointing out contradictions. The therapist also teaches in other more subtle ways, often without awareness. Certain types of probing behaviors, ostensibly used by a therapist to "bring unconscious material to awareness," are often utilized as teaching behaviors. The therapist may use the words "How much do you know about this?" to stand for "You should know more about this." For example, a certain therapist believed that his patient was too constricted socially. He also felt that it would be wrong for him to mention or recommend certain social activities, because the patient would have to react to the fact that the therapist had given the advice and might treat the suggestion in terms of their relationship rather than in terms of its wisdom. Even though the therapist felt that he should not give advice, he still wished that the patient would explore more adequate ways of social adjustment. In this situation the therapist was like the parent who thinks he knows what is good for the adolescent but has learned to keep quiet in order not to stir opposition.

The wish to lead the child, or the patient, in the right direction is frustrated by the knowledge that such leading will not accomplish the desired end. The result of this dilemma is often a subtle attempt at leading or teaching, sometimes with, sometimes without, awareness. In the therapeutic hour such leading occurs often enough—it appears in the way a statement is worded, in the sequence of questions, or in other covert ways which may betray the therapist's line of thought.

In the case just mentioned, the therapist was concerned about the social adjustment of his patient. He wanted his patient to broaden his social experiences, to join clubs (so he said), but he wanted to use subtle cues which would permit him to live in peace with his self concept of nonauthoritarianism. Teaching can also occur by the introduction of a new word or new concept.

Patient: "It was a miserable weekend. I got up late Saturday, spent all afternoon at home reading, and then went to the movies by myself. Sunday I repeated the routine. All day I felt so lonely, I just didn't know what else to do. I just have no one, and I felt I did not really want to see anyone. I guess it was my 'I hate all people' day."

Therapist: "Another of those lousy weekends."

The therapist did not know what the patient wanted to say and so he delayed. The patient's statement can be interpreted as having the following meaning: "I am lonely and feel terrible. What are you going to do about it?" The hypothesis may be formed that the patient was bidding the therapist, between the lines, to give him suggestions, perhaps even a scolding.

Patient: "Yea, it's getting that way too often. All week I just went to work, ate, and slept. This is something that I can do, I guess. But I just feel that there is nothing to look forward to, no relief. I did want to go to the "Y" to play chess, but I just didn't have enough interest."

Therapist: "You did not want to meet the people there."

Here the teaching intention comes through: meeting people is a problem the *therapist* introduces. He singles out this one event, at best hinted at in the patient's message and says, between the lines: "Let's talk about people." The teaching implication of his statement is likely to have a negative effect on their relationship. It is likely to reinforce the patient's syndrome of having others do for him that which he feels he cannot do himself. It will prevent him, at least at this time, from taking responsibility in this area.

Call to Reality

Other responses which frequently communicate an actual teaching intention to the patient travel under the justification of a "call to reality." Some therapists define maladjustment as a deficiency in the sense of reality testing—patients seem to distort stimuli and are not able to consider a phenomenon objectively. When a patient produces material which shows a lack of grasp of reality, the therapist may have the temptation to "straighten out" the misconceptions. This lack of reality, of course, is most pronounced in psychotic patients, where it is only too obvious to the other person. In the neurotic the distortion is more subtle and the "loss of reality" less obvious. It is well known that "calling for reality" is not very effective with the psychotic. In fact, the psychotic is often driven by such methods to hold on to his distortions even more tenaciously—perhaps with the difference that he no longer feels he can talk to the person who challenges him. With the neurotic, however, some therapists argue in favor of a different approach: the neurotic is considered to have more intellectual control, and calling him to reality may help him utilize his intelligence to break down automatic behavior. This, however, is a curious justification. The neurotic, after all, is ill because he is unable to utilize his intelligence in these areas, and it is puzzling to see him treated as if he were merely lacking in information. The neurotic uses his "stupid" behavior to solve important problems which he cannot solve in any other way. Thus, calling him to reality can hardly have any other effect than communicating to him that he has indeed behaved stupidly.

Many therapists who are convinced that "calling to reality" is useless nevertheless engage in this behavior. Straightening out misconceptions is a conventional behavior which easily enters the hour. Here is an illustration of how this behavior can occur:

Patient: "I was riding on Launer and was coming to State Street and the other car just ran into me. This blind bastard of a driver. . . ."
Therapist: "Isn't there a stop sign at Launer Street?"

One first wonders why the therapist wants the more specific information—he, after all, is not the judge or the insurance inspector. Of course, the therapist knows perfectly well that there was a stop sign, but simply wanted to call the patient's attention to the fact that he had left out an important element in the story. He responded in this way because the patient phrased the sentence as a sort of "demand bid": "Terrible things are happening to me because of irresponsible people and I am not to blame. Will you blame me?" The therapist fell in with the alternatives and answered the patient's covert question by an attempt to teach the patient to accept some of the responsibility; his communication was: "Yes, you are to blame." This response, rather than arousing uncertainty, confirms the patient's certainty that the world is against him. The statement "These people cause you a lot of trouble" would probably have been more effective and afforded the patient the freedom to explore or even to admit his own responsibility.

Magic Suggestion

Finally, a few words about another, more indirect form of teaching often observed in the therapeutic hour, which may be called "magic suggestion." In most of the examples cited so far the therapist attempted to teach the patient more social skills and a greater sense of reality so that he would be more in tune with society. In magic suggestion the intent appears to be to teach the patient to think the "right" thought in order to find a solution to his problem. This subtle form of teaching probably has its origin in the magic thinking of childhood. The child learns new labels and symbols and tries to apply his learning in manipulating events through these symbols. He says "milk" and learns that milk appears as if the name itself were the cause of the event. Occasionally the patient still relies on a similar form of magic. This patient introduces demands for a magical solution by requesting the therapist to give him the password. The therapist feeds these demands by developing a catechism of his own or of his school of thought. He trains his patient to learn the "lingo," and instead of being a means of more efficient communication, it becomes an end in itself. The patient is taught that he can solve his problems by repeating therapist-approved labels, by learning to think in terms of the catechism. The therapist seems to say: "Know this word and you will be well," and so the patient learns the magic formula.

The idea, so often presented in the movies, that the recognition of past trauma (and a specific past trauma at that) will change the patient's whole life is sometimes the only theoretical basis for the therapist's behavior. This is nothing but an illustration of the use of magic.

Patient: "My brother came over to my house and I cooked for him. On these occasions I miss having a wife. This time I had a chicken in the oven and it burned crisp. Black and crisp. That reminds me, the last three times I've had guests I burned the meals, and I prided myself on being a good cook."

Therapist: "You deny your 'female' component. You can no longer submit to your brother. Brother and daddy are no longer so threatening. You are growing up."

On the surface this may be not only an accurate interpretation, but actually a disengaging statement. After all, the patient reports a mishap, then reports that it happens too regularly to be merely a mishap, and that unconscious motivation should be considered.

The therapist might have delayed for further information here ("almost as if planned?"), but instead chooses to respond by telling the patient that he understands the dynamics: cooking represents the female component, and the unconscious refusal to be a good cook represents the idea of asserting rights and masculinity. The first part of the therapist's response could show the patient that his assertion does not engage the therapist. He, the patient, can take the responsibility for his refusal to play a female role and there are no drastic consequences; it has been a safe experience. The cues in the therapist's statement which do not enhance this safe experience, but instead promote a very different one, are contained in the words "daddy" and "you are growing up." These two symbols betray the therapist's intent of teaching. With them he tells the patient, "You must learn that your behaviors are childish; you no longer are a child; daddy is no longer as powerful as he once was, and you do not have to be afraid of him. Accept my new labels which imply that these behaviors are childish, and you can let go of them." With such an admonition he is more likely to encourage "childish" rather than "growing-up" behavior.

The few examples given here are only suggestive of the many ways in which the "therapeutic urge" of the therapist can cause interference. There are, of course, therapeutic approaches which do endorse teaching, to mention only Ellis' "Rational Therapy." Teaching is also practiced in guidance or rehabilitation. In fact, direct teaching is such a common human occupation that it would be surprising indeed if the therapist did not occasionally engage in it. The point of view taken here, however, is that the therapist's efforts in direct teaching are valuable only in that they teach us to understand his vulnerabilities.

Supportive Therapy

Some therapists believe in giving support to the patient on occasions when they feel that therapeutic measures would be too threatening. Supportive statements are designed to give the patient a sense of security and to keep him away from any such stress as may be involved in the therapeutic process. Supportive work in general does not aim at personality reorganization, but at maintaining the patient's present adjustment, tenuous though it may be. Sometimes outpatient clinics use supportive therapy in an attempt to keep the patient out of the hospital, particularly when and where professional help is thinly spread. The patient accepted for this "maintenance work" is generally an individual who could be expected to get worse if left alone but who, on the other hand, is too vulnerable to be placed under the stress of therapeutic work.

A supportive statement generally is supposed to reassure the patient. It is not merely an "accepting" response which communicates to the patient that it is safe to explore certain thought processes, but is instead a value judgment which offers the therapist's support for certain behaviors. As the patient's behaviors are often expressions of his neurotic symptoms, one may say that supportive statements tend to reinforce the neurotic symptoms of the patient. In this sense, supportive therapy actually communicates to the patient that the therapist has given up all hope of his ever achieving a greater sense of well-being.

The inexperienced therapist will often use supportive statements in the initial phase of therapy. He does so under the impression that he must build "rapport" with the patient, and that rapport essentially means a comfortable and unstressful relationship between himself and the patient. Rather than accept the patient's right to express any thought he wishes for the sake of rapport, he will give support, i.e., approval for certain behaviors. For example, a child may throw a tantrum to avoid going to the playroom alone. The therapist then permits the child's mother to go with him to the playroom so that he can familiarize himself with the strange surroundings in a comfortable manner. As the child's problem may very well be the separation from his mother, the therapist's permission to act out certain dependency behaviors actually reinforces the problem. The rapport achieved by this supporting behavior is likely to cause more hindrance than help in future work—the therapist has now identified himself as trying to take the easy way out. Under some circumstances such supportive behavior may in fact be necessary for the sake of the mother, but careful attention should be given to the covert information which is thereby communicated.

A more subtle way in which supportive behavior enters psychotherapy can frequently be observed when the patient is very shy and reluctant. He makes an appointment with the therapist, but then does not talk when he comes to the hour. By this behavior he is apt to create an emotional set in the therapist to take the initiative, to ask questions and probe for information. If the therapist does so, he provides the patient with both an experience of weakness and inefficiency and an experience of success in neurotic control. The more experienced therapist will sometimes also enter into supportive behavior, but he will not fail to communicate his recognition of the covert cues which set up the demand on him. By doing so, he transforms the patient's experience of inefficiency and neurotic control to an experience of uncertainty which may appear in the unspoken question, "Do I really need to control the therapist's behavior with my own inefficiency?" It is true that in the rapport-building phase of therapy the therapist must proceed slowly (by means of delay) because he cannot possibly have a clear understanding of the patient's intricate problems and needs time to experience and decode the covert information. Ordinarily there is very little justification for the supportive statement besides reducing the therapist's own discomfort.

Beyond the initial phase, therapists are most frequently caught in supporting behavior in matters of the patient's progress. After many hours of exploration, a patient finally learns how to drive a car, finds some friends, or changes his job. He then makes a strong bid for approval and the therapist frequently supports him, using supportive statements as a teaching device whereby he hopes to reinforce mature behavior. The chances are that this kind of support is quite detrimental to further progress because it diminishes the patient's responsibility for his acts: by supporting the "desired" behavior, the therapist accepts credit for it. At the same time he gives the patient valuable information about how he, the therapist, can be punished—by the patient's failure.

Supportive behavior, like other evaluative judgment, is essentially a response to the emotional demands of the patient, and its occurrence must be carefully evaluated for the covert information it provides.

CHAPTER VIII

CONTENT AREAS IN THE PSYCHOTHERAPEUTIC HOUR

THE content of discussion in the therapeutic hour varies widely and is largely determined by the thought processes of the patient, and perhaps the receptiveness and response of the therapist. However, broad categories are frequently used and can be usefully distinguished. Many patients, for example, describe their problems or talk of past traumatic events, specifically childhood experiences. Some discuss sexual episodes, dreams, and fantasies; others present a rapid succession of seemingly unconnected thought—they free-associate upon invitation. Choosing to discuss this kind of material may be partially due to the sophistication of a patient who has educated himself by reading books on psychoanalysis, or has become aware of popularizations readily available to the public. Nevertheless, to assume that these topics derive solely from the patient's intellectual acquaintance with them would surely be misleading. Actually, these popular media of communication between therapist and patient are established simply because they serve various needs which will be discussed in more detail.

Childhood Experiences

Recall of childhood events has a very special place in therapy. Freud, in fact, believed this type of production to be essential to the completion of an analysis, on the premise that such recall was significant in the process of restoring repressed ideas to consciousness. From a communication standpoint, however, childhood recollections serve a more direct need of both therapist and patient. The patient is seen as a person who wants to find new satisfactions, but does not dare to become vulnerable by giving up previous adjustment mechanisms. As talking is the medium through which he wants to reach his complex goal, one might say that he wants to talk to the therapist, but still wants to talk as safely as he can.

The use of animal stories by children and some adults as a medium of communication has been frequently noted (Klopfer, *et al.*, 1954). A child is likely to talk more easily about the feelings of his teddy bear than to state how he feels himself. Comic strip characters, mythological legends, and artistic productions also achieve such "safe" communication: the individual can experience and communicate threats and pleasures without being psychologically endangered. The reporting of childhood events serves a very similar purpose—it permits the expression of self-references without the responsibility which generally goes with such expression. The adult can say, "I hated my Uncle John," but he does not face the consequences that would result from expressing hostile feelings in the present tense.

In such statements about childhood experiences, the patient can talk quite safely about himself. This is not to say that he will not get quite involved or even anxious as he is reminded of past traumatic periods. The patient who reports past aggression by saying that when he was small he often wished his brother dead may feel deep remorse and perhaps anxiety in response to this memory, but in his immediate situation he is reasonably safe. The thought of aggression is only tested with the therapist, and retaliation would be absurd. Essentially the patient uses the medium of childhood experience to scan the therapist for emotional response without having to take responsibility for his feelings.

Dreams

An even wider range of feeling tones can be introduced via the medium of dreams. Dreams may contain intense and often violent scenes but they are, by convention, permitted to be irrational, and many otherwise prohibited wishes may be safely introduced. Even the interpretation of a dream leaves the patient in relative safety: although such interpretations communicate to the patient that his wishes can be recognized and have meaning here and now, they still leave him the defense that these wishes represent only that part of himself for which he does not have to feel directly responsible. Again, through dreams, he can scan the therapist's reactions to a great number of complex feeling tones and can safely bring forth ideas and wishes which he would have to hide carefully were he to take full responsibility for them.

Free Association

Free association as a medium of communication has yet other characteristics. First, it does not depend directly on memory function, but occurs mostly with the encouragement of the therapist. Thus the patient does not have the choice he has with dreams and recall of childhood experiences, where he can simply state that he does not remember any such events at a given time. But because he is asked by the therapist to produce free-associative statements, he accordingly has an even greater freedom from responsibility than he has with dreams. His statements are not only elicited by the therapist, but they are also predictably illogical and unclear, and their meaning is available only to the therapist. On the other hand, they appear to the patient himself as bewildering, discontinuous thought processes, and he generally has some anxiety about the technique. The typical patient must laboriously learn free association, perhaps because he feels that he is submitting to the greater wisdom of the therapist, who can find meaning where there was none before. The patient's feelings of submission, as well as his freedom from responsibility, are important characteristics of this medium.

Dreams, recollections, and free associations are thus media by which complex messages can be expressed safely and a large range of feeling tones scanned for their presence and explored. The structure and content of these messages permit both patient and therapist to be as much observers as participants in their discussions. The patient may ask the therapist, between the lines, "Let us assume that I am such and such a person, what would you do then?" The patient's covert expectations are introduced with an "as if" safety clause that helps the disengagement of the therapist. He can adopt the role of an observer with the patient and can more easily maintain an uninvolved emotional attitude. Although all these media permit the patient to create a situation in which he can safely explore new areas without severely risking his previous expectations, his statement still does not represent real feeling but only feelings from the shadowland of memory. In this manner prohibted wishes can be safely expressed and fears tested. No wonder these media have become useful tools.

While the advantages of these content areas are obvious, there are disadvantages which come from the same sources. Both the therapist and the patient become observers when they discuss material that has only a very indirect bearing on their relationship. As observers, they reduce direct participation with each other. In other words, the possible emotional impact on one another is reduced, and the experience the patient goes through is minimized.

Sexual Content

Messages concerning sexual behaviors are of a somewhat different dimension. This area is more daring, conventionally speaking, and the patient will often bring it up during the hour with a feeling of anticipation of great danger. At the same time, he can often more directly test the involvement or disengagement of the therapist via this important area. Discussion of psychopathic behavior and unusual sexual practices seems to make a great many people feel uneasy, including many therapists. Since the patient is always deeply interested in discovering the areas of the therapist's uneasy feelings, he will use statements with sexual content to test the therapist's defenses.

The sexual medium is also used to test the other person for his readiness for greater intimacy. A discussion of sexual behaviors often serves to emphasize the close, confidential bond between the patient and the therapist. Consequently, the sexual content area is often used by the patient to test out how much he can trust and depend on the therapist. Success in discussing material in this area (no anxiety on the part of the therapist) enhances transference phenomena and the patient learns to speak of "my analyst" or "the hour." The meaning of the sexual content area in these social feelings is of great significance and should not be overlooked.

The etiology of sexual problems may play a very special role in the development of maladjustment, yet statements with sexual content may also be quite incidental to the working through of sexual problems. Dependency problems are not necessarily worked through by the use of words which denote dependency. These problems are affected by the therapist's responses to the patient's covert acting out of dependency needs in the hour, such as asking questions, etc. Words that connote sexual meaning are not necessarily of great significance to the sexual problem. But the covert acting out of events which have their source in sexual problems (e.g., seduction, disgust, avoidance, and exhibitionism) will often have a direct effect on the therapist and may be of great importance in the process of working through sexual problems. Such problems represent experiences that the patient cannot successfully handle on the outside, and so he brings them into the hour to test his vulnerability. Consequently, statements of sexual problems may have little to do with beneficial experiences in the sexual area.

Memories

There are approaches in psychotherapy which maintain that memories of the past are of great significance, as in the historical emphasis of the psychoanalytic model. Other models place more emphasis upon discussion of more immediate, "real" problems. From the communication standpoint the important difference between these various uses of memory lies in the degree of responsibility with which the patient uses them. A patient may place a statement in the past because he wants to create a distance between his present self and his past self and in that manner express dangerous material more safely. What are the hidden meanings that such a statement of past events reveals to the therapist? By placing a memory of aggression against his father into an early phase of his life, a patient is perhaps testing, not very boldly, how the therapist will react to aggression. The age of the memory may very well be related to the degree of responsibility a patient wants to accept for a given feeling. By placing memories in the recent past, the patient may imply that he is now more ready to compete with the therapist, than he was when he still was concerned with early childhood experiences.

Problem Choice

Often in psychotherapy the patient is given the choice of the topic and is encouraged to talk about whatever he wants to, but the influence of the therapist on the patient's selections of topics should never be disregarded. Often the therapist is not aware of exercising this influence. He may report: "My patients never talk about sexual matters. The Freudians must have a peculiar sample of patients," illustrating both selective processes and lack of awareness. Not only should the influence of the therapist on the selection of content area be recognized, but it should also be utilized toward therapeutic goals. Rather than unconsciously reinforcing topics by covert cues of his own, the therapist should be aware of his influence and then make the most adequate choice of content in terms of a theoretical model. By utilizing the various content areas, the therapist can maximize both the amount of covert information he obtains and the beneficial experiences he provides.

Although each of the media discussed here has a specific yield, content areas as such are not of singular significance in the therapeutic process. As stated, any content area can be utilized by the patient to express and act out feelings which have very little direct relationship to the content itself. The sexual area can become a means of testing the social relationship; questions in regard to vocational choice can be a means of acting out dependency feelings; the report of failure can be the manifest cue for covertly acting out aggression against the therapist. The therapist can only try to obtain accurate information about covert cues by "listening with the third ear," in Reik's phrase, by broadening his attention to cues beyond the manifest content. He must listen to the manifest cues and then ask himself, "Why is the patient selecting this material now, and why is he telling it to me? What does he expect me to do?" Only when the therapist has formulated some answers for these questions and can point to the evidence, the specific covert cues on which his answers are based, is he in a position to understand the operations through which the patient perpetuates his problems. Content areas are then placed in the perspective where they belong: they are essentially varying sources of covert cues. The experienced therapist will listen to content areas with only partial interest—he knows that too much interest in the manifest problem presented can only lead to engagement and a very superficial understanding.

The process of therapeutic gain is based on experiences that follow asocial responses of the therapist with which he attempts to arouse beneficial uncertainty. To provide these experiences the therapist must learn to understand the patient's increased expectations covertly coded in his messages. Manifest media of communication give only indirect information about this behavior. Accordingly, it does not matter very much what the patient talks about as long as the therapist obtains the pertinent covert information.

EXTRATHERAPEUTIC INCIDENTS?

ROGERS was once confronted with this facetious attack on nondirective theory: what does the nondirective therapist do when a patient is about to jump out of the window? Tell him that you understand his feelings of wanting to jump and then "reflect" when he hits the ground? The implication of this all-too-clever comment is clear. There are obviously some incidents in the therapeutic hour which cannot be used therapeutically, where extratherapeutic activity is in order.

Surely on occasion the safety of a patient, of society, of the therapist himself demands attention. There is no time for reflection when the wastepaper basket is on fire. But how often do these emergencies occur? Generally speaking, the patient does not bring many situations to the therapist that cannot stand delay and inspection. When emergencies occur in the therapeutic hour, the therapist cannot proceed with therapeutic work because he must tend to the immediate; he must decide if an event is a true emergency or if it represents another "therapeutic" possibility. If we define "emergency" as an event which demands urgent action, it is likely that most events in the therapeutic hour demand therapeutic attention rather than immediate action or extratherapeutic measures.

As stated earlier, the patient is likely to express significant feelings with certain conventions of language in order to express these feelings safely and keep them unrecognized by the respondent. He will attempt to influence the therapist with the use of conventions that weaken his recognition of underlying meaning. Many seemingly extratherapeutic events will therefore be the patient's favorite hiding place. These events need special attention because many a therapist gets engaged in a social rather than a therapeutic role when seemingly extratherapeutic incidents are used with skill.

Some of the most frequent hiding places will be discussed here. They will be analyzed for the asocial responses they require, precisely because the social response is so obvious.

Change of Appointments

The predictable social response to a request for a change of appointment hour is often used by patients as a means of obtaining reinforcement for their neurotic dilemma. In trying to be sure of limiting the response activity of the therapist as much as possible, patients usually present rather convincing reasons for this request, in a manner that discourages the therapist from thinking of a therapeutic meaning. Note that this does not imply that the patient is trying to malinger or to present convincing reasons where he has none; nor is the patient lying. But in the analysis of any message, it is necessary to determine the usual social consequences of the conventions used, as they so often do serve as hiding places. The patient's message is designed to make the therapist look at his schedule for another appointment hour.

In an attempt to maintain some distance from the social expectations of the patient's message, some therapists try to detect whether the reasons given for wishing to change the appointment are fact or fancy. This judgment cannot be made, unfortunately, unless the therapist desires to become a detective. Some therapists acquiesce to the patient's demands with the conviction that it is his right to ask for a change of hour; and it certainly is his right to ask if he wishes to do so. Our concern is not with "his right," but with information he may be hiding beneath his social message. Is he using this message with its highly predictable social response to reinforce certain patterns of his behavior? It certainly is worthwhile to check into such a possibility.

The following illustrates a patient who used the request for an appointment change to hide very pertinent feelings.

Patient: "My mother is coming in from the East and will be at the airport at 5:30 tomorrow. I have to change my appointment."

This message was designed to give the therapist very little choice but to make arrangements for changing the hour. It is the very "patness" of this type of message, however, that should help the therapist disengage from its social demand. The therapist cannot properly judge how "truthful" the patient's stated reasons are. They may sound perfectly plausible, but the therapist still has the obligation to discover the extent to which the patient is using this information to achieve goals other than the obvious ones. The general rule is that a good therapist will not take the chance of reinforcing disturbed behavior, which is what he might do were he to respond socially. He must at least give himself the opportunity to obtain further information. In this case the therapist continued:

Therapist: "Oh, I see. Your mother is coming in at this time tomorrow and that means you cannot come to the hour."

The therapist was still unclear as to what he should do and his statement was one of delay. While he delayed he also gave the patient the hint to elaborate.

Patient: "Yes, that's right, and I thought perhaps we could find another hour this week."

The patient was strengthening his social plea. He chose to interpret the response of the therapist as one that still allowed him to hope for a conventional social reaction. He did not want his demand for a change to be treated as a therapeutic incident.

Therapist: "Now, let's see, another hour? Perhaps you can tell me more about this request of yours."

In the second part of the sentence the therapist asked for more delay. He apparently had begun to wonder if there were not some greater significance to the demand.

Patient: "You are so difficult; what is there to tell? My mother is coming to the airport and I am asking you for another appointment, and I don't see what thought I can have about that."

The patient increased the social demand of his message. He apparently intended to make the therapist look foolish. Or was he justifiably angry? Some therapists argue that the patient has a right to be angry when the therapist always clings to his role and asks foolish questions about the most obvious circumstances. But why should the patient's anger be called justifiable simply because the therapist is doing his job, is staying therapeutic even though the patient wants a "social" response? It is certainly possible that the patient's anger says, in effect, "Don't dare to treat this demand of mine therapeutically." The exchange continued as follows:

Therapist: "It made you unhappy and angry that I did not let this question go by, and that even here I have to psychologize."

The therapist was beginning to suspect that there was more significance to the demand than he thought at first, and he attempted to obtain further information. At the same time, there also seemed to be a need on his part to apologize because he was a therapist rather than a social "human being." He used the term "psychologize," perhaps in an attempt to minimize the patient's anger by recognizing the source. It should be noted that the therapist was not angry himself. He simply maintained a therapeutic role. The patient's anger, on the other hand, probably arose because he could not obtain the highly predictable response which he had identified as justifiable.

Patient: "Why do you have to needle me? Why do you have to analyze everything?"
Therapist: "That gives you no place to hide."
Patient: "I don't want to hide, I just want another hour. But you're refusing to give me another hour, is that it?"
Therapist: "It suddenly seems very important that I give you this other hour, that I give consent for you to go to see your mother."

The therapist was now fully disengaged at that point. His response to the patient's comment ("analyzing everything") was probably an accurate reflection. The therapist's message to the patient said, "Let's discover what emotions are associated with your demands." But then the patient rebelled.

Patient: "I don't need your consent. I'll go if it's the last thing I do."
Therapist: "After all, it's your mother or me, John" (with a smile).
Patient: (Pause) "I guess that is right." (Smiles and pauses for 60 seconds) "Mother wrote me that she wanted to come late in the evening, but I wrote her to take the earlier plane. I don't think that I really planned that her coming would interfere with the hour. As you know, I had to face a very similar problem when my parents got divorced . . . Father actually prohibited my seeing Mother. . . ."

In this illustration we notice how powerfully the patient tried to restrict the response activity of the therapist in order to make him conform to his demands. The patient's pressure to treat the incident extratherapeutically was rather severe in this case, but when the therapist maintained his therapeutic role some dynamics become apparent. Of course, it was possible that at the end of the exchange the patient simply wanted to please the therapist by recognizing the "significance" of his questions. Even this interpretation did not deny the necessity of asking questions. If the therapist had automatically consented to arrange for another hour, he might actually have harmed the patient by reinforcing his need to see Mother. By permitting the patient to succeed in such a scheme he might have reinforced the very problem' he hoped to solve. We note parenthetically that the therapist had the mannerism of saying "John" at an important junction, a communication which surely was not lost on John. The patient may have learned that the therapist occasionally had to apologize for his therapeutic role and that such an apology was expressed by a more intimate address. This kind of information can be useful to a patient if he later feels a need to ineffectuate the therapist.

Payment

Remuneration for services is a generally accepted convention in our society, yet there appears to be a feeling among many people that some services deserve payment more than others. Few people would argue that the TV repairman should "forget" his bill and be content with the fact that he is providing pleasure for them. The services rendered by the minister, the physician, or the psychotherapist, however, are often seen in a different light, almost as if charging for these services is taking some kind of advantage of people under stress. Excesses by these and other similar professions undoubtedly do occur; yet the feeling that these professions should not really charge for their services seems to go deeper, perhaps involving feelings of guilt over having to buy personal attention and friendship. This feeling of guilt also affects many members of the professions, although it has not prevented a substantial increase in professional fees over the last 50 years. Psychotherapists have their share of guilt feelings about charges, with the result that the topic of payment is often handled poorly from the psychotherapeutic point of view; consequently payments become one of the social engagements that the patient can use for purposes of control.

Many therapists who, with some pride, defend a disinterest in money (particularly if they practice therapy on a part-time basis and obtain their major income from other sources), seem desirous of indicating that they are really interested only in the patient and his welfare. On further questioning, some will admit that they are concerned lest the patient get the impression that they are more interested in his money than in him as a person. Other therapists claim that payments are good for the patient and that such an exchange helps to maintain the patient's self-respect and give him a sense of independence. This line of argumentation can also be interpreted to mean that the therapist is not really interested in money for his services, but is doing the patient a favor in charging a fee. Regardless of the therapist's attitude, the emotional involvements inherent in money matters often permit the patient to act out important feelings simply by payment or nonpayment of the fee. We think it is important to discuss these important issues thoroughly and to separate fact from fiction.

The treatment contract between therapist and patient is most likely a verbal agreement reached in the early hours of the contact. The patient selects the therapist he wants to work with, and the therapist then decides whether he wishes to accept the patient for treatment and under what conditions treatment can best proceed. Money is often discussed during the first few hours and the therapist sets the fee that he feels he must obtain for his services. It may be a token fee if the therapist feels he can afford this arrangement and is sufficiently interested in working with the patient. In other cases it may be arranged with regard to the patient's income. In still other cases there may be a flat hourly fee which the therapist charges anyone he accepts. In some clinics there is no fee at all; in such a setting the question of whether a fee is indeed beneficial to the therapeutic interview becomes especially important.

The position taken here is that the payment of the fee is totally irrelevant to psychotherapy. Like any other material of concern to the patient, the importance of a fee is in its discussion. In this sense the significance of the fee usually decreases as therapy goes on and as the therapist becomes more sensitive to other topics. That feelings of self-respect and independence are related to the payment of a fee is doubtful—a person can perceive his payments as a sign of weakness ("No one will help me except for money") just as easily as a sign of strength. Even when payment of fees is not part of the contract (as in some clinics), the chances are that other topics will serve as vehicles for working on these same feelings of "giving" or self-respect and value. In any event, it is not important what the financial contract stipulates, as long as both patient and therapist can live with it and are willing to use it as a guideline for the future.

If this contract is not lived up to, for whatever reasons, the relationship is technically dissolved and a new contract must be formed. When a contract between patient and therapist is dissolved, it is true that the therapist is responsible for either arranging a new contract or referring the patient for other help if this is judged necessary. But under no circumstances can the therapist simply overlook a breach of contract. The effect of nonpayment, once payment has been agreed on, may be as difficult for the therapist as it is for the patient, since the therapist often depends on the payment to sustain himself. In addition, nonpayments are likely to affect his attitude toward the patient, even though he may not always admit this to himself.

A contractual agreement between patient and therapist is a therapeutic event of the first order. There is a good deal of evidence to support this assertion. For example, a patient may have accumulated an overall debt of several hundred dollars but, despite having contracted for regular payments, be making only occasional, small payments. If the therapist neglects to discuss the matter, he may reinforce the patient's unaware mechanism of involving people by making them creditors. The patient may be testing the therapist's courage, his willingness to risk the total debt by challenging the patient, or even his trust and belief in him; such a need to test people's belief in him may be one of the patient's problems. The therapist, because of his own psychological involvement in the problem of money, may be engaged by the very mechanisms which he should handle and help to resolve.

Other patients will use payment or lack of payment as a vehicle to constrict the therapist's recognition of all sorts of feelings: aggression, demand for love, feelings of unworthiness, etc. In each case, such behavior demands disengagement by the therapist and a thorough discussion of what psychological use the patient is making of his obligation to pay. Whenever a contract is not honored the therapist should consider a new contract to replace a defaulted one. The decision regarding a new contract should be based on the therapist's judgment as to the conditions under which he can do his best work.

The following example illustrates the potential significance of the topic of payments for patient and therapist.

Patient: "Sorry, Doctor, I don't think I can pay you the full amount this month. My child needs an operation and with the hospital expenses I am running terribly short."

The tendency of many individuals brought up in our culture would be to sympathize with the patient who has had these special expenses. The message is (by emotion) specifically designed to evoke just that reaction, and the person who disregards such a request is in jeopardy of being seen as inhuman and greedy. The patient's message is designed to extend a strong emotional force, one likely to arouse highly constricted thoughts in most respondents brought up in our culture. Some readers will surely protest the insinuation that such a statement must be a manipulation. After all, what if it is true that the patient had these expenses? What if her child needs extended hospital care? Is the therapist not *also* a human being who should sympathize with the patient to the best of his ability? It is precisely the readiness with which many therapists accept these considerations that indicates most clearly how powerfully such a message structures an emotional climate in the respondent. The therapist's role is to help the patient, and understanding him properly is his best tool. Sympathy or any other emotion must not stand in the way of his best effort as a therapist.

Therapist: "You state this in a way which would make it very difficult for me to say 'no' to you."

The therapist here refused to react to the immediate social demand of the patient. Instead he stated his recognition of the emotional design of the plea, providing the patient with an opportunity to express any deeper significance of this event.

Patient: "Well, I have paid my bills most of the time and this is a real difficulty. I mean, the child needs the operation and I just don't know how I could pay you this month."

The patient was still aiming at a conventional end to the discussion, but one may note that she offered no solution other than nonpayment.

Therapist: "It would be inhuman if I said that my payments come ahead of those for your child."

The therapist disengaged from the demanded impact of the convention. His use of the word "inhuman" is perhaps rather dramatic, which may be one of the therapist's available behaviors.

Patient: "Well, I'm really sorry about it, but I think I can make it up next month. I will have to do some extra work, I guess; I've already arranged to do some work in the evenings."

The patient then discussed the issue and was not concerned only with consent.

Therapist: "I thought you didn't want to give me much choice. In a sense you didn't really ask me a question. But I believe you are asking now if you could delay one month in payment."
Patient: "Yes, I felt that you would understand that something like this can happen to everyone."
Therapist: "And I was unreasonable to hesitate. . . ."

Patient: "It seems to me that you're questioning whether my child really needs an operation. I'd be happy to give you the name of the physician. He said that it was absolutely necessary. He must have the operation. There certainly is no question in my mind."

Note that the patient again made a bid for consent from the therapist, rather than deal with the issue.

Therapist: "Again you're placing me in a position where I am inhuman if I'm not ready to help you in an emergency, like a friend who lets you down."

The therapist exaggerated again. He was impatient; he wanted the patient to look beyond the reality of her request.

Patient: "I guess you are right. For a moment I thought you didn't believe me. But the child does need the operation."

Therapist: "How am I holding up the operation?"

Patient: "Well, I have to pay you, too, and I cannot pay you both at the same time. While I think this hour is terribly important to me, I think the operation is even more so at this time."

Therapist: "What is really endangered then, is not the operation, as you would pay for it anyway, but your hour with me."

Patient: "I don't want to give you up. I have no one. You are the only person who will understand and it is in these hours that one needs . . ." (pause) "friends, people who will stand by when one really needs them." (Pause) "I suddenly realize what you meant before; that I did not give you much of a choice."

Note that the patient then gave up trying to evoke sympathy in the therapist, and instead attempted to create a different emotional climate to oblige the therapist. We may call it flattery or a play on his sense of obligation. She apparently believed that the therapist would respond more favorably to this message, but we should note that she still wanted to force him to consent to see her by using emotional impact. She was not yet discussing the therapist as a person who has the right to say no.

Therapist: "You want to find out how much I want to see you?"

With this response the therapist was again disengaged from the new impact (which he himself has perhaps elicited). He attempted to give the patient the experience that neither forcing her friends nor seducing them is a necessary mode of behavior.

Patient: "*Perhaps I can make arrangements with the hospital and pay in installments. Would it be all right if I pay you about half the amount this month and spread the other half to next month? I think I can handle it that way.*"

Here the patient has experienced that she could not get results by an emotional impact on the respondent but must deal directly with the issue.

Therapist: "*That sounds like a reasonable offer.*"

Patient: "*Of course, I could have asked my folks too, but I don't like to. With them it is always fight, fight, fight. My mother . . . (etc.)*"

Here the patient was no longer forcing the therapist through emotional impact to do her bidding. The therapist has used the information provided him to the best advantage of the patient. Had he responded to the social demands of the patient and immediately agreed to the delay in payment, he would have reinforced her neurotic behavior, perhaps the one of "forcing" people to do her bidding with an emotional impact solicited through sympathy and seduction. But the therapist was now in a position to tell the patient whether or not he was willing to engage in a new contract. The patient could leave with the experience that she must deal with the issues involved rather than trying to overwhelm others with emotional stimulation.

In summary, then, treating payment as a therapeutic incident does not spare the therapist from making decisions about money. However, these decisions will be based not on the patient's manipulations but on his own estimate of how he can best treat the patient.

Gestures as Communications

Patients engage in gestural behaviors—specific body movements, habits of speech, specific ways of sitting, means of smoking and so forth—which can only too easily be accepted by the therapist without further thought. However, these gestural behaviors may be safe ways of expressing significant information. In some cases the patient perhaps has experimented with them and established them as a successful means of communication. A person who habitually talks very softly may use this gesture to create a climate of being in "partnership" with the therapist, as well as forcing him to listen very attentively. Or a student closing his eyes during a lecture may wish to create a futile sort of anger in the teacher. The use of gestures, then, can serve in controlling the respondent's response activity without permitting him to counteract in a meaningful way.

Therapists, too, react to the emotional climate created by certain gestures, often without recognizing them clearly. By doing so they subtly reinforce the patient's schemes instead of arousing beneficial uncertainty. The significance of some of these gestures—apparently so harmless and yet so controlling—will be elucidated with an illustration.

A patient had the habit of standing next to her chair in the office until the therapist asked in a friendly way for her to be seated. This ritual had become rather thoroughly established, and the therapist had not given it any thought until he described the patient in detail to his "control therapist." When asked if he did this with all his patients, the therapist realized that the ritual might be of some special importance to this woman. He began to suspect that she acted out her feelings of dependency with this gesture. An excerpt from the interview, after the therapist was alerted, follows:

Therapist: "Good morning."
Patient: (Looks at the therapist and seems bewildered) "Good morning." *(Still standing)*
Therapist: (Sits down) "You are wondering. . . ."
Patient: "You seem to be very short this morning. . . . Oh, just an impression." *(Still standing)* "I don't know, I really have nothing to say today." *(Pause)*
Therapist: "Nothing to say? I notice you are still standing."
Patient: "Oh, yes, I guess I was." *(Sits down)*
Therapist: "You look dissatisfied. Is there something you don't like?"
Patient: "I don't know. I just feel disappointed."
Therapist: "Disappointed? In me?"
Patient: "No, I am not disappointed in you. In myself. It is all very confusing."
Therapist: "It seems that I am doing the wrong thing today."
Patient: "I don't know. It just is an off day. I feel blue."
Therapist: "I should do more for you."
Patient: "No, you do all you can. It is me."
Therapist: "That leaves me out. As if I really were not here at all."
Patient: (Laughs) "I wonder if you like me."
Therapist: "I did not prove it to you today: you had to sit down without my offering you a chair."

Here the therapist gave his punch line, but it should be noted that this bid of "insight" was not really necessary. Therapists simply are verbal creatures.

Patient: "Oh, yes, I can sit down on my own, I guess." (She cries.) "Lytha [her sister] was really mean. She said that I should get out of the house and grow up. I felt so small but I could not say anything and she kept nagging me. She does this once in a while. I wish she would leave me alone. I am not doing anything to her and I don't know what she wants from me."*

The patient had little awareness of the meaning of the sitting-down gesture. But the fact that the therapist did not reinforce her subtle bid to have him invite her to sit down (and in that manner give consent to her depending on him for the chair) brought forth exploratory behavior in the area of dependency.

In the following weeks this patient was able to assert herself more readily in the hour ("I can sit down without you"). Obviously the discussion of her gesture alone did not accomplish this, but it was a beginning. The therapist's recognition of the meaning of the gesture did result in his being more alert to her behavior that was designed to have him take the initiative in their relationship. When the therapist gave his punch line, he probably wanted to reassure himself that he had, in fact, understood. He had permitted the patient the experience that taking the initiative was not as dangerous as she had feared. The uncertainty aroused in the patient by responding to her gesture apparently served its function.

Gifts

Another event that is often not recognized for its therapeutic importance is the patient's use of gifts in his relations with the therapist. Gifts have a conventional connotation of friendliness with the expectation that the respondent will be grateful. The receiver is not to "look a gift horse in the mouth" and should not inquire into the value of the gift. Instead, he should gracefully accept the present and play the role of a pleased person. This role is so definitely expected that any deviation is likely to arouse painful and embarrassed feelings. When a seven-year-old girl brings the therapist a bouquet of flowers she has picked in the garden, the first impulse of any receiver is to say "thank you" and feel very pleased about this expression of gratitude and friendliness. Yet within the therapeutic situation nothing could be more wasteful. It is just because the gift is such a safe way of expressing feelings and setting up structures that some of the most therapeutically important feelings are likely to be hidden behind these expressions.

The therapist is placed in a situation which demands of him disengagement from powerful social conventions. Yet the gift must be treated as a therapeutic incident. It cannot be accepted, but must be set aside and the feelings involving it must be discussed. In some cases the therapist's disengagement will motivate the patient to take his gift back, while in others the patient may continue to offer it even after the therapist has disengaged from the imposed convention. The therapist might accept the flowers from the child, but only after exploring the giving with the child, lest significant problem behavior be reinforced.

Gifts need not always be objects. There are "gifts" like invitations, compliments, referral of other patients, and more subtly, gifts of the therapeutic "productions" demanded by the therapist. For example, a therapist wants the patient to talk about oedipal feelings and so the patient obediently talks about them—they are now gifts, to which the therapist may unknowingly respond with pleasure, and thus reinforce submissive behavior patterns in the patient. Such gifts are the most difficult to recognize, but the well-trained therapist will recognize his own pleasure and be able to disengage even from these subtle schemes.

The patient not only gives gifts, but also demands them. His demands may involve conventional and seemingly trivial gift objects such as cigarettes or matches, or they may involve the therapist's services. He may complain about the heat or cold of the office, or the noise outside. Sometimes the patient's demand to be pleased will even involve the way the therapist conducts his interview ("Please shut off the recording") or his verbalization ("I can't hear you" or "Don't talk so much"). The demand of a patient often seems rational enough, a justifiable request from one man to another. In fact, it must seem rational for the patient to achieve his ends. In some instances the therapist must deal with the rational demands extratherapeutically (as in a case of fire) but in most cases he can afford to look for unaware sources. We shall present an example which deals with a patient asking for cigarettes.

Patient: "I forgot my cigarettes. D'you think I could have one of yours?"

The patient demanded a gift that cannot easily be refused. Most people automatically respond by offering to help out. Here the therapist disengages.

Therapist: "I would be quite a heel if I refused you." (Does not offer a cigarette).

Patient: (Laughs) "Well, for the money I am paying you, I guess you can afford to give me one."

The patient persists in his request by trying to shame the therapist.

Therapist: "You are telling me that I owe you one."

Patient: "You are a hard man. You don't let me get away with anything. All I wanted was a smoke but I am losing my appetite for it fast. Can't you ever give?"

The patient was angered because he could not get his wish. Note that he threatened a loss of appetite, which happened to be one of his more consistent problems. The therapist picked him up on this.

Therapist: "You are disappointed because this safe way of making me 'give' was not so safe after all. You even try to make me feel bad by your loss of appetite because I didn't jump at the opportunity."

Note that the therapist disengaged from the demand but was not fully disengaged from the anger. The phrase, "jump at the opportunity," was not without anger.

Patient: "Now, about this woman I have been telling you about. . . ."

The patient changed topics. He had experienced that his problem of using a threat against himself to get his wish did not pay off. If it had, the therapist might easily have reinforced the very problem he was trying to help.

On the other hand, it may be the therapist who has forgotten his cigarettes and requests the patient to help him out. The rationale for this action is that the object is small and that it may help the patient to be treated as just another person. However, we cannot accept such reasoning. With such action the therapist introduces the social role which he must learn to avoid. It would be far wiser for the therapist to understand his own feeling of wanting to impose on the patient and to treat this feeling as an issue in their relationship. Some argue, however, that the therapist's request for a cigarette is analogous to his bringing his problem to the patient, a task that some therapists have experimented with in the name of decreasing their own omnipotence. We believe this to be an erroneous argument.

The following is an example of a patient who sends a gift at Christmas time. He sent the gift by mail, and the therapist brought the wrapped gift to the next hour.

Patient: (Sees the wrapped gift on the desk) "Oh, I have to tell you about a dream I had during the vacation. It was recurring and quite disturbing" (etc.).

This was an unusual opening and the therapist believed that the patient was bringing up material that he felt was important enough to prevent the therapist from discussing the wrapped gift.

Therapist: "I wonder why you start off the hour with something so very important. Has this something to do with the parcel here on this desk?"
Patient: "I saw that you hadn't even unwrapped it. Well, you handle it your way. Why didn't you even unwrap it? It would embarrass me if you unwrapped it in front of me."

The patient expressed some feeling of discomfort but still wanted to avoid the issue.

Therapist: "To discuss this present would be more difficult than discussing the dream?"
Patient: "I just went by the store and I saw that thing and I thought since it is Christmas time I wanted to enter the spirit of Christmas giving. I am disappointed that you did not unwrap it, because I expected that you would enjoy it very much."

The patient justifies his gift as an act of kindness. This, of course, is the conventional meaning of gifts, but the therapist was aware that an "act of kindness" can be in the service of other demands. He then attempted to better understand the reason for the gift.

Therapist: "Expected?"
Patient: "Oh, I bought it for you and I expected you to be happy with it. I just now thought that it doesn't seem to fit anymore—it's past Christmas and all. It is sort of a Christmassy gift. Why don't you unwrap it and see for yourself, or don't you want it?
Therapist: "You seem to feel now that I don't quite deserve your gift. I am making too much fuss about it—bringing it here wrapped."
Patient: "Well, do you? I mean, your bringing it in here

wrapped, and not saying thank you or anything else. You are treating it as if it were poison or shit or something. Don't you want to see it close?" (Laughs) "For all you know, of course, it might be shit."

The patient felt cheated of his pleasure and acted out his aggression.

Therapist: "I wonder why you laughed right then?"

The therapist could not quite deal with aggression directly and delayed by almost forcing the patient back to a more therapeutic discussion.

Patient: "It struck me funny, if you must know. You haven't looked, and it might be a piece of shit all wrapped up. Just my sordid sense of humor."

Therapist: "Are you saying now that this gift also could have been something I might not have 'enjoyed' so much?"

The therapist was now working on the hypothesis that the hostility was at least partly associated with the gift itself and not only with his nonacceptance of it. Perhaps there were ambivalent feelings in the patient's giving of it. Perhaps the patient wanted to express subtle aggression unnoticed, which was indeed one of his problems.

Patient: "It's a lighter, not shit. I bought it because you always seemed to be looking for matches." (Reaches for the parcel and places it in his pocket) "Permit me to take it back. I thought that it embarrassed you that you waste so much time with matches. Mind if I keep it now?"

Therapist: "I think that you already made up your mind."

Patient: "I will keep it as a reminder."

The presentation of a gift carried important meaning which could easily have been overlooked if it had been treated as an extratherapeutic incident. By neither accepting nor rejecting the gift, the therapist opened up the patient's behavior to inquiry. He did not reinforce the patient's secret wish to please or hurt by simply accepting it.

Demands

Many hard-to-refuse demands may be made on the therapist, designed to tempt him to provide services "outside" the hour. Such services include requests for reading material, for fee reduction, for changing the hour, for decreasing the number of therapy hours, or even for the name of a prostitute. Each of these events should be looked at as therapeutic incidents and not as simple "after-the-hour" comments.

Some might argue that the patient can legitimately ask some questions that deserve an answer, e.g., "How long do I still have to come?" Although this is not denied, it must always be remembered that the patient has learned to communicate his vulnerable wishes under camouflage of the obvious. The patient who requests the therapist to tell him "How long do I still have to come" has selected one particular question to "legitimately" force the therapist into a response. Yet with his question he can express many meanings: he may want to express fear, make an outright demand, display anger, apologize to the therapist, or even threaten to quit. Of course, the request itself must be dealt with on its own merits, and then answers can be given, but the more subtle meaning of the patient's communication must first be understood. The ever-so-rational demand itself is at times the means by which the patient attempts to perpetuate his maladjustment by forcing a reinforcing response. The therapist should not be overly concerned with the rationality of a given request but, as elsewhere, with the emotional climate it creates. Once the covert meaning of the request is understood, appropriate responses can be given.

An illustration of a "service demand" and one way of handling it follows:

Patient: "It is terribly noisy in here. Of course, it has been noisy all along, but today it just gets on my nerves. I don't know why they have to blow their trumpets so hard." (A band was marching by the building in which the office is located.) "No thought comes to my mind. Don't you think that this is true—I mean outside my neurosis? I wonder if we couldn't close the windows?"

Therapist: "We?"

The patient made a "rational" demand; the therapist did not unthinkingly fulfill it but inquired for meaning.

Patient: "I thought you'd want to close them. After all, it's your office. Would you mind closing them? I don't think I make that sort of request often, and you can see for yourself, or should I say, hear for yourself, that this is quite impossible. I can hardly hear a word you're saying."

Therapist: "I should close the windows because it's my responsibility to take care of my office."

This was a delay statement but the therapist recognized that the patient was using the noise to justify a bid for controlling his behavior. It happened that the patient had many problems with people because he made demands on them that he conceived as justified (and this, of course, is why the item was presented). Were the therapist to jump up and close the window he would reinforce (by rewarding) the problem behavior.

Patient: "No, that won't be necessary." (Got up) "I think I can close it myself." (Closed the window) "Well, now isn't this much better? At least it cuts out most of the sharp tones." (Went to the other window) "Well, this one is more difficult." (Attempted to close it but could not do it) "For Christ's sake, I can't close this one. What is the matter with it?" (Left the window open and returned to the couch) (Very softly) "I don't know what happened, I just can't close it." (Begins to cry) "I couldn't close it."

Therapist: "Makes you feel sort of helpless that you need me to take care of you."

Patient: "Leave me alone. I tried it, didn't I? It really is your responsibility. I don't know why I should close your windows. I did it just because I did not want you to have to get up. I tried it, but I couldn't do it." (Cries again)

Therapist: "There should be something left for me to do, why should you have to do it all? When you give a finger, who knows, I might be asking for the whole hand."

The therapist operated on the hypothesis that the patient's demanding behavior was a way of not allowing others to make demands of him. He had perhaps learned that those making demands on him were insatiable. The therapist worked on this therapeutic objective even though the social "window closing" demand appeared justified.

Some will argue that the patient's unhappy feelings arose from the therapist's refusal to respond to the justified demand. After all, the patient politely asked to have the window closed and the noise outside justified this as a reasonable demand. Rather than close it, the therapist proceeded to talk while the window remained open. The argument might go: Why shouldn't the patient be angry since his reasonable demand was not acted upon? No one likes a reasonable request to be forgotten under talk—in fact, one may ask what right the therapist has to refuse the reasonable demand of a patient and to avoid the responsibilities of his office.

The fact is that the therapist did not close the window, but neither did he refuse to close it—he merely insisted that the demand be discussed. What is more, it is very unlikely that the patient actually became angry because the therapist lacked "politeness." It is much more likely that he was anxious rather than angry—anxious because the therapist was not manipulated by the patient's "justified" demand that he follow a social role. Instead, the asocial "response" of the therapist made the patient uncertain about his making demands on people. Of course, the therapist could have closed the window himself and protected the therapeutic gain by discussing the demand later. The actual way of dealing with the problem is not so important as the therapeutic attitude toward subtle cues. We feel that the therapist did increase the impact of his social response by not obliging the social demand immediately.

Vacation

The patient's request for a vacation or "time off" can be difficult. The therapist may have taken a vacation himself, during which they had not met during hours ordinarily contracted for. The patient now comes with the same request and asks to be excused for a week or a month. His request is based on the convention that it is his right to have time off whenever he wants to, and he undeniably has this right. But we should note that he is not just availing himself of his right to take time off, but is asking for the therapist's consent to do so. He wants the therapist to agree with him that he can take time off, the implication being that if the therapist consents, it will not interfere with treatment.

As the patient has the right to accept or reject the absence of the therapist, so the therapist has the right to refuse his consent to a patient's demand for a vacation that in the therapist's best knowledge will interfere with treatment. The therapist should not be influenced by the fact that he has a waiting list of patients or that he himself took time off. He can only evaluate a patient's request for a vacation in terms of his own views on treatment. He must ask himself if he can continue to work with the patient under the new condition. This statement does not imply that there should be no vacation and absences or that both patient and therapist should not accept each other's absences. The point here is that an absence, for whatever reason, demands a discussion of the contract which the therapist has with his patient. The therapist, therefore, must deal with a request for time off from the point of view that it is consent which has been asked for. This turns the request into a therapeutic incident.

Number of Appointments

The patient sometimes demands a change in the number of hours he is seen during a week. How does the therapist arrive at an "adequate" number of therapy hours in the first place? Practices differ widely. Some therapists insist on seeing their patient a set number of weekly hours, while others permit the patient himself to choose. Some therapists use yet other criteria, such as the patient's financial resources, their own time schedule; or such "psychological" criteria as the estimate of resistance seen in the patient, the level of anxiety, etc. Some therapists adopt flexible schedules, telling patients that the number of hours will decrease as treatment progresses, while other therapists do not change the number of hours over time. There apparently is no agreement on meaningful criteria for determining the necessary number of hours for maximum benefit.

Some therapists see their patients monthly (such as in distant station Mental Health Clinics) and believe that there is a benefit in these visits, while others, like Rosen, work a 24-hour schedule on occasion and ascribe maximum benefits to this effort. New explorations are now underway with 15-minute sessions.

It is easier to say which criteria are inadequate than to point to adequate ones. It seems inadequate to use the financial resources of the patient as a criteria to determine the number of hours of maximal benefit. It is true that a patient's insufficient financial resources have to be considered and that a given therapist may want to reduce his rates or may not be able to afford to accept a patient, but it is difficult to justify consideration of financial resources in determining the desirable number of hours. Nor should this decision be left to the patient's judgment. Some may feel that to let the patient decide is a very permissive way of handling this problem, but it looks more evasive than permissive. It implies that the patient has more adequate criteria on which to base this judgment (a doubtful implication to say the least). The chances are that the patient has neither given this problem any thought nor had any experience on which to base a decision. The therapist is certainly in a somewhat better position in this respect and should not pass on responsibilities rightfully his. He has to discover reasonably defensible criteria for the number of hours during a week he wants to see the patient. His decision should be based on an estimate of maximum benefits under the specific conditions of the setting.

Psychological theory does give some clues for predicting rapport and transference. Many therapists, for example, are agreed that it is very hard to work with patients classified as "character disorders." The anxious patient who is very desirous of help may present a different problem than the involuntary patient sent in by a referring agent. The patient with somatic complaints often needs more time for rapport than others.

In the absence of pertinent research, the therapist can only use his own judgment, but in this he should develop reasonably objective criteria. The problem of hours is most complex. In fact, the very treatment goal of the therapist and of the setting he works in are involved in this decision.

When the patient demands a change in the number of hours he is to be seen, the therapist again must understand the demand in its therapeutic meaning rather than in terms of the "reality" of the question. Changing hours is inevitably a change in the contract. The demand may have many subtle meanings. A request for reduction of hours may imply a wish for reassurance of improvement; while a wish to increase the number of hours may imply a wish for greater dependency, or even the patient's desire for the therapist to tell him he is not making adequate progress. When this demand is treated extratherapeutically, the therapist often misses a significant therapeutic opportunity.

Interruptions

Therapists have established various ways of handling telephone calls, knocks on the door, noises outside the office, and other interruptions. The therapist is often unaware that he gives the patient much information about his own preferred behaviors by his way of handling these interruptions. For example, he may answer a telephone call at length, or apologize too profusely for a call, or refuse it altogether with obvious anger. Such occurrences may give the patient significant information about the therapist and his way of looking at the therapeutic relationship.

The helpless look, given to the patient while engaged in a long telephone conversation, the apology, or even the disregard of the interruption will all give the patient information for his scanning activity. The patient then will utilize this information for his own purposes. Aware of certain biases in the therapist, he is now in a position to arouse feelings in the therapist and thus to constrict the therapist's response activity when he senses danger to himself. It is probably true that the information gained from analyzing the way almost any practitioner handles interruptions could be significant in his success. It is sometimes useful to have another professional person observe the practitioner's office habits—as for example, his responses to interruptions in the office setting—in order to gain some insight as to idiosyncratic behaviors that typically affect his therapeutic relationship. Interruptions also may have other meanings to the patient, meanings that must be discussed in their own right.

It is impossible to avoid all disturbances, and the therapist's only safeguard is to be aware that disturbances, when they do occur, are an interference in the interpersonal process with his patient. He must discuss them with the patient, and in this way use them toward therapeutic gain.

It is not important whether these interruptions are "real" or imagined. In terms of the patient's feelings and messages, it does not really matter if someone is heard moving outside the door or apparently listening, or if the patient is just imagining it to be so. In either case, the "noise outside" demands discussion within the therapeutic hour.

Outside Calls, from Others, from Patients; Suicide Calls

For many years it was considered improper to talk to any other member of a family than the one in psychotherapy. (See Chapter XI.) The rationale was that such outside contacts would disturb the relationship with the patient. It was felt that were the therapist to confer with a patient's husband, he would not only arouse suspicion and fears but would also inform the patient that she was not fully responsible for her own behavior. Many therapists, therefore, have made it a practice to insist to the person calling on the telephone that the information conveyed must be information that can also be made available to the patient himself—it cannot be treated confidentially. While we agree with this conclusion, the original rationale for avoiding confidential contact seems faulty.

That the patient may experience suspicion, fears, or a sense of lack of responsibility is not really a critical consideration in therapeutic contacts with outside sources. After all, the patient can attach his fears to any half-worthy object, and the therapist cannot remove all such objects from the patient's life. These feelings are subject to therapeutic work and will yield many important experiences; the therapist must be prepared to discuss them with the patient. There is, however, a more valid reason for avoiding confidential information from outside sources.

This reason is that information from the outside that the therapist accepts under the banner of confidentiality limits his response activity with a patient. It limits the therapeutic instrument because the therapist himself must now weigh what he can and cannot say. He becomes less effective because he has aligned himself with someone outside his immediate relationship with the patient. There can be no "getting in cahoots" with a worried mother, an upset wife, or a concerned schoolteacher. However, there are other, proper means of bringing outside information into the therapeutic hour, as we shall discuss in the following chapter.

What are the responsibilities of the therapist when the patient himself calls between hours and wishes to talk to him? Therapists handle such requests in different ways. Some engage in therapeutic discussion, some hedge, and others discourage such calls altogether. The call itself, however, is a very special message: "I am worried and I have the right to ask that you talk me out of my worry—think of me, now." The message stands in the service of a plea for a social engagement. For example, a woman may call at 2:00 A.M. and say, "Please, it is urgent, see me now." We follow the practice of not responding to the patient's therapeutic material over the phone precisely because the act of phoning (and its plea to impose on the therapist in nonscheduled hours) may be one of the patient's problems. We reason that a response from the therapist would reinforce in her the behavior of getting extra time (love) by referring to special suffering (the reason for the call). From a social point of view, this argument sounds cruel and lacking warmth (who wants to let down someone in the hour of need?). However, the asocial response ("Thank you for calling, I'll see you at the appointed hour") provides the patient with the needed experience that "extra suffering" does not bring "extra love." This asocial response has its justification in the observation that by giving the engaged social response the therapist would actually maintain and perhaps increase the patient's suffering.

Is there a limit where the therapist must become a responsible social human being rather than maintain a therapeutic role? What if the patient threatens suicide? Should the therapist not enter the social stage at this crisis point and rush to the patient's help?

We believe that suicide behavior is learned behavior. Through thousands of messages, the patient has learned to force others to do his bidding by arousing guilt in them with threats of his own suffering or destruction. A patient who has been reasonably successful over a length of time in engaging others' sympathy for his suffering may, under particular stress, feel that he can also be successful with the therapist by threatening self-destruction. Were the therapist to accept the social role now and give extra attention, he would not only reinforce such behavior for the future but actually increase the possibility of the patient's following through with the threat at the present time. The patient's state of mind is such that arousing guilt in another person is more important to him than survival. If he experiences success, he is placed in a situation where he can commit suicide as a symbolic act: to die to be loved and remembered.

Some argue, however, that the patient is under great stress and it is more important to give him some extra love even if it does reinforce his maladjusted behavior. Furthermore, the argument goes, the rejection experienced by the patient when his desperate bid for love is not answered may give him the final "push" to follow through with his self-destructive act. The argument surely holds true for a new patient or a stranger who calls a suicide center. He might very well interpret a comment "I can see you Wednesday at 12:00" (three days hence) as a rejection of his immediate need. However, the patient with whom a therapist has worked for any length of time in a beneficial setting is not so likely to misread the therapist's cues ("I can see you at the appointed hour") as a rejection. This patient will also get the message that the therapist wants him to pull through under his own strength, and the show of confidence is more likely to discourage a suicidal action than a show of guilt.

However, there are occasions when the therapist does not trust the patient, when he is highly afraid of losing the patient, and when he will act in a social role either to provide extra help or advise a protective environment. After the emergency is handled in such cases, it is important to refer the patient to another source of help, because the therapist, by responding to his message, has now shown the patient that he has become ineffectual in handling him therapeutically. If the therapist does not refer the patient, the future of the therapeutic contact is likely to be dim. The patient has experienced that with desperate measures he can manipulate the therapist and force him to do his bidding. He has pushed the contact to the limit and has in this experience voided his hope for the future.

Breaking off Treatment

The patient's request to break off treatment is difficult to handle. It is generally understood in most voluntary therapeutic relationships that the patient has a right to terminate his contract with the therapist at will. It is this understanding that seems to make such a demand extratherapeutic. But again, one should remember that it is not part of this general agreement that the patient can end therapy at any time with the therapist's *consent*. When the patient comes into the hour with a request for termination, he may be more concerned with the therapist's consent than with the actual termination. Termination may have many underlying meanings and it must always be discussed. The patient may not really wish to break off treatment but rather to obtain the therapist's refusal. Or, he may try to arouse the therapist's anxiety by threatening him in his professional handling. He may even wish to test him with regard to the amount of control he will exert over the patient's decisions. Any such demand must be discussed therapeutically. And yet, that still leaves us with the question, when do we give our consent?

Patient: "I am through." (Pause) "Instead of getting better I am getting worse. I think that therapy has not helped me at all. I am sick and tired of giving up the little money I have and wasting hour after hour coming to your lousy office. There is no sense to it. I still can't live with myself any easier than before I came here. It's gotten worse. I don't know what I am going to do, but one thing I am sure, this is the last time I will see you."

Was the threat to break off the treatment used here as a vehicle to express other meanings? Did the patient really want to stay in treatment but also want to show anger and aggression to the therapist? Our answer to this last question is yes. We reason that with such strong feelings he would not have come in at all if he had given up the thought of further treatment. The underlying meaning is not yet clear. The patient may have been using aggression to cover up her increased (and deeply prohibited) wish to have a more loving relationship with the therapist. In the present case there was, in fact, some evidence that the patient wanted the therapist to commit himself as to his beliefs about her progress. Discussing termination at the start of the hour was designed to elicit such a progress report from the therapist.

The patient sets up the therapist to respond either by defending himself ("There has been some progress") or by agreeing ("We got nowhere"). Perhaps she tries to force him into a role of either accepting or rejecting her. Note that this "cornering" syndrome could be a problem of the patient, and she should be helped with it. If the therapist's response were to the social demand of the message (agreement or disagreement), it would reinforce her problem. However, the therapist cannot afford to reinforce the patient's present state of adjustment and must therefore disengage from it. The patient has the right to terminate the contact whenever she wishes to do so, but the responsibility of the therapist is to help the patient. Whether or not the therapist should give consent for termination should have nothing to do with the patient's request itself, but only with his estimate of whether the patient needs further treatment either by himself or others.

In his response to the termination threat the therapist said:

Therapist: "I wonder what you are so angry about."

By asking for further associations the therapist was delaying. He did not commit himself by either accepting or rejecting the demand to break off treatment.

Patient: "Angry? I have a good right to be angry. I am spending all this dough and nothing comes of it. Wouldn't you be angry? In any case, I just told you, and I am sick and tired of your asking me these silly questions."

The patient reacted to the therapist's lack of engagement. She wanted to force a social response.

Therapist: "You really are angry today."

Here, the therapist was floundering some. He apparently was surprised that the patient had not abated in the intensity of her hostility so he simply repeated his previous message. He lost sensitivity. Was he afraid of possible separation?

Patient: "Sure, I am angry but this is the last time I will be with you. I am sick and tired of your face, of your voice, of this office. I want to go."

The patient almost gleefully took advantage of her success. She seemed to enjoy her ability to arouse uncertainty in the therapist.

Therapist: "Why don't you go, then?"

This comment supported the patient's hypothesis that the therapist was worried about losing her, a gambit which apparently filled her psychological needs. (In other circumstances this might have been an adequate response.) In this case the comment was ill timed and played into the design of the patient to obtain reinforcement in her present state of adjustment.

Patient: "Okay, can I go now?" (Gets up)

The patient followed up her success in ineffectuating the therapist: she acted as if she finally had his consent for termination. At this point the therapist seemed to understand how he had been used. He avoided the comment which one might have expected ("Well, if you want to"), which would not have taken into account the fact that the patient was more interested in winning consent than in leaving.

Therapist: "I believe you want me to tell you to stay."

The therapist has sufficiently recovered and has disengaged from the "yes" or "no" alternative.

Patient: (Sits down) "I don't know what else there is to discuss but have it your way if that is what you want."

The patient was less angry but placed the responsibility for staying on the therapist.

Therapist: "You want it to be my responsibility that you stay here. That I would tell you I want to work with you."

The comments indicate the therapist's disengagement.

Patient: (Laughs) "I don't know, I had this uncontrollable anger [etc.]"

The patient had had a sequence of experiences very different from the ordinary ones in her life. She tried in the best way she knew to play on the emotions of the therapist and force him into commiting himself either to love or reject her. The therapist failed to reinforce this mode of behavior. It should be noted again that the question of consent to terminate treatment cannot possibly be given on the strength of a patient's request; it has to be based on those independent criteria which are concerned with the long-range welfare of the patient.

CHAPTER X

TECHNICAL PROBLEMS IN THE THERAPEUTIC PROCESS

Intake

A NEW patient has been referred to the therapist from an agency, another patient, another therapist, a physician; or the patient is self-referred and has heard of the therapist from friends, etc. It is important for the therapist to obtain a written release from the new patient permitting him to obtain available information. The reason for gathering such information is twofold. First, the therapist wants to be as certain as possible that he is treating a mental and not an organic condition. To the extent that he is a psychotherapist concerned with dealing with the patient's behavior, he wants the patient in good physical health. Thus, he would like to obtain information verifying the fact that there are no current neurological or medical problems of which he is unaware that could seriously hamper treatment efforts. A close team approach with specialists who are up to date in their respective areas is desirable for some patients.

Another reason for obtaining information from other agencies is to discover whether the patient has separated from them or if he intends to avail himself of several sources of help. This latter condition presents not only a therapeutic but possibly a delicate interprofessional problem. While the patient certainly should have a right to change his source of help, on some occasions his decision to change may be motivated by avoidance, and it might be wise to be aware of this. The rights of the patient to change therapists must be respected, yet the patient's welfare is the therapist's greatest concern. In some cases a therapist may not want to accept a patient who has been in treatment with a colleague if, in his estimation, this would not best serve the welfare of the patient. This becomes particularly significant in a case where the colleague is a friend and the patient is aware of this fact. Here the covert meaning of the act of changing may be of the greatest importance to the patient, as he may be attempting to create a competitive triangle. Whenever such information becomes available, the therapist must deal with it.

Not all therapists have a specific intake hour but rather use part of their first hour for this purpose. During this time technical biographical information and releases of information to be sent to other agencies will be obtained and the source of the referral noted. Some therapists also make inquiries into significant medical and psychological aspects of the patient's history. During this same intake time, both amount and manner of payment of fees will be discussed. It is wise not to avoid such topics but to spell out the "contract" as clearly as possible. The therapist will also want to discuss the number of hours he recommends for the patient and the times these hours are available. If there is a separate intake hour, the problems that bring the patient to seek help are ordinarily discussed. Occasionally the therapist will also discuss the length of the contract with the patient and possibly set a time for the evaluation of the outcome of the relationship. This latter practice has proved particularly useful when the patient seen is a minor or a dependent.

First Hour

The stranger is generally perceived both as a threat to our psychological existence and as a possible object of gratification. The therapist confronting the patient in the first hour is "the stranger" and should be aware of it.

The patient's first impression (often misleading) is based on scanning; perhaps he wants to discover where the stranger presents a "threat" to his particular areas of vulnerability. The therapist should realize that he threatens the patient's present state of adjustment by the very fact that he holds out his service as a therapist (hence the "headshrinker" label). The feeling that the therapist may be a possible threat determines some of the behavior of the patient. We can learn about the nature of this behavior by looking at everyday occurrences.

Thus, if we meet a salesman selling us a used car, we feel vulnerable if we suspect that he has no concern for us, but is merely concerned with ridding himself of the white elephant on his lot. It is not only that he threatens our pocketbook, but that he also threatens our skill in human interactions—we must "read" him accurately to gauge our safety. When we meet a stranger at a party we may not have a financial stake to protect, but we do protect our integrity. If the person appears to engage in behaviors which give us the feeling of vulnerability—be it in intellectual competition, suaveness, charm, wit, or whatever—we are likely to assess him as a danger and react in the customary manner in which we deal with dangers: we run, flatter him, engage him in a field where we are safe, fight him, try to outdo him, etc. In other words, *to the extent that the stranger threatens our psychological existence,* he will bring forth our most typical and consistent behavior to deal with this threat.

Even when on first impression we assess the stranger as a possible object of gratification or a person who seems attractive and worth cultivating, we will respond with our most typical "approach" behavior. This may range from showing indifference (letting others do the wooing) to obnoxious possessiveness. The first impression is ordinarily modified fairly soon as new exchanges follow, and before long we find both comfort and danger in the "good" stranger as well as in the "bad" stranger. We begin to move the individual out of the "stranger" category, and we feel we know him a little better.

The patient, being vulnerable by definition, will often see the therapist as a possible source of danger in the first hour, and so will reveal information concerning the more typical and consistent behavior pattern he uses to deal with possible threat. The therapist must be on the alert not to become engaged or all too interested in what he is saying at the expense of recognizing the purpose his statements serve.

The first hour presents the therapist with a unique opportunity to assess what hurts the patient, and he must not lose this by disregarding covert and subtle information. A patient may start with a description of how he has been "let down" by a previous therapist and has spent all this money without results. But he may add that he knows the new therapist is excellent because a friend of his had been helped. Instead of becoming engaged in the emotional climate of the flattery, the therapist could learn that this patient approaches the stranger with attempts to seduce him into competition with a third party over the patient. This may be the patient's device of trying to overcome his own apprehension in relating to others—a significant behavior to which the therapist ought to become sensitive.

Another patient may describe his problem in highly technical terms, telling the therapist how he "experienced his oedipal situation with a great trauma," etc. The facet of this patient's behavior to which the therapist may be alerted is his need to impress the stranger in the stranger's own area of competence. This behavior may permit the inference that the patient brings direct competition right into his relationship with the other person.

Another patient may be depressed and show how difficult it is for him to talk, thus creating an emotional climate in which the therapist may be expected to take the initiative. Still another patient may be on the verge of leaving the office the minute he enters, perhaps showing in this way his typical mode of response to danger.

The interpretations of these subtle cues are conjectures at this point, and they must be treated as such. Nevertheless, they do present information that is significant at this level.

The first few hours of contact should generally be utilized to gather information specific to the new confrontation, but should also serve two other functions: (1) they should help the therapist make a reasonable estimate of whether he feels he can help the patient, and (2) they should give the patient some idea what he can expect in the treatment hour.

Selection procedures take place long before the first hour. Many therapists make the decision about whether they can help a person from nosological and historical data, often without seeing the patient. A therapist may exclude psychotic patients, patients afflicted with an organic brain disorder, some problem groups (alcoholics, drug addicts), or certain age groups. Criteria for selection vary from therapist to therapist. The use of some such criteria is probably helpful, as the therapist will then select the patients with whom he feels most comfortable. However, there are some unfortunate consequences of these preselections, since some patient who may very well be helped by treatment are not seen by therapists because of their nosological classifications. For example, it has become accepted that "character disorders" are one category of patients who are hard to treat. This notion is probably due mainly to the fact that character disorders are exceedingly skilled in the game of manipulation, and understand how to immobilize the therapist through involvements. A character disorder who has been caught beating a woman in the city streets is not easily assigned the "sick" role. The feeling that his "senseless" and violent act should be punished rather than treated is widespread.

Since Freud, homosexuals also have been seen as people who are hard to treat, particularly if a therapist sees them as "unmotivated." This is another unfortunate prejudice on several counts. First, the lack of motivation: whether or not a patient states that he wants to get rid of a given symptom probably has very little bearing on his ability to leave the "libidinal position," i.e., to work through his problem. Most patients treat their symptoms as their problem, but the symptom actually serves an underlying problem that, most typically, the patient has automatically excluded from consideration. A patient's statement of willingness to get rid of symptoms is simply a gesture, a price which some professionals like to extract from their patients as a sign of good will. After all, it is a statement that consists of a few words and, in fact, has few real consequences.

Secondly, homosexuality may not really be a psychological problem at all, though it is a social problem in our society. Extracting a statement of willingness to give up homosexual behavior is like putting the cart before the horse. The therapist must first learn whether a given patient is using the homosexual outlet to fight a social battle, whether it stands in the service of a broader sexual problem, or whether he is one of those individuals who appears to be totally invested in this behavior. His overt wish to fit more adequately into the present mores of our culture would indeed have very little effect on treatment; and his stated willingness to give up homosexual behavior should not be a condition of accepting him into treatment. Most of us do not know what we really want.

Every patient has both the wish to be rid of his symptoms and a great deal of investment in them; a therapist cannot easily assess treatability from nosology. Preselection, i.e., a choice made even before a patient is accepted for the first hour, is often based on most inadequate criteria. A more adequate estimate of treatability—and that means *treatability by a given therapist*—should come from the therapist's experience with a given patient, provided, of course, that the setting in which the therapist works would be the proper treatment setting for that patient. There is no properly designed test for patient treatability or prognosis, though there are some claims for certain indices derived from tests like the Rorschach test, the Minnesota Multiphasic Personality Inventory, or the Thematic Apperception Test. At the present time, testing will not help the therapist in his task of selecting the patients whom he can help best. He must probably rely on his contact with the patient during the first few hours to estimate whether he can help the patient, whether he can gain some understanding about the patient's "hurt," and whether the patient shows some readiness to change.

During the early contact the patient should also have an idea about what he can expect from these hours. We do not wish to imply that the therapist should outline his goals for the patient. The point is that the patient should obtain enough information to make a sound estimate of what the therapist can do for him, to experience the uniqueness of the hour, and to estimate the value of their relationship.

The style of the therapist is not the main concern. Some want to be silent and have the patient talk for many hours—others commence immediately with interventions. The therapist's silence can structure the unique nature of the relationship as well as more conventional therapeutic responses. Whatever his style, the therapist must be concerned with treatment, giving the patient a chance to make a reasonable estimate whether or not he can work with him. Some therapists are concerned with building rapport rather than with treatment, and postpone treatment for this reason. In such instances, the therapist neither gains useful information himself nor gives the patient the basis for a reasonable estimate of what to expect from him.

As stated, the idea that building rapport belongs in the first hour has been advanced by many writers. English and English (1958) define *rapport* as a "comfortable and unrestrained" relationship of mutual confidence between two or more persons. We have nothing against rapport, which is certainly both a desirable and necessary condition for psychotherapy. What we are against is the use of the early hours to "build rapport." What does that mean? Does the therapist try to persuade the patient that he should have confidence in him and feel comfortable? Is the therapist so uncertain about himself or so scared of being misunderstood that he has to put effort in convincing his patient of his worth? Or is he hypocritical, in that he feels that he must first convince the patient of the comfort of the hour so that he can better withstand the discomfort of later hours? There is a legitimate reason for "timing" a response properly, but this reason is not to "protect" the patient. The timing of a response should depend on the therapist's estimate of whether a patient will be able to understand it properly at the time.

Perhaps we have overstated the case against rapport-building, but we feel that this behavior is out of place in therapy. The patient must get a reliable estimate of what he can expect from the therapist in the hour; and the therapist must not try to sell confidence, nor put his principal effort into creating a comfortable situation for the patient. Throughout their contact he must behave in such a way that the patient soon discovers for himself that he can place his confidence in the therapist. Therapist behaviors specifically designed to provide the patient with an experience of "confidence" are a type of persuasion we deplore.

Order of the Therapeutic Process

Some therapists have tried to discover an inherent structure in the therapeutic process. One of the most outstanding efforts can be found in Wilhelm Reich's *Character Analysis* (1949), which was written before Reich became obsessed with the Orgone. He saw a lawful relationship between the individual's "character layers" and his neurological and physiological structure. Each given character layer was thought to be responsible for certain behavior and was seen as specifically related to the organic structure of the person.

Reich wrote that a problem that had occurred early in a person's life could not be properly resolved in therapy until more recent character structures and their physiological correlates had first been worked through. This theory was designed to bring order into the therapeutic process by establishing a sequence of characterological behavior that could be discussed in the proper order during the therapeutic hour. Unfortunately, perhaps because of the unhappy later developments in Reich's career, this contribution was not as thoroughly discussed by the field as it might have been. Horney (1945) tried to bring order into the therapeutic process by suggesting a "hierarchy of symptoms," an interesting attempt based not on the person's history or learning, but on the interrelationships between his defenses.

Analysts are concerned with the problem of order, and often use both a historical model and the analytic relationship to establish a proper order within the analysis. By paying attention to the patient's earliest childhood memories, the analyst obtains a source of information that gives him cues for interpreting later disturbances. He establishes "ordering" by encouraging the patient to produce certain information to the exclusion of other productions. In terms of the relationship itself, the analyst's first concern is with building the transference relationship and learning about the use of this patient's use of resistance; only later does he proceed to "work through" resistance and with it the transference phenomenon. The analyst does not wholly "follow" the patient in his productions but selects from them the type of behaviors that he finds useful for the process.

Rogers, who had much impact on therapeutic procedures in the United States, originally was not concerned with ordering the process ("one should follow the patient"); but his latest book, *On Becoming a Person* (1961), introduces process in seven stages which follow each other naturally in successful therapy.

1. There is an unwillingness to communicate one's self. Communication is only about externals.

2. Expression begins to flow with regard to non-self topics.

3. There is a freer flow of expression about the self as an object.

4. The client describes more intense feelings of the "not-now-present" variety.

5. Feelings are expressed freely as in the present.

6. A feeling which has previously been "stuck" or has been inhibited in its process quality is now experienced with immediacy.

7. New feelings are experienced with immediacy and richness of detail both within and outside the therapeutic relationship.

These statements are merely the first condensed sentences of a more detailed exposition, but they give the trend of Rogers' thinking on the therapeutic process. Like others, he saw therapy as an orderly process that was a function of the development of the relationship—a process specifically related to the personal growth of both the patient *and* the therapist!

We feel that the shortcomings and dangers of such a description of sequential stages in personal growth are that it fits only some cases in treatment with certain therapists. We cannot find any universality in the suggested orders.

Order in the therapeutic process is essentially seen from two viewpoints: the "imposed order," i.e., the order that the therapist should follow to gain success with his patient; and the "hoped-for order," i.e., the order that the patient who is successful is likely to follow himself. The imposed order depends on the training of the therapist, who has learned to do certain things before others. He not only responds to the individual's messages, but selects specific patient messages in a systematic way.

Under the hoped-for order, the therapist would not systematically select messages to which he would respond, but instead would look at the patient's messages to assess or diagnose where the patient is in the treatment process at any specific time.

To our knowledge no research efforts have yet assessed the value of an imposed order, nor the diagnostic accuracy of a hoped-for order. We feel that, at the present time, the criteria for determining order in the therapeutic process are too limited. The only order we can discover lies in the perceptiveness of the therapist. His first duty is to be a sensitive instrument. We do not criticize a therapist who attempts to order his therapeutic efforts by encouraging certain messages or discouraging others. However, his ordering should be related to his wish to remain sensitive: he may pursue a given topic in order to understand the dynamics of a given behavior and discourage others that interfere with his understanding, for without such *in situ* ordering he could not make interpretations at all.

A patient says: "This chair is very uncomfortable." The therapist may read this statement as: "I am not so sure I should be here." If he chooses to do so, he may respond: "You were not sure you wanted to come today?" The therapist may now get the response: "Oh no, I am happy to be here." To interpret this response correctly for its covert meaning, the therapist has to have some certainty about the accuracy of his own interpretation. Were he to believe that he was accurate in interpreting the patient's uncomfortable state, he would assume that the patient now denies the discomfort. Thus the "meaning" of this patient's response would be "denial"; he does not want to be recognized by the therapist as aggressive or self-assertive. On the other hand, were the therapist not convinced that the patient's earlier statement was one of discomfort, he would not be able to interpret the patient's response as a "denial" but would have to interpret it as a "correction." This—quite contrary to the first interpretation —would be quite self-assertive!

By interpreting, the therapist certainly brings some order into the therapeutic process. He follows up some meanings and not others. As far as a lawfulness in the sequence of the overall process is concerned, we have not found it. We do believe, however, that an *individual* therapist, through his own beliefs, has the power to establish such a lawfulness and typically does so. He can, through attention to various phases of the patient's problems and through specific interventions, create an overall direction within the process. The order then is due more to his beliefs than to the inherent structure of psychotherapeutic endeavors.

Habituation

Through thousands of messages the patient is made uncertain of his style, of his former adjustment. He can tolerate this uncertainty, and actually will seek it (by coming to the hour), because he is learning that he can be daring, courageous, sad, or witty. He can test the repertoire of his emotional and intellectual endowments and his psychological skills without great risk to himself. He is in a pseudo-realistic situation, one that is not made of the gross realities of the world but only representative of them; the therapy hour is a sanctuary and, at times, even a playland. The question is really not why a patient becomes dependent on the hour, but why he wants to leave this situation at all.

Leaving psychotherapy is not easy for most patients. We know that many patients in hospitals seem to have great resistance to leaving the protective atmosphere (hence, the feasibility of an "open door" policy). We also know that many patients become habituated to the therapeutic process or to a given therapist, and, indeed, stay in these relationships for very long times.

Is habituation an inherent part of the therapeutic process? The answers vary. The Freudians feel that the transference neurosis, i.e., the introduction of an historic love relationship into the hour, is a dependency phenomenon essential for treatment and that this relationship has to be worked through properly before the patient can act independently. Rogers (1951) tried to discover a therapeutic relationship that did not involve dependency feelings. He felt that his model of a client-therapist relationship would eliminate dependency since he saw the more authoritarian model (the doctor-patient relationship) as a cause of dependency. This was apparently an erroneous assumption. More recently (1961) Rogers stressed the importance of a close relationship in which dependency feelings are more readily accepted.

Dependency on the therapist and habituation to the hour are probably symptoms which have their origin in early learning. Separation anxiety, as Rank (1929) so cogently pointed out, is a very basic experience and is based on the fact that the child depends on his mother in order to survive. The fear of losing a person on whom one depends is an early experience in human relations. Misery, a feeling of inadequacy, ineffectuality, and experiencing feelings of injustice have all been responses to the loss of a loved person. A child who has experienced trauma in this area may have learned to use these negative moods in his communication to others, in an attempt to forestall the anticipated loss. He may have been reinforced in this communication of negative feelings by his mother's response. Thus, he may have learned that if he is miserable, feels "blue," and otherwise shows his mother that he needs her, she will come to him and give him a sense of being loved to replace the feeling of loss. Misery then becomes associated with the communicative meaning of "having mother turn toward me." With this the expected reward, misery can become the prototype of a dependency relationship with the therapist. The patient needs to stay miserable to be loved, and sometimes continues to stay ill over a long period of time in order to justify continuing the therapeutic relationship.

There is an apparent contradiction: the patient comes to the therapist to get well, but he knows that when he does get well, he will lose the therapist. He does not wish to give up the therapist because this loss would reactivate his separation anxieties. The result is habituation to the therapeutic hour.

The resolution to the habituation problem lies in the pseudoreality of the hour. The patient may love or hate the therapist. He may emote or test various ways of involving the therapist, but he knows that these feelings are not really reciprocated. Both the setting of the therapeutic hour and the therapist's communications give the patient the information that the therapist is concerned: he wants to help him, he wants him to be free to explore new choices, and he may even want him to experience life with greater pleasure. But through thousands of asocial responses the therapist also informs the patient that he is not really the person the patient wants him to be; he is not really a friend or a lover and he does not really want to spend his time outside the hour with him. In other words, while the patient experiences a sense of bondage to the therapist and an experience of being better understood and more readily accepted than in the outside world, he also has the experience that this sanctuary is sterile. He begins to realize that there are no true reciprocated feelings of friendship and love (or at least, not with their customary consequences) and that there is no future.

It is this experience which works against dependency and habituation and encourages the patient to direct his newly found courage toward new objects, and toward people with whom he can have a real relationship and a future.

This analysis of the state of dependency may help us to understand the cause of unresolved dependency feelings in relationships where "habituation" has set in. What is likely to have happened is that the therapist has stepped out of his asocial role and has become a friend, a father, a lover. He may not act out these roles overtly, but through subtle messages (of which he himself may be unaware) he may lead the patient on to believe that there is a future in their relationship. Through the very length of the contact, the patient may have gained skill in arousing the therapist's anger, his love, his wish to be really helpful, his desire to be liked. And he may keep the therapist engaged in this role during the hour if the therapist has lost his representative role.

In many such cases the therapist himself is not aware that he has become deeply engaged with the patient and that, in being engaged, he is maintaining dependency and contributing to habituation. It is for this reason that we recommend that a therapist maintain a professional relationship with another qualified person for control purposes—to protect himself from the consequences of his own unaware communications.

As stated, considerable habituation seems to occur often enough and with enough patients that we recommend an exploration of this phenomenon in operational terms. A person "habituated" to psychotherapy may continue coming to therapy over a long period of time even though he feels that there are no further gains to be made (and though the therapist agrees with this conclusion). We would want to go over several hours of transcripts of such a patient's interviews. We predict that we would discover, in an analysis of messages and responses, a large number of continuous engagements or responses indicating that the therapist has lost his asocial status.

Identification

Although the readiness to try out new behaviors can probably be traced directly to the asocial response, the directions of this change need further discussion. We have stated that we do not believe that the wish for maturity is either inborn nor is it likely that it is simply liberated in the therapeutic hour (Rogers' growth principle). A "model of psychotherapy" has many variables to explain, and it can only sow confusion if it tries to explain the aim of the change as an inherent part of the model. *Change* and the *direction of change* are clearly two separate questions.

We once heard of an anxious bank robber who went into therapy. He evaluated himself and his capacity (cracking safes was his métier), then calculated that he had gotten caught only twice in 193 robberies; and so he decided to continue the probability game which had provided him and his family with a better-than-average income. Did the therapist fail him? He apparently helped him reduce his anxiety level even though the direction of the change was not toward better citizenship. Therapists like to justify the profession by thinking that they produce not only more effective people, but also better citizens. What is it that affects the direction of an individual's choices?

While we trust that the bank robber did not take his direction of change from identifying with the therapist, most patients seem to be doing just that.

While a child is growing up, he learns both to become more effective in dealing with his environment and to direct his new effectiveness toward new goals. How does he choose these goals? We believe he makes the choice of goals through the process of identification with one of his parents or through selectively drawing on both. His identification may be positive—he wants to be like his parents—or negative—he wants to create a distance between himself and the parent. A boy wants to become an engineer like (or unlike) his father, and to marry a girl just like the girl who married dear old dad—or else marry one quite opposite in character.

In psychotherapy it seems that this early developmental state is reactivated. The patient experiences a new sense of effectiveness and explores his world anew but has not yet found a goal. He searches for ways to apply his new effectiveness. Frequently, to obtain such new direction, he will look at the therapist as a person. Patients often go through an intensive search for an identity of their own, and so look to the therapist to discover if they can "borrow" some of his. The pipesmoking therapist may see his patient start to smoke a pipe. His patient may want to become a psychotherapist like him; he may take up the therapist's favorite sport, use similar phrases and gestures, look at problems through the therapist's eyes, and copy his style of living. One therapist even reported that one of his patients dreamed dreams similar to his own. (This, however, is indicative of counteridentification rather than identification.)

As a significant person in the patient's life, the therapist is likely to be at least one important source of identification and of new goals that the patient is now in a position to choose. There are, of course, other people who are significant to him; perhaps the patient will re-explore a past identification given up earlier, or find direction from previously submerged inner resources, or in some cases find his identity through reading. However, identification with the therapist represents the most frequent first attempt of the patient to "fill the vacuum" in his search for identity, and it is of therapeutic importance because in and by itself it is a means of communication.

The child who wants to become an engineer like his father may want to indicate something with this very act. For example, he may want to give approval, or to show his father up (by becoming more successful), or to demonstrate his own incapacity (by failing). When the patient identifies with a therapist, he also communicates certain value judgments to him. The message may be "Will you accept me if I make a different choice from yours?" or, on the other hand, "Will you accept me as capable of competing with you in your profession?" or a number of other attitudes. The therapist must be sensitive to these behaviors and disengage from them. In doing so he will help the patient not only to work through dependency feelings but also to find an identity of his own.

Replacement

A special case of identification occurs when we deal with a patient's wish for incorporation or replacement. Replacement fantasies can take two forms: the wish to find a replacement for his own person, or the wish to replace the therapist directly. A patient's wish to recruit new patients for the therapist often represents a wish to find a replacement for himself. This behavior entails an important message to the therapist. By finding someone else, the patient perhaps wants to please the therapist. Or, by finding a very difficult patient he may wish to test him for his strength and qualifications.

Beyond these obvious meanings, we discovered various covert communicative meanings with different patients who recruited new patients. Perhaps the patient wants to test the therapist's personal preferences—will the new patient receive more attention and love than he does? Or will he, the patient, be able to become an adjunct therapist and help out with background information? The second meaning of replacement implies more directly that the patient wants to "incorporate" the qualities of the therapist. In this case the patient wants to be like the therapist, taking over his qualities and achievements. By acting like him the patient wants to replace the therapist, to dethrone him. These wishes probably are activated because the patient begins to feel his "mettle," which perhaps reactivates his dreams of bettering the authority figure in his life. In some patients this feeling represents a great personal danger, as they have learned the association that "to replace means to kill."

We speculate on these generalities because we feel that the therapist should become sensitive to communications that imply replacement, as they are a very real personal challenge to him. Often these communications are designed to evoke in the therapist an emotional climate of threat and discomfort from which he must learn to disengage. Here the patient tests the therapist's ability to accept competition in the area of his own competency. The therapist's failure to disengage at this stage of the process can prolong therapy indefinitely. For example, a given therapist may feel threatened by a patient's newly found courage and subtly respond with his typical behavior under threat: to minimize the patient's aspiration, or to defend his own knowledgeability, or to shift the patient from this type of message to a more comfortable one. By doing so, the therapist is likely to reinforce the patient's feeling that his replacement fantasy is powerful and dangerous, and that he cannot directly aspire to equal or better authority figures.

When we talk about replacement wishes we speak of a widespread phenomenon which occurs in just about every therapeutic contact. That replacement fantasies are dangerous thoughts indeed was even experienced by Joseph in the Bible. His fantasy of colorful clothing setting him apart from his brothers almost terminated his career at the bottom of a well!

When the therapist is aware of this daring new behavior of the patient, he will try to give the patient the experience that he recognizes his struggle in his role in relation to authority. The therapist's therapeutic objective might be to have the patient experience that to replace does not necessarily mean to kill, that there is "room at the top." He might look with the patient at the consequences of this replacement fantasy. By assuming that replacing another person means to dethrone or destroy him, the patient actually excuses his own inactivity. The thought, at least in some cases, has become an alibi, a good reason not to act at all. It is a barrier to communication and shuts off exploration: by exaggerating the magnitude of his acts and dwelling on possible retaliation, the patient fails to discuss his fear of achieving that which he could achieve—he fails to deal with the possible.

Termination

There have been many efforts in the literature to find an objective criterion for termination. Unfortunately, most of these criteria are inadequate. Termination has been linked with achievement, a criterion that entails an assumption that change has occurred in that the patient is now functioning better in areas in which he failed before. However, we know of patients who appear to be functioning more adequately but still feel insecure and vulnerable and in need of help. Are they ready for termination? Termination can be linked with feelings and testimonials of "well being," but unfortunately, we also know that patient's testimonial are not reliable, and to some extent are subject to change depending on who is doing the questioning.

Another criterion has been discovered in the patient's "movement," or "growth" or "self-actualization." A patient was timid but is now more assertive; he was afraid but now faces up to his threats. Is movement or growth a reliable indication for termination? In their flight into health some patients make large steps forward only to retreat again; others move forward on peripheral problems only; and yet other patients do not seem to "grow" at all, but are able to maintain a "check" on the behavior pattern that previously got them into an increasing amount of trouble.

Improvement of social relations and a more hedonistic attitude toward life have been advanced as another set of criteria for termination. This suggestion is based on the theory that malfunction is related to social withdrawal and accompanied by an ahedonistic attitude. But are better social relations and a more positive attitude toward self reasons for termination? What if the patient is still functioning much below his potential? Some workers suggested using all these criteria, but would that not postpone termination indefinitely for some patients?

Some therapists believe that termination should follow the therapist's recognition that the patient is ready to leave. The therapist would take the responsibility for this decision, trusting his own judgment. A different view is taken by Rogers and his group, who first felt that the patient should make this decision and indicate it to the therapist. Later, however, Rogers thought that both therapist and patient should discuss the decision together and come to an agreement on termination.

In these views we are told where the responsibility for termination should lie, but no criteria other than the subjective opinion of therapist and/or patients are given. Rank experimented with yet another criteria, that of time. He told patients he would see them for just so many months. Some orthodox analysts see their patients for five years before they even consider evaluating for termination. Such an evaluation would be based on the analyst's estimate of the patient's state of transference and readiness to face himself and the world.

The problem of termination is complex indeed. We would find it most difficult to say how much education someone needs to be called "scholarly"—and it is at least as difficult to describe when a person is ready to "graduate" from psychotherapy. The problem is partially due to the fact that the term *psychotherapy* has been broadened by many to include both treatment processes for patients with mental problems and training procedures for people who want to achieve specific tasks. An example of the latter are the "creativity groups" composed of people who want to take a new look at their work and those who want to learn "how to relax" (through reinforcement principles). Whenever we have the medical model with the general goal of "health," we will have great difficulty in finding agreement as to what "health," and specifically "mental health," means. Where we have a "learning model" we can satisfactorily define the end result, but often have trouble meaningfully relating a given partial end result to a whole person.

It is our position that termination in psychotherapy has to be subjective. By definition it can be objective only when a specific goal has been set. Such specific training efforts, while relatively easy to define and evaluate, often seem rather sterile; they do not represent the type of goal many psychotherapists set for their patients, which carry such labels as "happiness," "a sense of identity," and "a reorganization of personality."

We feel that the decision for termination should rest with the therapist. (A patient may want to leave, but can do so with or without the therapist's consent.) The therapist's consent in most cases will be based on his impressions of the patient's state of well-being. Very few therapists are detectives or can afford to check out the "real" world of the patient. Thus the decision to give consent for termination will most often rest on the therapist's evaluation of what goes on within the therapeutic hour, and on what he directly experiences with the patient. He will have to evaluate the subtle meanings to which he has paid attention all along. He might discover that the patient is more ready and willing to take responsibility for his statements; this movement in the communicative process can be evaluated, because it is in the therapist's area of competence. From a given message he can discover whether the patient still desperately needs to hide meanings or appears to feel less vulnerable about them. He can discover by interpreting the patient's previous and current statements whether the patient has re-evaluated some of his automatic behavior, whether he asks himself further questions in areas in which he previously had to defend his answers, and whether he is on the way toward entertaining new choices. By evaluating the communication process, the therapist may not be able to establish whether the patient has reached the objective criteria of growth, self-actualization, or achievement, but he can assess the process of reaching out, of "growing," of the patient's now having a self-correcting device that will serve him in good stead in the future. The therapist's decision of "consent for termination" will rest on his conviction that this subtle attitudinal change on which he bases his judgment is of sufficient strength to permit the patient to encounter life on his own.

Special Applications

PART THREE

CHAPTER XI

COMMUNICATION ANALYSIS IN
FAMILY GROUP AND GROUP THERAPY

IN the United States, psychotherapeutic treatment of a relatively few individual patients occupies a large portion of professional time. This preoccupation with individual patients is quite in contrast to practices in other countries. The result is that only few people in our society obtain adequate services while the large majority are not reached.

The possibility of reaching larger numbers of people within our society was made possible with the advent of the tranquilizing drugs. Under the influence of these drugs, the patient became more manageable, and the psychological distance between him and his guardians was decreased. The tranquilized patient no longer made so many violent and unreasonable demands on those working closely with him (aids and technicians); and these workers became partners in the treatment process where formerly they had been helpers at best. Also, physicians began to prescribe these drugs for a relatively large segment of the population, and in so doing gave the professional the impetus to think of these larger numbers of people.

Attempts to give lesser but adequate training to selected individuals brought forth experiments in which housewives were trained to help other people with their problems (Rioch, et al., 1964). Selected parents of high school students have also been trained to help out with mental health needs in schools (Nielsen, 1965a; 1965b). Volunteer workers, as well as selected patients in hospitals, have been used as adjunct therapists. Professionals who were interested in broadening services became administrators, consultants, and teachers.

Another method of making services available to a larger number of individuals is based on the theoretical consideration expressed by the slogan "administration is therapy." In any large organization, there are many administrative decisions that change the environment in which people work. These changes might be beneficial in the prevention of mental breakdown and poor mental health. Becoming aware of their power to influence the psychological well-being of the people, administrators began to work for better communication upward and downward. They also attempted to recognize those individuals who created disturbances (to discover the "ill health" carriers) and tried to acquire a better understanding of the physical environment as it affected the well-being of people (for example, innovations in open door policies in hospitals, better housing for geriatric patients, etc.). The administrator needed help from professional consultants, for with a wise decision he was able to affect the mental health of thousands with a stroke of his pen.

Another method designed to reach larger groups of people (and one of special interest to us) was the attempt to increase the number of people one professional worker would see. Psychotherapists therefore began to work with families, youth groups, and other patients in group settings. In the last few years, the movement has approached the intensity of a revolution in the mental health field. Old established treatment methods, such as electric shock, insulin shock, and lobotomies, have been discontinued in the hospitals. Instead, community resources have been mobilized, volunteer workers employed, vocational outlets formed, and nursing homes integrated into a treatment plan. Community mental health clinics were set up in distant rural areas. Established rules were no longer followed, and the taboo against seeing family members was broken. Even the "fifty-minute hour" was questioned, and the discussions in the hour no longer followed established lines.

Theory, however, was lagging behind. There were sporadic efforts to justify the new behavior, but unfortunately the older theories of the mental health profession had been largely devoted to explaining individual dynamics. Currently, efforts are under way to replace these older and no longer adequate theories with such ideas as "operant conditioning"; but such learning principles are not theories at all, only isolated observations that have not as yet become organized into a body of knowledge. Still, a new picture of the patient seems to be emerging: he is no longer "mentally sick" or even a "patient," but is now seen as a malfunctioning individual. Sasz (1961) has led the field in viewing the person afflicted with mental problems as a person who learned the wrong behavior. In some instances he may have had a genetic disposition for learning so selectively, but he needed "retraining" and not "treatment." All the words of the older theories now began to haunt the theoretician: *patient, doctor, ill, health, sick, treatment, therapy,* all words definitely out of phase with the new model. These words had had a useful history, for they had replaced such words as "tainted" and "insane." They had brought the patient out of the "snake pit" because they were labels applied to the patient by the doctor rather than the judge, and implied both treatability and the need of shelter and protection.

The present attempt to discard the "sick" role, which was itself a great advance over the "insanity" role, has many arguments on its side. The sick role was doing its job too well, so that it often became all-inclusive in its protectiveness—patients became habituated to the role and developed "hospitalitis," the wish to remain forever in the safe hospital environment (or psychotherapeutic relationship). Also, the sick role was being used by too many people (victims and criminals alike) as an excuse, an alibi for unacceptable actions and criminal behavior. (See *West Side Story*, Bernstein, 1958.)

The "malfunction" role is thought to alleviate these disadvantages, by viewing the patient as only *temporarily* in need of a protective environment. Indeed, the temporary use of the mental hospital is reflected in the increased admission and discharge rates in these hospitals. The distance between a severely malfunctioning person and a mildly malfunctioning individual is no longer so great as when the sick role was in vogue. The new method of "training" is equally applicable to well-functioning individuals who want to change certain patterns. Thus, training groups for executives, engineers, sales personnel, university administrators, and principals are now in fashion.

In effect, the revolution in the mental health field has even broken down many differences between the malfunctioning and the well-functioning individual. Behavior therapy (a semantic mixture of new and old) is one of the new formulations underlying the training model based on principles of learning. Basic to behavior therapy is the communication process, with its analysis of persuasion and impact measures. In the following we shall describe two important treatment methods from the communication analysis point of view.

Family Group Therapy

Ackerman (1960), Jackson and his group at Palo Alto (1961), Bateson *et al.* (1961), Bell 1961), and Berne (1961), among others, can be given credit for the very sudden impact of conjoint family group therapy. They presented evidence that seeing a family as a unit and watching the individual members' interaction is a more useful tool for helping a given member than treating him individually.

This approach relies on the theoretical position that the malfunctioning member of a group can be helped most properly while the group interacts. All members of the group have some investment in the malfunctioning member and often they do all they can to protect their investment; they work hard to keep him malfunctioning. Conjoint family group therapy is a device by which each family member is given a chance to discover his contribution to the family structure. We essentially view a disturbed family as one where communication among its members is severely restricted.

The success of conjoint family group therapy rests on an increase in pertinent communication, following an analysis of the subtle cues of meaning in the communication process, which ordinarily serve to constrict communication in a family (double-bind hypothesis, Bateson, 1956). In our terms, the therapist brings to the attention of each member the subtle ways in which the speaker has constricted communication in the group. He "catches the speaker in the act," thus drawing the attention of the speaker and the group to information and feelings that were prevented from emerging by "family law." The therapist typically asks the members of the family to discuss their problem with each other rather than with him at the beginning of the hour. Although this is somewhat difficult at first, most families quickly adapt to it. It places the emphasis on communication from the start and avoids the "referee" role for the therapist. By staying with an analysis of the means of communication rather than with its content, the therapist avoids entering into the group dynamics directly.

We have adopted three guidelines for the therapist in such a setting, all designed to enhance communication of pertinent information among members:

1. The therapist intervenes when a member says or implies that someone else must change to solve his problem.

This is the device people use most frequently to shift responsibility away from themselves and thus maintain the status quo represented by the attitude: "I am just about blameless." When a wife said, "If John would only stop drinking," she used this device. The therapist responded with, "John surely knows your feelings in this matter. The question you should ask is why do *you* deserve a drinking husband and what are you doing to keep him drinking?" The message was: What do *you* as a member contribute to the conflict of this family? The response was both asocial and disengaging as it aroused uncertainty where there was none, and focused the patient's attention on her own behavior. The implication was that the patient had more control over her environment than she wanted to believe.

2. The therapist intervenes when any member makes a statement which is designed to maintain the past.

People use these conventions often. A husband said: "My wife wants me to be more aggressive, but I am what I am. I can't help it. . . ." The therapist responded asocially to this communication device with, "You are saying 'I am the way I am, I am not willing to accept the possibility for making any changes myself.' Perhaps you could ask yourself: 'Why do I want to keep my wife unhappy and angry?'" The therapist thus attempted to give the husband an experience of uncertainty by questioning his favorite past-clinging hiding place, epitomized by the "I am as I am" statement.

Historical remarks ("my mother never loved me") are also responded to as just another way of holding on to the past, and the therapist arouses uncertainty by pointing out that a patient is using such statements as alibis. Patients may also use feelings to maintain the status quo. A wife said, "I just feel cold toward him," and the therapist replied: "I sense that this was a very angry, cutting statement. Perhaps your husband deserves it—but why not discuss why *you* deserve to be frigid?" The therapist intervened to reopen a question which had been shut off by these devices.

3. The therapist also intervenes when a member constricts communication by asking "loaded" questions or by giving connotations of which he may not be aware.

A husband gruffly told his wife, "We always talk things over, don't we?" The therapist intervened: "Did you give your wife any *freedom* to answer this question? The way you said it only allows her to respond either with submission or a fight. Will this increase your knowledge of each other?"

A mother constantly nagged her child to speak louder, to sit still, not to lie, etc. The therapist intervened: "You repeatedly tell your child that he is not living up to your expectations. You know that your comments are not very successful. I almost have the impression that you would rather *not* have him talk, that you keep him silent by intimidation."

It should be noted that in such situations the therapist only analyzes the communication patterns and does not judge or take sides in the argument proper. He has to be especially careful that he does not spend all his time on the utterances of only one person. In the analysis of communications of the family and through the disengaging responses of the therapist, family members learn that they have excluded many pertinent areas of interaction from discussion. They often discover "hidden skeletons," problems which they denied even existed. Typically, a family with a delinquent child will quickly learn that the "black sheep" in the family serves a function for all members of the family. Often the delinquent child's function is to provide a distraction from the severe tension existing between the mother and father. Not infrequently, after the first few hours of family therapy, these tensions between the parents become the focus of their discussion. At the same time, the "problem" child begins (sometimes reluctantly) to lose his "problem." Owen Henniger, Jr., used this method at the Metropolitan State Hospital in California with groups of patients. He invited all close relatives of the ward patients to attend meetings and reported that these sessions were very successful in restructuring family interaction.

Communication analysis in family group therapy uses the *language of the family* as its source of information. The family members do not have to learn a new language to fit the therapist's theories and professional stereotypes. The therapist analyzes communications, be it words, gestures or innuendos, to discover the hidden family laws and rituals. He responds to the family's processes of hiding, not to what is hidden. As he works with a whole family which shares a history, any one of his responses is likely to create uncertainty in *all* members. This seems to increase the members' readiness to try out new interactions. We have noted that many families seen for fewer than 15 meetings have made marked changes in their interaction patterns.

Group Therapy

While family group therapy is concerned with a group that is cohesive and maintains continuous interactions outside the therapeutic hour, groups formed of individual patients often have neither a mutual history nor outside contact. In this case the members have to learn to interact with each other in an exploratory way—they can be more daring in testing each other, as there are only limited consequences to this behavior. Also, there are no fears that the group members will punish them if they explore new ways, a fear which is quite relevant in the family setting.

However, differences between family and traditionally formed therapy groups are not only in historical patterns and forces, but also in the motivational state of the patients. While the family group members have an investment in each other and often a goal of keeping the family together, the group therapy member has only a minimum and temporary investment in the other group members and ordinarily no interest in staying together as a group. Both the historical and the motivational differences have their consequences— the therapist will respond to interaction patterns differently. In a family setting the therapist can assume that members are familiar with the impact they have on each other, while in a group setting impact and emotional climate have to be explored from the beginning.

The Group Therapist in
His Role as Communication Analyst

The group leader is not just another group member, as some group therapists like to assume. Just as a father cannot be his child's pal without betraying his trust at the times when he must take responsibility for his child and exercise his authority, a group leader would be hypocritical to proclaim himself as just a group member. His purpose in the group is not to progress toward better functioning himself (though this sometimes can be a result) nor is he there to discuss his problems. He has a major voice in determining where and when to meet; and though meetings can go on without some members, the group is likely to fold without the group leader. Even when a group continues under its own inertia, it changes in character once it is leaderless. We believe that a leaderless therapeutic group is likely to be beneficial for some members at the expense of others. In support of this statement we reason that engaging and involving another person is the patient's greatest skill. Unless the group contains a person trained to disengage from the strong social demands made by some individuals, one who can show by example that disengagement is possible, the chances for therapeutic benefits are minimal.

The group leader as a communication analyst will see himself neither as a group member nor as a direct participant. He will occasionally interpret the emotional climate the group has created for itself or respond to a member and his bids for engaging him or other group members. His interest will be in analyzing the group members' communications for their subtle meaning and impacts; he will avoid entering discussions of subject matter. He will not become a referee. He will not even try to bring the silent member into the group's conversations. He will respond to the impact of silence on the group and verbalize the emotional climate it creates.

At the start he will typically make a comment to the effect that this group was formed because all members had some problems. After such a general statement some member may begin to talk to him or other group members, and some members will remain silent. The therapist will not make any further structuring comments. Should the group remain silent, he will comment on the emotional climate this silence creates in the group. As group members begin to participate, he will respond to the subtle cues he understands, always concerned with the emotional impact his statements have on the group.

For maximum effectiveness, the therapist should usually respond to the individual. This procedure has been subject to debate in group-therapy circles, and it has sometimes been argued that the therapist should avoid responding to the individual lest he only accomplish "individual therapy" in a group setting. However, we fail to see how individual therapy could ever be done in a group setting, since the entire group is necessarily involved with each exchange, be it between the group leader and one member or between group members.

When the therapist responds to an individual member, the others become participants in this exchange, though they may not have said a word. The subtle communicative meaning involved in singling out one member, the jealousies involved, the covert attempts of the member to use his prominence, and his wish to create a specific emotional atmosphere are all cues of importance to the group. These cues will affect the emotional climate of the group, engaging some of the members and thus restricting their response activity. The therapist will be on the alert to discover, *in situ,* any such imposed limitation on the communication exchange, and will utilize it to give other group members the experience that one can disengage from such involvements. We once worked with a group of near-dropouts and the youngsters were in a sullen mood. One boy started:

> *Dick:* "*I don't know why I should be here. I get laid every night!*"
> *Therapist:* "*Indeed, you live a happy life.*"
> *Dick:* "*And I drink too, a six pack every night.*"
> *Therapist:* "*You live a regular sort of existence too.*"
> *Dick: (desperate)* "*But I smoke also.*"
> *Therapist:* "*So?*"

The other boys laugh.

> *Therapist:* "*That was quite a trap.*"

This opening speech was certainly not only important to the boy who made it. The other boys indicated with their laughter that they had recognized Dick's need to find the enemy, and that they also were relieved to find the therapist able to handle this gambit. The asocial responses of the therapist gave them hope for a novel experience—perhaps they felt along with the first boy, that the therapist was not easily manipulated.

The therapist's response—"That was quite a trap"—was better than a technical discussion about the emotional climate Dick had tried to establish. The response provided the boys with the experience that it was all right to try out their games of interaction in this hour, in which they were games and did not necessarily have grave consequences. At a later hour the testing of the therapist followed hard and fast.

Tony: "Why should I go to school—it's for sissies. I think they teach you a lot of nonsense anyway."

Therapist (paradigmatically in an exaggerated tone of voice): "There is really no earthly reason to go to school. It's a ridiculous requirement."

Johnny: "But you can't be anything but a dishwasher if you don't go to school."

Therapist: "What's wrong with being a dishwasher?"

We note that Johnny could no longer stand the lack of authoritarian demand. He was forced to intervene with such a demand on his own. The therapist still responded paradigmatically and asocially, giving the boys the experience that values have to come from them and that their antivalues, touted against the imagined enemy, were designed to create an emotional involvement with the "authority figure," the therapist.

Dick: "Yeah, what's wrong with being a dishwasher?"

Johnny: "Nothing wrong really, but I just don't want to be one."

Lou (to Dick): "And neither do you!"

Therapist to Lou: "You are telling him what he should do, sort of ganging up against him. Will he be able to listen to you?"

Here the therapist went into the second phase of his work: he alerted Lou and the group into cognizance of the impact their statements had on each other.

Dick: "I got my girl and beer, who cares?"

Willie: "I'd like to have a girl too."

Johnny: "I think Dick is a sad case. I think he really wants to finish school."

The therapist recognized the dynamics of the interaction—Dick, on the slightest hint of authority, withdrew to his girl and beer image, and in this withdrawal he was joined by Willie. But Johnny wanted him to face the issues. The therapist did not enter these dynamics as such; he wanted the boys to understand the emotional climate they were creating for each other. He responded to the demands of the last message.

Therapist to Johnny: "*And you want to shame him into finishing school?*"

Johnny: "*He does not sound happy with that girl and beer stuff. He's just talking.*"

Willie: "*I would be happy!*"

Therapist to Willie: "*I get the impression you want to make friends with Dick.*"

Willie: "*He is a great guy. He's got everything I want.*"

This seemed to be a detour from the main theme. But after reading between the lines of Willie's comment, the therapist's goal became to provide the boys with the experience that the subtle demands inherent in their statements could be understood. It does not really matter what is being talked about, since the bids for involving another person are made with all sorts of messages. The therapist intervened when he thought he understood the subtle cues.

Therapist to Willie: (*with a smile*) "*If you could only get him to share his riches with you.*"

Johnny: "*I think I am going back to school.*"

Therapist to Johnny: "*I hear you say that the guys are too far gone. They are crazy. You have to go it alone.*"

Johnny: "*They are finks. Girls are okay, but they are no reason to foul yourself up.*"

Dick (to Johnny): "*That's my business. If I want to foul myself up it's my business.*"

Therapist to Dick: "*To hell with these bastards who want to tell me what to do.*"

Johnny: "*Sure, it's his business. I don't give a damn what he does or does not do.*"

Willie: "*To hell with school.*"

Therapist to Willie: "*If I could only have Dick as a friend.*"

Therapist to Johnny: "*And you are saying he is a bum, why should I help him?*"

Here, the therapist has begun to cue in on the language of the participants. He has become sensitive to Dick's desire for an enemy;

to Willie's need for an alignment; to Johnny's need for someone worse off than himself to straighten out; and the need of Tony and Lou to remain in the spectator role, unable or unwilling to commit themselves. This sensitization to the language used by the group members helps him to verbalize the suspected hidden meaning of their statements. His purpose, to provide each boy with the experience of uncertainty in his automatic behaviors, can now be more adequately performed.

The therapist provides the group with the experience of disengagement by giving asocial responses wherever he discovers unaware bids for engagement. He hopes that each member will experience a sense of uncertainty whenever he receives a response that recognizes the demands his message has made. The therapist thus attempts to create an emotional climate in this group in which the boys can no longer find reinforcement for their established automatic behaviors and so are forced to discover new choices.

Themes in Group Therapy

It probably does not really matter what themes a group discusses or even whether some members talk or are silent. Disregarding topic or silence, the skilled therapist still can discover the way an individual member tries to involve another person in his exchange of covert and hidden meanings. Even with the weather as a theme the essential information will still come through:

Member 1: "Nice weather today."
Member 2: "Oh, yes, I love a blue sky."
Therapist: "And the clouds are just beautiful. And the wind is blowing so sweetly. And the sun is sparkling, bright, and handsome."
Member 1: "Let's get going."

The paradigmatic response of the therapist was made with the intent of providing Members 1 and 2 with the experience that they were using the weather to maintain, conventionally speaking, a superficial contact with the group.

We have been associated with a hospital where the aides were given permission to act as group leaders with instructions to stay within a particular theme, such as "racing cars" or "sports." These instructions were thought to be a safety measure. While their safety value seems doubtful, these limitations did provide a sense of status to those giving the instructions; they underlined the differences between the activity level of a trained group leader vs. an untrained group leader. By giving the untrained leader what could be conventionally termed "inconsequential" themes, the trained leader perhaps made his own themes more important. We recognize that there is also a more serious consideration: the professional person wants to help the untrained leaders remain calm and is afraid that delicate topics such as sex, religion, politics. or childbeating would be hard to handle.

This reasoning, however, which helps to restrict the topic, seems somewhat faulty. We firmly believe that the topic itself is of little significance, since if authoritarianism is his problem, a poorly trained leader can use any topic as a vehicle to boss the patient around or impose his value system on another person. We believe that if the professional staff wants to use an untrained leader for a group, little value will come from it unless they put their trust in him. He must be carefully selected and should obtain some training centered on his ability to listen to another person. The choice of a leader should rest on his sense of empathy rather than on the themes which he is allowed or not allowed to discuss. The practice of prescribing topics for discussions led by the nonprofessional group leader is a practice without much merit, precisely because it fails to take the covert component of the communication process into consideration.

Hill (1961) and Hill and Hill (1961) devised an effective method of measuring the group process by evaluating the statements made by the participants, e.g., whether they were self-centered, group-centered, work- or issue-centered, leader-centered, etc. Although this attempt permits rigorous measurement of the group process, the question could be raised as to whether it even makes sense to create such categories or "themes." A so-called work-centered group may use a different set of themes to work out their problems than the self-centered group but, in spite of these differences, they can be equally effective in helping a patient make gains. To our way of thinking, Hill and Hill made a real contribution by introducing the problem of finding a systematic method of evaluating the group process, but we are far from convinced that their choices are based on the right principles.

Some therapists try to lead the group to "deep" and "meaningful" discussion and even speak of "peak experiences" within some sessions. We have already stated that we do not believe in the value of such selections, as we are more concerned with how these themes are used than with what they are. Our wish to minimize the significance of themes should not be read as an implication that one specific theme cannot yield more information than another once the therapist understands the patient's language. However, the therapist should be aware that a given theme may be of great interest and significance to one group member while quite peripheral to another. In other words, we feel that the therapist cannot afford to become interested in any given theme, not even Hill's so-called "work theme," lest he become engaged and ineffective in reading the meaning which the individual members attach to that theme.

Silence of Group Members

When a group member remains silent, and does not participate in the group, group therapy leaders have a tendency to become concerned. This is probably due to the therapist's having overlearned that talking is a good thing and his belief that patients must talk to get well. A patient can use his silence as an important communication to the group and to the therapist. To mention only a few possible meanings of silence, he can arouse concern with it, or create an emotional climate of guilt (because the group has been neglecting him), or anger (because he remains an outsider against some missionary efforts on the part of the group), or even fear (that he may harm himself). In silence, we see participation.

It has never been explained why a silent group member should have less of a therapeutic experience in the group than the talking member. In school the silent student certainly can get as good a grade as the noisy one. Why then do so many therapists assume that the patient should talk to get well?

We suspect that the silent group member (quite unlike the silent student) makes the therapist and the other group members feel uncomfortable. The therapist often becomes engaged with the silent member because he wants more conventional information (words and gestures) with which to read the patient. His therapeutic urge is the source of his engagement. The member himself perhaps has a different reason for his silence. Any group member is aware that he reveals what he considers intimate information about himself, and that he takes the chance of becoming vulnerable to attack by those present. The silent group member, though he may give an equal amount of covert information, does not volunteer this information. The participating group member may feel that his greater verbal output may leave him more vulnerable. While he thus reveals himself to the silent member, the silent member himself does not engage in risk-taking behavior. In other words, the silent member, by not volunteering information about himself, dampens the spirit of the other members and sometimes creates an emotional climate characterized by both apprehension and caution.

The therapist wants to encourage interaction and so gives special attention to the silent member in an effort to make him talk. However, to our way of thinking, the therapist is sacrificing the welfare of the silent member by singling him out with his attention in order to have more restraint-free interaction within the group. The word "sacrifice" is used because we believe that special attention reinforces the silent behavior rather than giving this member an experience of uncertainty through a disengaged response. We believe this reinforcement to be an error. The therapist should respond to the silent member in the same manner he responds to more talkative members, indicating that he understands the subtle information that is communicated by silence. He then will try to provide the member with the experience that his wish to engage others via the medium of silence can be recognized. With such an intervention, silence is not likely to succeed in constricting the group's behavior in the expected manner.

By treating the silent member as an equal in the group rather than a person who is not playing the game properly, the therapist will give all members the information that they are in a beneficial, protected environment. They will learn that they cannot fall into disfavor because they behave differently from other group members. This "democratic" acceptance (love of the least)—if we may give it this name—is probably a better guarantee of restraint-free interaction than singling out the silent member and not accepting his silence.

In conclusion, silence has to be dealt with as a communication, a behavior like other behaviors. As with all other behaviors, the therapist must be on the alert not to reinforce this attitude.

The Cues Creating
an Emotional Climate

Individuals appear to behave differently when they are members of a group than when they are alone. Although they have kept thinkers preoccupied for a very long time, the nature of these differences is not clear. An otherwise decent citizen may participate in a lynching when he is a member of a group formed to engage in this violence. A miser will contribute to a cause when the emotional climate of a group demands it, and a soldier will be braver and more effective when he is part of a daring unit. In times of war a whole nation may commit atrocities that an individual would reject as uncivilized and evil. What are the forces of influence which cause the individual to perform an act contrary to the values he ordinarily accepts? How does the group communicate these new values, and how does it cue the individual as to when the new values are to be used? We believe that we have something to offer by way of answer to these questions. Our contribution lies in the previously isolated process which we called the "shift of responsibility." We shall look at the subtle communication of group members with the attempt to discover just how an individual contributes to a given group climate, and how such a shift of responsibility takes place.

Individuals join groups for many reasons. When an individual joins a group he necessarily gives this group certain rights, such as the right to make economic or social decisions for him. He also hopes for certain gains—that these decisions will be of benefit to him. He hopes for the experience of magnification—the group is bigger than he is and more powerful and less vulnerable. By becoming a group member, he now can adopt group values for which he does not need to feel solely responsible, and these values can become more significant to him than any others he has known. Mankind (or any group) can become more important than life itself. An individual may face the idea of death itself with a sense of glory if he can feel that it will help his group, his nation, or mankind to survive.

What sort of information must an individual receive to make such judgments? What sort of cues does the group give him to help him to make these drastic decisions? (We are not denying the possibility of instinctual gregarious behavior in man, but are here concerned with individual differences.) One answer that has been advanced refers to the *identification process*. The individual receives information from the value and belief systems of a group; and to the extent that he assumes these values, he loses his own identity. Such a description is not very satisfactory, even if one accepts that identification plays a role in this transmission. We still are left with the task of specifying the information an individual receives which motivates him to become a member of a group. We can understand the nature of this information more adequately when we consider that modern communication devices permit most individuals to be in contact with many different groups. The willingness to identify with one's own group seems to decrease upon such contacts. As soon as the individual permits himself to differentiate groups other than his own and sees them as worthwhile, he receives information that is likely to modify his attitude toward his own group. He has learned that there are other roads to salvation.

The motivation to belong to a group is apparently related to an individual's sense of isolation. In our analysis we differentiate such motivating information into overt and covert components. We shall mention only a few of each of these components. Overtly, the individual will obtain information that motivates him to join by becoming acquainted with the particular work the group performs. He becomes aware of the economic advantages the group provides for its members. He becomes acquainted with the group's credos, pledges, bids for secrecy, punishments for leaving, romantic opportunities, particular clothing or food taboos, and, last but not least, its common language.

Covertly, the individual is motivated to join the group by becoming exposed to information that arouses strong emotional feeling tones in him. There may be messages that arouse fear of the common enemy ("They will destroy us") or enhance a sense of power ("We are strong"). There may be messages of hope ("We shall master our fate, yet we shall grow") or of praise ("We are the select"). Both overt and covert types of information are likely to affect the person's attitude toward the group and, if the messages have created their desired effect, the individual will identify with the group and shift responsibility to it; he will no longer feel isolated.

In group therapy there are somewhat similar forces at work even though the goals of this group are uniquely different from the goals of most other groups. The claim for uniqueness is based on the rather peculiar objective of the therapy group: it aims at its own dissolution. This objective demands that the group members perform entirely different tasks than they would in most groups. Instead of permitting the individual to obtain solace by shifting responsibility, this group is designed to facilitate each member's acceptance of responsibility for himself. The group leader provides the member with information that discourages dependency feelings or feelings of magnification. The very structure of the therapy group (in which the members often do not know each other and meet for only a limited time) provides the member with the information that there will be no lasting consequences to his attendance unless consequences are related to his own attitudinal change. Another unique quality lies in the fact that most therapy groups have a group leader who does not set common goals for the group. Rather he sees as his responsibility the helping of the individual member to find his own goals. While a member may join a group therapy session because of his sense of isolation, the information he receives in this unique group is designed to provide him with the experience that he does not need to be isolated and that he can make choices that may enable him to deal with isolation.

A number of other factors give subtle but important information to the group therapy members. One such factor is the group composition. The selection of an all-alcoholic group will in itself give different information to its members than the selection of a group of boys who have all stolen cars. Another factor giving subtle information is the motivation underlying the formation of the group. A group that has to meet in order to avoid going to jail is likely to start with a different emotional climate than the group composed of voluntary patients. The locale itself also seems to be a factor in determining the climate. If a group met in a school building, it might start out differently than if it were to meet at a mountain resort where people were "captive" for a few days. The therapist himself, and the way he sees his role, presents yet a further source of information determining the emotional climate in the group. An active group therapist will create a different climate than a passive one; a therapist who wishes to intervene often and for extended periods differs from the one who prefers to listen.

While these sources of information help determine the general climate of the group at its beginning, the significance of these determinants will decrease as the group works together. The alcoholics will forget that they all had a drinking problem, the location will no longer be of importance, the style of the therapist will matter little, and even the voluntary (or involuntary) aspect of group attendance will no longer play a role. The group member will be exposed to new and more immediate information, and will have to deal with people who affect him in specific ways. He will use his preferred skills with them, attempt to shift his responsibility to them, and thus become a member of the group and help to create its new structure.

Shift of Responsibility
through Engaging the Group

An individual who wants to shift responsibility from himself to others will often try to engage the other person. The child who is fearful and does not want to fight the neighborhood boys may "engage" his parents and elicit from them prohibitions against fighting. With this tactic he does not need either to fight or to see himself as responsible for his failure to stand up to the boys; after all, his parents are responsible for preventing him from doing so. It can often be observed that such a child will even refer back to his parents' prohibitions after his parents themselves are no longer concerned with them.

A group member who wants to shift responsibility to the group will try to engage the group in very much the same manner. He will give information in the attempt to create in the group an emotional climate that engages the other members. The subtle information that elicits the process of engagement for the group members will provide them with the experience of identification. For example, a patient in a hospital setting complained long and bitterly about the injustice of the hospital administration which would not permit him to go home. With this message he elicited sympathy for his trials from the other group members and succeeded in sharing his hatred of the hospital with them. Once he succeeded in arousing this emotional climate, he had found an alibi for himself, proving to himself and the group that he was well, but was being detained against his will. The fact is that he would not have dared to leave the hospital even if the staff had led him by the hand to the outside. The emotional climate he created was in the service of his alibi: the hospital, the environment, had become the reason why he could not leave. He had been sharing this "shift of responsibility" with the group, and he obtained a feeling of magnification from the fact that the group had been engaged by him. Up to this point, needless to say, the therapist had failed him by not helping the group disengage from this climate. He had reinforced the man's ill adjustment by allowing the *"They* keep me here" credo to engage the group.

Once a person has been successful in shifting responsibility to the group through "group engagement," other members will often feel highly encouraged to try their skills in engaging the group in their problems. This behavior and this type of message, when successful, seem to be contagious, and is likely to spread among the other group members who also wish to partake in the success. Such a bid for group engagement is motivated by the individual's wish to maintain his present state of adjustment. The very existence of an emotional climate that enhances group engagement should alert the therapist to his own engagement and ineffectualization. The group therapy session in which deep engagement in such an emotional climate has occurred takes on the character of a griping session; although it might give some momentary relief to the individuals involved, it probably has little significance in their lives. To the individual member, the group in this case comes to stand for *"us* equals good, *them* equals evil." While it serves the purpose of identification and magnification, it also reinforces the very behaviors the group process is supposed to make uncertain.

However, there are occasions where the contagious effect works for the benefit of the patient. This occurs when the therapist is successful in disengaging himself from the emotional impact of the messages and helps the group do the same. Rather than turn the group therapy session into a griping session, the group member who has received a disengaged response seems to wish to partake both in sharing his responsibility with the group and in accepting responsibility in return. This beneficial use of the contagious effect is most often achieved by the therapist who masters a sense of timing: he accepts the emotional climate and allows the group engagement to reach a certain intensity before he helps the group disengage from it. His disengagement then is representative and asocial and does not create any alignments within the group. This sense of timing and the skill in avoiding group alignments are, in our opinion, the necessary prerequisites for a good group response to the therapeutic efforts.

Timing is dependent on the skill of the therapist in adequately estimating the impact of his response on the group. Timing in a group differs from timing in the individual therapy hour in that the therapist has to assess whether his disengaged response will be properly understood by the whole group. A therapist with poor timing may make a disengaged response when one member will comprehend it and experience disengagement, but the others will not. In this way the therapist enhances alignments in the group. For example, the therapist's response to the patient who complained that the hospital administration unjustly kept him in the hospital might have been a paradigmatic exaggeration: *"They* keep you chained here, locked up behind heavy doors." The patient was, in fact, in an open-door ward, and such a response would have been designed to give the group the experience that the emotional climate created by this patient was a bid to justify his wish to stay in the hospital. But let us assume that only some of the group members were aware that the patient was in an open ward. Under these circumstances, the response would have divided the group into those members who comprehended the intended meaning and those who did not. The result would have been a division in the group, a minor division on the strength of a single response but a division nevertheless. Therefore, timing in a group demands that the therapist estimate how knowledgeable the group is in the area of his response.

Of course, we do not claim that a good response will provide the desired experience simultaneously to all members. There will always be some differences in comprehension and readiness, to say nothing of the members' different degrees of attention at a given time. We only suggest that the group therapist pay attention to timing and understand that alignments occur when he talks to just half the group.

A given statement at the right time can create laughter, tears, a sense of serious purpose, or a climate of relaxed play. The French nobleman about to be hanged from a lamp post by a revolutionary crowd during the French revolution is said to have remarked, "It won't help enlightenment to darken the lamp with my body," and the group suddenly changed its ugly mood and let him go free. He had been able to create group engagement with at least some of the individuals, and the engaged response had become contagious and spread to the group.

The possibility of a contagious effect is present in any number of people in the same proximity. Even travelers in the same compartment of a train may become a group. When a stranger enters, the group may act in unison to let the stranger know that he should look for a seat in a different compartment. The subtle response of some individuals to the intrusion of the stranger apparently creates a sense of engagement and the group acts under the emotional impact of this information. Perhaps the gesture which the first person used in response to the stranger's entrance was to push his briefcase a little further over on the seat, a subtle gesture indeed. It was enough of a cue to cause engagement and amounted to an encouragement for other travelers in this same compartment to gang up against the stranger.

In group therapy, group engagement often occurs on equally subtle stimuli. A usually active member may stay quiet and help create an emotional climate of boredom. Another group member may, by a friendly gesture, create an emotional climate of genuine liking among the members of the group. A third member, just through his manner of speaking, may create a climate of excitement and exhilaration. Not all gestures are successful in the sense that the climate they create spreads throughout the group; sometimes a group may be split into alignments, because the members may be split in their feelings about the gesture that demanded their engagement. However, even split alignments in the group present an emotional climate that is due to significant gestures by at least two members. It is the therapist's job, as we conceive it, to disengage from these climates once he has recognized them. An emotional climate will always constrict the communicative process of the group, and the constriction will distort the interaction.

In the following, we shall illustrate the sharing of an emotional climate by a group of juvenile delinquent boys (ages 15 to 17), with particular emphasis on the contagious effect.

This group was meeting for the third time, and at this point one boy felt encouraged to speak of an event in his life that appeared to bother him greatly. With tears in his eyes he told the group that he was responsible for the death of his mother. The previous Christmas Eve he had refused to go on an errand for her and get her some dope from the contact man (he had done this before). His mother had been furious and stamped out to get it herself. On her way back, she apparently stumbled over the curb and had frozen to death in the gutter. This message was not particularly designed to arouse sympathy in the group but was presented with a sense of anguish, with a plea to share the burden, to have the boys (and the therapist) share the responsibility with him. The message had an almost magnetic effect. Group members who had been cynical before began to relate how they were also guilty of committing acts of violence. They all spoke with great intensity of feeling. Perhaps they wanted to tell the boy that they were ready to share with him, that they also had feelings similar to the ones he had reported. The hour was characterized by the emotional climate of the confessional. Every member participated somehow in this meeting, all wanted to be heard. The emotional climate spread contagiously and created a sense of group engagement; it permitted the boy to shift responsibility away from himself to the group. He now could have a feeling of relief by sharing his burden. This sharing also created a sense of belonging and magnification in each individual; it lowered each member's judgmental and cognitive processes and certainly restricted his response activity.

The therapist became aware of the spreading of the emotional climate as each member participated in this group climate, and there was a sense of intimacy and intense feeling. When the therapist responded, he wanted to communicate to the group that he was listening without himself being engaged in the group climate. Some therapists commit the error of being intensely interested and even pleased when the group members become deeply involved in the discussion. With such special attention, the therapist communicates approval to the group and is likely to reinforce carthartic confessional behavior rather than uncertainty. The members of this group, in their confessional mood, obtained relief by sharing with the group the violence and crimes they had committed. Had the therapist shown his subtle approval and pleasure, the group members would have been reinforced in their feelings that violence and crimes are exhilarating behaviors, that deviant acts are a good reason for friendship and feelings of belonging, and that reports of violence enhance their status in the group. On the other hand, had the therapist censored such discussion, he would have communicated to the group that he was an outsider in the true sense of the word, that he did not understand the sense of belonging that came from such a group. The therapist wanted neither to approve nor to censor. He wanted to help the group separate out the sources of their experiences, to disengage from the climate itself. He had to stay disengaged in order to communicate to the group that he could understand the values, the sense of belonging, and the sense of sharing which the boys experienced and which they attributed to their all being delinquents. The therapist had to create a sense of uncertainty in the boys about the associations they had made in which they had related the idea of being a delinquent to the idea of belonging to a group. The therapist had to provide the boys with the experience of uncertainty that their wishes to belong, to share, and to find friendship were not necessarily related to behavior involved in committing crimes.

The therapist's responses were designed to accomplish this task. He remained disengaged from the emotional climate created by the group, and by his very attitude and presence he trained the boys not only to share the responsibility for actions with the group, but also to reaccept responsibility for their own behaviors. A boy said, "When I saw my father beating up Sis, I threw that pan with hot, boiling oil right into his face, and after that we did not see him for another two years." The therapist responded, "You chased him out of the house to protect your sister and you felt good and strong at the time. For some time you were the man of the house." This response was essentially an asocial disengaged response, since it did not follow either the boy's bid for approval, or his fear of disapproval.

The response subtly alerted the boy and the group to the fact that the violent act reported was not completely altruistic nor just designed to help the sister, but that the boy got some pleasure out of it. He had committed the violent act to feel like a man. In a very subtle way the therapist's response forced the boy to look at his behavior in a different way. Perhaps he was able to ask himself: "Must I really commit a violent act to be a man?" The therapist's response was disengaged but subtle, and in that sense counterpersuasive: it permitted the boys to view their group experience as something other than simply an act of sharing. The boys now also learned that these group sessions were a challenge and that they entailed a new way of looking at their behavior. The therapist was able to create a sense of uncertainty in the group, but a sense of uncertainty which was tolerable and challenging rather than threatening. He had created a sense of beneficial uncertainty.

On Size and Duration

Psychotherapists have a strong bias with regards to the questions of how large a group should be and how long contacts should last. They were reluctant to give up the one-to-one relationship as the most effective model of psychotherapy, and only hesitatingly accepted slightly larger groups for psychotherapeutic efforts. Psychotherapeutic work is very rarely planned for groups larger than 6 to 15 individuals, with the exception of ward or milieu treatment programs in hospital settings. Yet, in principle, we know that it is possible to have a significant effect on a larger number of people. We need only think of the impact that some church services or political addresses have. Even a powerful stage play can stir up people and cause them to think about their lives and their behavior. The proper information can arouse beneficial uncertainty in any group, regardless of its size. We believe that behavior modification is possible in large groups; even though we do not know as yet what the "proper information" is or how lasting or helpful these modifications are in getting people to accept individual responsibility for their behavior. It is our thesis that psychotherapists, because of their own bias, have failed to look at the possibilities of behavior modification in large groups. Through this oversight they have relinquished the opportunity to discover the variables in large group settings which could be utilized to help people improve in ways consistent with current psychotherapeutic goals.

The same comments apply to problems of duration of the psychotherapeutic contact. By and large, the amount of contact required to help a particular individual is dependent on the therapist's viewpoint. Among different therapists the desired length of contact ranges from short-term contacts encompassing a total of two to six meetings, to a five- to seven-year period of contact with five meetings each week. The range is large and the individual therapist, who typically has a fairly consistent view on the length of contacts required, probably takes into consideration the problems of a particular patient and the goals he has set for him.

But even this range, wide as it is, still neglects the two endpoints: on the one hand, the very brief contacts such as 15-minute meetings, and on the other, the lifelong contacts. We do not know whether contacts at these two ends of the contact range would be of any value to the patient, though the derivation of benefits at these extremes is certainly conceivable. It may be that some people can be helped best by seeing a professional person for a very short time but repeatedly over a span of many years. It also may be that some patients need to establish a lifelong contact in order to maintain their psychological adjustment and that such very long contacts are not necessarily failures in therapeutic skill.

Continuous contacts have been viewed as failures in therapeutic skill because of the mental health goals typically set for the patient. When the goal was to *cure* the patient, an exceedingly long treatment time was looked on with suspicion, and the critics would say that an unwholesome dependency had taken place or that a transference phenomenon which had not been "worked through" was hindering termination. On the other hand, if psychotherapeutic efforts are viewed as teaching methods whereby people discover consequences of their behavior and are confronted with a discovery of their automatic behavior, such "schooling" can go on for a lifetime without making an individual feel that he has become unduly dependent on another person. Just as a professional person will continue to accumulate knowledge in his given field by reading the journals and attending lectures and occasional refresher courses or institutes, it is conceivable that in his wish to be an "artist of living" *(Lebenskünstler)*, an individual may want to continue to keep up with his "field" throughout the years by occasionally seeking out such opportunities.

The concepts of "completing one's analysis," of "being cured," of "mastering one's own problems," are based on the idea that there is a state of optimum mental health that can be reached. However, this state is sometimes defined as one that permits the individual to have self-correcting devices at his disposal—methods of recognizing and meeting problems which permit him to make adequate corrections. In view of such abstract definitions of the state of mental health, one might believe that help should be needed only temporarily or until the person has succeeded in establishing these self-correcting attitudes.

This view of mental health, however, is highly abstract. Most individuals cannot be categorized as being either "self-actualized" or "self-correcting" or, on the other hand, as "sick" or "not self-correcting." The chances are that a vast majority of people are self-correcting with regard to some of their problems, while they are constricted in others. In our experience, even the most adequate and healthy person can profit by engaging in a therapeutic relationship, where he can look at himself and discover how he responds in the presence of another person and where he can inspect the behavior he has automated and discover his constrictions. He may not *need* psychotherapy as he is not malfunctioning or suffering, but he can nevertheless profit by the experience.

Continuous contact of many years' duration, though they may only entail attendance for a few weeks each year, seem particularly profitable where there are specific problems to be solved, as in cases where there is a mentally retarded child in the home. Under these circumstances parents can take a course in behavior, perhaps learning to deal more adequately with their problems and continuing to learn as problems change.

We as therapists should become a little uncertain about our automatic ways of helping people. We need to assess the information we provide to the group members as to its effectiveness in providing each one with an experience of freedom. We need to study whether such information should vary in nature with the size of the group, and we need to open up the questions of duration, of both the time required for each contact and that needed for the overall contact. The subtle information conveyed by the way we structure the contact should also be taken into consideration. Systematic experimentation is clearly indicated.

CHAPTER XII

THE CHILD'S COMMUNICATIONS
IN THERAPY

SILENT language is an important characteristic of all human interaction. The child, not yet fully accomplished in the nuances of language, perhaps relies even more heavily than the adult on silent language. He has not fully mastered the skill of hiding behind words and so expresses his wishes and fears in his behavior. Many of the subtle meanings that later will be incorporated into verbal language are now acted out. Yet we must not commit the error of assuming that he is less capable than the adult of powerfully affecting another person or of creating in him the emotional climate he desires. We shall attempt to isolate some of these skills of the child in his interactions and explore therapy with the child from this point of view.

The Concerned Parent

When a child is brought to the office of a therapist, we can be quite certain that in most cases he has managed to make his parents deeply concerned about his welfare. If a child is brought to a clinic, he probably has given his parents the feeling that they are incapable of handling him, that whatever they are doing only aggravates matters, and that time and money have to be expended to recover from this family trauma.

To elicit such feelings in the parents, the child does not need to behave with particular aggression. He does not have to be a misbehaving child. He can be a withdrawn child, a child with more than his share of accidents, or a child with psychosomatic complaints. He may be a child who is suicidal or one with problems of aggression. Whatever the complaint, the parents in their bewilderment and perhaps desperation are willing to delegate at least part of their authority to the therapist, and are willing to pay a price in effort and care. If we assume that the child desires that his parents expend extra effort and care for him, we must admit that he has been extra-ordinarily successful in achieving his wish. This is generally the assumption we do make.

More specifically, we assume that the child has learned that with certain behaviors he will arouse anxiety in his parents, perhaps giving them a feeling of impotence in dealing with him. By pursuing the "sick" or maladjusted role, he will get the parents' extra attention without demanding it directly.

We do not maintain that the child consciously schemes for such a devious reward, that he knowingly plans to upset his parents, or that he is necessarily unloved. But we assume that the child, through many thousands of messages, has learned that a given behavior will produce an upsetting effect in his parents. To the extent that he *wants* to upset his parents (for whatever reason), he is in a position to do so, even though there may be some pain or punishment con-nected with his behavior. The upset response of the parent apparently becomes rewarding, and the pain or punishment accompanying it peripheral in meaning to the child.

Thus far we have suggested that the child would be able to upset his parents if he wanted to do so, simply by using the informa-tion they give him daily. A given parent may be particularly involved in early toilet training. The young child senses that when he wets his pants he creates a great disturbance in his mother. Through hundreds of repetitions, the child learns that wet pants result in an upset mother. When "mother is upset" becomes a desirable goal for the child, he will use his knowledge and engage in the very behaviors which he knows will gain this end.

The question of why the child should want to upset his parents is a little more difficult to answer, in view of the fact that the child does not admit to himself or to anyone else that he has such intentions. Were the child to openly admit that he wants to upset his parents, the "why" question would be simple enough to answer. (The adolescent coming home late is often aware that he wants to "worry mother.") If such an admission were possible, we could then suggest that the child probably had a specific reason to "get even" with his mother. Perhaps he felt he was getting less candy than his brother, or was being unjustly yelled at, or had to stay alone too long, or was domi-nated too heavy-handedly. But the child creates upset with two qualifications: (1) he is not aware of why he is doing it, and (2) he also experiences something that is upsetting to *him*—some pain, a spanking, rejection, physical pain, or loss of a valued object. It is almost as though the child creates the upset in the adult at the same time he provides an alibi for himself. This alibi is based on the assumption that no one would voluntarily seek out pain. With his behavior the child expresses that: "I did not intend creating the upset any more than I intended being punished or feeling pain. I cannot be held repsonsible for this action."

Consequently, it is not enough to explain the child's behavior of creating upset in the parent in terms of simple retaliation. One must also consider the fact that the child wants to retaliate safely and without eliciting further retaliation from the parent. He wants to retaliate for wrongs received but feels he cannot afford to be recognized for his retaliation. Perhaps he has learned that overt retaliation against his parents does not only upset his parents, but makes them truly dangerous. His aggressive, retaliative behavior then must become subversive; it must occur without the parents having a legitimate way of fighting back. This sort of subversive behavior can be observed in every home in one form or another. One child accidently drops mother's best china ("He is so uncoordinated!"). Another forgets his schoolbooks just before the test, and still a third becomes the victim of the neighborhood children. While it would be absurd to claim that all such conditions are motivated, unconsciously or otherwise, in some cases there does seem to be sufficient evidence to call this a "safe" retaliative behavior. The child beaten up by the neighborhood boys (upsetting daddy with such weakness) may be observed seeking out and teasing the bullies. The child carrying his mother's best china may take it by way of the route where he is most likely to stumble. Some parents may respond with anger, disgust, or with anxiety to these behaviors. It is highly probable that the child has learned to find such negative responses rewarding and reads them as "concern," as a way of engaging the authority figures.

This "concern" that the child bargains for eventually culminates in the parents' recognition that they can no longer deal with these problems on their own. They experience a feeling of loss of competency and are ready to take some extra effort and go to some extra expense to bring the child into therapy. Our point is that the child has perhaps been successful in arousing such feelings in the parents. The "concerned" parent then is our first clue to the family interaction. The focus of our work is on the question: Why did the parents respond to this child in a particular way, and what experiences does the child encounter with his subversive retaliation?

The Child's Place in the Family

While the therapist may want to see the child in play therapy alone, it is nevertheless useful to meet together with the child and his parents, possibly with other siblings included. One or more such group meetings gives the therapist information that he may otherwise miss. Such meetings, though, do not replace the intake session in obtaining information on the specific problem with which the family is concerned. The intake session is also useful in obtaining releases for information from previous professional contacts, for assessing previous medical and psychodiagnostic information, and for discussing the necessary number of contacts and fees. The family group meetings are designed to give the therapist firsthand information on the interaction and communication patterns in the given family (see Chapter XI). The significance of this information to the play therapist is that he will become sensitive to certain idiosyncratic rules and laws within a particular family.

In one family a boy of nine had run away for the fourth time. The parents and the younger brother came to the first session and, upon the suggestion that the family discuss the problem among themselves, all three started to lecture the "prodigal son" on the evils of having the wrong friends. To a remarkable extent the discussion was led by the eight-year-old, who assumed a very serious mien and told his brother Johnny that he should always find out whether his friends come from a respectable family! The therapist not only learned that this family was preoccupied with respectability, which perhaps explained in some measure the particular "unrespectable" behavior in which Johnny was engaged, but he also gathered information about the cohesiveness of the 3:1 alignment. This alignment, hypothesized from this first interview, found much support in future sessions and sensitized the therapist to the sort of frustration Johnny was up against. In working with Johnny, the alienation from his family became an important issue, particularly Johnny's contributions to maintaining the very alienation he hated so.

We once interviewed an 11-year-old girl who, for the most part, lived in a world of her own. She described with real detail and imagination the beautiful garden in which she lived. She had been seen by four different agencies in addition to some private practitioners. In her heavy referral folder the most typical diagnostic label was "schizophrenic reaction." She was in a class for disturbed children on a third-grade level and was described by her teacher as extremely inattentive. Her mother had been interviewed and was described as a tense, well-educated woman who was overconcerned about her child. When we asked the whole family to come to a session, the mother told us that her two older sons could not come, as they had moved out of the home at the ages of 14 and 15. They lived with friends and she sent them money each month. However, father, Ruth (the patient), and a younger brother would come. In the first session it became quite clear from the interaction of these four people that the parents did not talk to each other and apparently had not done so for many years. The 9-year-old boy, with support from his mother, was "bossing" Ruth in a truly remarkable manner. He would strike her hard when she refused to play with him, and if she tried to play, would then yell at her and beat her for playing badly. The only response from the mother at these goings on was a shrug and the remark, "These children."

When the therapist commented that the mother and father had not said a word to each other, the father responded with tears: "How can I talk to her? Any word I'd say she would take as an offense or an insult; she'd run out of the house and take the car out and go racing through town. After our boy was born, I just could no longer talk to her."

The mother yelled back: "You know what you did to me before Tommy was born; you have no right to talk to me in this manner."

The children were so astonished at this exchange that they stopped fighting—the son went over to the mother, but Ruth made gestures implying that she was planting flowers in her garden.

From this dramatic exchange the therapist obtained useful information for a hypothesis regarding Ruth's place in this family. She apparently had learned that communication among family members has very dangerous consequences, that her father had "sold her out" to maintain peace, that her brother (acting out the father's wishes?) would enslave her, and that the one way in which she could retaliate was to escape and worry "them." With this behavior, she would have an impact on the family and be a person in her own right.

We do not claim that there is not more to this behavior—there is the possibility of a genetic predisposition and deeper historical sources —but we do believe that an analysis of such interaction does give the therapist important clues for his future work. At this point we only wish to show that full family sessions preceeding play therapy are indeed useful in sensitizing the therapist to important problems of his patient.

Unspoken Language

In adult psychotherapy, the therapist has to make an effort to transcend the social meaning of words and try to understand their implied meaning. In play therapy, the therapist has an advantage in that the child has not as yet learned as readily as the adult to hide behind words. Instead of words, the child may use gestures, silences, and facial expression to express emotions. He may even use spatial relations to be close or far away from the therapist, and he will use all these behaviors with less inhibition than adults. Toys, too, can take on a communicative meaning. The therapist will become sensitized to the unspoken language of the child and will be able to utilize it for the subtle information it conveys.

Most therapists prefer simple toys to complex ones. A therapist will find it easier to understand meanings expressed in playing with a wooden hammer than with, let us say, an erector set. In addition to a few simple toys such as fingerpaints, dolls, blocks, soldiers, cars, planes, a boxing bag, and sand and water, we have successfully used masks and a small house or tent in which the child could hide. While the adult can successfully hide behind words, the child should have more direct means of disappearing whenever he feels the need.

The Child:
an Involuntary Patient

In the analysis of the unspoken language one must not only consider vocal stereotypes and the nonverbal properties of speech, but also relevant information that is presented through context. These contextual cues include the information provided by the setting, and also that which is given to the child by the parents prior to the contact. The therapist is frequently asked by a parent what to tell the child before bringing him for treatment. We usually suggest that they tell the child they are worried about him and that they are taking him to see a therapist to help both him and the family overcome their problems.

It is important to discuss this question with the parents even if they do not bring it up themselves, since how they handle this question of motivating the involuntary patient to come in is of some importance. The parents of some patients we have treated paid their children for going to see the therapist. Other parents bribed their children with gifts such as a bike (to be given after getting a good "report card" from the therapist), and still others referred to the therapeutic hour as a school session and the therapist as a teacher. It is not our intention to correct the parents or to avoid misconceptions, but rather to point out the possible significance of the subtle information introduced into the therapeutic session through these suggestions. Threats or rewards will surely influence the child's approach to the therapist. A therapist sensitized to this information will become more effective in understanding the child.

The child essentially is an involuntary patient. He is rarely self-referred, nor does he typically wish to avail himself of therapeutic help. This fact by itself presents some contextual information. The therapist's final decision whether or not to see the child rests on the parents in most cases, and so contact with them is necessary. It has been our procedure to have all contacts with parents in the presence of the child so that there is a clear understanding by all family members as to what exchanges took place. The parents often seek contact with the therapist because of their concern about the progress the child is making. Sometimes they want to discover the "magic" the therapist uses to produce changes in the child and at other times they seek advice on how to solve specific problems. They may wish to direct the therapist's attention to certain goals which are important to them (e.g., "Can't you help me make the child want to go to church?"). The therapist's attitude toward the parent during such contacts will convey important information to the child. It has been our practice to involve the child in these sessions and suggest that the parents talk directly to him about the matters that concern them. The therapist must stay out of the role of adviser or referee lest he become directly identified with the parents and lose his unique relationship with the child.

Yet the therapist must always be aware of parental feelings; first, bcause he will then see the child's problem as it relates to the interaction within the family, and second, because the continuity of the relationship with his involuntary patient is dependent on the parent. (In a clinic it is often the practice to have the parent seen by another staff member.)

One therapist saw a child of five who was very dependent on his mother. When the child was separated from her to be taken to the playroom, he resisted and cried violently. Working under the assumption that he must have the child present to work with him, the therapist carried the boy into the playroom. Although views on this type of intervention differ, a case can be made for this procedure. After all, the mother had come a long way to get treatment, and permitting the child to control whether or not he received treatment at this point would have its own hazards. The therapist believed that he ought to let the child know that he understood his feelings of anguish, but at the same time he wanted to clearly set certain limits regarding this behavior. At that point the child began yelling with such intensity that his mother rushed in, grabbed the child, and left, thus closing the contact.

One could easily argue that the mother was not ready for separation and used the convention "my child suffers too much" in order to justify withdrawal. This argument is too pat. It would probably have been wiser to show concern for the mother's anxiety by inviting her and the child into the playroom for a family session. While one would temporarily be giving in to the son's need for control, through this gesture one would also communicate to him that the fear of separation is a family problem, not his alone. In addition one would enhance the probability that contact will continue.

When we call the child the "involuntary patient," we do not imply that he does not want to be helped. All patients are ambivalent about obtaining help, whether or not they report they want help. This is an observation on which Freud built his theory of resistance. Even the patient who claims that he wants help for his problems still clings to his present libidinal position, though he may deny it. The voluntary patient is often unaware of his wish to cling to his problems. The involuntary patient, on the other hand, is unaware (or denies) that he has any problems in the first place. Although there are ethical problems involved in giving therapy to a person who feels that he does not need it, it probably does not make much difference, in terms of the effectiveness of the therapeutic intervention, whether a person clings to his problems with or without awareness. In our experience, hospitalized patients exposed to a therapeutic milieu, delinquents referred by a court, or children brought in by their parents all seem to respond as well as voluntary patients who seek treatment. The behavior therapist cannot accept the assumption that only the voluntary patient, who seeks help, can be helped. Skillful persuasion can be effective as long as there is a person present who receives the information. Communication principles maintain that covert information can have an emotional impact on another person regardless of whether or not he actually sought this impact. Accordingly, the "involuntary" child brought to us by the parent does not present a problem in treatability, but rather a case where the child's awareness of needing help has not been established. The therapist should be sensitive to this distinction.

Structure

Therapists differ in what they tell the child upon entering the playroom. Some prefer to start the hour with a long list of "do's and don't's," while others refuse to provide any structure. In our opinion, verbalizing a given structure essentially serves the therapist rather than the child. The message, "You can do what you want here, but you cannot hurt yourself or me," is likely to give the rebellious child ideas, the docile child the feeling that the therapist is too strict, and the withdrawn child, at best, the information that the therapist is somewhat uncomfortable. The message, "You can do anything you want and you can trust me," is even more inadequate in that it invites the child into cahoots without consensual validation. The child's best guess about this message is the way we feel about a book title: will it fulfill its promise? The true structure of the interview will, of course, emerge within the treatment hours; and it is during the sessions that the child will find out how much he can trust the therapist, what he can get away with, and what he is expected to do.

It should be noted that structure is given not only by action, but that the therapist's silence also has communicative meaning. With a silent therapist, the child may experience that the therapist wants to wait him out without taking responsibility for the first move. In such an unstructured setting every gesture of the therapist will be of great importance to the child.

One often unnoticed gesture is the spatial distance between child and therapist. The child may stay at one end of the room with the therapist at the other. The question of who will make the first move to close the gap may seem inconsequential to the adult, but appears to be clearly perceived by the child and to be important to him. The adult's immobility may be interpreted by the child as indifference. With some cases, a move toward the child may be seen as a threat. We maintain that each of these spatial moves has a specific meaning to the child and that the therapist should be aware that these gestures, ordinarily unimportant to him, are likely to be meaningful to the child.

Another such subtle gesture often overlooked by the beginning play therapist is the child's use of silence. The adult can use silence effectively, but he also has the means to cover up silence with small talk. The child ordinarily has a somewhat smaller repertoire of behavior to cover his discomfort. He may play silently, thus leaving out the adult, or stare into space as if the adult were not present, or talk to himself. These are all gestures with meaning to the therapist.

They tell the therapist that the child wants to avoid the responsibility of seeking a relationship with him, perhaps because he is afraid of the consequences. He may feel hostile, or he may simply be silent because he wants to find out what method of approach the adult will use with him. We cannot know the reason unless we have further evidence. The therapist, in order to properly structure the interview, must read these subtle gestures and give the child the understanding that they are not lost on him, that he will make an effort to understand them.

Typical Problems

There are some specific problems often encountered by the therapist. What about rapport? Should the therapist try to be nice in order to elicit the child's giving of himself? Predictably, our answer is no. We feel that the therapist should not make any special social effort nor pretend that the hour is designed for the pleasure of the child. He should interact with the child and try to understand his hurt. At the same time he should provide the child with experiences that will permit him new choices both at the beginning and throughout the contact.

Some therapists sit in their chairs and let the child come to them, while others sit down on the floor with the child. Some always let the child originate the play and enter into it only on demand; others refuse to enter the play even on the demand of the child. Still others are willing either to originate the play themselves or to play with some objects such as fingerpaints in order to stimulate the child to explore these toys. We feel that none of these variations is of great significance by itself, but each presents a different structure to the child. The therapist must use the approach with which he feels most comfortable. If he feels that he understands the child better by sitting near him, he should do so. We encourage our students to try out some of the more unfamiliar approaches, approaches with which they can explore their own limits. They too will finally choose the approach in which they feel most comfortable. It is not the approach a therapist uses that makes the difference. The important point is whether, within his particular approach, he has found a way to respond in a manner that helps the child experience the freedom to explore new choices.

Another problem that often bothers the therapist is the child's leaving the room. The child may again and again ask to go to the toilet. He may make a plea to leave or just make a run for the door.

Within reason, we believe that the child should be kept in the room, even if the therapist finds it necessary to sit in front of the door. It is true that with this gesture he communicates to the child that he is bigger and that he insists that the child remain in the room. However, he also communicates that he wishes to maintain the relationship and hopes that he can help the child. By guaranteeing the child's presence, he probably enhances therapeutic effect. Some therapists deal with the child more permissively, on the assumption that he will eventually accept the responsibility of staying on his own volition when he is given the responsibility of making the decision by himself. These therapists are taking the risk that the parents will be content with a five-minute visit; more seriously, they simply have postponed the handling of *limits*. Even the most permissive therapist will set limits at some time. Many unspoken rules regarding the interview itself are in actuality "standard operational procedures" that impose immediate and direct limits on the contact. A therapist is ordinarily unwilling to see the child in the local bar or see him for four hours at a time on demand. We are inclined to make the presence of the child another such "standard operating procedure." We recommend enforcing his presence and using the behavior in which he engages in learning about his problems.

Limits

Bixler (1949) in a thoughtfully reasoned article wrote that limits *are* therapy. That is, the child is trained to accept responsibility by testing the limits of his environment. Testing limits is an essential part of play therapy. The therapist structures a new territory for the child and presents the child with unique limits. It is our intent to analyze the problem of testing limits from the standpoint of communication theory.

The behaviors traditionally eliciting therapeutic limits are the child's either endangering himself or the therapist, or, to a lesser extent, placing the play-therapy room equipment in jeopardy. The therapist ordinarily deals with these attempts by stating that he can well understand that the child wants to do a certain destructive act but that he will not permit him to do so.

In a playroom where the windows are not secured by a safety device, the child may attempt to climb out the window. First, he approaches it, then opens it, and finally climbs onto the window sill. What does this behavior mean? One could speculate that the child has learned that "taking chances" will arouse an adult's anxiety, and constrict the adult's behavior to prohibitional punitive responses. When the therapist finds support for his hypothesis that this is "testing behavior," he can then infer with reasonable certainty that the child has learned the use of this "high impact" behavior because milder behavior, such as jumping from a chair, did not elicit the response he wanted. We do not know as yet why he wants to constrict the adult into a "worry response," but we assume that his expectations are that he will obtain it. He has learned that climbing onto the window sill creates anxiety in his mother (who would not be likely to say, "Oh, Johnny, I see that you want to climb out of the window"), and that she will tell him to stop this nonsense. In other words, the child can force his mother to be concerned for his life.

Were the therapist to respond with a similar anxious and restricted response, he would most likely reinforce the child's testing behavior and enhance the chance of its recurrence. At this point the therapist has to set limits in a different manner than the mother and others have previously done. His response should be designed to give the child the experience that it is all right to test the adult, but that the particular testing behavior chosen is not acceptable. The therapist may say: "You want to frighten me, but you cannot climb out the window." If this limit is not successful, the therapist will have to constrict the child's behavior, but again with firmness and no anxiety. The communication involved in this gesture can be described as: "I will accept having to prevent you from killing yourself, but your thought of testing me in this manner does not frighten me; you have the right to think any thought."

Again, a child throwing sand at the therapist may attach certain expectations to this gesture. Since he is showing so much direct aggression, the child may assume (by convention) that the adult will get "mad" and punish him. If the therapist were to act out the expected social role, get mad and punish the child, he would possibly reinforce the inappropriate aggressive behavior. This child may perceive the expected response of anger and punishment as a reward. By separating the wish for aggression from the aggressive behavior proper, the therapist recognizes the right of the child to feel aggressive but limits the aggressive behavior itself. He may say: "It is really fun to throw that sand at me, but you cannot do this here." Should the child persist, he is essentially telling the therapist that this testing behavior is extremely important to him and is possibly being used to convey a meaning other than aggression.

The inexperienced therapist is given to repeating his statements when the child repeats his behavior, but such a repeated response quickly becomes inadequate. Instead, the therapist may speculate that the child continues to throw the sand to test him further. Perhaps the child has sensed that the therapist does not wish to punish him, and so his repeated aggressive behavior is a means of finding out just how far he can go and still get away with it. The therapist may respond: "You wonder when I will get really mad at you." If the child still persists, he might ask what we have called the "existence question": "You wonder when I will give up and let you go?" With this type of response the therapist recognizes the legitimacy of the child's wish to be aggressive but attempts to limit the behavior proper. In some cases no verbalization will stop the child from hurting himself or other people or from destroying objects. In such cases physical restraint is necessary. If the therapist is anxious about or unable to provide such restraint, he may have to refer the case.

Neill (1960) has claimed that a child who is left relatively unrestricted, that is, where the limits are extremely broad, will eventually find his own limits. If you let him destroy property (for instance, break a window), he will eventually discover that he does not need to do that to establish himself. We do not share all of Neill's basic assumptions. When the child learns that he can obtain a punitive response from the adult, he also learns that the controls for his behavior lie outside himself and that he does not need to accept responsibility for his behavior since some adult will do this. However, when the expected response does *not* follow his act, the child is faced with an experience which demands that control come from within.

One could agree with Neill to the extent that broad limits help to retrain the child. However, there is another consideration. It is questionable whether the child's experience must in fact include testing all limits with his actions before he can accept responsibility for his acts. Does such a model perhaps confuse wish and deed? We believe that the *wish* to destroy the window is actually as significant as the deed itself. It is the wish that motivates the testing behavior. The deed becomes necessary only if the wish itself is not dealt with. By helping the child differentiate his wish for aggression from the aggressive deed, one helps him to differentiate: "to wish" and "to do" are separate behaviors. With the therapeutic responses, "I can understand how you would want to feel strong and break the window. That would show me," the child can learn that there is nothing wrong with the wish itself, but that the deed may not be necessary to prove his point.

In this connection we can comment on the contradiction in the educational goals to which the child is so often exposed, particularly in reference to aggression. The male child, in particular, is supposed to be reasonably aggressive, willing to compete and ready to assert himself. Yet the responses to his messages connoting aggression, competitive feelings or self assertion not only leave him unrewarded, but actually punish him. The punishment would be understable were it administered only for aggressive deeds, but more often than not he is also punished for his wish for aggression. Typically, punishments almost seem designed to "throw out the baby with the bathwater." The parent says, "You are a bad child; you should not hit your brother." This statement, "You are a bad child," is designed not only to discourage the boy from hitting his brother, but actually to make even his wish to hit his brother suspect. "You are a bad child" means just that: "You and your behavior are unacceptable." Perhaps the boy has just been hit by his brother or he has seen his brother preferred in some reward by his parents, and his wish to hit him is simply a manifestation of his desire to assert himself. He wants to compete, and his aggressive act serves his need of self-assertion. "You are a bad child" is a statement designed to discourage these feelings.

What the child should really learn is not that he is bad for wanting to hit his brother but that the actual deed of hitting him is unacceptable, and that there are more adequate ways of asserting himself. The trouble is that many parents do not guide the youngsters toward "more adequate ways"—such as discerning the child's feeling that he was an object of injustice—and the child simply learns that he is not permitted to assert himself when he feels that an injustice has been done to him. When his parents discourage even his wish for self-assertion, the child is placed in a "double bind." He is expected to be self-assertive, but cannot afford to be self-assertive enough to have such behavior seem meaningful to him. By differentiating the wish from the deed, the therapist helps the child escape this "double bind."

A related problem with which play therapists have to deal is the destruction of property. Trained to be permissive, the tendency of many beginners is to constrict the child as little as possible. This permissive type of response is often of great importance to the therapist but probably somewhat less so to the child. For example, in allowing the child to squeeze the whole tube of fingerpaints instead of a limited amount, the therapist tells himself that he is in a unique, asocial situation where acceptance of the child is mandatory. Actually, the quality of his therapy is not dependent on the number of inches of fingerpaint he permits the child to use. If the child squeezes the whole tube on the paper, he will do so either because he has the understanding that this is permissible or because he wants to challenge the therapist. If he acts because he has not been instructed to conserve, a simple limiting statement would correct the child's behavior. On the other hand, if he squanders because he wants to find out at what point the therapist will set limits, the problem becomes an interpersonal one and is no longer related to the fingerpaint.

At this point a statement of limits such as, "I know you like to use more of the paint, but that is all I can let you use," would attempt to recognize the child's wish to squander but would set the limit in much the same fashion as when the child wanted to climb out the window. If the child was trying to elicit a scolding or punitive response by his squandering of paint, setting limits without scolding is indeed a new experience for him. He will frequently persist in testing further limits as though obtaining the punitive response was of great importance to him. This often means that he will increase the activity that has become the vehicle for his current test. This increased challenging activity, vociferously demanding the expected response, is designed to test the adult in a "matching of wills." Many adults grow impatient with the test and become punitive. If the therapist does become anxious, he rewards the child with the expected response, thus reinforcing the very problem he wishes to solve. With an anxious, punitive therapist, the child quickly learns that the therapist's acceptance of his wish to assert himself is only skin deep, and that this adult too, has to be engaged and controlled by more subtle means.

The child's testing of limits does not necessarily directly involve threats against himself, others, or property. Challenges are often much more subtly introduced by the child. The following exchange will illustrate this.

Child: "Can you spell my name?"
Therapist: "You wonder if I can spell your name?"

This response was a simple delay response which asked for further information. As all delay responses, it avoided the social response (J-o-h-n-n-y) which this message was set up to elicit.

Child: "Can you spell it?"
Therapist: "You wonder if I can spell it."

This response was a perseveration. It no longer was a quest for further information, but communicated to the child that the worker was having some difficulty in responding. Possibly the child had the feeling that the therapist was not permitted to give a direct answer, and so he wanted to challenge the therapist's involvement with this restriction.

Child: "Can you?"
Therapist: "You wonder if I am able to spell it?"

Here the therapist became "engaged" in the demand of the child. True, he did not spell the child's name, which in response to the first message would also have been an act of engagement. At this point the child most likely was no longer interested in having his name spelled, but appeared to want to "call" the therapist on his own restriction of not giving a direct answer. The ineptness of the repetition permitted the child to sense that he had succeeded in being "one-up" in rendering the therapist ineffectual. One might say that by being repetitive, the therapist reinforced the child's notion that he could get satisfaction by confusing an adult. He apparently enjoyed his victory and maintained his role:

Child: "Why don't you spell it?"
Therapist: "You want me to spell it."

At this point the therapist played the role of the confused adult to perfection. The child might very well ask: "How dumb can you get? I told you four times that I want you to spell it."

Child (angrily): "Yes, spell it."
Therapist: "You are quite angry that I haven't spelled it yet."

This reflection was more adequate. Apparently the therapist has begun to pull out of the engagement. This response indicates that he realized that spelling the name was no longer really significant and that he was dealing with a matter of control.

Child: "Please spell it for me."
Therapist: "It is very important to you that I can spell it. It would show you that I care for you."

The therapist responded to the sudden change to pleading in the child's voice. He introduced his interpretation (the translation of "Can you spell it?" into "Do you care for me?") with skill. With it he told the child: "Your challenge (Can you spell my name?) is a substitute for such words as 'Do you like me.' What is so dangerous about this inquiry?" With this response he stopped reinforcing the child's attitude he must control and mislead adults in order to get a response indicating that he is liked. Had the therapist spelled his name right at the beginning of the exchange, the child would have been reinforced in his syndrome of obtaining a "liking response" only by first hiding the meaning of his message.

Of course, it is possible that the child had little awareness of the meaning entailed in his first question ("Can you spell my name?"). The subsequent reluctance of the adult to answer turned this exchange into a question of control and then one of liking. Even so, it would have been an error to spell the name at the beginning of the exchange, as the therapist was still unclear as to what this question implied.

After the therapist had disengaged, the child responded.

Child: "If you like me you will spell my name."
Therapist: "That would really prove it to you."

The therapist was fully disengaged at this point. The child still wanted to force the therapist to like him, and the therapist responded to this minor attempt at blackmail.

Child: "I think you like me a little."
Therapist: "You are not quite sure, but it seems that way."

In terms of providing the child with the experience that he does not have to use subtle methods of coercing others to express liking for him, this was a good response. At this point the therapist could even have spelled the name without an overlay of meaning, though this behavior would probably have met his own needs for completion rather than those of the child.

In this exchange, the child tested the limits of the therapist in a more subtle manner than by destroying property. The chosen testing ground was in the area of the therapist's self-restriction. Again, the child's benefit did not derive from unrestricted freedom, but from the asocial responses of the therapist who managed to disengage from the social demand of the message.

The Asocial Response in
Play Therapy

While the disengaged response used with an adult is predominantly verbal, a disengaged response with a child can more readily take a nonverbal form. We have already mentioned that the spatial relationship between the child and the adult plays a role, as do gestures such as sitting by the child on the floor or cooperating with him in his play. We once worked with a student who treated a very withdrawn child who sat very still at the far end of the room and stared at the wall. The student apparently grew bored and pulled some papers out of his pocket and started to read, occasionally looking at the child to see if there were any changes. This gesture of inattention was certainly most inept, as the child's testing behavior was possibly concerned with the meaning that his presence would have to the adult. The therapist perhaps became engaged in the child's attempt to elicit a response, and confirmed his view that "adults just do not care."

In the following we shall discuss nonverbal gestures as disengaged responses in a number of settings.

The Silent Child

Many therapists work with children who come to the room and sit inertly in a corner, presumably in a state of self-preoccupation. Assuming that we know the child is medically sound and of normal intelligence, we can use the information presented by the child's apparent inertness for a tentative answer to the question: Where does this child hurt? We can speculate that a child who meets the stranger by ignoring him may have learned that any show of interest or participation equals some kind of commitment. "Commitment" may appear dangerous to him—he may have experienced that "they will take the whole hand if offered a finger." On the other hand, he may have found that "commitment" is typically responded to with indifference. In addition, the child may have learned that his behavior not only serves a defensive purpose but also has the effect of eliciting commitment on the part of the adult. That is, it serves to arouse feelings in the adult, perhaps anger ("He is sulking, he acts deaf and dumb") or perhaps love and sympathy ("Poor kid, come talk to me"). These speculations are merely tentative, as they are based on very little information; yet to us they seem necessary in order to formulate some meaningful approach to the silent child.

Viewed in terms of such speculations, we would want to be careful in committing ourselves by using methods such as encouraging the child to talk, responding with indifference or anger, or reading in his presence to make a point of our inattention. We would want him to experience that his act of ignoring us arouses neither sympathy nor resentment. A verbal delay response might be:

Therapist: "You wonder what coming to this playroom is all about."

The therapist attempted to disengage from the idea of commitment and tried to let the child know that it is all right to be silent. The response was probably more adequate than those we often come across in our transcripts: "It is hard for you to get started" or "It is hard for you to talk to me." These two responses show concern for the child but have the ring of engagement, as they imply that the child in fact wants to get started or wants to talk. The silent child all too easily can read these responses as encouragement to talk or a form of sympathy, perhaps the very responses he wanted to elicit from the adult. Their occurrence would reinforce his silent behavior as a "successful" mode of interpersonal relations.

A verbal response is not really necessary, and probably serves more as a means of anxiety reduction for the adult than as a method of help for the child. By the act of talking itself, the therapist defines the structure. He communicates to the child: "One ought to discuss events here." It is questionable whether this communication is actually beneficial. An alternative would be to sit quietly with the child with one's interest centered on him, provided this can be done without anxiety or a sense of failure. We do not claim that the therapist's feelings will mysteriously be communicated to the child, but we believe that such waiting behavior, with one's interest maintained in the child, is an indication that the therapist is in the proper frame of mind to disengage from the child's message of silence. By avoiding gestures of restlessness and by showing interest even in the face of silence, the therapist helps the child have the experience that adults do not necessarily either have to talk or impose on youngsters.

We find that such cases often take a typical turn of events. Eventually the child admits his awareness of the presence of the other person by glancing furtively in his direction and perhaps by making some slight efforts to acknowledge the therapist's presence by reaching out for nearby objects. The therapist's silence, combined with attention and interest, is a disengaged response under these circumstances. After the therapist obtains additional information he can soon enough label what is going on and talk to the child at a time when these activities would be of help. Eventually he may want to respond to a furtive glance with: "You wonder what I am doing" or "You wonder why I am not talking." Yet, we know that even this behavior of labeling the child's state of mind is an invitation for a reply, and the therapist would have to be concerned lest his inviting the child to give a reply be perceived as coercion. An acceptance of the furtive glance with interest but continued silence is probably more adequate, but often more difficult for many therapists to accomplish.

A variation of the silence theme is presented by a child who comes to the playroom and immediately occupies himself by playing with finger-paints, thus ignoring the presence of the therapist. In this variation, the message is more ambiguous. The therapist does not know if the child really wishes to ignore him or if he perceives the play situation as an event similar to the kind of supervised play which he may have experienced in school. In that case a verbal response may be indicated as it may help to clarify the child's motivation.

Therapist: "You like to play with these paints."

Such a response again represents a mild invitation to take cognizance of the therapist's presence, and the therapist can gauge from the child's response (or lack of comment) what sort of feeling was involved in the ignoring behavior.

A nonverbal response can be useful for disengagement in a situation where the child tries to hide. In some playrooms there are tents or children's houses where the child actually can hide. However, this convenience is not always present. Without physical facilities for escape, hiding may be attempted with an act that symbolically represents the desire to "not really want to be seen." The child can accomplish this in an ostrich-like fashion by simply not looking at the therapist. However, by constantly staring at the child, many therapists do not permit hiding. The nonverbal gesture of keeping one's gaze on the child at all times can be most disconcerting to the watched child. There are times when it would be wise to shift one's gaze to other objects. This gesture is actually not very different from the behavior, used in adult psychotherapy, in which the therapist does not always give the interpretation or the response which comes to his mind, but "times" his responses so that the patient has the feeling that he can proceed at his own speed, that he can take time to rest and time to hide according to his needs. The child also needs this freedom to proceed at his own speed, and the nonverbal gesture of averting one's eyes, minute as it is, can communicate the therapist's understanding for such a need.

This gesture would be particularly important if the therapist were to become engaged with the child through visual cues. A little girl had performed a dance for the therapist, and the therapist became aware that he had been quite caught up by the beauty and grace of the child. The child expected this response, and it is likely that her very seductivity was part of her problem. Were the therapist to be seduced by her gesture, the child would most likely be reinforced in using it for her purposes. Therefore, the therapist's therapeutic objective should be to give this girl the experience that she can be liked without resorting to the use of seduction. To provide her with this experience he may very well say: "You like it when a lot of people admire you for dancing so prettily." Since the cues have been visual, the therapist should be cognizant of where he directs his gaze in order to help the child experience that he is not engaged by her exhibition.

One "extraverbal" cue we observed many times in the supervision of play therapy is the use of "children's talk" by the therapist. Many adults have adopted a particular way in which they approach children, whereby they let the child know with every message (in terms of adjuvant cues) that they think of him as immature. The child is, of course, immature in certain ways, but we feel that this special language unduly restricts him. This behavior probably derives from a generalized feeling of uncertainty that many adults have when they deal with children. Most adults have learned to make some allowances for the child's behavior, and the child in our society does have certain rights of exploration which we do not allow the adult. He can be a little more dirty, and when he is vain he is considered cute. Crying is not a crime, and even yelling on occasion is permissible. Furthermore, children, along with drunks, are considered as people who tell the "truth": if they do not like you there must be something wrong with you. Consequently, children are often seen as a threat by the adult, and many adults feel uncomfortable with the child's greater freedom. Some therapists bring such feelings into the therapeutic hour. A therapist may talk down to the child, for which many children resent an adult. To the extent that he is not aware of the subtle information he transmits, the therapist will be a blunt instrument and less effective than he could be.

Sometimes the therapist faces a different dilemma in play therapy: verbal creature that he is, he will use words beyond the understanding of the child. Play therapy is a real challenge in this respect but, in essence, no different from therapy with adults. The therapist has to leave his academic way of talking and think of the impact his comment may have on the child. A good way to illustrate this point is to think of a driver in a car who slowly cruises by a gas station. He wants to find out if he is going in the right direction. Were he to say, "Sir, would you be kind enough to tell me whether I am going in the right direction to get to Ogden?" he would probably get less of a response than if he were to yell, "Ogden?" and point in the direction he was headed. Many therapists still need to learn how to give a clear message, and play therapy with children makes a very special demand on this ability.

As in adult therapy, the therapist will formulate a therapeutic objective for the child. The evidence for this objective comes—just as with adults—from recognizing the child's unaware expectations of the therapist. Within the structure of the play therapy setting, these un-aware expectations are most easily recognized from the actions and gestures of the child. A child was playing with some marbles, looked at the therapist, and placed a few marbles in his pocket. The therapist responded:

Therapist: "You would like to take these marbles?"

This was an exploratory type of remark which communicated to the child that the behavior was noticed and that some significance was attached to it.

Child: "May I take them home?"
Therapist: "You would like to have something from the playroom at home."

The therapist still wanted to explore the feelings involved. He was not yet certain what the child expected from him. This delay response also communicated that he could understand the wish of the child to extend the playroom, though he could not as yet be sure that his speculation would be supported.

Child: "Will you let me take them home?"
Therapist: "No, I cannot let you take them home. I know you wish I would let you."

The therapist placed limits on the behavior, but tried to indicate that it was all right to have the wish.

Child: "Please let me take them. I need them."
Therapist: "I am a meanie for not letting you take them."

The therapist used "children's talk," perhaps because he felt that he really should have let the child take the marbles home. At the same time, he followed the child's expectations well; he recognized that the child was no longer concerned with the marbles but with coercing the adult into giving him something.

Child: "Please, just these few marbles."
Therapist: "You wished that I would give you something. That would show you that I really like you."

The therapist was disengaged, and continued with an asocial response. He realized that the child expected him to give in or perhaps was asking for a rejection in order to experience the feeling that "nobody loves me." By verbalizing the feeling, the therapist gave the child the information that these feelings can be understood without danger to the child. This is one way of providing the child with the experience that it is not really necessary to hide feelings and control the other person by eliciting "high probability" responses.

Child: "I just want the marbles."

Therapist: "You want to make it really easy for me to give them to you."

Apparently, the response was still disengaged. The therapist was well "tuned in" and changed his response with each new repetition in terms of possible new meanings. He had been sensitive to the child's need and had maintained his asocial response pattern. The child pulled the marbles out of his pocket and placed them in the drawer.

Child: "What about this drawing, can I take it home?"

From this exchange the therapist could make certain formulations as to where the child hurt and what his therapeutic objective might be. He reasoned that the child had learned that there was some significant reward involved in making adults give him things, and that the object itself was unimportant so long as there was a gesture of giving (e.g., marbles or drawing). The child may have learned at home that he could feel loved when his parent made the gesture of giving him something, or perhaps that this was the only way he could elicit a "loving" response. The therapist could then formulate the tentative hypothesis that this child had learned that he could not be certain whether or not he was wanted, and that he was vulnerable in his fear of being unloved unless he himself could produce a "giving" response. Many people have to force others to love them, with the tragic result that they can never be sure whether these feelings expressed by other persons are "genuine," or merely "elicited." The therapeutic objective in this type of case would be derived from this hypothesis: the child has to experience that he can have a meaningful relationship with another person even though this gesture of giving is not present. Sensitized to this pattern in the child's behavior, the therapist then will proceed to arouse what we have called "beneficial uncertainty." He will provide the child with the experience that "making an adult give me things" is not the only way of achieving the feeling of being liked. He will avoid responding directly to the social demand of the child (in the above case, either by giving the drawings or refusing to give them) but will communicate that he can accept the child's wish for a gift, even though he cannot accommodate by giving one.

It is quite possible that the child's demand for a gift had a more specific and highly differentiated purpose than fulfilling the general desire to prove he was loved. One hypothesis is that the child wanted to extend the permissiveness of the play hour to his home. He wanted to be exposed, through the object, to the therapist's presence even outside the playroom. In formulating his hypothesis the therapist has to be aware that any current therapeutic objective will most likely change as his understanding of the child's behavior changes.

Sometimes the social expectations of the child are far more subtle. A girl of eleven played with some dolls and the furniture in a toy house set. While "playing house" she typically placed the mother and a baby doll in an oversized refrigerator while the father and a girl doll were alone in the house. The child seemed very absorbed in the play and went through a day's activities, including preparation of breakfast, father going to work, the girl preparing supper and making the beds, etc. What expectations were involved in this "classic" play? We assume that the choice of playing this game in front of the adult had to do with the child's motivation to test whether this adult would accept her replacement fantasy. The girl stacked the cards in her favor because she could predict that the therapist was not likely to chide her, and yet she apparently wanted to find out how far she could go with this play before sensing some disapproval. The exchange went as follows:

Therapist: "The little girl wants Daddy all to herself while mother and baby are kept in the refrigerator."

Then the child took another baby doll and placed her in the bedroom.

Child: "There is the baby."
Therapist: "They have a baby of their own."

The therapist introduced the words "of their own." He tried to provide the child with the experience that her replacement wish could be understood and was not in itself subject to punishment. Had the therapist said: "*Mommy* had another baby" or some other response excluding the possibility that the girl was responsible for the baby, he would have reinforced the child's feeling that the adult rejected her because of her wishes to identify and replace. Adult disapproval and rejection of her *wish* for replacement would also have reinforced her replacement fantasies, assuming that she saw "obtaining disapproval" as rewarding. By not providing this reward and by accepting her wish, the therapist reduced her need to indulge in these fantasies.

From these conjectures, the therapist could develop the hypothesis that this child hurt in her competitive feelings with her mother.

Perhaps she had the experience (along with many other children) that her mother punished this fantasy of identifying as an adult female (since it often includes wooing the father). Punishment became a reward for this girl because it proved to her that she was a threat to mother! The therapist's therapeutic goal at this point was to provide the girl with the experience that punishment is not necessarily always associated with competitive feelings or adulthood.

The asocial response then is essentially one that does not follow the expectations the child has learned to associate with the wish. This asocial response helps both to extinguish the punitive association (by failing to reinforce it) and to provide the experience that the wish is acceptable to another person. The hope is that the child will find new choices for fulfilling this wish (for adult female identity) rather than having to maintain the original choice which centered on testing her mother.

CHAPTER XIII

THE THERAPIST AS A CONSULTANT

THE therapist has been trained to be an observer and a participant in human interaction. He is specifically cognizant of the subtle cues in communication and has learned, using himself as an instrument, to make inferences from such information as to where people have developed psychological deficits. Even though his understanding of the processes that cause people to change and "seek new territory" may yet be very incomplete, he is able to make some significant contribution in providing for such change. His skills in the analysis of communication processes and his ability to facilitate meaningful intervention have been applied to many other than patient-therapist relationships. In the following, we shall illustrate a few applications of communication principles in settings outside the usual or typical settings of the therapist's work.

The Behavior Consultant in the School

(1) *Working with a teacher.* Various modes of subtle communication affect learning in schools. The design of the school, the personality of the school superintendent, the teacher's relationship to other teachers, the student's perception of his tasks—these are just a few of the factors. To illustrate an application of the analysis of a communication pattern to one of these factors, we shall select as a problem the effect of a teacher's personality on her students. We shall send the school consultant to a classroom to observe her interactions in the student-teacher relationship.

It appears that some teachers have fairly consistent behavior problems in their classes while others do not. Some classrooms seem deeply devoted to learning, others are not. Not all differences are consistent—a teacher can also differ in his behavior from class to class. He may vary with different age groups or react strongly to certain individuals in his room.

In the analysis of the communication process in the classroom, our consultant focuses on covert information and is specifically interested in the impact such information has on the respondents. With this emphasis, he may discover the various devices a given teacher uses (often unaware that he does so) to maintain his classroom in a state of restlessness. These subtle communications are effective and not lost on the class. Yet, they are so subtle that ordinary measures used to differentiate good from poor teaching have not considered them.

Our behavior consultant was asked by a teacher to consult with her, sit in her class, and comment on the type of cues he observed. The teacher, Miss R., was interested in having an impartial observer present because she was having discipline problems with her class. Some of her students apparently did not mind her, talked during class time, wrote notes, and occasionally threw spitballs. Miss R. told the consultant that she had once complained to another teacher about her problems. She was, in effect, asking the teacher for advice on how to handle her class. The other teacher said, "Oh, that is simple, when the class is about to get out of hand, I just look at them!" She gave a sample "look" and one could well understand why the class shut up in fright. Miss R., on the other hand, apparently did not feel that she had the necessary cues of terror at her disposal.

It should be noted that Miss R. did not have trouble with all her classes, but there seemed to be at least one class each year that she complained about. Most often this was an advanced class that she taught. It was not the consultant's intent to collect a psychological history of Miss R. in order to show why she selected one class each year with which to have trouble. He was mainly concerned with the information that Miss R. utilized to accomplish her unhappy task of having trouble.

When Miss R. entered her class, the consultant felt that she looked confused. This emotional climate was created by an uncertain gait, a bewildered facial expression, and the way she looked at the floor. These cues gave him the feeling that she was afraid that she might stumble. When she sat down the class went on talking as if she had not yet entered the classroom, and Miss R. apparently disregarded this lack of respect. She opened a number of books, laid them aside, reached for them again, and put in small bookmarks which she tore out of her notebook. The class responded to these preparatory tasks with indifference and total disregard of her presence. After a minute or so Miss R. looked up, looked at the class, moved her glasses so that they would fit more tightly, and said: "John Brown, you are talking. If you go on talking, you can go on talking to the principal."

For a moment the class was quiet. Miss R. then began her lesson in arithmetic. She seemed to know what she was talking about and was clear in her presentation, but sounded bored. The subtle cues of her own boredom were clearly communicated to the class in both her facial expression and her monotonous voice. Her boredom was reflected by the students with sporadic yawns. Miss R. proceeded to explain the lesson, brought a few students to the blackboard to solve problems, and totally disregarded the increased restlessness in the class. The children not only continued to get noisier, but also got up and walked around the class, made visits to other students, and even did some sham fighting. Apparently, they, as well as the consultant, received the information that the teacher either did not really care or felt unable to control the class. This attitude appeared to arouse a feeling of challenge in the class, and they wanted to find out to what extent Miss R. would tolerate the disorder. It was almost a mass testing of limits.

Miss R. hardly ever looked at the class, but went on talking about the lesson. Since she did not raise her voice, much of what she said was lost on the class. Most of the time she had her face turned toward the blackboard where a student was at work. She gave her attention to the student at work at the blackboard, who seemed to put some effort into solving the problems demanded of him. The restlessness of the class seemed to increase in time, and Miss R. suddenly turned around, faced the class, and said in a tired voice: "Vansluiten, I saw you, you gave a piece of paper to your neighbor. You will stop misbehaving or I will send you to the principal." There was a giggle which was disregarded, and the teacher turned back to another student at the blackboard.

It was not the consultant's purpose to criticize Miss R. for poor teaching habits. Actually, she was known as a reasonably good teacher, and the classes that responded to her peculiarities seemed to learn well. She gave the impression that she had mastered her subject matter and showed concern for the individual student. It is easy to describe a good many teachers in terms of their peculiarities, but it accomplished little, because it is well known that some people are able to make their peculiarities work for them while others cannot.

The consultant wished to describe Miss R.'s peculiarities only with the purpose of speculating on the general impact that this behavior had on her class. He wanted to find out at what point her peculiar approach to teaching reached a state of "no return" and accounted for the trouble about which she complained.

There are a number of generalizations possible even from this short description. First of all, the class obtained the information that the teacher was interested in the individual, not in the class. Miss R. disregarded the class and devoted her time to teaching the individual student who happened to be at the blackboard. Also, upon severe provocation, she singled out one particular student for punishment, again disregarding the restlessness of the other students.

The second generalization is that Miss R. appeared to communicate that she was scared of the class, that she felt that it was beyond her power to handle them, and that she was there reluctantly in the first place. She gave this information through her boring and monotonous voice, through her lack of interaction with the class, and by referring to the principal as a source of punishment without ever attempting to take discipline into her own hands. She also supported this impression that she would rather not handle discipline problems by the fact that she permitted the restlessness to build up to a high degree before she entered the problem.

A third generalization is that the class can sense a feeling of fatigue and reluctance to teach, and that some of the children can be expected to take advantage of the opportunity to make an adult look ineffectual. The children in this class experienced that they could best accomplish this task of teasing the teacher by mass action rather than by individual cunning. Perhaps this also accounts for the fact that the advanced classes give her more trouble.

Miss R. gave much of this information without awareness, and elicited student responses without knowing to what extent she was responsible for them. Miss R. stated that she wanted to be an effective teacher, one who would inspire confidence and keep her class in good command. Could she learn to be what she apparently was not?

The behavior consultant can help Miss R. and others like her by using a "communication profile" to help her recognize what impression she makes on her class and, to some extent, how she does it. He can sensitize her to the behaviors involved in her teaching style. He can expect that such information may effect a new awareness. Miss R. listened to the consultant and responded: "I am too old. The things you have said might be quite true, for I certainly recognize some of them. I am more interested in the individual student than in the class. I am scared of the class and I am not happy teaching it, it is true. It is also probably true that I present the children with the picture of disinterest and that I am the one they can take advantage of. They surely are doing it."

Miss R. agreed with the profile presented to her, but implied ("I am too old") that there was little she felt she could do about it. We noted that she was quite successful in some of her other classes each year, which gave the information that even with her peculiarities she still could teach well and command a class. Did she have a deep-seated psychodynamic problem that called for periodic failure and the seeking of reasons to complain? If she had such problems, why study the "how" in the first place? What possible use could it be to Miss R. to know *how* she created her problems, particularly since she appeared aware that she was creating them? However, the behavior consultant was also telling her something quite new: though she knew and admitted that she was scared of the class and reluctant to teach, she did not know that these feelings could be read by others. She did not know that her feelings could be recognized by the way she behaved, or that each of these behaviors was directly associated with a certain response. The very fact that some of the behaviors that created problems were singled out and labeled was likely to have an impact on her future actions. She had evidence that others recognized her behavior and read the feelings she thought were hidden. She began to realize that she might be directly responsible for the responses she elicited, and this recognition experience was likely to produce some modification in her behavior.

This prediction is based on the observation that if a person knows that certain private feelings are laid bare and can be read, he will be stimulated to discover ways either to hide these feelings more adequately or, in other cases to explore alternate ways of behaving. As it turned out, Miss R. supported this position. Miss R. was deeply affected by these tentative observations on the reinforcement pattern she was using to elicit unwanted responses from her class. After some searching, she decided that she was not "too old," but wanted to stay in teaching and at least experiment with her problem class. She responded to the challenge of facing the class rather than the individual student, and there is some information that indicates this new attitude was reflected in her behavior. It is not claimed that these tentative and brief interventions made a "new person" of Miss R., but they seemed in this case (and that is why we are reviewing it) to have been a stimulus to explore new choices.

(2) *Working with children.* Children who have problems in school have been studied from many different points of view—their socioeconomic status, their intelligence, their family background,

their relationships with peers, and their personality have all been made the focus of investigation. In the following we shall apply a communication model to such problems, discuss some aspects of their training toward school delinquency, and analyze some experimental methods of retraining.

Children learn that certain of their behaviors will elicit certain responses from the adult. A parent may have very little respect for "book-learning," and his verbal message to the child may not coincide with his more subtle communications. He may tell the child to do his homework but at the same time imply that the "important tasks" have to be done first, such as babysitting or running to the store. By many thousands of messages, another parent may communicate to a boy that he should excel in sports and that studying is just a bit on the "sissy" side. The child then can elicit enthusiastic responses from his parents by telling how many home runs he made, but only experiences parental disinterest when it comes to homework. Other children may have learned that their parents pay a great deal of attention to school performance but typically communicate dissatisfaction. The child begins to associate the feeling that he cannot please his parents with his school work no matter what grades he gets; one can say that his parents' repeated communications reinforce a negativistic value system in the child. He may even learn to obtain pleasure from failing, as he can thus punish his parents for what he conceives of as unjust behavior.

Parents may wish to communicate to their child that it is good to have good grades in school and that it is important for one's future to stay in school. They may wish to implant in their child the understanding that it is utterly foolish to get a police record for stealing a car or be caught in a fight. Yet their subtle communications tell a different story. In some families a child is singled out to bear the brunt of family dissatisfaction—the parents, rather than arguing with each other, express all their dissatisfaction toward the child. And so the child learns that he can elicit intense attention from his parents by being a misfit. He may even learn to perceive that a police record, failing grades, and being in trouble are tokens of success, as he is constantly reinforced by the parents' intense attention to these matters in the absence of good will directed to other things.

Through subtle communications the child learns that the parents permit him to excel only in the role of misfit. An example of such communications can serve to illustrate this type of covert training. Here a very competitive father, afraid of his growing boy's talents, says to the consultant in front of the boy:

Father: "He is very bright. He learns fast and has a good memory. But he is lazy, never looks at a book."

Boy: "I have too. I have a B average in school."

Father: "You know you can do better than that. And he never takes care of his things."

Boy: "You won't let me use your tools; you don't give me a chance to take care of them."

Father: "How can I? You never put them back into place."

Boy: "That was once, Dad, once!"

Father: "You don't even take care of your own things."

Boy: "I did clean the bike you complained about; you just did not see it."

Father: "That reminds me—how about that rust on your gun you left lying around?"

Boy: (desperate) "But I did clean it all up. It's shiny now!"

Father: (raising his voice also) "And what about your fooling around with this girl. . . ."

The father's last comment was perhaps the significant one from a psychodynamic point of view. But the general exchange can only communicate to the boy that whatever he does will cause a dissatisfied response. The father's skipping around from one topic to the next, his failure to deal with the issue under discussion, his way of bypassing the boy's achievements will help train the boy to see himself as a misfit. Not that the boy is an innocent victim. He surely does his share to keep these competitive feelings alive. He too constantly feels that his father is wrong, and he is far from being as helpful as he claims. The boy had vandalized his school, which would be an indication that he has begun to reverse his value system. To be called to the principal as a misfit was a rewarding event; to be brought before the judge as a misfit was a minor victory. All these events have taken on the characteristics of a reward because the boy has been trained to associate a sense of strength (as a competitor) with the misfit role. We should note that the father has now become truly impotent: all the punishments he can hand out are rewarding, and therefore reinforce the very behaviors they are supposed to subdue. This very impotence felt by the adult is, of course, what the child is aiming at. It makes his father helpless; he cannot discover any method of correction, while the boy can obtain gratification in counteracting the adult's desperate attempts to straighten him out.

These children's communications are designed to create certain emotional climates in the adult. A combination of anger and impotence seems to be the emotional climate desired by the child. He produces these feelings of anger and ineffectuality in the adult via a number of different behaviors. Sometimes the cues are subtle (when the child does not want to be held responsible for eliciting anger) and sometimes they are given overtly. The child's cues are of sufficient impact to gain their ends with most adults. The adult will typically respond in terms of the child's expectations, and consequently rewards him, training the child still further in his misfit behavior. The adult wants to make the child pay a high price for this kind of control: a teacher may want to throw the child out of the class or send him to the principal or bring him to court. But these communications are not likely to be corrective in more severe cases, as all they communicate to the child is that he is still in his preferred line of battle.

One way of correcting for this behavior would be to use punishments that would be so unexpectedly devastating to the child that the noxious behavior would be extinguished immediately. The communication to the child is clearly "authority is not impotent and your games have not ineffectualized it." This method, certainly not without its advocates, would probably work efficiently to correct the specific behavior, though it is questionable whether society would permit the type of punishment necessary (an estimate which the child may be counting on). It would have to be a very severe punishment, indeed, reminiscent of the laws that demanded a thief's hand for stealing. Modern society does not engage in such retaliations, as massive punitive assault is also known to have predictable after-effects, both in the way this individual would treat others and in terms of the behaviors that would come to the fore when this severe punishment was no longer applied. Massive punishment does not seem to provide the desired answers.

A more therapeutic approach would cope with the problem through individual psychotherapy, family group therapy, or group therapeutic efforts for parents with children who have school problems. Here the interaction pattern would be analyzed, and the family would learn to disengage from the demands of the child, hopefully giving him less reinforcement through punitive behavior and more of an opportunity to discover new values. Many parents feel that the school should be doing more for their children along these lines, but this shift of responsibility to the teacher needs to be analyzed itself for communicative value. It seems to us that the parent is saying that he himself can do little to correct the problems and that, in effect, he is not able or willing to change his own interactions with the child. The behavior consultant in the school system could be most effective in working with families who have school problems, possibly even in their own homes. Many well-trained school psychologists have begun to play such a role, even though much of their time is spent with testing programs and emotionally disturbed children. School problem clinics attached to schools are still the rarity; often the consultants deal with private referrals. Once a family starts working with a consultant, the communicative meaning of the "wish for help" (that is, the implied shift of responsibility) can be discussed, and the parent's interaction can be utilized in the corrective work.

Can the teacher be expected to be a therapist and disengage from the manipulation of the child? The teacher has already been too heavily burdened with mental health rather than learning problems. The teacher would neither have the time, the inclination, nor the setting where he could afford to let a child violate the rules and use therapeutic devices. He has to become engaged and the child knows it.

Beyond psychotherapeutic efforts there have been a few other interesting attempts in retraining. In England one was tried utilizing a random punishment method on delinquent boys (Burns, 1957). They lived together in a school setting and were simply punished and rewarded on a random schedule. If they engaged in one of their preferred acts that was intended to elicit a specific response from authority, the expected response was not forthcoming. Instead, the child would perhaps be rewarded at this particular time. But at another time the child might engage in quite acceptable behavior, and still not necessarily gain approval. His rewards and punishments were programmed in a random fashion, independent of his actions. The method was based on the theory that because of the uncertainty created, previous associations would become extinct, and the child would be motivated to explore new systems of values. The author claimed rather extensive success for this method of treatment. The subtle communications of the adult to the child were "I shall not be manipulated by you."

A different approach was taken by Slack (1960) who paid delinquent boys money to attend meetings in group therapy. He reported that his method motivated the children to attend the meeting, that his therapeutic efforts were successful, and that some of the boys even volunteered at a later date to pay for services received. By paying, Slack subtly provided his boys with an alibi for coming to a "headshrinker."

Another noteworthy study was reported by Nielson (1965a; 1965b),

who used parent volunteers to work with children who presented
school problems. He trained the volunteers to respond to the children
without becoming engaged in their subtle demands. These workers
were trained in a relatively short time not to criticize the children and
not to engage in an effort to teach them. They were told that they
should play the role of listening companions. This program was
intended to communicate to the child that he would be given attention and care regardless of his specific behavior. This work appears
promising but still needs to be evaluated.

Looking at the expectations of the child with the knowledge that
he may find punishing behaviors desirable and that he is willing to
pay the price in pain for exercising control over the adult will give
us the opportunity to search for the type of experience that may
enhance the possibility of a change in values. Currently we tend to
reinforce the child's noxious behavior pattern, and our attempts to
describe the conditions most conducive to change have not been
very successful so far. We do know that these children need a special
situation in which they do not receive their peculiar "rewards." We
also know that we need to hold their interest and attention long
enough for them to tolerate a state of temporary uncertainty and
explore new values. We have at least a hunch that these new values
will come through identification and imitation. The psychotherapeutic
relationship seems to provide such a condition but is costly and
cannot be applied to all individuals in need of such an experience.
The behavior consultant in the school will have to discover new
approaches that can be made available to more people; and he will
have to try to enlist parents, volunteers and machines to help with
the work.

The Behavior Consultant and the
Training of Parents

Can parents be trained in the use of some therapeutic techniques
so that they can help their children and others? The question has
often been answered in the negative. There are good reasons why
such efforts were thought to be likely to fail. (1) The parents were
seen as being directly involved with their children, and it was felt
that their own needs would interfere with the use of therapeutic
tools. A parent has "an ax to grind," an investment in maintaining
a situation that may be rewarding to him. (2) The family member
who makes a therapeutic effort could not, and perhaps should not,
deny his authority and responsibility. (3) Information given by one

family member in a parentally created therapeutic setting may later become dangerous to him. That is, he gave the information in a favorable emotional climate, but once the climate changes, he may regret having given it. In a confidential setting, the parent using therapeutic techniques may hear that his daughter is interested in a certain boy. How will this information be used when the father has to make the decision whether or not to let the two young people meet each other? These arguments are particularly valid if one holds the view that the therapeutic process is based on empathy, deep understanding, understanding of the historical roots of a problem, and acceptance.

When one thinks of the assumptions of the behavior therapists, these considerations are not quite so significant. The reason that behavior therapies are not subject to the same restrictions is that they are based on the principle that change can be effected through reinforcement of certain behavior. The family members' levels of motivation to understand their level of psychosexual development, or even their possible reluctance to look at the deeper sources of family interaction, are only peripheral to the task of changing behavior. If a parent wants to train a child to read better, he may be advised to experiment with a system of immediate reward for reading improvements. The parent can become a reading therapist provided he is willing to learn a good method and sets time aside to use it. Though he himself may have psychological problems that help maintain the child's poor reading skills, the routine he needs to follow to help the child improve his reading is so clearly spelled out that his reluctance would soon be obvious to all concerned. If we compare this type of recommendation with the suggestion that parents be "more permissive" as was customary some years ago, the differences are apparent. Few parents would know how to go about being more permissive, but most parents could learn to stock small candies and give one for every correctly read word.

The real question is not whether a family member can learn to handle certain reinforcement techniques but to what extent such techniques have anything in common with psychotherapy. As stated earlier, there is very little agreement on this point. The argument between the value of psychotherapy vs. the behavior therapies centers around the symptom. Psychotherapists claim that reinforcement techniques and behavior therapies attack the symptom alone and fail to provide any reorganization of the personality. Some therapists think that an individual so treated develops a new symptom to replace the one lost.

A child who cannot read well may have learned to use this symptom to act out certain feelings about his family. One possible reason for this might be a severe intellectual competition with his brother. Thus, the poor reading symptom would give him some reward, both as an excuse or alibi for his failure in this competition and as a way of getting more attention from the parents. What happens to these needs when the child learns—almost against his better judgment—how to read well? Will he have to find another and better alibi to soothe his feeling about the competition with his brother? Will he not need to find other devices to get the attention of his parents? Unfortunately, this argument has generated more heat than light.

Actually, there is very little research data to support either view. Symptom replacements are described in case records. These reports are often, at best, anecdotal and post hoc. To our knowledge, one of the few experimental studies on symptom replacement was done by Seitz (1951, 1953), who used hypnosis to suggest inhibition of a present symptom. While his findings supported psychoanalytic theory and suggested that symptom suppression merely forced other symptoms to the fore, the use of hypnosis, to our mind, minimized the validity of this study.

We feel that this question is unanswerable at this time. New symptoms may or may not develop, and an intervention with one significant symptom may or may not be called a personality reorganization. At the moment, whether one considers a symptom change as a personality change depends more on value judgments than on facts.

In the last twenty years, giving advice and teaching for better mental health have become thought of as undesirable or ineffective therapeutic techniques. The field had largely accepted the notion that the individual has to be helped to discover his own solutions to his problems, that advice coming from the outside would violate the internal values of the individual. It was felt that advice is essentially rendered on inadequate information, as the total forces acting on a problem cannot be available to another person. Perhaps the case against advice has been made not only on rational grounds but on emotional ones as well. The full information on a given problem is probably as little available to an outsider as it is to the individual himself. Sometimes terms like nondirective or "democratic processes" were used to describe the therapeutic process, while advice was described as "directive" or "authoritarian." These terms make us a little suspicious—actually, the dictionary defines advice as an "opinion recommended to be followed," which still leaves the decision to accept or reject the advice with the advisee.

The distaste for giving advice probably came from the recognition that many advisors claimed an authority they did not in fact have. In the "Dr. Anthony" sequences, the client would present a short description of his problem, and the good doctor, under the title of "expert," would dispense advice on how to solve it. In the feeling of many, he assumed an authority which he did not warrant. The term *advice*, however, contains only these two elements: the opinion itself, and the recommendation that it be followed. Becoming sensitive to the authoritarian quality ("to be followed") of this definition, the field tried to dispense with advice altogether.

Is it really true that advice for solving mental problems is either undesirably authoritarian or ineffective? Perhaps there is a useful function to its use. For example, we see nothing wrong with the advice to an individual under great emotional strain that he might benefit from seeing a psychotherapist. Here an opinion is rendered together with a certain recommendation "to be followed," and as long as we are considered competent to render this opinion, we would not be criticized. On the other hand, consider the case of a parent who asks us after a PTA meeting: "Now, doctor, how do I handle my little girl? She is lazy and does not want to practice playing the piano." Were we to advise this mother to use a specific technique, such as forcing the child to play or letting her discover the joys of playing by herself, we would be criticized. We would not be seen as competent to render this advice in the absence of further information, and it is doubtful that the advice, even if followed, would be effective for long. The consultant, therefore, has to be aware of the problem and whether or not it is in his area of competency. He must consider the information available to him and decide whether the advice he gives can provide a solution to a problem. Advice seems to be feasible (1) where it does not constrict the freedom of the person seeking it, (2) where it is rendered with competency, and (3) where it presents a possible solution.

We note that as "experts" in human behavior we do not seem competent to advise the mother of the reluctant child pianist simply because we cannot give competent advice without pertinent information. Perhaps we are competent as consultants to this mother, and could explain some general principles of behavior related to discipline problems which she might be able to apply. For example, a consultant may tell this mother that the problem is not likely to be due to laziness but may reflect some tensions in the parent-child relationship. He may add that some children even get something out of being reminded and pressured by their parents. Were our family consultant to make this statement, he would hardly be criticized for giving advice outside his area of competency, though he might be criticized for arousing anxiety in the parent without providing much in the way of a solution for it.

What would be useful advice to a parent in this short-term contact? Let us assume that this mother's attention has been drawn to the broader problem of tension in the house. She may respond: "Maybe you are right. I think this child is trying to get me angry." How useful is this thought for this mother? Probably it will do very little to solve her problem with her daughter, but perhaps her interest in learning about behavior will be somewhat increased. It may be that she will focus more on family interaction rather than just her daughter's behavior. The consultant's objective in giving such teaching advice is not to solve this problem but to alert the mother to the possibilities of learning something about human behavior.

Ellis' system of rational therapy is formulated around the idea that the therapist can utilize a person's ability to reason and his wish to live a reasonable life. Thus, he can advise others on their "problems" in a much more direct fashion than was formerly believed. We too believe that many of the theoretical formulations which have been developed and found useful in the field can also become topics of advice to the family. The consultant ordinarily knows more than the general public about methods that people can use to learn about their unconscious motivations and methods of developing a feeling of shared responsibility for problems occurring within the family. There is no reason why a family consultant cannot share this information with those seeking it, and indeed, it may make a difference in the way a family solves its problems. This is not psychotherapy in its orthodox sense, but rather a form of teaching certain principles of human behavior to those seeking this information.

It seems reasonable to say that not all people need long-term treatment and that learning even some principles of human interaction may provide them with useful information. The short-term contacts of a family consultant may be of some benefit, although there are also dangers that one ought to take into consideration. The main danger is that the "student" will misapply what he was taught and that his new knowledge, incorrectly imparted to others, may not be correctable by his later contacts. In this case the consultant may be cast in the role of an "authority figure" who had "advised" new maladaptive behaviors. There is also the hazard that the information given was rendered on too little knowledge of the family problem. Both dangers are very real and must be considered. Yet, the question "How effective is consultant teaching?" certainly is of great importance. Were we to discover that lectures and other short-term teaching devices can have an important impact on the behavior of the family, we would have available a way of reaching many more people than we do at the present time using individual or small group therapy methods.

In Bandura's interesting article (1962) in which he discussed Boardman's case of Rusty, he pleaded for a refocusing on the "advice giving attitude" of the therapist. In many cases, parents who want to help are eager for advice. They could be enlisted as allies. Rather than work on the parental psychodynamic disturbances (as some clinics do by inviting the parents into psychotherapy), it might be wise to inspect with them their schedules of reinforcement for the disturbed child.

Bandura's plea was to inform the parents on: (1) the cues eliciting the child's undesirable behavior, (2) the response-reinforcement contingencies maintaining that behavior, and (3) the manner in which reinforcement contingecies must be modified if clearly specified therapeutic objectives can be reached. This approach assumes that the parents can profit from the information informing them how they should act; it is designed to remove the reinforcing responses that the child's behavior elicits from them. We have experimented with this approach by having parents "behave" with the child in our presence and then pointing out, at the *time of occurrence,* the responses that elicited the undesired behavior. Bandura's suggestion may have a greater impact on family members in a setting in which the therapist can point out those family interactions responsible for problems as they occur, rather than by advising them indirectly. We shall illustrate such an approach in the following case, which rather speedily brought out family tensions. This case was limited to just two visits, a predetermined agreement with the referral source at the child's school. The therapist accepted these terms in order to investigate the possibilities of very short-term contacts.

All we knew of Johnny's problem was that he did not want to go to school. We asked both parents and 9-year-old Johnny (an only child) to come to the therapeutic hour.

Therapist: "You apparently have a problem with Johnny. I understand he does not go to school. I would like you to discuss this problem with each other and Johnny while you are here."

Mother: "There is not much to discuss. We have discussed it many times. He becomes nauseous every morning so we took him to the doctor. The doctor said that there was nothing wrong with him, but he is still nauseous every morning and refuses to get up."

Therapist: "You are talking to me, and I appreciate the information you gave me. But I would like you to discuss this problem with your family; it will give me some idea how you talk to each other."

Mother: "Well, dad, you go ahead."

Father: "The boy should go to school. He is just lazy."

Mother: "He isn't just lazy. You should talk! You are never home. You work all night and sleep all day. How do you know he is lazy?"

Father: "You see, there is not much sense in talking about it, is there?"

Therapist: "I can see that it is not easy. You made me feel like you did not try very hard either. You seem to give up rather quickly."

The therapist wanted to have the father experience that he also contributes to the disturbance in the family.

Mother: "That is it. He never stays around long enough to discuss anything. He always goes to his room and stays there the rest of the day."

Therapist: "Your tone of voice—it was pretty harsh. I almost got a little scared. . . ."

The therapist wanted to help the mother look at herself rather than her husband.

Mother: "I know. I am just so worn out. I know I make it difficult for him to talk to me. I should know better than that."

Therapist: "I have the feeling that when you blame yourself you are really saying that you have no intention of changing your behavior. I guess I got this feeling by reading between the lines."

Mother: "Johnny, you say something. The doctor wants to know how we talk to each other."

Johnny: "I'd like to have my room back."

Mother: "But Johnny, father says he needs a room of his own. He comes home tired and needs to lie down."

Father: "Why don't you tell the doctor that you say I snore and that is why you sleep with the boy in the other room?"

Mother: "It is all my fault again. You may remember that you were the first to suggest that you take the boy's room when you took your night job."

Father: "*I couldn't stand the nagging all day when I was supposed to sleep.*"

Therapist: "*You are fighting each other. This gives me the impression that you want to leave things as they are. Maybe fighting gets you as close to each other as you want to be. I also noted that Johnny is very much in the center of this fight.*"

The therapist tried to give the parents the experience that their fighting was a meaningful behavior, the purpose of which was to avoid facing each other and perhaps more painful family problems.

Johnny: "*They are always fighting.*"

Father: "*You sit still, will you?*"

Mother: "*He is only a little boy; you don't have to be all over him.*"

Therapist: "*I noticed that Johnny is directly involved in the fighting. Dad corrects him and Mom defends him. How can he go to school when he is needed at home to become involved in his parents' skirmishes? And Johnny is sleeping in mother's room. . . .*"

The therapist tried to provide all three family members with the experience that they each contributed to their dilemma. He also implied that Johnny, in his role of helping his parents avoid talking about their differences, had become such a meaningful "pawn" in the game that he perhaps was needed at home. Johnny interrupted him.

Johnny: "*I want my room back.*"

Mother: "*I guess we have to discuss that, though I think that Dad could not keep his night shift if he doesn't have a room of his own.*"

Did the therapist make an error in his response by failing to point out how desperately mother wanted to keep father out of her room and Johnny in it? (By this time Johnny had become alarmed at the obvious manipulation and now wanted to withdraw.) We do not think so since, first, it would have been poor timing (i.e., would have frightened the family rather than provided a beneficial experience), and second, the therapist also wanted to stay with the problem this family had presented. He did not want to involve the parents in psychodynamic interpretations in such short-term treatment.

In this excerpt the therapist attempted to discover, with the family, how they were reinforcing each other in the maintenance of their present situation. We note that he did not enter the debate of who should sleep with whom or if they should or should not send Johnny to school, nor did he venture directly into psychodynamic areas. In his last comment he began to center on a few specific behaviors he had observed in order to arrive at some tentative therapeutic objective. He had recognized that (1) the parents were reinforcing the boy's role of a behavior problem child with their skirmishes. Johnny was given the power to divide his parents by being a problem child, which must have been a highly rewarding response. With his problem behavior he could indeed control his parents. (2) The parents avoided discussing the reason for the distance between themselves by centering on the boy. By fighting with each other over Johnny's welfare, they felt able to maintain their marriage and avoid discussing their real differences. During the two visits, the therapist brought these two reinforcement patterns into the discussion and made these people sensitive to the consequences of their poor communication patterns: the marginal marriage and the school problem. In this case the parents were able to let go of Johnny (who returned to school), though there is some doubt that their marriage improved.

Another way of affecting the child's behavior by converting the parents to allies was suggested by Guerney (1964). He suggested that parents could be trained to do play therapy in their home. He trained groups of parents in training meetings and discussed play therapy with them. He suggested that his method was worthy of further exploration because he encountered greater parental motivation to learn and more readiness to accept the difficult behavior of their children than he had anticipated. Freud (1959) perhaps was the originator of filial therapy. In his case of Little Hans he analyzed the father and then helped him with the analysis of his son. It is quite possible that the widely held assumption that parents fulfill their own needs in their behavior towards their children needs revision. Perhaps they have greater freedom to change their responses than previously assumed.

Colston (personal communication) reported a similar approach in which he recommended the institution of a "listening post" in one home, whereby the parents would permit all members of the family to state whatever gripes they had about each other. One condition was that each member had to listen without attempting to defend himself even against unjust accusations. It has been our experience with similar recommendations that such a device is not likely to be maintained for any length of time. This is because the later consequences of such listening behavior do not always enhance further sessions in which people will "let their hair down."

Finally, there is a rush of reports on therapy with specifically handicapped children, where specific reinforcement schedules were used. Handicaps in reading, spelling, writing, and arithmetic have been worked on using scheduled reinforcement methods whereby the child was given an immediate reward (such as a piece of candy or praise upon success). One of the most noteworthy attempts in this direction was undertaken by Lovaas and his students (1965), who treated four autistic, very self-destructive children in California. One of the children had bitten his finger off and nibbled on the next, another child had scratched himself to the bone, etc. The therapists discouraged such behavior with various means of negative reinforcement, such as slaps, yelling, or electric shock, and reported immediate success in stopping the self-destructive behavior. As none of these children was able to talk, therapists first tried to teach them the use of words by listening to the sounds they made and reinforcing them for appropriate sounds. They soon changed this approach to reinforcing imitation behavior, and rewarded the child when he correctly imitated the therapist.

Their preliminary findings were very encouraging indeed, but we note that their best results were accomplished when the reinforcements were no longer contingent upon a specific response (such as a specific word) but an attitude (imitation). Lovaas was severely criticized by Bandura (1965) for not taking cognizance of motivation and acting as if these children were devoid of any history. Bandura felt that there was ample evidence to show that these children in fact had a history and had learned to discriminate rather effectively.

One of these children behaved destructively only after his father had left the home, and was rather subdued when his father was around. Bandura reasoned that these children were not simply "deficient" but essentially behaved in terms of "rewards" that are generally unacceptable to others.

Currently, other attempts to work with children's deficiencies in terms of scheduled reinforcement are underway. Peterson (1965) is attempting to toilet train children by a scheduled reward system. While these attempts appear very promising, one can only hope that the field will not be swept with the kind of passion that characterized the introduction of psychoanalysis, which worked to exclude other possible directions.

We feel that these various experimental approaches of modifying children's behavior are most noteworthy and that we need to inspect many of our cherished beliefs. The model presented here, however, cannot go along with the concept that a given behavior can be changed without affecting the motivational state. We agree with

Bandura's criticism that even autistic children have learned to discriminate, and we would assume they too have an "ax to grind." Understanding how individuals reinforce each other's behavior is only the first step toward a solution. The next step—so it seems to us—has to be to provide the person with experiences which affect his attitudes rather than a given behavior.

The Behavior Consultant
Visits a Home

Play therapy and family therapy ordinarily require many contacts before they can achieve objectives such as changes in family interaction or more adequate functioning. It may take many years for therapists working with severe family disturbances to achieve psychotherapeutic gains. It stands to reason that behavior which has been learned over a lifetime may require an extended and intense effort on the part of the therapist. Yet it is also quite possible that the therapist, just by being continually exposed to problems which need his attention over a long time, tends to overlook occasions where people can profit from very short-term contacts. Some support for this statement comes from experience with graduate students in psychology who have been trained in mental hospital settings. When shown the psychological test record of a normally functioning individual, they have the tendency to discover many serious pathological deficits and recommend treatment. This professional problem of narrowly focusing on the pathological aspects of the person may have prevented us from rendering appropriate short-term help to those people who may indeed profit from it.

Reid Morrill (personal communication) reported to us that he visited the homes of people who had problems with their children. He met with the whole family in their own home and learned about their communication patterns directly from their interactions. He reported that even a very few visits seemed to make a real difference in the way the family members behaved toward each other. Zimet, in a personal communication, reported about a new and hitherto unpublished home visit program conducted by the staff of a Colorado hospital. A team of professionals visited the homes of applicants to the state mental institution. The still-unofficial report is that many of the families withdraw their applications for hospitalization in order to try new methods of dealing with the individuals in the home.

The following report describes a visit to the home of a family that wanted to avail itself of some help as a preventive measure rather than as assistance for any particular behavior problem. In family group therapy (see page 141) a consultant interacts with the family members and tries with his interventions to enhance communications between them. He is on the alert for ways in which the participants engage each other and constrict the flow of information among themselves. In the home visit, on the other hand, the consultant places his emphasis on observation rather than intervention. He observes the subtle communications that are characteristic of the family. His only intervention is presenting the family with a report. As we envision this experiment, the home visit represents a diagnostic rather than a therapeutic experience. As with some diagnostic procedures, beneficial changes may occur through this sort of intervention.

The parents who had asked for this house visit reported that they were happily married, they loved their children, and their children did not seem to have any particular disturbing problems or shortcomings. Even so, they felt that they would like to have a professional person visit with them, perhaps to get a fresh look at the things they were doing or to discover if there were any particular behaviors to which they should pay attention. We accepted this venture on an experimental basis only, as we had some idea that the presence of a consultant or observer in a home would not necessarily yield the most reliable data. As it turned out, we now have the impression that the observer can discover important interactions even though his presence does affect the information he obtains. Important behavior is often not under conscious control of the person involved but is communicated through subtle cues, and therefore is not easily hidden from a trained observer.

We were invited as a house guest and spent two days with this family. The father was an engineer and the mother looked after the home. There were two young daughters, three and seven years of age. The family lived in a small private home in the suburbs of a large city. The father was absent about ten hours each day and about four hours on Saturday when he had a golfing engagement. The mother spent most of the time at home, though we all went shopping on Friday afternoon. We ate all our meals with at least some members of the family, but stayed in the living room or the garden to read for several hours each day. During these times we occasionally visited with the mother or the children. In other words, our presence was not constantly emphasized, as it would have been had we played with the children or talked to the mother all day.

We shall discuss our observations in terms of the interactions of the parents with each other and with their children. We realize that

the limited data gave us a right to no more than hunches and speculations at this point, but we also feel that we obtained some supporting
evidence for these hunches.

It appeared to us that this couple had established a relationship
which we may best label with the term "matter-of-fact." Mr. and
Mrs. G. each had their work which had to be accomplished, and it
was expected that there would be only a minimum of communication
in this work area. Mr. G. expected that his meals would be served
properly and on time. He typically sat down for all his meals at a
given hour and began to eat as soon as he was served. He let his wife
eat whenever she was ready, that is, when she was through serving
him. The children did not eat with them. There was no talking during
the meal except for specific requests to pass the salt or some dish.
Mrs. G. did not have to call her husband to dinner; he was always
ready at the expected time. The meals were eaten quickly and
with efficiency; Friday night dinner lasted about 14 minutes.
There was no attempt to recognize the effort which went into it,
but neither was there any inquiry by Mrs. G. about her husband's
work. This lack of communication did not give us the impression
that this couple did not want to talk to each other but merely
that there was a certain compartmentalization of functions, and
eating was eating.

After breakfast Mr. G. would relax in the living room, and when
Mrs. G. had finished eating she would join him. There they divided
the morning paper (they offered us part of it) and discussed with
each other particular news items that they had found of interest. They
had apparently established some sharing behavior in this area, and
we gained the impression that they were both ready to interrupt their
own reading and respect each other's opinions. When Mr. G. left
for work there was no affectionate farewell of any kind. Mr. G. just
looked at his watch, got up, and left. Mrs. G. stayed in the living
room reading for a while, and then proceeded with her work and
caring for the children.

However, when Mr. G. walked into the house at 5:40 in the
afternoon, he took Mrs. G. into his arms and kissed her, and also
showed some affection for the children. Apparently returning from
work was a more significant affective event than leaving for work.
After the evening meal the family again returned to the living room
and spent about an hour together. Here the exchanges between the
husband and wife were of a more personal nature. They discussed
some of their friends, planned when they would invite them over,

and again made some comments on the political scene. The father also engaged in some play with the children.

The only note of irritation we noticed came when Mr. G. announced that he would play golf the following day. His wife responded that she had hoped that they all would drive out to the fair. Mr. G. seemed to respond to this notion as an interference with his plans but did not offer an alternate date for the fair nor an excuse for his golfing date. A somewhat similar exchange took place on Saturday when Mr. G. was asked if his next business trip would have to take a full week. Here Mr. G. again answered with annoyance and simply with a "yes," as if to imply that the question should not have been asked in the first place. No attempt was made to explain or assuage his wife's feeling that she was being left behind. We also noticed that after each of these attempts to keep her husband with the family were rejected by Mr. G., Mrs. G. would get up and leave the room with the motive of looking after the children. On Saturday afternoon when Mr. G. returned from his golf engagement, there again was an embrace. The family then spent the afternoon together in the yard reading, without much talk but, in our opinion, without much tension either.

The above is a sample observation of some of the behaviors which this couple had established. Here are our inferences:

We had the impression that these two people liked each other and had found a way of living together; they complemented each other in raising the family. There was not a great closeness, nor was there much common ground for activity. Both Mr. and Mrs. G. traveled their own road most of the time, but they still had sufficient feeling for each other to spend some time together. They seemed to respect each other's opinion and competency within their assigned areas of function. They did not go out of their way to make each other feel good or bad; they simply seemed to accept the distance that the compartmentalization of their lives imposed on them. However, when this distance was questioned, as in the two attempts of the wife, limits were imposed. The husband apparently arranged his work and play in such a manner that it reassured his feeling of independence. Mrs. G. was told in no uncertain terms that any effort to control him would be rejected. She probably could have predicted the annoyance responses by her husband, but it was apparently important to her that she annoy him slightly with the feeling that he was neglecting the family a little.

This bid for annoyance becomes more understandable when one considers that the only observable affective demonstrative behavior occurred upon Mr. G.'s return. It was almost as if Mrs. G. used her gesture to tell him that he should feel at least a little guilty about leaving the family behind, and that he should be closer and more affectionate when he returned. It should be noted that with this annoying gesture the wife possibly reinforced the husband's "leaving" behavior, because it gave him the information that he had to guard against her wish to control. On the basis of this speculation, we can make the further inference that Mrs. G. possibly wanted to arouse some annoyance in her husband and with it give him an excuse for leaving. At the same time, she seemed to want to bring the leaving behavior ever so lightly under her control. Her turning to her children after she had created the annoyance was perhaps the most telling gesture, i.e., "You leave me and my children and I will leave you." This was apparently a satisfying counterthreat. We learned, incidentally, that this counterthreat was not merely a threat but to some extent a "hope"; she was an oldest sibling and had had to take care of her family after her father's premature death.

The communicative meaning of these subtle exchanges between the couple provides us with at least some understanding as to where this family had its strengths as a unit and where it would be sensitive in times of crises. Here we have seen two people engaged with each other in a meaningful way, a couple that has accepted the team concept in living their lives. Their philosophy of marriage might be paraphrased as "we collaborate where necessary and go our own ways the rest of the time." On the other hand, they had not ordered their lives in ways that would lead to greater closeness by doing things together. They made sure that the limits they had imposed on themselves for the purpose of maintaining a feeling of independence were adhered to.

We noted three separate behaviors to support our hypothesis that the mother was rather concerned with maintaining control of their children and giving her husband only a minor role in regards to them. The children did not participate at the meals but were always fed before the husband came home. Mr. G. was never mentioned during the day even if one of the children questioned Mrs. G. about him. In the evening, when the father did play with the children, it was Mrs. G. who called the shots, such as saying, "Go over to Daddy now."

We do not imply that Mr. C. was an innocent bystander in this. He seemed to like things the way they were and made very little effort to initiate contact with the children himself. Even in times of crisis, periods when many mothers refer to father as either the punishing or helping agent, Mrs. G. would never mention her husband. The ritual in this household was that the bringing up of children was mother's work. While many families may have adopted such a division of labor, it appeared to us that these rules were very stringently enforced in this family. The children never once became a topic of discussion between the parents, and while the father was nice to the girls, there was never a show of affection between them. We observed several subtle cues with which this family reinforced this rule. At one point father had lifted the younger child above his head and was bringing her down slowly; for a second there was the possibility that their faces would touch. At this time the mother, who had been looking on, called the girl and told her to come over to her. Father put her down and the little girl immediately went to mother. Father was not beyond teasing Mrs. G. with this "danger of closeness with the children," even though we are quite sure that he was not aware of this teasing. While the mother was watching, he would occasionally hold out his hand to the child and draw her close, but then let her go before there was any close contact. We may have overinterpreted this behavior because it fit in so well with our hypothesis, but we did observe a frown on Mrs. G.'s face on these occasions. Although the couple never once directly discussed the children during our stay, we read between the lines that the couple had made the unwritten agreement that Mr. G. could have his freedom and independence provided he did not arouse Mrs. G.'s jealousy about the daughters.

The younger girl was rather aggressive and had quite a temper. She occasionally threw objects and created some damage. Once she hurt her sister by throwing a wooden block at her. On yet another occasion she pulled her sister's hair so violently that she emerged from this contact with a whole lock of hair in her hand, swinging it over her head like a victor. Both parents were concerned with this aggression, and her mother in particular tried to tell the child that this was unacceptable behavior. We noted, though, that her words were rather discordant with her gesture. She not only gave much extra attention to this girl, but also almost totally neglected the older sister who was victim of the aggression. Though the older sister was crying and holding her head, the mother took the little sister in her arms and gave her a serious talking-to, telling the crying sister only that the pain would soon cease. We felt that mother acted out the exact expectations of the younger girl and thereby rather reinforced her aggressive behavior, at the expense of the older sister.

The older sister seemed to notice her mother's preference for her younger sibling, and we noted that when the older sister was hurt, she moved closer to daddy (who, for reasons of his own, was not a very satisfactory ally). Daddy was ready to tease his wife but was not inclined to alienate her by giving too much attention to the older girl. We felt that the older sister, because of her position in the family, had already sensed the subtle competition in which she lived and had adjusted to it by playing on her own, not relying on either parent nor her sister for much comfort. Sometimes she communicated her withdrawal to her parents as if to say "Come and seek me out; do involve me too"; but for the most part these subtle bids were followed by a reinforcement of her feeling that she had been right in the first place, that she had to go it alone.

We wondered whether we were witnessing the parents' use of subtle communications to make their children act out their own unconscious wish; isolating the older daughter with the help of the younger aggressive daughter in order to keep the marriage intact. We felt that this hypothesis added one further thought about the behavior of this family. Father's "leaving" behavior was not only designed to give him a sense of independence, but also contained the communication that his wife should be a little uncertain about his whereabouts—uncertain as to whether he still remained devoted to her. The embrace upon his return, then, was more than a gesture of closeness; it was actually a gesture of reassurance, whereby the husband said, "I still want you."

We made a good many conjectures with this very limited information; and perhaps by emphasizing problems in this family we may have given the impression that we saw them increasingly as problem-ridden. This, however, does not really represent our thinking. Whatever family one studies, one will discover idiosyncratic characteristics and uncover covert streams of tension among its members, just as a well-functioning society will show certain weaknesses and strains in spite of its overall health. We were invited into this family with the request that we give them some statement regarding our observations of their interactions, so that they might have the benefit of an outsider's reaction. It may be argued that this very request carried the information that these people felt that there was something wrong with their family life. However, we felt that the motive for the invitation came from the thought of prevention rather than from the belief that disturbances existed.

We condensed our conjectures into a very few statements: we commented that we had noted that the parents did not wish to communicate with each other about Mr. G.'s absences and that we thought that this was a problem which had meaning to them. We mentioned that we felt that the younger girl's aggressive behavior was reinforced by the responses she obtained and added that we felt that the older girl, in our opinion, appeared somewhat isolated from the family. We added that we thought we had had enough information to make these tentative statements as a stimulus for further discussion.

The parents reacted with surprise, more at the comment on their own relationship than at the statements about their children. They apparently had conceived of their own relationship as highly satisfactory, and the "absences" had been taken as a matter of course. It was interesting to note, though, that without further intervention by the therapist, they directed their attention to a discussion of "doing more things together." They used this opportunity to reopen a question which had been automatically shut out from discussions because of its emotional loading. With the outsider observing subtle cues of communication related to this topic, they seemed to feel a greater readiness to re-discuss this issue.

With this family we did not feel that the problem behaviors identified here were of such magnitude that therapeutic intervention was indicated. We did feel that it might be helpful for them to pinpoint a few problems that they could inspect, for the strength of their relationship would possibly permit them to make some gains in these areas without outside help. We supported each of our statements with examples of behaviors we had observed, in order to make the family aware of what their gestures communicated to the outsider. We felt that the mere knowledge that someone could recognize hidden meanings (provided they were accurately interpreted) would stimulate them to question whether the choices they had made in building their marriage and their family were necessary ones.

We cannot say with any certainty that our observations were accurate, nor whether our time spent with this family was of particular value to them. We have no evidence that their initial discussion had any consequence in their subsequent behavior. But we do believe that, in principle, such efforts may be truly useful with some families, as they may help them discover problems before they become "malignant." As far as we are concerned, this visit was an experimental effort at preventive work. Although we are far from satisfied with either the procedure or the findings, we shall encourage such experiments in the future.

The Behavior Consultant
in the Professions

(1) *Working with a lawyer.* We had the opportunity to consult with a criminal lawyer. He had contacted us "to gain some knowledge about himself" regarding his courtroom procedure. He had become quite aware that he frequently aroused antagonism in members of the jury, yet he could not understand why this should be so. Upon his invitation, we visited the court with him.

Most of this lawyer's clients were criminals, some with a substantial record. Typically they had only limited means, and their parents and relatives often obliged themselves to pay the lawyer's fees; as often as not they did not pay at all. The lawyer himself, who had worked his way through law school, had come from an impoverished home and now felt that it was his duty to defend these cases, though he made only a marginal living doing so. He was an intelligent man and had won some important cases, resulting in his being offered a partnership of substance which, however, he had refused. We noted that he was most conscientious and spared neither time nor effort in his careful and detailed research efforts for each case. When he spoke of his clients he talked about them with loving care and we got the impression that he was highly identified with them. He also gave us the impression that he was extremely lax in collecting fees even when they might have been available. His communications with us were characterized by caution. Though he had decided to seek us out in order to discover something about himself, he gave us the feeling that he was annoyed at having to contact anyone. He seemed particularly reticent about the "loving care" relationship with his clients.

Upon talking to him, we advanced the hypothesis that this man "hurts" in that he identifies with his clients and wants to help them, but that his identification is too close, so that, at least covertly, it includes the criminal's rebellious relationship with authority. We reasoned that this lawyer probably not only represented his clients but fought the court. Hypothetically, his design, his hidden wish, was to blame the injustice of the world (and possibly the injustice of his own childhood) on the ignorance and prejudices of the jury, whom he usually called "those righteous citizens." When we complied with his invitation to visit the court, we found evidence to support this hypothesis. The lawyer "talked down" to the jury, and his statements reflected his own ambivalent attitude: the members of the jury should be respected for the power they held, but they would probably misuse it. "Those who are called upon to judge others may themselves have broken the law at times" was the paraphrased biblical quotation which appeared a number of times in his summary. But the way it was said did not make it sound like an appeal for understanding but more like an attack on the ability of the men sitting in front of him.

We speculated that the lawyer, through his all-too-close identification with the criminals, unknowingly communicated his feelings to the jury that they were punitive, foolish people who had no right to sit in judgment. The lawyer had little awareness that he helped to fulfill his own prophecy by the manner in which he addressed the court. Through his subtle cues he expressed his doubts about the integrity of the men sitting in front of him. By creating this negative emotional climate in the members of the jury, he probably did color and constrict their judgmental process, verifying his own views.

After one interview and one visit to the court, we had only a very limited sample of behavior to draw from. Yet the nature of subtle communication as expressed in the lawyer's attitude both in the interview and in front of the jury gave us a beginning understanding of the problem. When we discussed our impressions with the lawyer, our first objective was to sensitize him to the subtle cues that possibly helped create the undesired impression on the jury. This gave him the experience that his disdain for the jury was communicated. When such unaware behaviors are called to a person's attention, a sense of uncertainty is created. This uncertainty very frequently makes the person center his attention on the behavior isolated, with the result that new coding and new choices are now possible where automatic behavior was formerly the rule.

With this uncertainty, the lawyer, through this short-term contact, could then judge to what extent he had to express his disdain in just this manner, and to what extent he had to rebel against the court to the disadvantage of his clients. Sometimes the depth of questions raised by such a confrontation gives the person the impetus to continue with the exploration. This was the case with our lawyer. His original reluctance to enter into a therapeutic relationship gave way to the hope of being able to profit from further contacts.

(2) *Consulting with lawyers on broader issues.* Another experience of consultation should be included here. A group of lawyers interested in legislative questions arranged a seminar to which the consultant was invited. The seminar was concerned with the topic: "The law and the image of the law." The consultant's role would be to express his speculations with regard to the manner in which

certain laws are perceived by the public. For instance, a certain law may be enacted with the intent of deterrence, but may be perceived as "challenging one's ingenuity," as being "impossible to enforce," or even as humorous. (In the state of Utah there are regulatory laws on the books specifying the nature of sexual relations in which one may engage with one's wife in the privacy of one's bedroom. People who hear about these obscure laws find them amusing.)

In this seminar the lawyers were interested in certain aspects of communications and in the overt communication of the law, its lexical meaning and "official intent." They were also concerned with the hidden or covert meaning of the law—the way it is perceived and the way it affects individual behavior. The behavior consultant was encouraged to look at the consequences of certain communications; a few of these discussions will be presented here. The issues were broad indeed. One has to keep in mind that these issues were discussed by a group interested in legislative questions; the lawyers wanted to expose themselves to an experience in which they looked at issues from different points of view. To aid in providing this different view, the consultant decided to take a "marketing" view in which the law was seen as a product, and the public, or law violator, as its customers or potential consumers. Within this framework the specific question became: how does the consumer perceive the product?

For example, the present trend of the U.S. Supreme Court decisions is to require increasingly greater protection for the rights of suspected criminals. Recent decisions make a more careful investigative procedure mandatory, particularly with regard to arrests and the obtaining of testimony. Such decisions are made with the understanding that police and court procedures should not endanger the rights of citizens. Police officers loudly protest that their work is made harder and that more criminals will be on the loose; that is the response of some "interested consumers." It would be interesting to discover what this ruling means to other concerned consumers, the criminals themselves. Does this message: "We [society] want to protect your rights carefully even though you have violated our laws," mean to most criminals that it is now easier to commit a crime? And, assuming that criminals do feel that there is "greater ease," does this mean that a larger number of crimes will actually be committed? It is not inconceivable that this type of covert information may indeed have the opposite effect and will be interpreted by the "consumer" as "crime is no longer a challenging activity." If the criminal perceives his crime as a challenge to authority, the crime rate may very well be reduced by such court decisions, at least in times of prosperity.

From studies by traffic engineers there is more interesting information available on the perception of "unjust authority." When the speed limit at a given road is set too low relative to actual traffic flow, people will actually drive faster than when the speed limit is set at a more reasonable rate. If the speed limit on a certain road has been set at 30 mph, people may drive at an average speed of 43 mph, but when the speed limit is set at 40 mph, people will actually drive at 41.5 mph on the average.

Apparently a rule or a law can be perceived by the citizen as reasonable or unreasonable. The establishment of rules perceived as unreasonable may result in rebelliousness and with it more violation. Research on the communicative values of certain laws may give us critical information as to what certain laws actually mean to people; and this type of information may improve the relationship between the government and the public.

The lawyer group also discussed a widely debated question: whether capital punishment is in fact a deterrent or merely a challenge to the criminal—or perhaps just the expression of society's impotence and anger. Both those people who want to abolish capital punishment for humanitarian reasons and their adversaries will often fight on the basis of imaginary data. Here too we need "consumer response" data.

In a later session the group debated the use of "mental problems" for purposes of mitigation of sentence, as well as the use of an insanity plea and the impact such usage has on the public. The communicative meaning of such usages as perceived by the criminal "consumer" would be most interesting. Although many people seem to assume that the criminal will use such pleas as a means of reducing his sentence, it is not at all clear whether the majority of the criminals want to do so. An occasional criminal may make the headlines when he "avoids justice" and is admitted to a mental hospital, but it is not at all unlikely that many others dread the hospital and the sick role even more than they dread prison. Some such criminals certainly want to be seen as strong aggressive people and not as insane. The consultant helped the discussion group in raising this question, even though no pertinent answers are available so far.

In yet another meeting the group became interested in viewing violence and crime as communicative behaviors. Here we assumed that some criminals commit a crime in an attempt to communicate a message to others—they want others to see them as bold, independent, and rebellious. In other cases they seem to be concerned with highly idiosyncratic messages. The professional burglar is not only out to enrich himself or to violate a norm, but it appears that he also has a rather specific "ax to grind." Very often the police can identify a specific burglar from the act he committed. It is almost as if many burglars carry out their crimes so as to leave a rather special signature, a personal message. Some burglars will leave a room to which they have forced entrance if they find a sleeping child there, since they do not like to commit the act of stealing in front of any person. Others will take money but leave jewels behind, or vice versa. Still others will enter only very special locations, such as food markets or liquor warehouses or hotel rooms on the fifth and seventh floors. Some will only enter rooms with a challenging lock to pick, leaving rooms with less intricate locks intact. These highly specific behaviors are often a "give-away message" and certainly appear otherwise unreasonable in terms of the supposed goal. Yet the fact that people are attracted to crime because it permits them to engage in some very meaningful expressive behavior has rarely been studied scientifically.

Were we to understand what these people want to say with their actions, we might be able to find out where they "hurt" and what other choices of expression may be available to them. We know that delinquents steal cars and that we punish them for their aggressive acts. With an understanding of the psychological meaning of the act and the type of message a boy wants to communicate, we may be in a better position to correct his behavior. A boy engages in behavior that carries with it a high probability that he will be brought before the court. Looking at the meaning of his message, we may speculate that this boy, on some level of awareness, wants to "get even" with his family. He wants to be heard and perhaps through his acting out is saying, in a loud and desperate voice, that he has the power to strike back for whatever injustices he feels have been done to him. Our understanding of the communicative meaning of a crime should give us some lead in studying just how a person learns to express his feelings using one given message in preference to another form of expression. With this line of inquiry we can now ask this question: what type of rewards or reinforcements have taken place in his family setting to make a delinquent mode of expression become dominant? By being sensitized to the communicative meaning of an act, one is in a position to make sound inferences about the forces that potentially could modify an individual's behavior.

The group of lawyers had asked the behavior consultant to contribute to a discussion of the "image" of the law, a new perspective on the way law is perceived by the law "consumer" or public. This seminar afforded the consultant an opportunity to look at the subtle communicative meaning of the institutional messages—covert messages that come to us through the structure of our laws—and the form of our government. These covert, institutional messages which change relatively slowly over time, transmit very important meanings to us and probably determine our sense of values. Perhaps they even represent the memory of society, and in this sense present us with the type of information that provides for relative consistency over the generations. An individual law may change but the subtle meanings representing the attitude of the law remain largely constant.

(3) *Meeting with a dentist.* Dr. F. was a successful dentist. He treated mostly adults but his aspiration was to specialize in child dentistry. He said he liked children and preferred to work with them. To his disappointment, most of the parents who brought their children to his office seldom returned with them for further treatment. He questioned some of the parents carefully as to why they had not brought their children back but only obtained what he considered "noninformative" excuses. He invited us to be with him in his office while he was treating children and instructed us to see if we could find any cues. We agreed to visit with him. We stayed for a total of two days in his office, and during this time he treated seven children. We wrote our observations on his treatment of each of the children and there emerged a rather striking similarity among our observations. The following single case illustrates the subtle exchanges which took place.

Mother arrived with Peter, age nine, and addressed the dentist:

Mother: "Here he is. Hope that he doesn't need anything serious."
Dr. F.: "Well, we'll see. He is a nice child."
Mother: (Smiles) "He can be quite a stinker. He did not want to come today."
Dr. F. (to Peter): "You should always come to have your teeth checked. Then you won't have any pain later on."
Mother: "Listen to the doctor."
Dr. F.: "Ready? You are going to get a nice elevator ride, Peter."
Peter: "I don't want to."
Dr. F.: "Well, how else can I see your teeth?"

Peter sat in the chair, rode upward, and was very apprehensive.

Dr. F.: "Wasn't that a nice ride, uppity-up, just like a nice elevator? Now, Peter, open your mouth, just open it wide."

Mother sat in the adjoining room reading. Dr. F. began checking the teeth. Peter made small noises as he was being checked.

So far we could not advance any hypothesis as to where Dr. F.'s approach was deficient, though we could formulate certain hunches. Going over the messages and responses of each of the participants, we noticed that the mother, by using the words "Hope that he does not need anything serious," might have increased the child's apprehension. Dr. F.'s response, "He is a nice child," was somewhat irrelevant, but if anything, would have been slightly reassuring. His second statement, though, was moralistic and probably created a distance between himself and the child. His implied threat (". . . have your teeth checked, then you won't have any pain later on") was not reassuring but was not really an alarming statement either. When Dr. F. made his first comment that Peter was to have a nice elevator ride, he was trying to put the boy at ease. At this point we noted that Dr. F. maintained the fiction of the nice "uppity-up" ride in the face of Peter's discomfort. This was somewhat heavy-handed, almost like saying "You better feel good when I tell you to feel good." We formulated a hunch about Dr. F.'s lack of sensitivity in this area.

Dr. F. proceeded to check Peter's teeth and apparently found a cavity.

Dr. F.: "Peter, we found a little something here. We are going to put a little silver mine in that tooth. Just a pretty little silver mine, and I am going to show it to you too. This whirl here is just like a birdie, it's singing. Keep your mouth wide open."

Peter was very apprehensive. He slowly shut his mouth, biting the drill. Mother was still reading.

Dr. F.: "You must not bite the birdie. Just keep your mouth open."

Peter opened his mouth momentarily but then shut it again. Dr. F. then forced Peter's chin down by laying his thumb and index finger against Peter's nose. Dr. F. was firm with his grip, but did not appear brutal. Peter struggled and whimpered a little but his mouth was open.

Dr. F.: "So, so, there we go, we will not bite this birdie again. It just sings a little and it is a pretty little song."

Peter whimpered more loudly. The mother stood up and looked at the chair. Dr. F. firmly kept his hand over the child's chin and continued his work. He said to mother:

"Peter sings a little with the birdie. He is a nice boy."

At this point we were struck with the discordance between Dr. F.'s sweet words and his firm actions. Dr. F.'s actions appeared strictly functional; he was interested in proceeding with his work and he did so with firmness and apparent competence. However, his colorful sweet talk, introduced to deny the discomfort, seemed to give his firmness a quality of brutality because it was so discordant with his words. The "silver mine" or the "birdie" might be too faulty an image even to a receptive child, one who wanted to collaborate with the denial, but Peter was *not* collaborating and his apprehension probably increased upon the impact of these images. To Peter the images must have meant that this big man was not honest with him, not sensitive to his feelings, and that he could not predict what further discomfort and pain was in store for him. He probably felt quite helpless and, though he felt pain, he could not get his message across. The boy intermittently yelled and tried to shut his mouth, but Dr. F. finally had his silver mine after all. He reminded Peter not to bite his treasury but to use his toothbrush to fight this battle with the little germs. Even the mother seemed to have sensed the discordance, as her last comment was an attempt to correct it.

Mother: (to Peter) "I know it hurts, but it's all over now."

After the patient had left, it took us a little while to disengage from the impact of the experience, but in front of us we noticed this very friendly face with naive eyes and a puzzled expression.

Dr. F.: "That went rather well, don't you think? Of course, I tried a little harder because you were here."

We then told Dr. F. that we had noted the discordance theme between his competent action and his sweet talk designed to deny any discomfort on the part of the patient. He responded that he had learned this new sweet language in a book that highly recommended the euphemisms; he also recognized his own wish to "re-explain" the child's feelings to him. He stated that these re-explanations (his term) were meaningful and should help the child forget his pain. Dr. F. then said "How can a child love God when he learns how much pain there is in the world?" This statement helped us understand Dr. F.'s missionary zeal.

Peter did not come back to Dr. F., along with four of the other children to whom he had "re-explained" feelings. On some level of awareness, the dentist must have known that his way of denying pain just did not work and that his re-explanations made the children more uncomfortable rather than helping them to master the situation. To the children he must have appeared dishonest: this message came through loud and clear. Why did Dr. F. use his ineffective persuasive power again and again? In view of his continued lack of success with this behavior one would assume that he would learn to alter it—unless, of course, there was some reward in being an incompetent persuader. In a psychotherapeutic intervention, one probably would eventually discover the psychodynamics related to being dishonest with children about their pain and having them reject him. But in this diagnostic kind of intervention, the aim was to find the how and not the why. We assumed that Dr. F. was not a patient, but a person who experienced a peripheral disturbance that he might possibly be able to overcome out of his own resources.

In order to help him have a choice in these behaviors in which he appeared to engage automatically and without awareness, we pointed out the subtle communicative meaning in his talk to the children as we ourselves had experienced it. We told him our impression was that not all children can accept the recommendation to deny their discomfort, and that his talk of "the birdies" would appear to them as rather deceptive. Our aim was to provide Dr. F. with the experience that his behavior, which he automatically labeled as "helpful," could also be labeled as dishonest. We also alerted him to the consequences of his discordant messages: that some of the children could see him as being dishonest and reject him as not being trustworthy. Although we are aware that such short-term methods entail possible dangers in that such statements may seem threatening, we feel that many well-functioning individuals can often profit greatly from such a confrontation with their preferred behaviors. The dangers can be met by further availability of the consultant if required.

We shall add some general comments on the communicative meanings of certain behavior in dentistry. At the dentist's office the child will have to open his mouth and he will expect at least some discomfort. The mouth historically stands for an early pleasure experience, and the passive role of enduring discomfort by keeping one's head still and mouth open is an experience that is contrary to previously learned behavior. The dentist trains the child to have negative feelings about opening his mouth by conditioning methods: every time the child holds his head still and his mouth open, discomfort results. No wonder many children (as well as adults) have a tendency to postpone visits to the dentist and have altogether negative feelings about having dental work done. If one analyzes the training to which the child is exposed in the dental chair, one marvels that so many patients are able to compensate and hold their heads still and their mouths open for undifferentiated future gains.

It might be useful to explore how such training, particularly with children, could be altered in order to provide the new patient with positive reinforcement for his new behavior. If such training were successful, the patient might even learn to like his new position and to endure the discomfort as part of a pleasurable experience instead of anxiously concentrating on pain alone. Many dentists give children small presents such as a little ring or toy after the work is done, in order to provide some sense of pleasure in the total setting. It might be wiser to think of an immediate reward after the earlier behaviors occur, after the child opens his mouth and holds still and to reinforce with small reward each step in the total dental procedure.

Another problem is inherent in the image of dentistry held by many parents. Dentistry has drastically changed in the last few years, to the point where there is discomfort rather than severe pain. (The shot to reduce pain may be the event of greatest discomfort.) But adults who have in fact experienced acute pain in the past communicate their fear of the dentist to the child and in this way increase his anticipatory fears. The mother in the above example transmitted her own anticipatory fear with her first statement, "Anything serious?" and so trained the child to become anxious. "The poor child has to go to the dentist" is a feeling often communicated, and Dr. F. actually supported this subtle negative image of dentistry by his extra efforts to assuage the child. Some dentists have begun to counteract this image by giving lectures on oral hygiene to the adult patients and introducing a new role—the teacher-student role—which produces another image altogether. However, many dentists still focus on pain. Even such methods as "white noise," television sets, or music designed to divert attention from pain do, in fact, maintain the general subtle image of pain. It seems that both patients and dentists have a difficult time in abandoning the pain image, though the actual discomfort has significantly decreased in our time.

The Behavior Consultant in Industry

A more thorough understanding of communication also finds its application in industry. In labor management problems especially, communication skills are of importance, not just in the bargaining discussions at contract renewal times, but throughout the year. The image of labor and the image of management are subtly communicated through behaviors that often seem insignificant but that may create conditions of great tension or of well-being, as the case may be. Much has been written about the supervisor in industry and his particular dilemma of identification with both management and labor. His attitude is not necessarily revealed through gross acts but may be communicated through subtle behaviors; he can make or break the relationship between the factions with whom he is in contact. There are a number of behavior consultant corporations staffed with high level clinicians who help top management with communication problems. The analysis of communicative processes is helpful not only for problems within the company, but also for an assessment of the impact the company has on the consumer. The image a given company has on the consumer, the effectiveness of its advertising campaigns, even the use of subtle cues in packaging with regard to consumer motivation are legitimate concerns of the behavior consultant, as he has something to offer in assessing the impact of this information.

The following section describes one behavior consultant's effort in the training of sales personnel, illustrating the type of consultation that seems to be a natural outgrowth of the communication theories described in this book.[4]

There is a certain amount of discomfort in discussing principles of consultant work as it applies to sales personnel. This discomfort comes from a consideration of the ethical questions involved—will such training be used for purposes of persuasion and manipulation? Industry wants to sell, and all sorts of cues are being used in advertising to accomplish this task. At what point do we call the use of subtle cues manipulation? The covert cues used to make a specific merchandise desirable are often irrelevant to the quality of the product. In order to sell, advertisers present cues that arouse feeling tones ranging from patriotism to personal embarrassment or a sense of imminent danger. Advertising is only controlled to the extent that advertisers can be prosecuted for *false claims* as related to the merchandise; to our knowledge, no one was ever prosecuted for an advertising claim which had to do with the *covert* implication of the ad. A cigarette advertisement can no longer feature the word "health," but it can show a sportsman who is the picture of health strutting along while he smokes. Another advertisement shows the picture of a girl in the arms of her man—she, the caption claims, is using a certain deodorant. The implications are clear to every girl: you, too, can find your man if you use product X. Was the company ever sued by a girl who failed to find her man in spite of complying

4. This section is based on notes made by the author in his role as consultant to Xerox Corp.

with the directions? The use of subtle cues always provides a margin of safety from responsibility.

The contact the salesman establishes with his customer can be characterized along a continuum of persuasiveness, from merely acquainting a person with the merchandise to practically forcing him to buy it. This continuum of persuasiveness is, of course, not an exclusive characteristic of sales talk. One suitor can send flowers to his girl to win her love, while another may threaten suicide to gain his ends. Although some kinds of persuasion have public sanction, persuasion is almost always seen as an undesirable behavior if the "persuader" uses control that limits the individual's rights to make a reasonably free choice.

These ethical problems concerning the rights of the individual should certainly govern the conduct of the salesmen as well as that of the behavior consultant. The salesman uses certain techniques to close a sale, and he should consider the ethical problems. However, his techniques themselves are probably of less importance than how they are used. The salesman should behave ethically no matter what techniques he uses, for he can misuse both good and poor techniques. We want to make this point particularly clear because we believe that the information becoming available through research on communication provides increasingly powerful tools in behavior modification and can therefore be put to dangerous use. So far, the only safeguard against misuse has been the dissemination of such information to both potential senders and receivers of persuasive messages. Silence or suppression of such information has been alien to our views.

Here are some of the basic considerations of our behavior consultant as he approaches the problem of training the salesmen: The salesman is, at least to some extent, engaged in the business of behavior modification, and his goals are rather specific. If he is an ethical salesman he does not want to sell a customer goods that are useless or worthless; he wants to sell merchandise or services that will both satisfy the customer's needs and live up to his expectations. The salesman's long-range goal should be to offer his goods or services only where they are needed and where the customer is likely to be satisfied with what he receives. When a salesman is able to communicate this attitude to the customer he uses subtle cues in the best sense of the term.

This sort of communication is violated when a hard sell approach, with its atmosphere of pressure, is directed toward closing a sale rather than winning the ear of the customer. When this fine distinction is overlooked, as is often the case, the consequences are very disadvantageous to the maintenance of a continuous or an ethical business relationship, as the communication implies lack of concern with the customer's welfare. There are, of course, some salesmen who specialize in hard sell techniques when closing the sale. They are not concerned with either continuous relationships or ethics, but this kind of promoter would probably be found in any profession.

In the following we shall select a limited problem for discussion. The behavior consultant will address himself to the question posed by a salesman who wants to contact a new prospective customer. This salesman wants to modify the prospect's behavior so that the prospect will be motivated to spend enough time with him to find out what goods or services are available. What are the principles involved in motivating another person to give time and attention to something he had not thought about?

Most authors on sales techniques seem to agree that the salesman first has to "sell himself." We have no particular disagreement with this principle. To "sell oneself first" demands a keen understanding of the communication process. In this context, "selling oneself" means that the respondent is to experience the feeling that this stranger—the salesman—has certain specific qualities. The salesman should convey the impression that he is a person who will not take advantage of the customer, that he has an understanding of the customer's needs, that he knows what he is talking about, and that he is worth listening to. These qualities are largely brought across through covert information. The customer will make up his mind about the salesman and his products only partially on the basis of what is being said. He will base his judgment more directly on the subtle cues he receives from the salesman himself.

The feeling that another person is concerned about us certainly cannot be communicated with the sentence "We are very concerned about your satisfaction," simply because of the redundancy of this sort of information. The individual has heard that before and since he has often found the sentence unrelated to its inherent promise, he discounts its meaning. He not only discounts it but even may respond negatively with the thought, "another one of those glib salesmen."

Even where the content of a statement is of importance (for example, where a salesman ought to know the machinery he is selling), the salesman does not necessarily convey the information that he "knows what he is talking about" simply by having the information at his fingertips and presenting it. Most people have had a teacher who knew his information well but through covert cues gave the impression that he was talking over everybody's head, that he did not understand the students' problems in grasping the material, or even that presenting it was boring. The salesman has to do more than have his information handy. He has to be able to present it in such a manner that his covert cues give the customer the information that he does know what he is talking about and that he can also make the customer understand what he is talking about. He has to "program" the information in such a manner that he can be understood; he has to show interest in the customer and be alert to the degree of understanding achieved with his statements. In other words, in addition to being knowledgeable, he has to be sensitive and able to listen to the customer. It is not difficult to train a reasonably intelligent person to be knowledgeable, but it is far more difficult to train him to understand what information he communicates to a respondent through the covert components of his message. It is in this area that the behavior consultant can be effective in the training of sales personnel.

The information involved in first selling oneself to the customer is based on the adjuvant or additional cues that one transmits. Training of sales personnel should include an emphasis on understanding the impact the salesman makes on his respondent. First of all, he has to learn what his "natural" inclinations are, what impact he has on others without attempts at modification. This first step is of importance as the salesman may try very hard to copy another successful salesman in his company and still be unsuccessful, since the techniques used by another man may not fit his particular strengths and inclinations. He has to know what sort of "climate" he creates in the other person, and he must become familiar with the subtle cues he transmits in different situations and with different individuals. This, in fact, should be the first step in his training.

Once the salesman has a grasp of what emotional climate he creates in the customer, and of which cues create this climate, he can then learn to modify the impact by trying out new and less "natural" approaches. There are some people who object to the idea of behaving "artificially" on the grounds that such behavior is not genuine. This criticism, however, has somewhat mystical overtones, since the history of each individual includes his learning, because he has to adjust to his culture, behaviors which do not "come naturally." The man who is learning how to ski will feel that his natural inclination is to walk and that sliding is most unnatural for the human being. Most skiers, however, discover that the new behavior very quickly becomes "natural" and that to lift one's legs as in walking would be unnatural and awkward. However, the critic may still state that skiing is one thing but changing personality traits is a different matter altogether.

It is probably true that there is a basic and fairly consistent approach that people learn early, and that this approach is not easily changed. But, just because certain behavioral consistencies are stressed, the leeway within them must not be overlooked. A person may have learned that the world cannot be trusted and so may be very uncertain about himself. When he approaches a novel situation he may be indecisive lest he take the wrong step. He may ponder all the alternatives and find some good in each. This approach may be very consistent in him, but within it he can still either achieve greatness, as Adlai Stevenson did, or falter and come to naught. In other words, he can use his approach of uncertainty and arrive at most thoughtful decisions or, at the other end of the continuum, he can collect injustices and feel sorry for himself. There is at least some possibility that the same "consistent" uncertainty approach still permits important choices.

In his training, the salesman has to learn first about the "natural impression" he makes on another person. He has to understand the cues he uses to create a certain emotional impact on others. Second, he has to learn to have freedom in modifying the cues that create the emotional climate in such a manner that he will be free to communicate with greater freedom of choice. How can the salesman be best trained for sensitivity in these two phases? His training must clearly include both theoretical knowledge and practical type of training.

Within the province of theoretical knowledge, the salesman has to learn to distinguish between the cues he uses to give the covert information to his customer. These cues are (1) paralinguistic cues, such as tone of voice, choice of words, pauses, inflections, and the way he makes his themes hang together; (2) visual cues, such as those of appearance, gestures and body posture; and finally (3) contextual cues which have to do with the setting, location, history of the contact, and its broader meaning and purpose. A clear understanding of such cues and their communicative significance would be the object of the theoretical phase of this training.

The practical phase of training would include feedback from a sensitive and objective person as to the impact which had been created on another person under various conditions, as well as training in how to listen for subtle cues from this third person, how to "read" him and decode meaningful information. The reaction of the customer to the person of the salesman should provide the most adequate information on the impact he has made. When read properly, this "other person reaction" will provide the salesman with a self-corrective mechanism to check himself throughout his life.

For example, a salesman may notice that he typically creates in many of his customers a climate that can be labeled by the term "tenseness." The customer seems to respond to the presence of this salesman with cues which give this covert information back to him. The cues indicating this might be a rising pitch in voice, quickening of movements, irritation in facial expression, and vexed choice of words. The salesman should be trained now to look at himself and try to discover to what extent he contributes to such a reaction. Another salesman may find that his customers typically listen carefully to his exposition, only to lose interest after a few minutes. By first discovering this behavior and labeling it properly, he then can try to discover where his own contributions in the communicative exchange have helped to create this loss of interest. He might discover that he loses the customer by his use of language, by talking too much, by the monotonousness of his voice, or even by presenting the wrong product.

All the behaviors described here are not only utilized by the good salesman, but are used every day in one form or another by most people. However, most often such decoding mechanisms are engaged in without awareness. The good salesman simply has the "knack" to sense what he is doing and can assess his impact. An understanding of the communicative processes and an awareness of the meaning of covert cues will help in the training of the salesman until this new attitude, his new "impact" as well as the self-correcting mechanism, has become established and automatic.

Through the self-correcting mechanism, the good salesman will both know what he is doing and be able to modify his behavior as the occasion demands. Through such training the individual will learn to find the possibilities within his own repertoire of approaching another person. Just as people who want to learn how to ski can learn to slide and feel "natural" in this new activity, the salesman can learn to explore various ways of mastering himself in the impact he makes on the other person. A number of behaviors—the ones most frequently observed as being related to persuasion—can be distinguished in this "impact on others" area. Each behavior presents a different attitude, which will be discussed in more detail. The most adequate setting for the training might be a "simulation" training in which a salesman can explore new ways of behaving without exposing himself. Like anyone else, the salesman needs a training situation that is reasonably free of threat and retaliations, as few people cherish being evaluated and possibly condemned while they explore behaviors about which they feel awkward.

The response categories to be discussed are not all useful or even desirable. They have been observed in a variety of situations and will be discussed in order to identify the type of covert information they give to the respondent. They are (1) teaching and preaching, (2) request for a response, (3) being in cahoots, (4) guilt arousal, (5) encouragement to talk longer, (6) broadening the class of meaning, and (7) avoiding emotional engagement. These seven categories are not meant to be all-inclusive nor are they intended to cover the entire field of responses. They are simply mentioned to illustrate that an approach which is concerned with the covert meaning of the communication can be labeled in a meaningful way.

1. *Teaching and preaching.* This label designates the specific behavior of a salesman who wants to convince the respondent about his product. He tries to instruct the customer in its use and its advantages over other products, and uses forceful language to create a belief in the quality of the product. By teaching the customer about the product's useful functions and preaching to him on its quality, he gives the customer the subtle information that he, the salesman, sees the customer in the student role and possibly also as a person who can be converted. Teaching behavior makes sense only if the customer wants to see himself in the student role, ready to learn new ways. Teaching is worse than worthless when there is no student; a person who is taught without being ready for it will feel that the uncalled-for teacher is placing him in a somewhat inferior role. For the "teacher" to achieve the positive gains he hopes for, he must accurately gauge when the respondent is ready to be taught.

Preaching is a somewhat more serious behavior. Inherent in all preaching is the message that the preacher assumes that he knows the truth while his poor respondent is quite ignorant and has yet to discover it. Teaching has to do with objective information; preaching, on the other hand, deals with an evaluation of information. It is fairly safe to speculate that most preaching of this sort is discounted, and that is fortunate. Yet, a certain amount of preaching is tolerated and even expected ("Does this salesman not like his own product?") However, if there is too little restraint, preaching may give the respondent the information that the salesman is trying to "talk him into something" and the customer's resistance is likely to increase.

2. *Request for a response.* A number of cues can be observed that would give the respondent the information that he is expected to say

something. A typical covert cue of this sort is the convention of slightly changing the inflection in the last word of the sentence. This is one way of asking a question without appearing to do so. Other ways are by using the gesture of looking expectantly at the respondent or by pausing after a response. Of course, a question can also be asked overtly and lexically.

The reason attention is paid to this particular response is that cues designed to encourage the customer to enter the conversation are often given inadequately, halfheartedly, or even not at all by a remarkable number of people. With teachers it is often a professional disease to give only lip service to even such lexical requests as "Any questions, please?" by not pausing for a response. It is not easy to give the respondent a chance to reply if one is afraid of the reply. It is almost as if the person's wish that the respondent should *not* reply is expressed in the message, as the invitation to reply is clearly an empty gesture. The source of the contradictory wish for a non-reply may differ from person to person but, with some people at least, one gets the impression that they rather prefer a non-response because they are not so certain that they can adequately cope with the expected response. Actually, this discordant message is a self-protective device designed to avoid the wrong answer yet still go through the motions of asking for a reply. The trouble with this device is that it fools no one but the sender himself. It is he who is satisfied that he had requested a reply and it is he who knows that he did not get one. The respondent, on the other hand, is hardly ever fooled. He knows that he cannot get a word in edgewise, and is more likely to feel resentment at the attempted intimidation.

A true request for a response is a different matter altogether. Here the respondent is told that his thoughts matter and that his partner in this exchange is willing and able to handle the reply. A salesman who has adopted the former habit of discouraging a reply should be trained to ask himself what sort of response he expects and how he could deal with it in more adequate fashion than through use of intimidation.

3. *Being in cahoots.* This type of response is very frequently used. It is the nature of any persuasive task to give the other person the feeling that there is some sort of "togetherness" between him and the persuader. The "being in cahoots" response ranges from bringing up the name of a mutual friend to finding out beforehand the potential buyer's attitudes toward church or politics, or his favorite sport. The "being in cahoots" response, however, does not have to be based on such blatant information. The simple comment, "You know," which is

a repetition compulsion with some people, is a device that, said in the right confidential manner, will give the respondent the bid for engagement. Other devices include certain self-references, as in "I am a hearty eater," or "That reminds me of my younger years," or "Oh, you also have two sons." The response is designed to engage the respondent and make the interview more personal and correspondingly less related to the object. It is a plea which stresses the common ground with the implication that the customer, whether he can use the product or not, should feel personally obliged to buy it or at least develop a favorable attitude toward it.

It is probably true that this type of plea is often effective, as high customer expense accounts might indicate (another form of getting in cahoots). On the other hand, a line can be drawn between selling oneself as a person and selling out. A person selling himself should rely more on selling himself as a friendly, competent person than as a long-lost friend. Actually, the "cahoots" response backfires rather severely when it is recognized for the "oneupmanship" it is. Here the customer gets the information that the salesman tried to "worm himself into his good graces," and he is more likely to show him the door than invite him to tea.

One particular deviation of the "being in cahoots" theme is seduction. This can be done by tone of voice, gestures of the eye, or a smile. Seduction is the "you are worth wanting" type of response, and many people, regardless of their sex, seems to have pleading, seductive mannerisms. The wish is not a sexual one, though this may be its origin. (We took short speech samples of a number of people and had the voices judged by others to determine whether there were mood consistencies in particular speakers' voices. The judges' rating of "seductive" was a fairly common one and was often consistently used in rating a given voice regardless of what the person was saying.) A seductive response is essentially flattering because it sets up a climate in the respondent which gives him the feeling that he is a desirable person, one worthy of being courted, revered, or looked up to in deference. This climate, when achieved, gives the customer either a sense of well-being (depending on his object choice) or a sense of guilt and perhaps disgust (this fellow is "gooey"). It is a response which is often automatic with people, and training should alert the salesman to this behavior so that he can become aware of what he does.

4. *Guilt arousal.* Many individuals have learned in early youth to control adults in authority by arousing their guilt feelings. Children are often rather successful in achieving their wants by hinting to their

parents that they have been wronged and deserve a reward ("You are going out again, Mommy? Will you bring me a present?") It is no wonder that this type of response is deeply ingrained with many people and used often in sales talks. Many times it is introduced in very subtle ways via such behaviors as going to very elaborate efforts to demonstrate the product and in this manner obliging the customer ("I worked so hard, you owe me something"). It is often brought more into the open by an actual denial of the obliging gesture: "Just because I spend a few hours on you and go to all sorts of trouble, you are under no obligation, you know." More often guilt arousal occurs through the introduction of self-references, either verbal or nonverbal, into the sales talk. These references imply that were the customer to decide against his product he would also decide against the person. Even the conventional response, "I believe in my product," is such an attempt to tie the product to the person. If, under this adage, the customer chooses not to believe in the product, he also chooses not to believe in the salesman.

Seductive cues (as discussed in the preceding section) also have some of the characteristics of guilt-arousal responses because with them the person tries to oblige the respondent by implying that a return is expected. Promises of services ("I will get you these hard-to-get theatre tickets") essentially serve the same purpose, though they are somewhat different in that a service is performed in exchange for the hoped-for favors. While this response has become customary in many settings and undoubtedly has many successes to its name, it has the disadvantage to the salesman that to some extent he is "selling out" rather than "selling himself." Mother will bring the present to her child because of a feeling of guilt, but she will also increase the distance between herself and the child and be more guarded in the future. The customer may buy because he does not want to hurt the poor soul, but he is not likely to cherish the contact. This response is mentioned here because in his training the salesman should at least become aware of whether or not he utilizes guilt arousal. If he discovers that he does, he can then make a choice as to whether he wishes to continue to behave on this basis.

5. *Encouragement to talk longer.* Many subtle cues have been invented to tell another person that one is listening and that he should go on talking. The response presently preempted by the therapist's "Hm, hm" is such a cue, as is the gesture of nodding one's head. Others are the devices of repeating the last word spoken by the respondent or the repetition of a significant word in his statement. These devices are used to permit the customer to talk more and

specify more precisely what he wants, what objectives he has, and what feelings he has toward the product in question. These are legitimate devices to encourage feedback and are not often mastered by the person entering the field. There are also some dangers to such requests. As many people have the need to be listened to, the permissive atmosphere created by careful listening may bring personal material into the conversation, material which the person may later regret having revealed. Listening can be directive as far as the trend of the conversation is concerned. The interventions of the respondent (the "Hm, hm," etc.) will specifically create this direction. The salesman should be trained to understand that these responses are subtle but powerful methods in the communicative process and that they can produce personal references which are beyond his scope of competency.

6. *Broadening the class of meaning.* This type of response is of great importance in the communicative process and should be carefully analyzed in a training program. A customer may be talking about the qualities of a rival product. The salesman agrees with him that this product has its merits, and thus he broadens the class of meaning of his statement. He states that it is his conviction that competition is a worthwhile event for the economy because it stimulates his company to produce better products in the attempt to match the rival products. He then perhaps describes his product's qualities. This is an illustration of a response that broadens the class of meaning. In this case it ties the "rival product" in with the "value competition." This response uses subtle cues in order to communicate to the customer that the salesman can deal with a challenging message, that he is not afraid of it.

The subtle meaning of this interaction is of significance here. The communicative meaning of the customer's praise of the rival product is perhaps that he is asking some legitimate questions as to the quality of the salesman's product, but it is also a way of testing the salesman for his competency in dealing with an aggressive statement. Will the respondent become aggressive under pressure; will he remain composed or will he run? The response which broadens the class of meaning includes the meaning of the original message. Otherwise, it would be a *"change* in class of meaning" response, which has an entirely different communicative value. The salesman could have changed the meaning altogether and asked, "How are the wife and the kiddies?" Such a response would possibly have been perceived as avoidance of the dangerous topic. "Change of class of meanings" is learned early. For example, the child will sense "avoidance" when the parent talks about the merits of baseball after the child has asked where babies come from. Avoidance is a measure often interpreted as fear, and changing the class of meaning in the above example may have been interpreted that the salesman was afraid of dealing with questions about the rival product. When he responds with a broadening of class of meaning, the respondent meets the challenge and subtly lets it be known that he can indeed deal with the given question.

7. *Avoiding emotional engagement.* The response above is actually related to the engagement category of responses. In "broadening the class of meaning" responses, the customer tries to engage the salesman in an emotional climate and the salesman has to learn to disengage. But the "disengagement response" warrants a category of its own and, though it can, it does not necessarily include a change of meaning. Through the engagement of another individual, a person attempts to obtain a *constricted* response from him. He creates an emotional climate in which the respondent is supposed to become involved through subtle cues of the message.

For example, the customer may make some oblique attack on the integrity or prestige of the salesman or the company he represents. He may do this by turning to his secretary and asking her for the time of the next "important" appointment, the implication being that the present one is not really very important. The point here is that the customer uses the arousal of an emotional climate to ineffectuate the salesman. If the salesman becomes anxious because of the subtle aggression, if he becomes angry, if he shows bewilderment in his sales talk, or if he gives signs that he is caught up in the emotional climate that has been created for him, he gives the customer the information that he is an incompetent person who can be teased and controlled. He is indeed ineffectuated. The salesman should be trained to disengage from the "climate" of the message and reevaluate his objective under the given circumstances. A sales interview after a ten-minute discussion of the product, might proceed as follows:

Customer: "I don't think you really have anything to offer in addition to what I have now."

The statement may be an attempt to terminate the interview, but it also contains a possible dissatisfaction with the presentation itself. The personal reference "I don't think *you* have anything to offer. . . ." might be a bid for engagement, a personal emphasis to make the salesman feel unhappy about his personal failure, feel defeated, and leave. If the salesman, however, remains disengaged from the emotional climate set for him, he may then want to assess whether he still has a chance with this customer or whether he should change his objective. He obviously cannot continue with his previous sales talk. He has to respond to the message and perhaps request a response:

Salesman: "I can understand that you feel that we should offer more than what you have now. Perhaps I did not present our advantages as clearly as I should have."

This sort of response has the communicative meaning of delay in that it permits the salesman both to test whether the customer is ready to discuss things further or if he definitely wants to terminate. It also permits the salesman to change his objective if that seems necessary. Instead of making a sale he now may want to create good will for the future. The salesman here has learned to disengage from the emotional climate created for him; and he succeeds in giving this information to the customer through a response that shows both acceptance of the customer's statement and a subtle bid to continue with the discussion.

One should not assume that bids for engagement always contain subtle aggression. Actually, most responses are bids for engagement. For example, the salesman "engages" the customer through guilt arousal, seduction, etc. The customer, of course, will invariably use his own skill to counterengage the salesman. He may show impatience and arrogance or he may praise the salesman's product and accept every recommendation (except for the last one, to buy) with an enthusiastic nod, or play the cahoots game in reverse. The salesman should be trained to learn to decode this information and learn to disengage from the climate created for him if he wants to deal with the customer competently.

The behavior consultant's role in a training program for sales personnel was outlined with the purpose of showing how knowledge of subtle communication can enhance the salesman's skills. Such knowledge will help a man have a greater awareness of what kind of impression he makes on others, how he can modify such impressions, and how he can develop self-correcting mechanisms by carefully listening to the customer. This selection was presented only to illustrate the applicability of communication analysis to sales work, without claiming by any means, to offer a thorough coverage of the area.

The Behavior Consultant
in Government

There seems to be an increasing interest in government agencies in seeking out the behavioral scientist as a consultant both for the decision-making processes and for giving information. The contributions of the behavioral scientist have long since gone beyond poll-taking and attitude assessment. Government agencies have availed themselves of the help of such "brain trusts" as the Rand Corporation and Systems Development Corporation, both employ hundreds of Ph.D.'s to find a crystallization of questions and answers that are important and sometimes central to the welfare of the country. Some behavioral scientists hope that there will be a time when political world leaders will be evaluated for competency rather than for popular appeal or skill in playing power games. Not everyone shares such hopes, and many people feel that creating a "superpower" consisting of these behavioral scientists who set the criteria for selection perhaps would be more dangerous in the long run than the popular appeal criterion.

The behavior consultant concerned with international communication problems also has had his share of work. Attempts to read the mood of the leaders of foreign nations by evaluating the subtle cues communicated in their messages is an old political game. A given statement by a foreign power has to be evaluated for its meaning: Was it made for domestic consumption, and therefore not to be taken literally, or was it a message to a possible opponent? Did it have the intent of threat or bluff or was it meant "dead seriously?" Was the statement made to feel out world reaction to a given proposition, to test alignments, or to announce a new line of action?

Perhaps one of the reasons that Hitler lost World War II was that he made an enormous and costly miscalculation about the readiness of the United States when he assumed that we would not enter the war in force. France also made a most costly miscalculation by taking Hitler's gesture of occupying the Rhineland as an act of aggression rather than a test of will. We know now that German orders to withdraw troops were ready had the French not tolerated this violation. In domestic politics the American Medical Association possibly misread both the statements of political leaders and the popular support for the "medical care of the aged" question. With cash and publicity they engaged in opposition up to the very time the bill was passed, rather than becoming an effective force in modifying it, which might have been a more adequate objective for their purpose. The way the AMA led the opposition actually increased the benefits promised by the bill.

Reading the meaning of subtle cues has so far been done largely by the expert who is familiar with the source and supposedly can assess information more adequately by being familiar with past events and future trends, but some attempts are being made to find more objective means of evaluating such cues. Starkweather (personal communication) used the computer to process-list the words used in speeches by Krushchev, hoping to find some objective changes in both word usage and themes when new directions occurred.

A number of reports assembled by the brain trusts seem to have been based on communications from various sources and include psychological inferences. We remember a related paper by Hamburg (1955) which compared the United States with the U.S.S.R. in terms of psychological needs. The report stated and supported with some evidence his contentions that both countries need an enemy to maintain their own unity and both countries have a similar symbol of hatred (for the U.S.S.R. it is Wall Street; for the U.S. it is the Communist party). Also both countries believe that the true popular support of the opposing government is slim (the Russian leaders and the party do not really represent the people; Wall Street does not represent the workers), and they both assume that science stands in the service of the state (scientists are seen as having to support the capitalistic or the communistic system of government). This latter belief, however, was somewhat shaken when Sputnik went up, and there was a growing feeling of mutual respect for each other's achievements. In addition, both countries firmly believe that there is no political freedom on the other side. Both countries also assume that *time* is on their side. Enumerating these likenesses in feeling tone for both countries may permit certain inferences as to readiness for war or peace or for a hard or soft line of political maneuvers.

Wars are often engaged in with the belief that one's side has an advantage or that one has no other choice. An assessment of the opponent's belief will help to gain a clearer understanding of the subtle meaning of his utterances. At the present time, for example, there is a growing belief that Red China is the coming enemy; the Soviet Union is thought to hold the same belief, even though there are many messages coming from the U.S.S.R. that, on the basis of their lexical value, would not support this proposition. Our skill in assessing these contrary statements as bluffs or truths will determine our freedom of action on the political scene and perhaps our survival.

Scientific approaches toward making a more objective assessment of the meaning of such utterances need to be discovered; and an evaluation of the supporting evidence may avoid costly errors in decision-making.

Another application of communication theory on the political scene was made by Osgood (1964). He suggested that reinforcement principles also operate on the international scene; and that we have learned well in that we have accelerated the cold war, but that we still have to learn that peace efforts also can be accelerated. Thus, in the war acceleration, an aggressive action of the opponent is responded to by an aggressive act on our part, which, by reaffirming the fears of the opponent, forces another aggressive action on his part, and so on. Why not, Osgood asked, put the same principle to work for the lessening of tension whereby, without pressure or immediate crisis, we would relax tension in some spot in the world and thus give the opponent the opportunity to do likewise and top us in this tension-reduction endeavor? Maintained by reinforcing peaceful moves in each other, this competition for tension reduction would result in peaceful coexistence. With nuclear power in the background, such risks as one would take in relaxing tension would not be irreversible because an opponent had misread such an act as weakness. With the proper controls, nuclear power itself could eventually become subject to such peace moves.

This proposal was immediately hailed as dangerous and unrealistic. But then, any new untried way of thinking at a time of great stress will evoke such responses rather than any attempt to assess what part of such a proposal makes sense. We decribe it here because it was an effort to use subtle communication (the gesture toward peace) in influencing world events. President Kennedy was deeply concerned with the image of the "Ugly American" and developed the gesture of the Peace Corps. This also was a political move concerned with communication.

Unfortunately, many other gestures, often engaged in because we feel we have no other choice, counteract this picture of a helpful United States. An assessment of the communicative value of sending troops into a neighboring country is probably evaluated by the government in terms of the public image (we want to be seen as strong and not encourage our opponents by being seen as a "paper tiger"), but it remains to be seen if such gestures do not have just the opposite effect. For instance, we may thus be seen as an enemy of the independent, underdeveloped countries, and our gesture may give them a reason to unite against the enemy. Research and a careful evaluation of how and by whom such cues are perceived is essential in finding sound answers to these questions.

The behavior consultant has only recently discovered that he has contributions to make on the political scene. The political scientist had preempted this field, but without having a thorough knowledge of human behavior in the sense that the clinician has. There are currently some efforts underway in psychology to train individuals in areas such as government and politics at the same time they receive thorough psychological training. At the University of Wisconsin and at New York University courses are offered in political psychology; at Utah there is a dual program in which clinical psychologists may obtain training in political science along with practical government training. The behavior consultant in government is likely to ask new questions. He will bring his research skills, his understanding of human functioning, and his increasing knowledge of processes of communication to bear in order to discover useful ways of obtaining accurate information in this arena—which has for so long been a playground for human emotions.

Special Problems

PART FOUR

CHAPTER XIV

COMMENTS ON THE
TRAINING OF THE THERAPIST

WHEN we focus our attention on the subtle cues in human interaction, certain aspects in the training of psychotherapists become significant. We have to train the therapist in using himself as an instrument, in becoming sensitized to the sort of information a patient produces in order to involve him, and in the discovery of his own engagement patterns. This training is prerequisite to making adequate responses to the patient, since these responses will necessarily follow from a clear understanding of the patient's messages. The purpose of the supervisory session and later of the "control" session is to create in the inexperienced therapist a sense of awareness of his own participation in the demands of the patient; and to sensitize him to "read himself" and learn about the patient from his own involvement. His response to the patient's message must come from the recognition of the hidden or covert demands that are made on him.

Supervision in Psychotherapy [5]

In order to supervise a student in psychotherapy, it is important for the therapist-supervisor to let him know where he stands in terms of his own theoretical model. The supervisor may want to give the student great liberties of exploration, or he may want him to become proficient in psychotherapy within one particular model. In either case, it is important to state the "bias" or the basis on which the student's work will be evaluated. Our statements are best summarized in the following five points:

1. The first assumption is that the patient "hurts," in that he lives

5. This discussion is based on a paper by the author published in *Psychotherapy*, 1964, 1, 91-95.

with some discomfort and feels vulnerable in his dealings with himself and with others. The patient will approach an interpersonal relationship with an attitude of imminent danger, which justifies his attempt to control this relationship in order to protest his vulnerability and survive psychologically. Perhaps one of the most severe fears lies in the experiencing of indifference in others. This is one of the factors motivating the "engagement" of other individuals, i.e., controlling them in a specific way.

2. Like any individual who senses possible danger, the patient will try to protect himself, most often by hiding his vulnerabilities from the respondent. But, unlike individuals who are physically hurt, the patient in his psychological "hurt" needs to seek out experiences in the area of his vulnerability. Perhaps he does this to keep up his hopes that he will learn to master his vulnerabilities. He accomplishes this compromise between "seeking" and "protecting" by acting out within the area of vulnerability. He will constrict the respondent's awareness of the true intent of these behaviors through cues which are not easily identifiable. We have called this process "interpersonal repression." The patient first baits the respondent into his problem area and then, by creating a specific emotional climate, he dims the respondent's awareness in order not to be held responsible for his behavior. The patient's psychological survival appears to depend on his ability first to test himself out, and then to constrict the respondent's (and his own) awareness regarding his responsibility for certain behaviors. This process permits the patient to feel alive by experiencing significant behaviors which originally had met with trauma; at the same time he avoids the feared consequences associated with them.

3. The mechanism of "interpersonal repression" is a mode of behavior that the patient uses to perpetuate the type of adjustment he has found or has been forced into. The mechanism isolated here appears to be of significance with regard to the question of how people re-create their own problems. People give information of which they themselves are not aware. They constrict their own and the respondent's awareness with great skill and are then totally surprised when they obtain responses for which they cannot account, though they unknowingly worked hard to elicit such response activity in the first place.

4. Within the therapeutic hours, the patient will introduce his particular compromise of living out his problems, and at the same time he will constrict awareness. He will "scan" the therapist for ways of "engaging" him successfully, trying to obtain useful information

about the areas in which he can most easily constrict the therapist's awareness and so protect himself properly when necessary. He will test by trying to please, threaten, seduce, frighten, or flatter the therapist in order to find out in which of these emotional climates the therapist becomes preoccupied with himself. Whenever the patient succeeds in engaging the therapist into being concerned with himself, he has also succeeded in maintaining his present state of adjustment. When this occurs, no possible therapeutic gain can occur, and the patient has simply reinforced his view of the world.

5. The uniqueness of the psychotherapy hour lies in the fact that the therapist is a social human being who will respond to the conventions of our language and will therefore necessarily become engaged with the patient. But he is also trained to look at himself, to use himself as an instrument, and to learn from his own engagements what ails the patient. Rather than respond within the emotional climate expected of him and reinforce the present adjustment of the patient (as most of the patient's respondents will usually do), he can *disengage* from the patient's expectations. He can thus provide the patient with an unexpected response in which he changes the class of meaning altogether. For example, he might respond to a patient who told him that "the office is dirty," not with anger, which would be self-concern, but with such a response as: "You're quite uncomfortable being here." It is this unexpected response of the therapist, which represents concern for the patient rather than self-concern, that forces a change in the patient's experience. The patient has failed in his attempt to engage the therapist and yet has remained both safe and free from the feared consequence—indifference. The therapist did not become preoccupied with himself but acted out his continued concern for the other person.

In this model the therapist provides an experience that will change the patient's behavior, though we do not know as yet the direction of such change. He keeps to his objective of creating uncertainty in the patient, and it can be hoped that the uncertainty will be beneficial to new exploration. Whether or not the new exploration will, in fact, be beneficial to the patient is probably dependent on media of information other than those which provide for change. One might speculate that the identification processes and other influences in his environment that are valued by the patient will be utilized in his creation of a new concept of himself.

The above summary of our theoretical position appears necessary in order to discuss problems inherent in the supervisory process as we see it. Perhaps we should start by disclosing a procedure of training which we have found to be immensely useful. In teaching students to become psychotherapists we require them to pair up, whereby one becomes the "therapist" and the other the "patient." The "patient" can either invent a problem, imitate a patient he knows, or adopt any role he wishes. The "therapist" is specifically instructed to be attentive to the covert or latent information that comes his way. He is taught to look for the type of expectancies that the "patient" has of him. He will learn to use the manifest content of the information only to find consistencies in covert meaning, such as contiguity of words, sequence of thought, etc. The major emphasis is always on the questions: "How does the patient try with subtle cues to involve me in the relationship? Where does he create 'emotional climates' that make me concerned with myself and my own feelings?"

The somewhat frightening experience of the student who plays the patient's role is his growing awareness that role-playing does not help cover up certain consistent patterns of his behavior. The student learns that in whatever role he assumes he gives out information he does not necessarily intend to give. He creates involvements of which he has little awareness. As it is the objective of our first course to understand how we ourselves, as therapists, affect the patient, this somewhat unpleasant experience via role-playing is the very cornerstone in the learning of future work.

The student who plays the role of the therapist learns that he can identify information which is consistent and from which predictions can be made, disregarding the fact that his "patient" has "faked" a role. He also learns that he has to disengage himself from the social impact of the manifest information presented to him. He is trained to listen to manifest information by qualifying it with the question: "Why is the patient adopting this role now?"

At this time we usually instruct the students to be attentive to the media of communication in terms of their specific interpersonal implications. It is not by chance that certain media such as free association, the recounting of dreams, childhood experiences, etc., have become so popular. These media of communication are all effective ways of expressing feelings and thought processes for which the patient does not have to take any direct responsibility. Thus, when telling a dream or recalling an event long passed, he can express some fearful thoughts and still say, "I am really not responsible for having these thoughts." Looking at media of communication in this manner the student very quickly learns that a discussion about sex may have nothing to do with the sexual problem of the patient but may be a message acting out feelings of trust. Along the same lines, a patient's discussion of his dependency may have nothing to do with his dependency problem, while the occasions during which the patient asks questions of the therapist may in fact be a covert way of acting out feelings of dependency. Much emphasis is placed on the student's skill of analyzing communication for these covert acting-out processes.

There are three major questions that the student will learn to ask himself:

1. He will learn to ask, "Where does the patient hurt?" He will learn about the patient's hurt not from what the patient says manifestly, but rather from his own experience with him. To evaluate these experiences effectively, the student will learn to discover the emotional climate that the patient's message creates in himself. Thus, he might say to himself, "The patient talks about my being inexperienced and looking too young. He wants to create some distance between us. Perhaps this behavior of creating distance by minimizing the qualities of the respondent is, in fact, one of the patient's problems. Perhaps that is where the patient hurts." This hypothesis, of course, is formulated on very limited information. The student does not necessarily have to respond in terms of this information, but it does offer him at least some first idea of how the patient makes his own problems.

2. The second question the student will learn to ask is, "What evidence is there for my hypothesis?" In social life we can experience a great number of feelings, such as anger, joy, jealousy, and sexual arousal, without having to account for the cues that promote these feelings in us. The therapist, on the other hand, must understand what affected him and to what extent the patient was responsible for it. By understanding specifically how the patient creates an emotional climate in others, the therapist begins to isolate the processes with which the patient keeps himself in a state of maladjustment. But he must also estimate the extent to which the evidence upon which his hypothesis is based is convincing or weak; that is, he has to make a probability estimate of the evidence. Should the therapist intervene with a response, this probability estimate becomes particularly important. For example, if the therapist responds to a message that showed no clear evidence of anger with "You feel angry," a denial by the patient cannot be interpreted in the same way as when the patient's message was more clearly an angry one.

3. The third question the therapist has to ask himself is: "What is the therapeutic objective; what experience do I want the patient to have now?" Let us assume the patient says, "When I woke up this morning I thought I had missed the appointment. I was much relieved

when I saw that I was still early." On this very limited information the therapist can make a number of hypotheses concerning "where does the patient hurt." Perhaps the patient wants to express some positive feelings about the hour and is fighting to overcome his own uncertainty about the therapist. One hypothesis might be that the patient hurts in that he cannot express his wish to trust the therapist openly. With subtle cues the patient might want to say, "Although it is not easy for me, I want to tell you that you are very important to me, that I am successfully fighting my negative feelings." One can also speculate that the patient perhaps had very demanding parents, and that any recognition he gave them may have resulted in further demands. He is subtly testing the therapist to determine whether it is safe to express his wish for trust in the therapeutic setting.

In spite of this limited information, the therapist can, at least hypothetically, form a therapeutic objective for the patient. Perhaps the information suggests that the patient has to experience that expressing a wish to trust does not necessarily create a devouring type of response. The response of the therapist will have to be coded to provide for this particular objective. The student has to learn to avoid a social response to the patient's statement: ". . . I was still early" ("I am so glad you made it"); he also must learn not to simply verbalize his own insight ("You want to test to see if you can trust me as yet"), as such a response may not be understood by the patient at this time. The student must be trained to think of the patient and to code his responses in such a manner that they will provide an experience in line with the objective. He must code this response from his knowledge of the patient and must be prepared to justify his response and explain why he believes it will have an impact on the patient.

In accordance with these three questions we often play only five minutes of the student's tape during one supervisory session; and analyze with him each single message and its response with the view to anticipating what sort of experience the particular response may evoke in the patient. Looking at the anatomy of messages and responses is a very cumbersome process, but in our opinion it provides the student with an experience that alerts him to watch for covert cues and have concern for the patient.

Supervision: Engagement

By discussing each message and response, particular attention is given to the patient's messages that were successful in engaging the student. By analyzing the patient's specific communicative devices with the student, we expect the student to learn to disengage from the patient at his next encounter. As we have no intention of doing therapy in the supervisory process, we must assume that proper information about being engaged will dissolve the "social countertransference." So, for example, we might tell the student who got angry at his patient and wants to discontinue seeing him that he must understand that "making people angry" is most likely a significant problem of the patient. We also inform him that it is the student's "job" to understand specifically how the patient succeeded in creating this anger in him. Ordinarily, the student can utilize this "control" information properly and then proceed to handle a problem in which he became engaged through the social skill of the patient. Should we discover that the student engages in terms of true countertransference, I would have to refer him to a therapy experience of his own, as stated earlier.

In summary then, we try to assist the student in his attempts to decode the covert aspects of the patient's messages, in learning to use himself as an instrument, and in learning to express himself in such a manner that he can provide the experience most helpful to the patient in terms of a specific therapeutic objective. We try to teach him that he must not lose sight of the fact that the patient hurts somewhere. We ask him to be on the alert for the specific ways in which the patient tries to involve him. We let the student understand that an analysis of those ways will give him a maximum of information, and thus teach him to respect each single message and its response and their meaning in the therapeutic hour. Finally, we try to teach him that, in the broadest sense, his deepest concern must be for the patient: the patient should be helped to experience "uncertainty" about formerly automatic behaviors, with the goal of greater freedom in exploring new choices.

Countertransference

We have used in the above description the somewhat esoteric term *countertransference* because it is closley related to the concept of engagement. But it becomes necessary to distinguish countertransference from *social* countertransference. The term *transference* was introduced into psychoanalytic language when Freud wanted to describe the patient's wish to transfer to the therapist "libidinal" feelings which he had experienced toward significant members of his family. *Countertransference* was used to describe the counterinvolvement of the therapist with his patient, whereby he brings his own historical feelings to bear with the patient and consequently experiences a loss of freedom in responding to the patient.

We introduce the term "social countertransference" because there are engagements that do not appear to be deep-rooted and can be dissolved with reasonable ease. This is not to say that some therapists may not become engaged with their patients in some way that dates back to their own earliest experiences, with the consequence that a resolution of such engagement demands further analysis or psychotherapy. To give an extreme example: Should the patient suddenly stand up and pull a knife on the therapist and threaten him, the therapist will most likely become engaged by this social gesture to the extent that he cannot respond adequately in terms of the welfare of the patient. This social engagement, however, does not necessarily have any bearing on the type of problems the therapist may have himself. In fact, one might say that should he be totally unresponsive to this gesture, he is likely to have problems!

"Pseudo-" or "social countertransference," of course, often occurs in more subtle ways. It has been the thesis of this book that this engagement is the aim of the patient and occurs with many messages. The patient is seen as a person who, for the maintenance of his psychological adjustment, has to engage the other person in the best way he knows. By using subtle conventions that are likely to affect the other person, he is able to exercise control and constrict the other's response activity. The patient aims at establishing social countertransference because he needs the therapist's engagement, both for a modicum of pleasure and to satisfy his need for safety. This engagement, however, is more easily resolved than true countertransference, as it does not involve deep-seated personal problems of the therapist. One could probably state that the training of the therapist is concerned with his abiilty to disengage, to resolve pseudo- or social countertransference. The therapist learns to disengage by recognizing in himself the effect of the patient's social messages.

A young female patient came to the office wearing a new dress with a few white roses pinned to it. She looked radiant, quite different from the way she had looked at the previous hour. We certainly do not know whether she specifically dressed up for the therapist. Yet being dressed this way in the morning hour would cause many people to ask the question, "What is the occasion?" The therapist found himself reacting to the young lady's apparel with, "It's a pretty dress," apparently reassuring the patient that he had noticed it. But the therapist also noticed that his own response was not just a delay statement, a quest for further information; his "It's a pretty dress" came forth with a smile and a feeling of admiration for the girl. Being well trained, he then asked himself: "Why does the girl want me to admire her now?" He asked himself this question not because he was really sure the dress had been put on for him, but because he noticed he had become "engaged" in this subtle message.

One could argue that it is hardly a problem if a young girl dresses up and wants to be admired. But that is not true. It might be (as it happened in this case) that the girl never dressed up for anyone but her father. Had the therapist simply made his admiring statement and let it go, he would have most likely reinforced the girl's fantasy that "father figures" can be seduced by dressing up. The therapist continued.

Therapist: "This morning it seems important that I admire you."

(This subsequent statement may have been somewhat too speculative, but was an asocial response that failed to reinforce the girl's fantasies about father and so opened up this automatic behavior to question.)

We argue that the therapist's behavior indicated that he was engaged when he made his first affective statement. He was involved in the social cue given to him, and his response activity was restricted. But was he in a state of countertransference? Is it predictable from his engagement that he had deep-seated emotional problems that have to be worked through before he can again enter the arena of therapy? There is, of course, the possibility of deep-seated problems, but in the above case the therapist was able to disengage from his involvement. The engagement was temporary and easily resolved, which is ordinarily not consistent with the definition of a deep-seated problem.

When we train the student to become aware of his engagements, we actually train him to learn a new language. He must learn this new language without forgetting his old one. In other words, he must understand what the patient is saying and what his social and conventional messages are, but he also must understand what the patient is hiding behind his words. He must learn from his pseudo-countertransference what the patient is trying to accomplish with him and must learn to distinguish cues that he ordinarily would disregard. The patient says "Good morning" in a gruff way, and the therapist will not only know the discomfort of being addressed in this manner, but may recall the last hour, which had been very demanding on the patient. He will go beyond the social impact of the image and not respond in the expected way (perhaps showing disturbance about the gruff address) lest he reward the patient and reinforce the behavior.

Students often wonder if they have committed an "error" when it is pointed out to them that they have become engaged. In response to such questions we suggest that engagement is only an error when we are dealing with a true countertransference, when there is an inability to master the engagement. Any therapist is enough of a social being and enough a child of our culture (i.e., indoctrinated in the social meaning of words) to have thoroughly overlearned covert meaning in everyday life, where one would expect him to become engaged. The new language the therapist has to learn with each patient can only be learned when the therapist becomes sensitized to the engagement wishes of the patient. The therapist learns to disengage only after he has been engaged many times with each patient.

One way to give the student the experience that he actually has *some* awareness when he is engaged with a given patient, though he cannot label it, is to permit him to talk about the patient. The student will often unwittingly introduce value judgments in his descriptions and will recognize the source of such judgments when they are called to his attention. A student had been seeing a husband and wife who were contemplating divorce. The student described the couple to the supervisor; the following is from a taped recording of this section of the supervisory hour.

Student: "He is a steady sort of fellow who is holding his job, has friends and hobbies. It seems that several years ago he got involved with a girl and now his wife just cannot forget it. She makes his life miserable. She is constantly nagging him at home and I think he finally cannot take it any longer."

Here is where the therapist interrupted.

Therapist: "I can tell you where your sympathies lie."
Student: "Well, yes, she is quite a nag. That's the way I size it up."
Therapist: "I don't think you can help her much with the feelings you have and, in fact, I doubt that you can help him either because you don't seem to understand his contributions to the trouble. Reading their impact on you, I guess the ritual, the specific idiosyncratic law in this family is that the husband is a good fellow who, for an offense which should have been long forgotten, now has to suffer the fury of his wife. Perhaps he believes that, and so does she. But where do these people hurt? Is it not here that they have successfully engaged you? You come in here feeling that she is just about solely responsible

for the family trouble. To me, this suggests the possibility that the frictions which he creates are very subtle and that her angry and nagging responses are just a little too obvious. You cannot help these people as long as you remain engaged in their ritual. In order to help them realign their preferred behaviors, they have to experience with you that he too contributes to the trouble. He must try to discover where he deserves a 'nagging wife,' where he triggers her responses. You can help them to the experience that both contribute to their trouble."

In subsequent hours, new information was obtained that the husband had maintained clandestine relations with another girl. The "nagging wife" apparently was his alibi; he could feel less guilty because of it. The wife suspected such a relationship and "nagged" in order to avoid discussing it. By no longer accepting the family game, the therapist had enhanced the possibility of their taking more direct responsibility within the family for discussion of this central issue. The engagement of the therapist, which had made him at the time quite ineffectual, had prevented him from helping the patients.

We have also used another device to help a student become aware of his engagement. We had him read from a transcript the words spoken by his patient. He read the patient's comments and took the role of the patient talking to the therapist; the supervising therapist read the student's own responses from the transcript. The impact of this device has often been useful. The student can often realize the patient's frustration in the therapeutic setting. The student read the patient's statement; the supervisor read the student's responses.

Patient: "What is the time?"
Student: "You want to know the time?"
Patient: "Yes, I want to know the time."
Student: "You want to know the time badly?"
Patient: "Yes, I want to know the time, but not badly. I just don't have a watch."
Student: "And I should tell you the time."
Patient: "Well, in the absence of anyone else, I guess that would be my expectation."
Student: "And when I tell you the time, you would be happy."
Patient: "Not happy, I just would have gotten an answer to my question."
Student: "You want me to answer your question."

When the final response was read, the student pleaded to stop.

He felt that he had experienced the frustration the patient must have felt at that exchange, and he blamed himself for being so inept. The therapist, however, was less concerned about "ineptness" than "engagement." While this exchange does show lack of skill, it also shows that the patient was utilizing the vulnerability of his respondent to make him feel impotent. It is this attitude of the patient—taking advantage of the vulnerability of the respondent—which perhaps gives us useful information about his problem. The patient could have responded in many different ways, but he apparently had noticed that the therapist was caught in that time question and was not able to handle it satisfactorily. The patient, with his cynical and angry replies, only added to this confusion. Between the lines he told the therapist that he never had met such an inept fellow. From this pattern of the discussion, we can learn much about the patient. If a person has the need to "needle" his respondent, to confound his confusion, we can speculate that this behavior would provide the patient with many enemies and with many people who are scared of him.

The supervisor told the student that his "ineptness" was not all of his own making, that he had become engaged, and that he should use this information for his hypothesis of where the patient hurts. Role-playing gives this type of learning a very real meaning, as the student can experience both the impact of his own responses and the feeling tone of the patient.

Control Supervision

Sometimes there are indications that a student cannot profit from supervision and training because he is governed by his own problems to the detriment of understanding the patient. In such cases, the student cannot properly gain from the information given him and needs time out to learn about the hindrances he experiences in this learning situation. We might ask a student to take a year off and avail himself of psychotherapy. This sort of recommendation is important as we do not want to provide psychotherapy for the student in the supervisory session but rather take for granted that the student can gain from the knowledge provided him. This recommendation to take time out for psychotherapy is the exception rather than the rule.

Some claim that all budding therapists should complete their personal psychotherapy in order to be ready to help other people. While we do not wish to raise any serious objections to this recommendation, we are weary of the implication that a "completion" of personal psychotherapy really should be the aim. The student completes his studies and he may complete an experience of psychotherapy for himself, but as long as he works with other people, he will become engaged with the patient and will profit from some kind of professional supervision (control). In fact, we firmly believe that supervisory sessions should continue as long as the therapist is in the business of helping people.

Although we believe that personal psychotherapy for the therapist may be helpful, we feel strongly about the possible misuse of the word "completed." The therapist is required to keep up with the developments in the field and he therefore never really "completes" his studies; moreover, he should also be very concerned with his continued personal experience in supervision. By having a working relationship with another professional person even for as little as an hour a week, the therapist can discuss some of his cases and obtain information about his social engagement with his patients that will make a real difference in the quality of his work.

The model we have been describing claims that even the most experienced therapist will become engaged with his patient, regardless of the effectiveness of his personal therapy. He will be forced, through the skill of the patient, into some of these engagements, and at times they will be very subtle. A "therapeutic plateau" due to engagement can last a long time and can be dissolved most efficiently through discussion with another professional person.

We have been working with a "control therapist" who, when we described a case to him, commented: "I never heard you being so bored with any other patient." This subtle involvement with the patient, elicited through such cues as the patient's monotonous voice and insipid comments, had blinded us to his problems. By complaining all along about a very boring life, he gave us the very example of how he perpetuated this kind of life. He had put us to sleep. This comment from our control helped us to break through a plateau with this patient which had lasted for many hours.

In another case we mentioned to a therapist who complained that he was not satisfied with his work with a female patient that he never seemed to have reacted to the girl's seductive games. Again and again she mentioned the names of boyfriends to the therapist and always implied unsatisfactory relationships. We wondered why the therapist had not responded to this possible attempt of the patient to make him jealous. The therapist realized that his omission was part of the "silent contract" he had reached with the girl, to the effect that he was happily married and therefore was not a love object!

The therapist had become "engaged" with the patient by ruling himself out as an object of seduction. When he was alerted to these feelings, he broke the "plateau" and discussed the girl's fantasy about himself with her.

Currently there are voices in the field who feel that talking to patients is not enough and that a helping hand, a caressing hand, an expression of anger and other "honest" emotions are more powerful tools in human interaction than mere verbal responses. We firmly disagree with such efforts, as we feel that such nonsymbolic gestures are essentially engaged responses. Were this "mutual acting-out" technique ever to become fashionable, we would indeed need a chaperone rather than a control supervisor to help the therapist help the patient.

CHAPTER XV

NEEDED RESEARCH IN PSYCHOTHERAPY:
A Cursory and Highly Selective Journey[*]

Evaluation and Outcome

WHILE many of the studies evaluating the results or "outcome" of psychotherapeutic endeavor are inconclusive, they do help us crystallize some of the problems inherent in such research. Few of the studies reviewed used comparable definitions of patients, process of psychotherapy, adequate criteria control groups, or comparable criteria for failure or success. The result is that evaluations are often both incomplete and unconvincing. In addition, many studies leave the reader with the impression that the investigator had a definite ax to grind, either pro or con, and that his selection of patients and his designs were geared to this intent.

The confusion is probably due in part of the absurdity of the question: "Is psychotherapy effective?"

A comparable question might be "Is playing tennis an enjoyable sport?" or "Does education help man to fulfill himself?" It is most probable that these questions cannot be truly answered unless one is willing to resort to highly artificial "operational definitions" which limit the question in scope. Some individuals may object to this comparison and argue: "Don't psychotherapists claim that psychotherapy helps people to be happier? What is wrong with measuring whether they are successful?" But is "being happier" really an agreed-upon, measurable goal? We believe that reading the literature suggests that there is probably no single universal goal in psychotherapy; not even the more convincing ones such as "living more happily" or "functioning more adequately." Secondly, the goals, even if agreed on, are still too wide in scope to permit sensible answers.

6. In the bibliographic reference section there will be four topical reference lists on: Research on Operant Conditioning; Research on Non-verbal Cues in Language; Research on Outcome of Psychotherapy; and Models of Psychotherapy.

The confusion comes from the fact that the practice of psychotherapy was modeled in the image of the doctor-patient relationship, a model which has since moved ever so lightly into the psychological realm, resembling more closely a teaching model. Psychotherapy is no longer used exclusively for treatment. Theoretical models of psychotherapy used to be treatment models for teaching an adequate state of mental health. Today, many of the models presented, including the one presented here, are behavior models designed to explain changes in human functioning. The hospital patient treated with psychotherapy differs greatly from the scientist who attends a sensitivity group therapy meeting with the hope of discovering new reference points and a goal of achieving greater creativity. With such diverse goals, how is one to measure the effect of the process objectively? In one case, one may consider hospital or psychotherapists' discharge rates as a measure; in another case, greater achievements in creativity than prior to treatment; and in yet another case (such as in the geriatric patient) an improvement in feeling tone.

There is a further difficulty with regard to goals. Can one really set a sensible general therapeutic objective without considering the specific patient? Who can set these goals? A patient may come into therapy to save his marriage but, as he obtains some distance from his behavior, makes the decision for divorce. Yet he feels quite satisfied that he has profited from psychotherapy. Another patient wants to find friends but instead of doing this, he pulls out of a marginal job and embarks on a brilliant scientific career. He is still unhappy, though, and perhaps feels that therapy did very little for him.

What are adequate measures? What happens when the patient does not improve at all, but is able to maintain his (unhappy) state of adjustment rather than spiraling to a breakdown? Who is going to serve as a control group in this case? Attempts to accept every second patient from a waiting list and then compare the two groups (treated vs. untreated) are also fallacious. We can speculate that the decision to seek treatment and the hope to obtain it can alter attitudes significantly. Let us assume that the researcher's control group is selected from those individuals who no longer want to avail themselves of treatment after an extended waiting period. In this case he would deal with a highly selected sample and, in addition, he could never be sure what the act of resignation itself had done to the hopes and aspirations of this person.

We maintain that approaches that attempt to evaluate the efficiency of psychotherapy by measuring "success" are bound to falter, as they are devoid of sensible measures. General outcome studies geared to the medical model of psychotherapy are not very meaningful since too many questions are left unanswered. We have isolated seven such questions which confound most studies in this area. They are: (1) What constitutes a patient with mental problems that differentiate him from the nonpatient? (2) What are the goals of the specific model of psychotherapy under investigation? (3) Is the time of contact controlled for all patients measured? (4) Are the therapist equally experienced individuals? (5) Does the control group have "equal" mental health problems? (6) What are the outside influences to which the control group is exposed? (7) What is the measure of success (or failure)—individual growth and maturity, social improvement, professional betterment, freedom from symptoms or what? We believe that many of these questions which confound our research efforts on evaluation of psychotherapy result from an inadequate model, a model which was never devised to encourage measurement in the first place.

There may be some hope in the type of study, under a psychological model of learning, that measures the efficiency of the process in terms of specific objectives for a given patient. This sort of measurement is most easily done with the conditioning therapies in which the objective is limited and defined from the start, although many therapists feel that the meaning of such studies is too constricted. We grant that we would have to be modest in generalizing from this kind of research, as many conditioning ventures are very specific and concerned with isolated behaviors of the individuals concerned.

When Lovaas (1965) declares that he wants to rid autistic children of their punitive behaviors or that he wants them to learn to speak certain words, he surely can evaluate whether or not he has accomplished this objective. He can do so because he proposed a specific unit of measurement in his therapeutic goal. Someone may point out that though the children learned the words, they still may not have learned to use them appropriately; Lovaas could reply that appropriate usage would have to be the objective of a second study, and so forth.

Our model, based on information exchange, suggests some promising evaluation procedures. Suppose a given therapist discovers a suicidal blackmail syndrome in a given patient, whereby the patient threatens his respondent with suicide unless he has his way. The therapist could define this type of message as a unit of measurement; and then measure its frequency of occurrence and evaluate the efficiency of the process that reduced its occurrence. He would have a limited unit of measurement since it would take a second study to relate it to peripheral or secondary areas of function. Though he cannot generalize to the mental health of the patient, the therapist can state whether or not his first therapeutic objective was reached. We believe that with this modest approach to evaluation one can gather meaningful data.

Utilizing a communication model of psychotherapy, one could use message and response as a unit of measurement. This is more feasible now than it has been in the past, due to the increased sophistication in the use of the computer, which may yet prove to be the long-sought-for microscope of the behavioral sciences. Stone *et al.* (1962) at Harvard and Starkweather (1964) at the Langely Porter Clinic have devised programs that actually move toward evaluation of such verbal productions. Starkweather and Decker (1964) "process-listed" twelve hours of the patient productions of a therapeutic interview, in which all his words within given time intervals were counted. They also attempted a statistical analysis of those word meanings which belong together (such as words relating to denial: *no, none, never,* etc.). They prepared graphs of the sequence of occurrence of such clusters showing the distribution of these factors during the interviews. They could then answer such questions as "Does 'denial' increase or decrease as therapy progresses?" They plan to discover similar factors for the therapist and eventually hope to show what sort of change a therapist produces with a given set of responses.

The implications of this approach are both interesting and exciting. Through such programs one may be able to discover therapist behaviors that effectively reinforce a given patient behavior. More specifically, one would be able to inspect whether a given set of therapist behavior (set of words, gestures, etc.) can be used by any therapist, or whether they can only be effectively used by their originator. With this procedure the researcher can measure problems of generalization and take some important steps in evaluation. A number of questions, important for both training and the process of psychotherapy, would be opened to inspection.

Surely, such "microscopic" studies on process, with such limited objectives, will only partially answer the ambitious question, "Does psychotherapy work?" This question, encompassing the differing value systems of a large mass of people, will perhaps never be answered satisfactorily. Holistic answers to this question will be attempted largely by partisans in battle who like to back their wishes with the authority of research. The legitimate question of the psychotherapist—"Is my work effectively doing what I am setting out to do?"—will have to be carefully reworded before it can be answered. As in so many other areas of behavioral research, our first task is to discover the proper question.

Experimental Setting

Since the psychotherapeutic process appears to be related to (but not entirely identified with) behavior change, we can use laboratory methods for evaluating the conditions under which such change occurs. Research studies with a learning orientation claim to examine persuasion, attitude change, and response to stress. Operant conditioning studies are also included in the general category of learning research. It is not our attempt to summarize these studies here (though we shall include a bibliography on the most recent studies related to the therapeutic process) but to point out research needed in this area. We shall include three areas that we feel have not been given their proper place in the laboratory.

1. *The state of awareness*. The problem of awareness has been neglected because it is exceedingly difficult to define. Subception research tried to formulate a number of laboratory experiements with such formulations as the "perceptual defense hypothesis." These studies have not been unequivocal in their findings, precisely because "reportability" seemed to be the only operational definition of awareness used. There are many variables involved that prevent a person from reporting events, and it is difficult to decide where to draw the line between reportability or nonreportability of a given event. We may see the color of the wall in a strange room and possibly it has an effect on us. Yet we may not always be able to label the color properly, though we may be able to do so once our attention is directed to it. To what extent are we actually aware of the color? One probably could argue that the probability of the occurrence of the correct response is the best estimate of awareness, but where does such a statistical concept leave the idea of the clinical meaning of consciousness?

The role of awareness has been recognized in market research (Packard, 1957). Hard sell techniques are based on the understanding that the individual will respond to the emotional climate (associations) created for him. Music in supermarkets is said to increase sales. Would it still increase sales if one were to have a large display stating, "We know that music stimulates a customer to buy more. That is why we play music here"? Or "We have packaged our soap in yellow paper, because we have found that yellow paper is appealing to customers"? This message would bring the "climate" which has been created to awareness, and would at least give the customer the chance to use judgmental process instead of emotions. We think that such awareness would probably also be detrimental to sales.

Awareness also seems to play an important role in the therapeutic process. What effect does the emotional climate created by the therapist have on the patient? We refer to such cues as the setting of the therapist's office, his demeanor, tone of voice, the many subtle cues which show concern for the patient, and his way of dress or manner of opening the door. The therapist's asocial messages are designed to extinguish certain previous associations. Are they effective because the patient is unaware of their intent, or would they work equally well even if this "beneficial manipulation" of the therapist were called to his attention? Is the impact of certain responses dependent on the state of the patient's awareness? Does the impact of a therapist's response on the patient *generalize* as readily when the patient is aware of the intent?

We do not know the answers to these questions, but some of them at least can be investigated in an experimental setting. With new equipment, the effect of generalization can be accurately measured in the laboratory. A person undergoing psychotherapy could be asked to carry a small voice-actuated tape recorder, and the generalization effect of certain new and relevant responses might then be measurable. Such a method could even serve to measure the generalization effect under different states of awareness. This and other such laboratory techniques may be applied to gain new knowledge in this difficult area.

2. *Communication process.* Research with nonverbal stimuli is another area which seems pertinent at this point. (A bibliography in this area is given on page 294). Studies such as the one by Kramer (1964) have tried to evaluate the meaning of sounds in the absence of the lexical meaning of words. A number of methods are being used in this area, such as that of Starkweather (1956), who limited the sound frequencies so the message could not be understood. Another was Kramer's (1963) constant content methods, where the same word or series of words was said in different moods in order to portray different vocal stereotypes. In our own laboratory we produced a tape which contains 48 items, each expressing one of six moods (happy, sad, angry, flirting, fearful, indifferent). These items were standardized with a large number of subjects to assess to what extent these vocal stereotypes could be recognized by delinquents (Humphrey), schizophrenic patients (Robinson), patients in therapy (Ravsten), individuals who had been shocked by a stress film (Estrine), and males and females and various age groups (Donoviel). Plans are

under way to play the tape to individuals in foreign countries (are there internationally meaningful sounds?), and to families of schizophrenic patients (do these families have greater idiosyncratic communications among their members and less ability to decode conventional vocal stereotypes?).

These types of studies are possibly useful for studying the therapeutic process since they will give us some information as to what extent disturbances in the patient are related to a deficit in the communication and decoding processes. A more sophisticated approach to these questions will become available when factors other than audio cues can be used for evaluating the decoding skills. Setting and visual cues are important determinants of meanings and should eventually be included. Also, total verbal output (both for content themes and type token ratios, etc.) may give some information about the subtle verbal behavior of the patient and the generalization effect of the new attitudes that become represented in his verbal behavior in the hour.

The communication process in psychotherapy could also be investigated by postulating a reinforcement model such as the one under consideration by Lovaas (1965), in which he rewarded verbalization in autistic children. One of the problems in using this model is in specifying those responses that represent a reward to the patient. Such reward responses may be highly idiosyncratic and differ from patient to patient. (Neither praise nor money is a universal reinforcer.) If one could discover the type of response a given patient has designated as a reward, one could improve the therapeutic process by measuring the effect of various schedules of learning. We shall briefly present a speculation with regard to a learning model that would take more cognizance of the complexities of the therapeutic process. It is difficult enough in the laboratory to assume that a given stimulus is a reinforcer; the same problem occurs in manifold ways in therapy because a one-stimulus model is simply not easily applied to the complexities of learning in psychotherapy. If we postulate a model in which extinction of one behavior and reinforcement of another occur simultaneously, we would have a model more adaptable to our observations.

In psychotherapy a given response *seems* to accomplish both these tasks simultaneously. For example, a child has learned to topple over the milk bottle to arouse his mother's anger. By punishing him, the mother hopes to extinguish his obnoxious behavior. While she may succeed in eliminating one behavior, she has also reinforced another. Depending on the intensity of the punishment, the child both unlearns the obnoxious behavior and learns that aggressive behavior engages his mother and brings a highly predictable state of attention. To the extent that the child desires attention from his mother and identifies her anger as a state of attention, the mother's reaction may extinguish immediate aggressive behavior but increase the likelihood of aggressive behavior in the future. This particularly holds true if we take the liberty of classifying certain covert forms of behavior as aggressive. If the punishment is severe, the milk-toppling behavior may be stopped, but other and possibly more subtle means of aggression are likely to increase in frequency. This reasoning leads to a model where one response simultaneously extinguishes some behavior patterns in the child but reinforces others.

What would happen if our hypothetical mother responded with love rather than anger to her child's aggressive behavior? The child turns over the milk bottle, hoping his mother will get angry and notice him. This time, instead of spanking him, she hugs him and says, "My little boy, how much you must have suffered to have to use such desperate means in order to get my attention!" What would this mother's dramatic response do to her child? We assume that it would reverse the above pattern; i.e., the child had identified "anger" as a state of attention and therefore as a reward to the extent that he wanted her to be angry. The mother would help extinguish the annoying behavior by not rewarding the boy (the reinforcing anger was absent). In addition, she would also reinforce his experience that mother can give him attention other than anger. One might predict that in the future some of the annoying behavior will still appear (to test the new form of attention) but that the association anger–attention will be weakened.

We shall apply these speculations to psychotherapy. When the therapist gives an asocial yet attentive response to the patient, he is essentially in the position of the mother who reversed her behavior: he helps extinguish the occurrence of a given behavior because he does not reward it in the expected manner. Through covert cues he also trains the patient that another person can be concerned for him even though that person is not "engaged" in the customary manner. A child may be pounding on the window to arouse the anxiety of the therapist. From previous behavior the therapist assumes that this act means: "Can you love me even when I am so annoying and dangerous?" He responds:

Therapist: "You wonder if anyone can like a boy who tries to break windows."

This message is asocial in that it is not the socially expected reprimand or restriction; and therefore it should contribute to the extinction of the noxious behavior, i.e., the therapist did not "reward" the child by becoming anxious. This exchange also has additional ramifications.

The response reinforces the feeling in the child that someone can be concerned for him without being anxious; it weakens the anxiety–attention association. The response simultaneously helps extinguish the noxious behavior and reinforces a positive feeling tone in the child. After the child has been exposed to a number of asocial responses in this area, we would predict that he will engage in the "testing for anxiety" behavior less frequently. We would also predict that he will engage more frequently in behaviors reflecting a positive feeling tone. Thus the response activity of the therapist can be used as a unit of measurement, as long as we know what the patient has learned to identify as a reinforcer. In this manner we can bring the communication process into the laboratory.

3. *Physiological-clinical research.* While we have stressed the value of the computer as a tool in assessing the communication process, new discoveries in psychophysiological areas are certainly of equal importance. We know of at least one U.S. government-supported research program that has important implications for the future. The theoretical structure of this work is grounded in both the psychoanalytic theory of persuasion and results from pharmacological studies of the brain. We refer to the environmental enrichment studies, which relate environmental enrichment to later chemical properties of the brain (Rosenzveig *et al.*, 1962).

On a broader scale, the "Operation Head Start" took 3- to 6-year-old lower-class children, who have a predictably higher future incidence of dropouts and unemployables, and exposed them to an "enriched" environment. This consists of food, clothing, medical care, and general cultural and social stimulation. This program needs to be carefully evaluated. There have been somewhat similar programs in Russia, Denmark, and Israel; and after evaluation of Head Start and these similar programs abroad, we will gain important clues to the understanding of the maladaptive process.

Further research on the pleasure and pain centers of the brain may yield a clearer understanding of the psychophysical counterparts of the ahedonistic attitude so often observed in the neurotic patient. Psychogenetic studies (Meehl, 1962) seem to imply that genetic dispositions for certain behaviors are necessary but not sufficient conditions to explain neurosis. When these dispositions are better understood, we will be confronted with those needs of the organism which operate independently of prior learning experiences. They too will have to be taken into consideration. For example, obese individuals often have been fat babies (Heald, 1960). Is overeating learned or is it genetic? Is it a direction or a disposition? New, widely used drugs such as tranquilizers, antidepressants, stimulants, and hallucinogens, with their known effect on the emotions, need to be further evaluated as to their influence on psychotherapeutic work. One new psychophysical method of assessment, the "evoked potential" of the brain (Shagass and Schwartz, 1965), is a promising tool for the eventual discovery of relationships between various parts of the brain and thought processes. While there is no claim that this tool can as yet specify these relationships, there seems to be some hope of applicability, possibly even to diagnostic work.

Esoteric measures, such as the response of the pupils in the eye as a measure of attention (Hess *et al.*, 1965), may also be promising tools in the investigation of attention states and may serve in research to discover attention states in the psychotherapeutic process.

Developmental Psychology

In this cursory and highly selective journey into research needs as they relate to the process of psychotherapy, we would like to mention a few rather specific needs concerned with the developmental process. In this area we need to know more specifically to what extent the child's early learning engenders his adult behavior, and to what extent consistent personality patterns are formulated in these early years. At the same time we also need to look at the other side of the coin, that is, how much freedom for change exists within these limits of consistency.

A child may learn early in his life that his environment does not reliably respond to his needs and that he cannot trust anyone. In later life he may develop an untrusting attitude which may be consistently displayed. Yet, within this attitude there may be more freedom than we had formerly assumed. The child may develop into a self-defeating, suspicious individual or, on the other hand, into a detective. Consistency in certain behavior may very well be an outcome of early learning, but a capacity for change also exists. We need to differentiate these qualities and, in addition, discover the conditions that enhance either consistency or change.

Over and above what Bandura and Walters (1963) report, we need to know more about the "imitation" behavior that seems to be a basic characteristic of the normal developing child. Imitation seems to enhance his learning from the environment. Which experiences enhance the wish to imitate and which do not? Studies in birth order (Denber, 1964; Schachter, 1964) are attempts to assess the lawfulness of social interaction learning in the family setting. One can ask to what extent a certain position in the birth order (e.g., first or last) results in some behavior in later life that a different placement would not have produced. Speculating that a certain position in the birth order is a necessary but not sufficient condition to produce neurotic behavior, one could try to discover the adjuvant conditions that relate to birth order. Language studies of children are particularly significant, since language is both a vehicle for communication and a media for maintaining or changing behavioral consistencies. Understanding specifically how the child learns his language, to what extent his language formulates his world, and what changes can be effected by learning new meanings and new words is a very central problem. Within the therapeutic process one could even define the therapist's work as teaching the patient a new language to effect his behavior.

Community Interaction

Finally, we want to direct our attention to some selected research needs in the area of social processes constantly going on in the family, the community and the nation. Can we really assume that a "mature" or "healthy" person will function more adequately in society than a sick one, or even that he will be a greater benefit to society than the maladjusted person? Is it not possible that the "maladjusted" beatnik, with his loose and undifferentiated values, represents an attempt to maintain individuality in a highly structured world, and a serious and courageous attempt at that?

We do not propose solutions here, but we do point out the need to think through what roles individuals play in society and what values they contribute. We also need careful research work on the problem of interaction between the community and the family. What are the mechanisms that discourage certain groups of people from seeking help when they suffer from mental conflicts? Have these groups found devices other than known methods with which they can help maintain the individual neurotic or psychotic member in their community? What are the social factors of spontaneous remission? What are the extratherapeutic devices that some societies provide for their members to overcome a state of despair? What are the characteristics of an individual's resistance to breakdown? Why is there a lesser mental health problem during a war?

Toward Making the
Therapist Dispensable

One author has called psychotherapy "the bought friendship," and traces the demand for psychotherapy back to loneliness. Others stress the demand for conformity, which is supposedly increasing in modern society, as one of the reasons for seeking psychotherapy. We are not at all sure about the conformity thesis: one can easily argue that demands for social and moral conformity were by far greater when neighbors knew each other. At present, with large masses of people living side by side without knowing each other, we can argue just as easily that we have a society which has almost too little demand for conformity (which can be enforced) and therefore leaves the individual too much room for individual decisions.

Not having any clearly defined standards to live by, the individual can set his own standards. He often sets them in such a manner that no opportunities for pleasure are missed. He behaves like the little boy who is not satisfied with his own toy precisely because all the other boys together have so many more than he has. Stimulated to high aspirations of satisfaction, the individual now compares what he desires with what he has found and finds himself dissatisfied. When he goes to seek psychotherapy, he does so because he has not found satisfactory standards and is trying to find a set of values to adopt and perhaps live by. If our aim is to make ourselves as psychotherapists truly dispensable at some time in the future, we have to discover the individual and social conditions that will give us the information as to why individuals seek this type of help. Our speculation, that the patient is essentially trying to discover a satisfactory set of values, would have consequences both on our views of society and on the treatment process itself.

Over the last few years we have asked students to visit individuals offering "psychological" help to people through newspaper advertising. We visited prayer women, scientologists, phrenologists, palm readers, and various doctors of "relaxology" and related disciplines. Before visiting them we informed them of our university association and said that the visit would be one of inquiry, but this statement was often seen as an "excuse" or "alibi" ("No one wants to admit that he needs help," said one). We did not visit members of this group to criticize them, but rather to understand why these people are sought out for help and what help they are likely to deliver.

We found that some generalizations were possible from our visits. We got the impression that their clients were from low socioeconomic income levels, and that the psychotherapist would not ordinarily feel comfortable with this same type of client. He neither dresses up for his visits nor is he ready to learn a new language. He primarily wants answers, answers for possible and speculative questions. By and large, this type of client did not obtain his answers here, except in very ambiguous terms. Efforts were always made by members of this group of "fringe therapists" to secure a second visit from our students, sometimes by threats and sometimes by vague promises. In about 25 per cent of the cases, the healers tried to sell merchandise, insurance, or books and pamphlets. Our students also felt that these people have some real skill in adapting to the language of the customer; and, although (or perhaps because) they frequently engage in a hellfire approach, they seem to give their clients the feeling that it is within their own power to resolve their problems or sins. Generally speaking, we learned that these practitioners do "reach" their clients, that they aid in cathartically reducing some immediate pressures, and that a fairly large number of them take advantage of their clients.

We have to understand what troubles people have and which kind of help they are seeking. We have to understand that social class still determines attitudes and aspirations. We have to consider the individual's value system more thoroughly than we have in the past, in order to become more effective and thus help the individual to become weaned from the psychotherapist.

CHAPTER XVI

THE ETHICAL PROBLEMS OF
CONTROL OF BEHAVIOR

WHEN Socrates led his respondents in dialogue through the "Socratic way of questioning" toward a certain goal, he was confronted with an ethical problem. In its simplest form, the problem was how to justify his manipulation of his respondents by this way of talking. Socrates' response to the ethical problem is of some significance here because it lasted some two thousand years. Socrates' first comment on ethics is contained in this statement: "For is not the discovery of things as they truly are, a good, common to all mankind?" (Jowett, 1937). That is to say, to the extent that Socrates helps toward the discovery of "things as they truly are," he cannot really fail to be good.

A second answer to Socrates' ethical problem is found in young Theaetetus, who does not really have to learn from his better but who can bring forth his own knowledge with another person's help. Socrates says, "I only know just enough to extract. . . . I shall say nothing myself but shall endeavor to elicit something from our young friend" (Jowett, 1937, p. 163). Socrates is the facilitator, the "mid-wife" who does not see himself as imposing his own ideas on the respondent, but, at best, helps to bring forth the respondent's ideas.

Both of Socrates' answers are reflected in many of the theories which have governed the practice of psychotherapy. Just as Socrates justified his behavior on the grounds that it would lead to the well-being of his friends, psychotherapeutic theory, generally speaking, conveniently theorizes that psychotherapy is a method to help a person "to get well," "to adjust," or "to function more adequately."

From Socrates to the present day, many theoreticians have provided us with theories which assume that to help our respondent we use our knowledge and methods to work toward two goals: (1) the discovery of truth (the ideation of the true self) and (2) the dis-

272

covery of the respondent's own true thoughts and desires. Defining our work as beneficial *ipso facto,* we are clearly led astray from accepting responsibility for any of the dangers to the individual that may be due to our methods of changing another person's behavior. With his conviction that asking questions leads to a better knowledge of self and brings forth only the person's own wishes, Socrates cannot even ask the question: "What harm can I do by questioning; what values will I impose on the other person?" In order to evaluate our methods, we must first accept the fact that we are utilizing methods which have to do with behavior change (better or worse) rather than adjustment (better only).

Bergin (1964) lists an impressive number of studies that (some upon reanalysis) contain data indicating that clients in psychotherapy both improve and lose in adjustment measurements when compared with control groups. Bergin calls this the "deterioration effect." It is certainly an effect frequently overlooked by our researchers, who generally ask only the question of how much improvement occurred in a given group of clients.

Krasner (1962) speaks of psychotherapy as a form of behavior control that uses methods of exerting influence, persuasion and manipulation of behavior. Psychotherapeutic techniques utilize both the therapist's total behavior and the structure of the interview. These are the "social reinforcements" which are the tools of the hour. Krasner (1962) says:

> . . . a behavioristic viewpoint might argue that apparent spontaneity on the therapist's part may very well be the most effective means of manipulating behavior. The therapist is an individual programmed by his training into a fairly effective behavior control machine. Most likely the machine is most effective when it least appears like a machine. (p. 200)

While one may argue about the labels, that is, whether a person who at least consciously wants to help another person to help himself can be called "controlling," there seems to be accumulating evidence that the therapist's behavior does determine patient behavior and values. This occurs whether the therapist wants it or not. There is no doubt a difference between a friend who tells a patient that he ought to get married and the therapist who gives paralinguistic cues of approval or shows an increased degree of interest ("hm, hm") when the patient talks about marriage. The friend gives advice and will easily admit that, to the extent of this advice, he wants to control the person's behavior. The therapist, on the other hand, may rightly deny that he had any wish to control behavior. But to the degree that he has learned to be a keen observer of himself, he may admit that he was in fact influencing the patient (perhaps even more effectively than the friend who made a direct statement). He may even admit that values were communicated and that a form of persuasion (conscious or unconscious) occurred. We know that even the length of our statement in therapy is predictably related to the length of the patient's reply (Matarazzo *et al.*, 1965). Thus, it is most likely that the paralinguistic, nonverbal behavior of the therapist affects the patient and determines certain of his responses. To what extent is the therapist responsible for his behaviors which influence and perhaps persuade another person but which he neither "intends" nor recognizes?

The problem of ethics is certainly not unique to the psychotherapist. Behavioral scientists are entering every conceivable field of activity, from schools, industry, and politics to just about any organization with two or more members. If our knowledge of behavior change through such subtle devices as reinforcement of covert cues increases, Brecher and Brecher's quotation in Krasner's (1962) article may be representative of public fears. It concludes that: "New methods of controlling behavior now emerging from the laboratory may soon add an awe-inspiring power to enslave us all with our own engineered consent" (p. 201). Although this quotation is overstating the case, one can add that these "new methods" utilizing subtle cues can circumvent any ethical consideration altogether.

When we are looking at processes of behavior change proper, unalleviated by a convenient referral to the subterfuge that "we adjust only," fearful vistas appear to both the behavioral scientist and the public. The cries of invasion of privacy, misuse of testing (for instance, the Motorola case), and behavioral control have to be taken seriously even though they are often based on half-accurate information. We cannot discontinue scientific work on methods of persuasion any more than the physicist could discontinue work on splitting the atom. The comparison may sound grandiose, but were we to have a breakthrough in understanding the processes of persuasion, the impact on society would be enormous. We must try to guard now, in principle, against misuse of persuasive power by identifying properly where it occurs, by keeping all information public, and by giving "equal time" to the study of protective devices.

Such words of caution are not really enough to deal with the immediate problem in psychodiagnostics and psychotherapy. More specific guidelines are necessary. Carter (1964) recently reported on Brim's report (1965) on "American attitudes toward intelligence tests." The following *ethical considerations* (in reference to diagnostic tests) can be categorized: (1) confidentiality of test data; (2) evaluation of the question of invasion of privacy by asking certain questions which "no one has the legal and ethical right to ask"; (3) better validation of tests to discover whether their use in early life can legitimately determine outcome; (4) better validation, again to discover if abilities measured are in fact the only ones to be considered (Is a high intelligence rating really necessary for a given career?); and (5) a concern by the profession that tests are not used "consciously or *unconsciously* [author's italics] as means of discriminating against culturally deprived groups" (p. 1696). These categories are more specific and give more adequate guidelines to the profession than a mere general reminder.

The impact of reinforcement theory on the practice of psychotherapy has changed the nature of the ethical problem. No longer can ethical considerations be concerned only with gross misbehavior of the therapist. Here is an attempt to identify a few specific problems for discussion:

1. *The "conscious or unconscious" impact of the therapist on the value system of his patient, to the extent that such an impact is identifiable.* This responsibility of a psychotherapist to be concerned with his subtle impact on the patient means that a responsible psychotherapist will seek professional consultation (control) about his therapeutic hours in order to obtain information about and distance from the type of reinforcement he practices. Although the psychoanalysts proposed that a new analyst be "fully analyzed," reinforcement theory does not permit such a finality. Psychotherapy is a mutual and ongoing process, and constant control may be of the essence. The therapist has to be alert as to precisely what he communicates to the patient, and he cannot always rely on himself to discover his own attitudes, which determine at least some of his messages. Therefore it becomes important for him to have some contact with another professional person who can help him see himself clearly in a given relationship and with whom he can discover what his attitudes toward the patient are. Here we are not thinking of an hour of controlled supervision, but of a continuous professional relationship for the person engaged in treating others; this would serve the purpose.

2. *The problem of the patient's consent.* Freud and Rogers both could say that their therapeutic methods were effective only if the individual was asking for help. This appears no longer to be true; we probably can affect a person's behavior whether he wants it or not. Persuasion appears to work with the voluntary and the involun-

tary respondent. Once we understand his feelings, the hostile delinquent sent by a court is probably not any more difficult in therapy than any voluntary patient. We have to begin to evaluate under what circumstances we are willing to engage another person in therapy and to spell out the conditions which must be satisfied to keep the effort from being an "invasion of privacy." New rules are obviously necessary.

3. *Discussion of goals.* Socrates could see himself as a "midwife," just helping others to "give birth." Today we have some indication that the therapist is at least to some extent also the father of the baby. The goals may be very broad (such as encouraging the person to explore new choices) or very specific ("This patient should face the fact that he is hurting others by his silence" or any other such immediate therapeutic objective). Since the therapist will encourage the patient toward such goals, he should at least label them for himself and ask himself if they are the goals he wants to set for the patient. A frank discussion of goals seems necessary.

4. *Increased powers of persuasion on the society.* What limitations should be imposed to safeguard the individual from being exposed to increased skills in manipulation? Should there be considerations given where society needs protection from the persuader?

5. *The validation problem.* We need to know the extent and limits of our power of conscious and unconscious persuasion, its effectiveness and its dangers. Also as part of validation, we should consider the duration of the contact. Perhaps we should keep a patient in therapy only until he starts explorations rather than until completion of full analysis. It may be that we overtrain most patients and maximize habit action effect. New knowledge always presents a challenge to a profession, and we are now at the point where we have to consider this challenge seriously.

The Communication Process
in Psychotherapy

PART FIVE

CHAPTER XVII

SUMMARY:
The Communication Process in Psychotherapy

THAT one can control another person's behavior with words and other information is obvious, but that this control can occur without the awareness of either sender or respondent is less well known. This chapter is an attempt to discuss in summary statements the problem of such subtle control in human interaction.

Communication in the psychotherapeutic process lends itself particularly well to analysis: it represents a very conscious effort on the part of the therapist to affect a patient with information, but the information exchange actually goes both ways. The psychotherapeutic process, therefore, can be regarded as a prototype for other communicative processes.

Man communicates more about himself, his character, and his wishes than he consciously intends to. We assume here that he does so through subtle cues of which he is ordinarily quite unaware but which are part of his message. These cues include contextual cues (where the situation, or context, determines meaning) and adjuvant cues (where changes in meaning are due to additions such as tone of voice, gestures, etc.). An individual is frequently quite unaware of just which subtle cues he uses to change nuances in connotation in order to affect respondents. The use of these cues is part of his habits and automatic behaviors. Such subtle cues may or may not be hidden from the sender's awareness, but their purpose is to create an emotional climate in the respondent that is beneficial to and desired by the sender.

Almost all human communication includes subtle "hidden" cues. These are very frequently used to effect slight changes in the meaning of the message. They are also used where they are either discordant with the lexical meaning of the message or convey an entirely independent meaning. The result is that the respondent finds the decoding of the message difficult because of the ambiguity of the coding.

Almost all messages are sent with the purpose of influencing the respondent. That is, a message is designed to create certain "sets" in the respondent which, in turn, create predictable, expected responses.

Not all individuals are willing to accept their wish of influencing others with their message. It is through the covert cues attached to a given message that such messages serve to hide the sender's intent. The person's intent to influence others can become hidden even from himself; the message camouflages this information from the respondent. The extent to which a message can be understood for its intent to influence others represents the degree of responsibility the sender wants to accept for having sent this particular message. Responsibility in communication, then, has to do with accepting one's own wish to influence others.

Here are two illustrations: In the following message the sender takes responsibility for the intent of his message and permits full exposure of his intent to influence the respondent by creating in him a negative emotional climate. "Go to hell," said in the right tone of voice and at the right time, can be a message where the intent of aggression is admitted by the person. He does not hide his intent, as he uses a convention which is redundant as a vehicle of aggression.

With another message, however, an individual may not permit the respondent to fully recognize his intentions. "Gee, your city has a little smog, too," said perhaps in a pleading yet friendly manner, may be such a statement. Its intent (or in this case, the underlying feeling) may be just as aggressive as the intent in the statement above. That is, the manipulation, the desired effect of influencing the respondent, may be achieved just as effectively as with the overt statement, "Go to hell." In the smog example, the sender is careful not to use the conventional language of aggression, and by his ambiguity he is ordinarily able to confuse the respondent. Should the respondent recognize the intent and challenge the statement anyway ("You always see the worst of everything"), the sender can then capitalize on his use of covert rather than overt cues. He can escape taking full responsibility for his intentions to set up discomfort in the respondent because he did not expose himself fully.

Subtle cues are actually the means by which a sender *constricts* the response outcome. He uses these subtle cues to influence and control another person's responses to his own ends with only a minimal risk of being exposed for his attempts (persuasion).

In addition to constricting the respondent's possible recognition of his intentions, an individual can, as stated earlier, also hide the meaning of his manipulation from his own awareness. With his subtle hidden cues he can influence the respondent and bid for and provoke certain responses, yet maintain that he is quite innocent, that he really had no share in triggering these response activities (evoking message).

The mechanism described here allows the sender to "engage" the respondent and at the same time reduce the possibility of exposing his own intentions. The concept of engagement leads to new observations helpful in the analysis of the communicative process, particularly with reference to understanding certain practices in the psychotherapeutic process.

It is probable that "hidden cues" and "engagements" are learned in infancy and serve to protect the child from areas of vulnerability. When a child discovers that expression of certain thoughts and wishes produces responses that he finds unmanageable, he learns to hide these thoughts and wishes. In the future he will also learn to express them in such a manner that they will not be fully understood by the respondent; he discovers ambiguity under which to hide. He develops skills for controlling the exposure of his now vulnerable intentions in order to avoid responses with which he cannot deal. Areas where such control becomes necessary comprise the individual's *areas of vulnerability.*

Defenses against one's vulnerability are expressed by engaging another person through discordant messages. The adult may no longer be aware of the specific thoughts and wishes that made him feel vulnerable. What remains is the behavior that he has learned to use in order to compensate for his feeling of vulnerability. Vulnerability, then, gives rise to certain preferred behaviors in interaction, which are his ways of engaging and involving another person. When carefully analyzed, these "messages" seem to yield the ideas that made the individual vulnerable in the first place. An individual's preferred modes of interaction are not merely defenses; they are also behaviors that seek out certain responses in the environment. They trigger responses that are safe (as the sender has created an emotional climate in the respondent by which the response activity has been constricted) and apparently are also rewarding. They give the patient the experience that he is still dealing, still "alive" in the area of his vulnerability.

In his wish to avoid exposure of his vulnerability and his desire to engage another person for certain rewards, the person appears quite willing to pay a price. As he constricts the responses of another person through his use of covert cues, he shuts out a great deal of information which would come his way were he to give the respondent greater freedom of expression. This constriction of information flow is perhaps the basic reason for maladjustment and disturbance. The individual elicits constricted responses which seem to serve his purpose of obtaining protection while still remaining "in the battle." But the curtailment of the information flow diminishes the self-correcting devices available to the individual. He no longer is fully capable of directing his attention to the solution of problems.

In addition to the deficit arising from curtailment of the information flow, the individual may also elicit primary punitive responses. A child may want to be close to his mother, but has learned to hide this wish to be loved by her. He now directly elicits a punitive response to achieve his end; he forces his mother to pay attention to him and yet not recognize his prohibited wish. He seems to be willing to pay the price, to experience some pain, to obtain the attention; that is, he appears to repeat his behavior again and again regardless of consequences.

Evidence for the fact that an individual seeks to obtain a certain response from another person cannot be obtained through the sender's own "testimonial." Such evidence must come from the analysis of the communication itself; the frequency of occurrence of a specific "bid" and its particular response is perhaps the most telling sign that a given person is not simply victimized by his environment but that he elicits certain responses.

An individual activates behaviors in vulnerable areas. An individual will not only perpetuate his state of adjustment with his communications, but will actually seek out and select situations in his area of vulnerability. Man apparently is his own prophet; he can make his predictions come true without being aware of his own contribution. He feeds information to others without knowing it and so obtains certain responses that in turn give him both an excuse to behave the way he wanted to in the first place and an alibi for this behavior. He has a great deal of skill in collecting injustices. He appears to defend himself but he actually seeks out behavior that permits him to assume the defensive posture. By these means an individual maintains consistency of behavior, his present state of adjustment.

The more "vulnerable" the individual, the more "skillful" he will have to be in affecting the emotional set of others. The more vulnerable an individual feels about a given area of his world, the greater skills will he develop in eliciting constricted, highly predictable responses in other people. He urgently needs to avoid responses with which he cannot deal, and he gains at least some sense of existence by engaging others in predictable ways. The maladjusted person has greater skills in the use of subtle cues than the person not so affected, simply because he needs them more urgently to maintain his psychological existence.

In the therapeutic situation, the patient introduces his hidden expectations into the relationship with the therapist; he attempts to engage him in his typical manner. Any and all behaviors in the hour may serve to express hidden meanings and covert ways of affecting the therapist, and thus may be of therapeutic significance. The unique quality of the hour is that it is a pseudosocial situation where social engagements can be tried out without the customary consequences. Even the topics themselves, such as dreams or childhood remembrances, are excellent media of communication for this pseudosocial situation. This is true precisely because the patient can talk about dangerous events without taking full responsibility for them—he can introduce these thoughts to the therapist in relative safety.

Hidden cues are largely designed for emotional impact in order to create emotional climates beneficial to the patient's unaware wishes. To recognize the meaning of these communications, the therapist must learn to use himself as an instrument and understand which of his feelings are due to the information conveyed to him by the patient.

The therapist is most effective when he provides disengaged responses that do not reinforce the patient's present behavior. The therapist's responses not only interrupt the patient's expectancies (and in this manner extinguish association) but, being disengaged, are actually designed to give the patient the experience of "beneficial uncertainty." This experience provides a challenge to explore new choices in a nonthreatening situation. The patient should experience with the therapist, message by message, that he can tolerate the uncertainty and even utilize it for the discovery of territory previously prohibited to him. He will experience that in this "sanctuary" he can forgo the dangers and pleasures of being misunderstood, and so his messages will become less discordant.

Through the disengaged response, the therapist trains the patient to give more freedom to the people he encounters. This democratic training occurs because the therapist, through the use of beneficial uncertainty, lightens the burden of the patient's need to engage others at all costs and constrict their responses. As the patient begins to tolerate uncertainty, his psychological existence is no longer at stake, and he does not have to constrict the response activity of others to obtain only highly predictable responses. Identifying those communications which enhance an individual's giving of greater freedom to others appears to us as an observation having some political significance.

The patient has lifelong practice in his hidden manipulatory skills, and the therapist will necessarily become at least temporarily engaged in some of these manipulations. The therapist's skill does not consist in avoiding all engagements, but rather in learning about the patient from these engagements, and in being able to disengage in due time. Because of the patient's great skills, the therapist should consult with another professional person who can often help him to disengage from his involvements with the patient's messages more efficiently than he could using only his own resources.

Another consequence of this model is that the patient can be "persuaded" to change, whether or not he wants to change. He needs neither insight nor the "wish to get well" in the therapeutic setting. When provided with the proper experience, a person apparently can be significantly affected. This "change in spite of himself" emphasizes the significance of the ethical questions involved.

In the therapeutic hour, specific experiences, message by message, reinforce or extinguish the patient's unaware states. This model is useful for a more systematic investigation of psychotherapy. We feel that concepts such as "insight," "understanding," and "warmth of the relationship" have proved too elusive in the past, and that a message-response unit of measurement is a more heuristic formulation.

BIBLIOGRAPHY

ABRAMSON, J. H., SINGH, A. R., & MBAMBO, V. Antenatal stress and baby's development. *Arch. Dis. Childhood*, 1961, *36*, 42.

ACKERMAN, N. W. Family-focused therapy of schizophrenics. In S. C. Sher and H. R. Davis (Eds.), *The out-patient treatment of schizophrenia.* New York: Grune & Stratton, 1960.

BANDURA, A. Punishment revisited. *J. consult. Psychol.*, 1962, *26* (4), 298-301.

BANDURA, A., & WALTERS, R. H. *Social learning and personality development.* New York: Holt, 1963.

BANDURA, A. (discussant), LOVAAS, O. I. (chairman), PERLOFF, B., MEISEL, JOAN, KASSORLA, IRENE, SHEARMAN, R. WHALEN, CAROL. Reinforcement theory approach to an experimental treatment program for childhood schizophrenias. Paper read at Western Psychol. Assoc. convention, Honolulu, 1965.

BARKER, S. C. Behavior therapy for transvestism: A comparison of pharmacological and electrical aversion techniques. *Br. J. Psychiatry*, 1965, *111* (472), 268-276.

BATESON, G., JACKSON, D., HALEY, J., & WEAKLAND, J. Toward a theory of schizophrenia. *Beh. Science*, 1956, *1*, 251-264.

BATESON, G. The biosocial integration of behavior in the schizophrenic family. In N. W. Ackerman, F. L. Betman, and S. Sanford (Eds.), *Exploring the base for family therapy.* New York: Family Service Assn., 1961.

BECKETT, S. *Waiting for Godot.* New York: Grove Press, 1954.

BELL, J. E. Family group therapy. *Pub. Health Monogr.*, 1961, No. 64.

BERGIN, A. E. Some implications of psychotherapy research for therapeutic prediction. Paper read at American Psychol. Assoc., Los Angeles, September, 1964.

BERNE, E. *Transactional analysis in psychotherapy.* New York: Grove Press, 1961.

BERNSTEIN, L. *West side story.* New York: Random House, 1958.

BIXLER, R. Limits are therapy. *J. Consult. Psychol.*, 1949, *13* (1), 1-11.

BRIM, O. G., JR. American attitudes toward intelligence tests. *Amer. Psychologist*, 1965, *20* (2), 125-130.

BURNS, M. *Mr. Lynward's answer.* Boston: Beacon Press, 1957.

CARTER, L. F. Psychological testing and public responsibility. *Science,* 1964, *146,* 1695-1697.

DENBER, W. N. Birth order and need affiliation. *J. abnorm. soc. Psychol.,* 1964, *68* (5), 555-557.

ELLIS, A. *The theory and practice of rational-emotive psychotherapy.* New York: Lyle Stuart, 1964.

ELLIS, A., FELDER, R., & ROGERS, C. R. Taped interviews of Loretta. Listed: *American Academy of Psychotherapists newsletter,* 1963, 8 (2), 1963.

ENGLISH, H. B., & ENGLISH, AVA C. *A comprehensive dictionary of psychological and psychoanalytic terms.* New York: Longmans, Green, 1958.

FELDMAN, M. P., & MacCULLOCH, M. J. A systematic approach to the treatment of homosexuality by conditioned aversion: Preliminary report. *Amer. J. Psychiat.,* 1964, *121* (2), 167-171.

FREUD, S. *The future of an illusion.* New York: Liveright, 1953.

FREUD, S. The analysis of a phobia in a five-year-old boy. *Collected papers,* Vol. III. New York: Basic Books, 1959.

FULLER, P. R. Operant conditioning of a vegetative human organism. *Amer. J. Psychol.,* 1949, *62,* 587-590.

GREENSPOON, J. Verbal conditioning and clinical psychology. In A. J. Bachrach (Ed.), *Experimental foundations of clinical psychology.* New York: Basic Books, 1962. Pp. 510-553.

GROSSBERG, J. M. Behavior therapy: A review. *Psychol. Bull.,* 1964, *62* (2) 73-88.

GUERNEY, B., JR. Filial therapy. *J. consult. Psychol.,* 1964, *28* (4), 304-310.

HAAS, S. A study of a method of teaching Spanish utilizing selected electromechanical devices in the elementary school. *J. exp. Educ.,* 1964, *33* (1) 81-86.

HAMBURG, C. Logic and foreign policy. *J. Philos. and phenomenological Res.,* 1955, *15,* 493-499.

HARGREAVES, W. A., & STARKWEATHER, F. H. Voice quality in depression. *J. abnorm. Psychol.,* 1965, *70* (3), 218-220.

HEALD, F. Obesity in the adolescent. In L. T. Meiks and M. Green (Eds.), *Pediatric clinics of North America,* Vol. 7, No. 1. Philadelphia: W. B. Saunders, 1960. Pp. 207-220.

HESS, E. H., SLETZER, A. L., & SHLIEN, J. M. Pupil response of hetero- and homosexual males to pictures of men and women. *J. abnorm. Psychol.,* 1965, *70,* 165-168.

HILL, W. F. (Ed.) *Collected papers on group psychotherapy.* Provo, Utah: Utah State Hospital, 1961.

HILL, IDA, & HILL, W. F. *Hill and Hill interaction matrix.* Provo, Utah: Utah State Hospital, 1961.

HORNEY, KAREN, *Our inner conflicts.* New York: W. W. Norton, 1945.

ILLOVSKY, J. Experiences with group hypnosis on schizophrenics. *J. ment. Sci.,* 1962, *108,* 685-693.

ISAACS, W., THOMAS, J., & GOLDIAMOND, I. Application of operant conditioning to reinstate verbal behavior in psychotics. *J. Speech and Hearing Disorders,* 1960, 25, 8-12.

JACKSON, D. D., & WEAKLAND, J. H. Conjoint family therapy. *Psychiatry,* 1961, *24,* 30-45.

JOWETT, B. (Translator) *The dialogues of Plato.* New York: Random House, 1937.

KELLY, G. A. *The psychology of personal constructs,* Vol. II. New York: W. W. Norton, 1955.

KLOPFER, B., AINSWORTH, MARY D., KLOPFER, W. G., & HOLT, R. R. *Developments in the Rorschach technique,* Vol. I. New York: World Book, 1954.

KORZYBSKI, A. *Science and sanity.* Lancaster, Pa.: Science Press, 1941.

KRAMER, E. Judgment of personality characteristics and emotions from non-verbal properties of speech. *Psychol. Bull.,* 1963, *60,* 408-420.

KRAMER, E. Elimination of verbal cues in judgments of emotion from voice. *J. abnorm. soc. Psychol.,* 1964, Vol. 68, 390-397.

KRASNER, L. Behavior control and social responsibility. *Amer. Psychologist,* 1962, *17,* 199-204.

KROGER, W. S. *Clinical and experimental hypnosis.* Philadelphia: Lippincott, 1963.

LOVAAS, O. I. (chairman), PERLOFF, B., MEISEL, JOAN, KASSORLA, IRENE, SHEARMAN, R., & WHALEN, CAROL. Reinforcement theory approach to an experimental treatment program for childhood schizophrenias. Paper read at Western Psychol. Assoc. convention, Honolulu, 1965.

MACHOTKA, P. & SPIEGEL, J. P., *Presentation of the body in human communication.* Cambridge: Harvard University Press, 1966. (in press)

MATARAZZO, J. D., WIENS, A. N., SASLOW, G., ALLEN, BERNADENE V., & WEITMAN, M. Interviewer "mm-hmm" and interviewee speech durations. *Psychotherapy,* 1965, *1,* 109-114.

MEEHL, P. E. Schizotaxia, schizotypy, schizophrenia. *Amer. Psychologist,* 1962, *17* (12), 827-839.

MORENO, J. L. *Psychodrama.* New York: Beacon House, 1946.

NEILL, A. S. *Summerhill: A radical approach to child rearing.* New York: Hart Publishing Co., 1960.

NELSON, MARIE C. *Paradigmatic approaches to psychoanalysis: Four papers.* New York: Dept. of Psychology, Stuyvestant Polyclinic, 1962.

NIELSON, E. The use of volunteers in areas of sparsely distributed mental health workers. Unpublished manuscript. Granite School District, Salt Lake City, 1965. (a)

NIELSON, E. The use of volunteers to assist teachers of emotionally disturbed children. Unpublished manuscript. Granite School District, Salt Lake City, 1965. (b)

ORNE, M. T. The potential use of hypnosis in interrogation. In A. Biderman and H. Zimmer (Eds.), *The manipulation of human behavior.* New York: Wiley, 1961. Pp. 169-216.

OSGOOD, C. E. The psychologist in international affairs. *Amer. Psychologist,* 1964, *19,* 111-118.

PACKARD, V. O. *The hidden persuaders.* New York: David McKay Co., 1957.

PETERSON, D. R., & LONDON, P. A role for cognition in the behavioral treatment of a child's eliminative disturbance. In L. P. Ullman and L. Krasner (Eds.), *Case studies in behavior modification.* New York: Holt, 1965. Pp. 289-295.

RANK, O. *The trauma of birth.* New York: Harcourt, Brace, 1929.

REICH, W. *Character analysis.* New York: Orgone Institute Press, 1949.

REIK, T. *Listening with the third ear: The inner experience of a psycho-analyst.* New York: Farrar, Strauss, 1948.

RIOCH, MARGARET J., ELKES, CHARMAIN, & ARDEN, A. F. Pilot project in training mental health counselors. *P.H.S. Publications,* 1964, No. 1254.

ROGERS, C. R. *Counseling and psychotherapy.* Boston: Houghton Mifflin, 1942.

ROGERS, C. R. *Client centered therapy.* Boston: Houghton Mifflin, 1951.

ROGERS, C. R. *On becoming a person.* Boston: Houghton Mifflin, 1961.

ROGERS, J. M. Operant conditioning in a quasi-therapy setting. *J. abnorm. soc. Psychol.,* 1960, *60,* 247-252.

ROSENZWEIG, M. R., KRECH, D., BENNETT, E. L., & DIAMOND, MARIAN C. Effects of environmental complexity and training on brain chemistry and anatomy: A replication and extension. *J. comp. physiol. Psychol.,* 1962, *55* (4), 429-437.

SCHACHTER, S. Birth order and sociometric choice. *J. abnorm. soc. Psychol.,* 1964, *68* (4), 453-456.

SCHRAMM, W. *The research on programmed instruction: An annotated bibliography.* Washington, D.C.: U.S. Govt. Printing Office, No. FS5.-234:34034, 1964.

SEITZ, P. F. D. Symbolism and organ choice in conversion reactions: An experimental approach. *Psychosomatic Medicine,* 1951, *13* (4), 254-259.

SEITZ, P. F. D. Experiments in the substitution of symptoms by hypnosis: II. *Psychosomatic medicine,* 1953, *15* (5), 405-424.

SHAGASS, C., & SCHWARTZ, M. Visual cerebral evoked response characteristics in a psychiatric population. *Amer. J. Psychiat.,* 1965, *121* (10), 979-987.

SLACK, C. W. Experimenter subject psychotherapy: A new method of introducing office treatment in unreachable cases. *Ment. Hygiene,* 1960, *44,* 238-256.

SNYGG, D., & COMBS, A. *Individual behavior.* New York: Harper, 1949.

STARKWEATHER, J. A. Content-free speech as a source of information about the speaker. *J. abnorm. soc. Psychol.,* 1956, *52,* 394-402.

STARKWEATHER, J. A. Variations in vocal behavior. In *Disorders of Communication,* Vol. XLII. Research Publications, Assoc. Research Nerv. and Ment. Disease, 1964. Pp. 424-447.

STARKWEATHER, J. A., & DECKER, J. B. Computer analysis of interview content. *Psychol. Rep.,* 1964, *15,* 875-882.

STONE, P. J., BALES, R. F., NAMENWIRTH, J. Z., & OLGILVIE, P. M. The general inquirer: A computer system for content analysis and retrieval based on the sentence as a unit of information. *Behav. Sci.,* 1962, *7,* 1-15.

SULLIVAN, H. S. *The interpersonal theory of psychiatry.* New York: Norton, 1953.

SZASZ, T. S. *The myth of mental illness, foundations of a theory of personal conduct.* New York: Hoeber-Harper, 1961.

WATSON, G. Class lecture, Columbia University, New York, 1947.

TOPICAL REFERENCE LISTS

THE following four topical reference lists: "Research on Operant Conditioning," "Research on Non-verbal cues in Language," "Research on Outcomes of Psychotherapy" and "Models of Psychotherapy (annotated)" were selected to complement the discussions in the book. They were included here so that the student of psychotherapy interested in a more thorough acquaintance with these areas will find sources for additional reading.

No claim is made that these reference lists are all inclusive and represent the total efforts in the area, and this disclaimer is particularly true for the annotated bibliography on models of psychotherapy, which is highly selective and necessarily leaves out many noteworthy contributions. Yet, incomplete as it is, it represents the background material that was utilized in formulating the model presented in these pages. The thoughts formulated here incorporating, discussing or debating many of the contributions made by these authors owe a debt to them. So this bibliography too has been included to help the reader follow up on some of the references listed.

A. Reference List for Selected
Research in Operant Conditioning [7]

ADLER, P. T. The relationship of two types of dependency to the effectiveness of approval as a reinforcer among a group of emotionally disturbed children. *Dissert. Abstr.*, 1962, 23, 697.

ALLEN, K. EILEEN, HART, BETTY M., BUELL, JOAN S., HARRIS, FLORENCE R., & WOLF, M. M. Effects of social reinforcement on isolate behavior of a nursery school child. *Child Develpm.*, 1964, 35, 511-518.

AYLLON, T. Intensive treatment of psychotic behavior by stimulus satisfaction and food reinforcement. *Behav. res. Ther.*, 1963, 1, 53-61.

AYLLON, T., & AZRIN, N. H. Reinforcement and instructions with mental patients. *J. exp. anal. Behav.*, 1964, 7, 327-331.

AYLLON, T., & HAUGHTON, E. Control of the behavior of schizophrenic patients by food. *J. exp. anal. Behav.*, 1962, 5, 343-352.

7. Messrs. D. Miller, M. Rardin and I. Severtsen assisted with the gathering of these references.

AYLLON, T., & HAUGHTON, E. Modification of symptomatic verbal behavior of mental patients. *Behav. res. Ther.*, 1964, 2, 87-97.

AYLLON, T., HAUGHTON, E., & OSMOND, H. O. Chronic anorexia: a behavior problem. *Canad. psychiat. assoc. Journ.*, 1964, 9, 147-154.

AYLLON, T., & MICHAEL, J. The psychiatric nurse as a behavioral engineer. *J. exp. anal. Behav.*, 1959, 2, 323-334.

AZRIN, N. H., & LINDSLEY, O. R. The reinforcement of cooperation between children. *J. abnorm. soc. Psychol.*, 1956, 52, 100-102.

BACHRACH, A. J. Some applications of operant conditioning to behavior therapy. In J. Wolpe, A. Salter, & L. J. Reyna (Eds.), *The conditioning therapies.* New York: Holt, Rinehart & Winston, 1965. Pp. 62-78.

BACHRACH, A. J., ERWIN, W. J., & MOHR, J. P. The control of eating behavior in an anorexic by operant conditioning techniques. In L. P. Ullman & L. Krasner (Eds.), *Case studies in behavior modification.* New York: Holt, Rinehart & Winston, 1965. Pp. 153-163.

BAER, D. M. Laboratory control of thumbsucking by withdrawal and representation of reinforcement. *J. exp. anal. Beh.*, 1962, 5, 525-528.

BAER, D. M. A technique of social reinforcement for the study of child behavior: Behavior avoiding reinforcement withdrawal. *Child Development*, 1962, 33, 847-858.

BANDURA, A. Behavior modifications through modeling procedures. In L. Krasner & L. P. Ullman (Eds.), *Research in behavior modification.* New York: Holt, Rinehart, & Winston, 1965. Pp. 310-340.

BANDURA, A. Psychotherapy as a learning process. *Psychol. Bull.*, 1961, 58, 143-157.

BANDURA, A., LIPSHER, D. H., & MILLER, PAULA E. Psychotherapists' approach-avoidance reactions to patients' expressions of hostility. *J. consult. Psychol.*, 1960, 24, 1-8.

BANDURA, A., & WALTERS, R. H. *Adolescent aggression.* New York: Ronald Press, 1959.

BANDURA, A., & WALTERS, R. H. *Social learning and personality development.* New York: Holt, Rinehart & Winston, 1963.

BARRETT, B. H. Reduction in rate of multiple tics by free operant conditioning methods. In L. P. Ullman & L. Krasner (Eds.), *Case studies in behavior modification.* New York: Holt, Rinehart, & Winston, 1965. Pp. 225-263.

BARRETT, BEATRICE H., & LINDSLEY, O. R. Deficits in acquisition of operant discrimination and differentiation shown by institutionalized retarded children. *Amer. J. ment. Defic.*, 1962, 67 (3), 424-436.

BIJOU, S. W. Experimental studies of child behavior, normal and deviant. In L. Krasner & L. P. Ullman (Eds.), *Research in behavior modification.* New York: Holt, Rinehart & Winston, 1965. Pp. 56-81.

BRADY, J. P., & LIND, D. L. Experimental analysis of hysterical blindness. *AMA Arch. gen. Psychiat.*, 1961, 4, 331-339.

BREGER, L., & McGAUGH, J. L. Critique and reformation of "learning theory" approaches to psychotherapy and neurosis. *Psychol. Bull.*, 1965, 63 (5), 338-358.

CHAPMAN, L. F., & WOLFF, H. G. The cerebral hemispheres and the highest integrative functions of men. *Arch. Neurol.*, 1959, 1, 19-82.

ELLIS, N. R., BARNETT, C. D., & PRYER, MARGARET W. Operant behavior in mental defectives: Exploratory studies. *J. exp. anal. Behav.*, 1960, 3, 63-69.

EPSTEIN, R. J. Need for approval and the conditioning of verbal hostility in asthmatic children. *J. abnorm. soc. Psychol.*, 1964, *1*, 105-109.

EYSENCK, H. J. The development of moral values in children: VII. The contribution of learning theory. *Brit. J. educ. Psychol.*, 1960, *30*, 11-21.

FERSTER, C. B., & DEMYER, M. K. A method for the experimental analysis of the behavior of autistic children. *Amer. J. Orthopsychiat.*, 1962, *32*, 89-98.

FLANAGAN, B., GOLDIAMOND, J., & AZRIN, N. H. Operant stuttering: the control of stuttering behavior through response-contingent consequences. *J. exp. anal. Behav.*, 1958, *1*, 173-178.

FLANAGAN, B., GOLDIAMOND, I., & AZRIN, N. H. Instatement of stuttering in normally fluent individuals through operant procedures. *Science*, 1959, *130*, 979-981.

FREDERICK, C. J. Group psychotherapist or group discussant? Paper read at 6th Int. Congr. of Psychother., London, August, 1964.

GROSSBERG, J. M. *Behavior therapy in a case of speech phobia ("stage fright")*. Technical Report No. 3, Grant RD-892P-63.Washington, D.C.: United States Department of Health, Education, and Welfare, Vocational Rehabilitation Administration, 1963.

GROSSBERG, J. M. Behavior therapy: A review. *Psychol. Bull.*, 1964, *62* (2), 73-88.

HARRIS, FLORENCE R., JOHNSTON, MARGARET K., KELLEY, C. SUSAN, & WOLF, M. M. Effects of positive social reinforcement on regressed crawling of a nursery school child. *J. educ. Psychol.*, 1964, *55*, 35-41.

HART, BETTY M., ALLEN, K. EILEEN, BUELL, JOAN S., HARRIS, FLORENCE R., & WOLF, M. M. Effects of social reinforcement on operant crying. *J. exp. child Psychol.*, 1964, *1*, 145-153.

HASTORF, A. H. The "reinforcement" of individual actions in a group situation. In L. Krasner & L. P. Ullman (Eds.), *Research in behavior modification*. New York: Holt, Rinehart & Winston, 1965. Pp. 268-284.

HAUGHTON, E., & AYLLON, T. Production and elimination of symptomatic behavior. In L. P. Ullman & L. Krasner (Eds.), *Case studies in behavior modification*. New York: Holt, Rinehart & Winston, 1965.

HINGTGEN, J. N., SANDERS, BEVERLY J., & DEMEYER, MARION K. Shaping cooperative responses in early childhood schizophrenics. In L. P. Ullman & L. Krasner (Eds.), *Case studies in behavior modification*. New York: Holt, Rinehart & Winston, 1965. Pp. 130-137.

ISSACS, W., THOMAS, J., & GOLDIAMOND, I. Application of operant conditioning to reinstate verbal behavior in psychotics. *J. speech hear. Disord.*, 1960, *25*, 8-12.

JONES, H. G. The behavior treatment of enuresis nocturna. In H. J. Eysenck (Ed.), *Behavior therapy and the neuroses*. New York: Pergamon Press, 1960. Pp. 377-403.

KING, G. F. Merrell, D. W., Lovinger, E., & Denny, N. R. Operant motor behavior in acute schizophrenia. *J. Pers.*, 1957, *25*, 317-326.

KING, G. F., ARMITAGE, S. G., & TILTON, J. R. A therapeutic approach to schizophrenics of extreme pathology. *J. abnorm. soc. Psychol.*, 1960, *61*, 276-286.

KRUTCH, J. W. Calipers on the human mind. *Saturday Review*, June 19, 1965.

KRASNER, L. Verbal conditioning and psychotherapy. In L. Krasner & L. P. Ullman (Eds.), *Research in behavior modification*. New York: Holt, Rinehart & Winston, 1965, Pp. 211-228.

KRASNER, L., & ULLMAN, L. P. (Eds.) *Research in behavior modification*. New York: Holt, Rinehart & Winston, 1965.

LANG, P. J., & LAZOVIK, A. D. Experimental desensitization of a phobia. *J. abnorm. soc. Psychol.*, 1963, *66*, 519-525.

LAZARUS, A. A., DAVISON, G. C., & POLEFKA, D. A. Classical and operant factors in the treatment of school phobia. *J. abnorm. Psychol.*, 1965, *70* (3), 225-229.

LINDSLEY, O. R. Operant conditioning methods applied to research in chronic schizophrenia. *Psychiat. res. Rept.*, 1965, 5, 118-139.

LINDSLEY, O. R. Characteristics of the behavior of chronic psychotics as revealed by free-operant conditioning methods. *Dis. of nerv. System*, 1960, *21* (Monogr. Supp. #2), 66-78.

LINDSLEY, O. R. Direct measurement and functional definition of vocal hallucinatory symptoms. *J. nerv. ment. Dis.*, 1963, *136*, 293-297.

LINDSLEY, O. R. Geriatric behavioral prosthetics. In R. Kastenbaum (Ed.), *New thoughts on old age*. New York: Springer, 1964. Pp. 41-60.

LINDSLEY, O. R., & SKINNER, B. F. A method for the experimental analyses of the behavior of psychotic patients. *Amer. Psychologist*, 1954, *9*, 419-442.

LOVAAS, O. I., FREITAG, G., GOLD, VIVIAN J., & KASSORLA, IRENE C. Experimental studies in childhood schizophrenia: Analysis of self-destructive behavior. *J. exp. child Psychol.*, 1965, *2* (1), 67-84.

MICHAEL, J., & MEYERSON, L. A. A behavioral approach to counseling guidance. *Harv. educ. Rev.*, 1962, *32*, 382-402.

MISHLER, K. B. Of people and pigeons. *SK&F Psychiatric Reporter*, July 1964, No. 15.

NEALE, D. H. Behavior therapy and encopresis in children. *Beh. Res. Ther.*, 1963, *1*, 139-149.

NELSON, H. UCLA breaks barriers of children's isolation. *Los Angeles Times*, January 10, 1965 (Sec. H, p. 7).

ORLANDO, R., & BIJOU, S. W. Single and multiple schedules of reinforcement in developmentally retarded children. *J. exp. anal. Behav.*, 1960, 3, 339-348.

PATTERSON, G. R. A learning theory approach to the treatment of the school phobic child. In L. P. Ullmann & L. Krasner (Eds.), *Case studies in behavior modification*. New York: Holt, Rinehart & Winston, 1965. (a)

PATTERSON, G. R. An application of conditioning techniques to the control of a hyperactive child. In L. P. Ullman and L. Krasner (Eds.), *Case studies in behavior modification*. New York: Holt, Rinehart & Winston, 1965. Pp. 370-375. (b)

PATTERSON, G. R. Responsiveness to social stimuli. In L. Krasner & L. P. Ullman (Eds.), *Research in behavior modification*. New York: Holt, Rinehart & Winston, 1965. Pp. 157-178. (c)

PETERS, H. N., & JENKINS, R. L. Improvements of chronic schizophrenic patients with guided problem-solving, motivated by hunger. *Psychiat. quart. Suppl.*, 1954, 28, 84-101.

PETERSON, D. R., & LONDON, P. A role for cognition in the behavioral treatment of a child's eliminative disturbance. In L. P. Ullman & L. Krasner (Eds.), *Case studies in behavior modification.* New York: Holt, Rinehart & Winston, 1965. Pp. 289-294.

REYNA, L. J. Conditioning therapies, learning and research. In J. Wolpe, A. Salter, & L. J. Reyna (Eds.), *The conditioning therapies.* New York: Holt, Rinehart & Winston, 1965. Pp. 169-179.

RICKARD, H. C., DIGNAN, P. J., & HORNER, R. F. Verbal manipulation in a psychotherapeutic relationship. *J. clin. Psychol.*, 1960, 16, 364-367.

RICKARD, H. C., & DINOFF, M. A follow-up note on "verbal manipulation in a psychotherapeutic relationship." In L. P. Ullman & L. Krasner (Eds.), *Case studies in behavior modification.* New York: Holt, Rinehart & Winston, 1965.

ROGERS, J. M. Operant conditioning in a quasi-therapy setting. *J. abnorm. soc. Psychol.*, 1960, 60, 247-252.

SALZINGER, K., FELDMAN, T., COWAN, JUDITH E., & SALZINGER, SUZANNE. Operant conditioning of verbal behavior of two young speech deficient boys. In L. Krasner & L. P. Ullman (Eds.), *Research in behavior modification.* New York: Holt, Rinehart & Winston, 1965. Pp. 82-105.

SALZINGER, K., & PISONI, STEPHANIE. Reinforcement of affect responses of schizophrenics during the clinical interview. *J. abnorm. soc. Psychol.*, 1958, 57, 84-90.

SALZINGER, K., & PISONI, STEPHANIE. Some parameters of the conditioning of verbal affect responses in schizophrenic subjects. *J. abnorm. soc. Psychol.*, 1961, 63, 511-516.

SASLOW, G. A case history of attemped behavior manipulation in a psychiatric ward. In L. Krasner & L. P. Ullman (Eds.), *Research in behavior modification.* New York: Holt, Rinehart & Winston, 1965. Pp. 211-228.

SHERMAN, J. A. Reinstatement of verbal behavior in a psychotic by reinforcement methods. *J. speech hear. Disord.*, 1963, 28, 398-401.

SHERMAN, J. A. Use of reinforcement and imitation to reinstate verbal behavior in mute psychotics. *J. abnorm. soc. Psychol.*, 1965, 70 (3), 155-164.

SIDMAN, M. *Tactics of scientific research: evaluating experimental data in psychology.* New York: Basic Books, 1960.

SINGER, ESTELLE, BLANE, H. T., & KASSCHAU, R. Alcoholism and social isolation. *J. abnorm. soc. Psychol.*, 1964, 69, 681-685.

SKINNER, B. F. *Science and human behavior.* New York: Macmillan, 1953.

SLACK, C. W. Experimenter-subject psychotherapy: a new method of introducing office treatment of unreachable cases. *Ment. Hygiene*, 1960, 44, 238-256.

SOMMER, R., GWYNNETH, WITNEY, & ASMOND, H. Teaching common association to schizophrenics. *J. abnorm. soc. Psychol.*, 1962, 65, 58-61.

SPRADLIN, J. E. Effects of reinforcement schedules on extinction in severely mentally retarded children. *Amer. J. ment. Defic.*, 1962, 66, 634-640.

SWENSON, E. W. The effect of instruction and reinforcement on the behavior of the geriatric psychiatric patients. Unpublished doctoral dissertation, Univ. of Utah, 1965.

THOMPSON, G. N., & BIELINSKI, B. Improvement in psychosis following conditioned reflex treatment in alcoholism. *J. nerv ment. Disord.*, 1953, *117*, 537-543.

ULLMAN, L. P., & KRASNER, L. *Case studies in behavior modification*. New York: Holt, Rinehart & Winston, 1965.

ULLMAN, L. P., KRASNER, L., & COLLINS, BEVERLY J. Modification of behavior through verbal conditioning: effects in group therapy. *J. abnorm. soc. Psychol.*, 1961, *62*, 128-132.

ULLMAN, L. P., KRASNER, L., & EDINGER, R. Verbal conditioning of common associations in long-term schizophrenic patients. *Behav. res. Ther.*, 1964, *2*, 15-18.

WEISS, R., KRASNER, L., & ULLMAN, L. P. Responsivity of psychiatric patients to verbal conditioning: "success" and "failure" conditions and patterns of reinforced trials. *Psychol. Rep.*, 1963, *12*, 423-426.

WILLIAMS, C. D. The elimination of tantrum behavior by extinction procedures. *J. abnorm. soc. Psychol.*, 1957, *59*, 269.

WOLF, M. M., RISLEY, T. R., & MEES, H. I. Application of operant conditioning procedures to the behavior problems of the autistic child. *Beh. Res. Ther.*, 1964, *1*, 305-312.

WOLPE, J. *Psychotherapy by reciprocal inhibition*. Stanford, Calif.: Stanford Univ. Press, 1958.

WOLPE, J. Reciprocal inhibition as the main basis of psychotherapeutic effects. In H. J. Eysenck (Ed.), *Behavior therapy and the neuroses*. New York: Pergamon Press, 1960. Pp. 88-113.

WOLPE, J. Isolation of a conditioning procedure as the crucial psychotherapeutic factor: A case study. *J. nerv. ment. Disord.*, 1962, *134*, 316-329.

WOLPE, J., SALTER, A., & REYNA, L. J. *The conditioning therapies*. New York: Holt, Rinehart & Winston, 1964.

YATES, A. J. The application of learning theory to the treatment of tics. *J. abnorm. soc. Psychol.*, 1958, *56*, 175-182.

ZIMMERMAN, ELAINE H., & ZIMMERMAN, J. The alteration of behavior in a special classroom situation. *J. exp. anal. Beh.*, 1962, *5*, 59-60.

B. Research on Non-verbal Cues in Language

ALLPORT, G., & CANTRIL, H. Judging personality from the voice. *J. soc. Psychol.*, 1934, *5*, 37-55.

AUNGST, L. F., & FRICK, J. V. Auditory discrimination ability and consistency of articulation of /r/. *J. Speech Hear. Dis.*, 1964, *29* (1), 76-85.

BERNSTEIN, B. Linguistic codes, hesitation phenomena, and intelligence. *Language & Speech*, 1962, *5* (1), 31-46.

BLACK, J. W., & DREHER, T. Non-verbal messages in voice communication. *USN Sch. Aviat. Med. Res. Rep.*, 1955, No. NM001, 104,500.45.

BOWERS, J. W. Language intensity, social introversion, and attitude change. *Sp. Monogr.*, 1963, *30*, 345-353.

CANTRIL, H., & ALLPORT, G. W. *The psychology of radio*. New York: Harper & Bros., 1935.

CASTELNOVA, A. E., TIEDEMANN, J. G., & SKORDAHL, D. M. Individual differences in transcribing voice radio messages embedded in atmospheric noise. *USAPRO Tech. Res. Note*, No. 137, 1963.

COHEN, A. Estimating the degree of schizophrenic pathology from recorded interview samples. *J. clin. Psychol.*, 1961, *17*, 403-406.

COMPTON, A. J. Effects of filtering and vocal duration upon the identification of speakers, aurally. *J. acoust. soc. Amer.*, 1963, *35*, 1748-1752.

DAVITZ, J. R. Social perception and sociometric choice of children. *J. abnorm. soc. Psychol.*, 1955, *50*, 173-177.

DAVITZ, J. R., & DAVITZ, L. J. Correlates of accuracy in the communication of feelings. *J. Comm.*, 1959, *9*, 110-117.

DAVITZ, J. R., & DAVITZ, L. J. The communication of feelings by content-free speech. *J. Comm.*, 1959, *9*, 6-13.

DIMITROVSKY, LILLY S. The ability to identify the emotional meaning of vocal expressions at successive age levels. *Dissert. Abstr.*, 1964, *24*, 2983-2984.

DITTMAN, A. T., & WYNNE, L. C. Linguistic techniques and the analysis of emotionality in interviews. *J. abnorm. soc. Psychol.*, 1961, *63*, 201-204.

DUNCAN, M. H. An experimental study of some of the relationships between voice and personality among students of speech. *Sp. Monogr.*, 1945, *12*, 47-61.

DUSENBURY, D., & KNOWER, F. H. Experimental studies of the symbolism of action and voice. II. A study of the specificity of meaning in the abstract tonal symbols. *Quart. J. Speech*, 1939, *25*, 67-75

EISENBERG, P., & ZALOWITZ, E. Judging expressive movements. III. Judgments of dominance-feeling from phonograph rcords of voice. *J. appl. Psychol.*, 1938, *22*, 620-631.

FAIRBANKS, G., & HOAGLIN, I. W. An experimental study of the durational characteristics of the voice during the expression of emotion. *Sp. Monogr.*, 1941, *8*, 85-90.

FAY, P. J., & MIDDLETON, W. C. Judgments of occupation from the voice as transmitted over a public address system and over a radio. *J. appl. Psychol.*, 1939, *23*, 586-601.

FAY, P. J., & MIDDLETON, W. C. Judgments of Spranger personality types from the voice as transmitted over a public address system. *Character and Personality*, 1939, *8*, 144-145.

FAY, P. J., & MIDDLETON, W. C. Judgment of intelligence from the voice as transmitted over a public address system. *Sociometry*, 1940, *3*, 186-191.

FAY, P. J., & MIDDLETON, W. C. Judgment of Kretchmerian body types from the voice as transmitted over a public address system. *J. soc. Psychol.*, 1940, *12*, 151-162.

FAY, P. J., & MIDDLETON, W. C. The ability to judge the rested or tired condition of a speaker from his voice as transmitted over a public address system. *J. appl. Psychol.*, 1940, *24*, 645-650.

FAY, P. J., & MIDDLETON, W. C. The ability to judge sociability from the voice as transmitted over a public address system. *J. soc. Psychol.*, 1941, *13*, 303-309.

FAY, P. J., & MIDDLETON, W. C. The ability to judge truth-telling or lying from the voice as transmitted over a public address system. *J. gen Psychol.*, 1941, *24*, 211-215.

FAY, P. J., & MIDDLETON, W. C. Judgment of introversion from the transcribed voice. *Quart. J. Speech*, 1942, *28*, 226-228.

FAY, P. J., & MIDDLETON, W. C. Judgment of leadership from transmitted voice. *J. soc. Psychol.*, 1943, *17*, 99-102.

GOLDFARB, W., BRAUNSTEIN, P., & LORGE, I. A study of speech patterns in a group of schizophrenic children. *Am. J. Orthopsychiat.*, 1956, *26*, 544-555.

GOTTSCHALK, L. A., GLASSER, G. G., & HAMBRIDGE, G. Verbal behavior analysis: Some content and form variables in speech relevant to personality adjustment. *AMA Arch. Neurol. & Psychiat.*, 1957, *77*, 300-311.

GRIGG, A. E. Experience of clinicians, and speech characteristics and statements of clients as variables in clinical judgment. *J. consult. Psychol.*, 1958, *22*, 515-519.

HARGREAVES, W. A., & STARKWEATHER, J. A. Vocal behavior: An illustrative case study. Paper read at Western Psychol. Assoc., Seattle, June, 1961.

HARMS, L. S. Listener comprehension of speakers of 3 status groups. *Lang. Speech*, 1961, *4*, 109-112.

HOBERMAN, S. Z., & GOLDFARB, W. Speech reception thresholds in schizophrenic children. *J. Sp. Hear. Res.*, 1963, *6*, 101-105.

INNES, G., MILLAR, W. M., & VALENTINE, M. Emotion and blood pressure. *J. Ment. Sci.*, 1959, *105*, 840-851.

ISAAC, D. M. The relationship of personality factors to some aspects of verbal behavior. *Dissert. Abstr.*, 1964, *24*, 2985.

KAUFFMAN, P. E. An investigation of some psychological stimulus properties of speech behavior. Unpublished doctoral dissertation, Univ. of Chicago., 1954.

KNOWER, F. H. Analysis of some experimental variations of simulated verbal expressions. *J. soc. Psychol.*, 1941, *14*, 369-372.

KRAMER, E. Elimination of verbal cues in judgments of emotion from voice. *J. abnorm. soc. Psychol.*, 1964, *68*, 390-397.

KRAMER, E. Personality stereotypes in voice: A reconsideration of the data. *J. soc. Psychol.*, 1964, *62*, 247-251.

LAFFAL, J., LENKOSKI, L. D., & AMEAN, L. Opposite speech in a schizophrenic patient. *J. abnorm. soc. Psychol.*, 1956, *52*, 409-413.

LEVILL, E. A. The relationship between vocal and facial emotional communicative abilities. *Dissert. Abstr.*, 1962, *23*, 1783.

LEVY, P. A. K. The relationship between the ability to express and to perceive vocal communications of feeling. *Dissert. Abstr.*, 1962, *22*, 4082-4083.

LIFT, J. Differences in prediction based on hearing versus reading verbatim clinical interviews. *J. consult. Psychol.*, 1951, *15*, 115-119.

LYNCH, G. A. A phonographic study of trained and untrained voices reading factual and dramatic material. *Arch. Speech*, 1934, *1*, 9-25.

MABRY, MARIE. Language characteristics of scattered and nonscattered schizophrenics compared with normals. *J. Psychol.*, 1964, *57*, 29-40.

MALLORY, E., & MILLER, V. A. A possible basis for the association of voice characteristics and personality traits. *Sp. Monogr.*, 1958, *25*, 255-260.

MERKEL, N. N., MEISELS, M., & HOUCK, J. E. Judging personality from voice quality. *J. abnorm. soc. Psychol.*, 1964,*4*, 458-463.

MOORE, W. E. Personality traits and voice quality deficiencies. *J. Sp. Hear. Dis.*, 1939, *4*, 33-36.

ORTLEB, R. An objective study of emphasis in oral reading of emotional and unemotional material. *Sp. Monogr.*, 1937, *4*, 56-69.

OSTWALD, P. F. A method for the objective denotation of sound of the human voice. *J. Psychosom. Res.*, 1960, *4*, 301-305.

OSTWALD, P. F. *Soundmaking: the acoustic communication of emotion.* Springfield, Ill.: Charles C Thomas, 1963.

PEAR, T. H. *Voice and personality.* London: Chapman & Hall, 1931.

PFAFF, P. L. An experimental study of communication of feelings without contextual material. *Sp. Monogr.*, 1954, *21*, 155-156.

POPE, B., & SIEGMAN, A. W. An intercorrelational study of some indices of verbal fluency. *Psychol. Rep.*, 1964, *15*, 303-310.

POLLACK, I., RUBENSTEIN, H., & HOROWITZ, A. Recognition of "verbal expression" over communications systems. Paper delivered at the 59th meeting of the Acoustical Soc. of America, 1960.

RAMM, K. Is monotonism an indication of maladjustment? *Smith Coll. Stud. Soc. Wk.*, 1947, *17*, 264-284.

RUESCH, J., & PRESTWOOD, A. K. Anxiety: Its initiation, communication and interpersonal management. *AMA Arch. Neurol. Psychiat.*, 1949, *62*, 527-550.

SAUER, R. E., & MARCUSE, F. L. Overt and covert recording. *J. Proj. Tech.*, 1947, *21*, 391-395.

SKINNER, E. R. A calibrated recording and analysis of the pitch, force and quality of vocal tones expressing happiness and sadness. *Sp. Monogr.*, 1935, *2*, 81-137.

SOSKIN, W. F. Some aspects of communication and interpretation in psychotherapy. Paper read at American Psychol. Assoc., Cleveland, September, 1953.

SPILKA, B., HANLEY, T. D., & STEER, M. D. Personality traits and speaking intelligibility. *J. abnorm. soc. Psychol.*, 1953, *48*, 593-595.

STAGNER, R. Judgments of voice and personality. *J. educ. Psychol.*, 1936, *27*, 272-275.

STARKWEATHER, J. A. Content-free speech as a source of information about the speaker. *J. abnorm. soc. Psychol.*, 1956, *52*, 394-402.

STARKWEATHER, J. A. The communication value of content-free speech. *Am. J. Psychol.*, 1956, *69*, 121-123.

STARKWEATHER, J. A. Vocal behavior: The duration of speech units. *Language and Speech*, 1959, *2*, 146-153.

TAYLOR, H. C. Social agreement on personality traits as judged from speech. *J. soc. Psychol.*, 1934, *5*, 244-248.

THOMPSON, C. W., & BRADWAY, K. The teaching of psychotherapy through content-free interviews. *J. consult. Psychol.*, 1950, *14*, 321-324.

THOMPSON, DIANA F., & MELTZER, L. Communication of emotional intent by facial expression. *J. abnorm. soc. Psychol.*, 1964, *68*, 129-135.

298 : *Topical Reference Lists*

VOIEERS, W. D. Perceptual bases of speaker identity. *J. Acoust. Soc. Amer.*, 1964, *36*, 1065-1073.
WEISS, I. H. Phonetic symbolism re-examined. *Psychol. Bull.*, 1964, *61*, 454-458.
WOLFF, W. *The expression of personality.* New York: Harper, 1943.

C. Research on Outcomes of Psychotherapy [8]

ALLPORT, G. W. Foreword. In E. Powers & Helen Witmer, *An experiment in the prevention of delinquency.* New York: Columbia Univ. Press, 1951.
ASSUM, A. L., & LEVY, S. J. Analysis of a non-directive case with follow-up interview. *J. abnorm. soc. Psychol.*, 1948, *43*, 78-89.
ASTIN, A. W. The functional autonomy of psychotherapy, *Amer. Psychol.*, 1961, *16*, 75-78.
AULD, F., JR., & MURRAY, E. J. Content-analysis studies of psychotherapy. *Psychol. Bull.*, 1955, 52, 377-395.
BALES, R. F. *Interaction process analysis.* Cambridge, Mass.: Addison-Wesley, 1950.
BANDURA, A. Psychotherapy as a learning process. *Psychol. Bull.*, 1961, *58*, 143-159.
BANDURA, A. *Behavioristic psychotherapy.* New York: Holt, Rinehart & Winston, 1964.
BANDURA, A., & WALTERS, R. H. *Social learning and personality development.* New York: Holt, Rinehart & Winston, 1963. Pp. 224-259.
BARRON, F. B., & LEARY, T. F. Changes in psychoneurotic patients with and without psychotherapy. *J. consult. Psychol.*, 1955, *19*, 239-245.
BELLIN, H. The prediction of adjustment over a four-year interval. *J. clin. Psychol.*, 1957, *13*, 270-274.
BERDIE, R. F. Changes in self-rating as a method of evaluating counseling. *J. counsel. Psychol.*, 1954, *1*, 49-54.
BERG, I. A. Measures before and after therapy. *J. clin. Psychol.*, 1952, *8*, 46-50.
BERGIN, A. E. The effects of psychotherapy: negative results revisited. *J. counsel. Psychol.*, 1963, *10*, 244-250.
BINDRA, D. Psychotherapy and the recovery from neuroses. *J. abnorm. soc. Psychol.*, 1956, *53*, 251-254.
BLOCK, J., & THOMAS, H. Is satisfaction with self a measure of adjustment? *J. abnorm. soc. Psychol.*, 1955, *51*, 254-259.
BORDIN, E. S., CUTLER, R. L., DITTMAN, A. T., HARWAY, N. I., RAUSH, N. L., & RIGLER, D. Measurement problems in process research on psychotherapy. *J. consult. Psychol.*, 1954, *18*, 79-82.
BORGATTA, E. F., & COTTRELL, L. A., JR. Control-group experimentation in psychotherapy. *Psychiat.*, 1959, *22*, 97-100.
BRADY, J. P., REZNIKOFF, M., & ZELLER, W. W. The relationship of expectation of improvement to actual improvement of hospitalized psychiatric patients. *J. nerv. ment. Dis.*, 1960, *130*, 41-44.

8. Messrs. D. Boutin, S. Donoviel, J. Grundvig and P. Sartoris assisted with the gathering of these references.

BRILL, N. Q., & STORROW, H. A. Social class and psychiatric treatment. *Arch. gen. Psychiat.*, 1960, *3*, 340-344.

BUTLER, J. M., & HAIGH, G. V. Changes in the relation between self-concepts and ideal concepts consequent upon client-centered counseling. In C. R. Rogers & Rosalind F. Dymond (Eds.), *Psychotherapy and personality change*. Chicago: Univ. of Chicago Press, 1954. Pp. 55-75.

CALVIN, A. D. Some mis-uses of the experimental method in evaluating the effect of client-centered counseling. *J. counsel. Psychol.*, 1954, *1*, 249-251.

CAMPBELL, D. T. Factors relevant to the validity of experiments in social settings. *Psychol. Bull.*, 1957, *54*, 297-313.

CARTWRIGHT, D. S. Effectiveness of psychotherapy: a critique of the spontaneous remission argument. *J. counsel. Psychol.*, 1955, *2*, 290-296.

CARTWRIGHT, D. S. Note on "changes in psychoneurotic patients with and without psychotherapy." *J. consult. Psychol.*, 1956, *20*, 403-404.

CARTWRIGHT, ROSALIND D. Effects of psychotherapy on self-consistency. *J. counsel. Psychol.*, 1957, *4*, 15-22.

CARTWRIGHT, ROSALIND D. The effects of psychotherapy on self-consistency: A replication and extension. *J. consult. Psychol.*, 1961, *25*, 376-382.

CARTWRIGHT, ROSALIND D., & VOGEL, J. L. A comparison of changes in psycho-neurotic patients during matched periods of therapy and no therapy. *J. consult. Psychol.*, 1960, *24*, 121-127.

CHANCE, ERIKA. *Families in treatment*. New York: Basic Books, 1959.

COLBY, K. M. Psychotherapeutic processes. *Annu. Rev. Psychol.*, 1964, *15*, 347-370.

COMBS, A. W. Follow-up of a counseling case treatment by the non-directive method. *J. clin. Psychol.*, 1945, *1*, 147-154.

CROSS, H. J. The outcome of psychotherapy: a selected analysis of research findings. *J. consult. Psychol.*, 1964, *28*, 413-417.

DECHARMS, R., LEVY, J., & WORTHEIMER, M. A note on attempted evaluations of psychotherapy. *J. clin. Psychol.*, 1954, *10*, 233-235.

DENKER, P. G. Results of treatment of psychoneurosis by the general practioner. A follow-up study of 500 cases. *New York State J. Med.*, 1946, *46*, 2164-2166.

DIMASCIO, A., & BROOKS, G. Free association to a fantasied psychotherapist. *Arch. gen. Psychiat.*, 1961, *4*, 513-516.

DREVER, J. *A dictionary of psychology*. Middlesex, Eng.: Penguin, 1956.

DYMOND, ROSALIND F. Adjustment changes over therapy from self-sorts. In C. R. Rogers & Rosalind F. Dymond (Eds.), *Psychotherapy and personality change*. Chicago: Univ. of Chicago Press, 1954.

ELLIS, A. Outcome of employing three techniques of psychotherapy. *J. clin. Psychol.*, 1957, *13*, 344-350.

ENDLER, N. S. Changes in meaning during psychotherapy as measured by the semantic differential. *J. counsel. Psychol.*, 1961, *8*, 105-111.

ENGLISH, H. B., & ENGLISH, AVA C. *A comprehensive dictionary of psychological and psychoanalytical terms*. New York: Longmans, Green, 1958.

EYSENCK, H. J. The effects of psychotherapy: an evaluation. *J. consult. Psychol.*, 1952, *16*, 319-324.

EYSENCK, H. J. The effects of psychotherapy: a reply. *J. abnorm, soc. Psychol.*, 1955, *50*, 147-148.

EYSENCK, H. J. *The dynamics of anxiety and hysteria.* London: Routledge & Kegan Paul, 1957.

EYSENCK, H. J. Learning theory and behavior therapy. *J. ment. Sci.,* 1959, *105,* 61-75.

EYSENCK, H. J. *Behavior therapy and the neuroses.* New York: Pergamon Press, 1960.

EYSENCK, H. J. The effects of psychotherapy. In H. J. Eysenck (ed.), *Handbook of abnormal psychology.* New York: Basic Books, 1961. Pp. 697-715.

FAIRWEATHER, G. W., & SIMON, R. A further follow-up comparison of psychotherapeutic programs. *J. consult. Psychol.,* 1963, *27,* 186.

FAIRWEATHER, G. W., SIMON, R., GEBHARD, M. E., WEINGARTEN, E., HOLLAND, J. L., SANDERS, R., STONE, B. G., & HEAHL, J. E. Relative effectiveness of psychotherapeutic programs: A multicriteria comparison of four programs for three different patient groups. *Psychol, Monogr.,* 1960, *74,* (Whole No. 5).

FEIFEL, H., & EELLS, JANET. Patients and therapists assess the same psychotherapy. *J. consult. Psychol.,* 1963, *27,* 310-318.

FIEDLER, F. E. A comparison of therapeutic relationships in psychoanalytic, nondirective, and Adlerian therapy. *J. consult. Psychol.,* 1950, *14,* 436-445.

FIEDLER, F. E. Factor analyses of psychoanalytic, nondirective, and Adlerian therapeutic relationships. *J. consult. Psychol.,* 1951, *15,* 32-38.

FORGY, E. W., & BLACK, J. D. A follow-up after three years of clients counseled by two methods. *J. counsel. Psychol.,* 1954, *1,* 1-8.

FORD, D. H. Research approaches to psychotherapy. *J. counsel. Psychol.,* 1959, *6,* 55-60.

FORSYTH, R. P., & FAIRWEATHER, G. W. Psychotherapeutic and other hospital treatment criteria: the dilemma. *J. abnorm. soc. Psychol.,* 1961, *62,* 598-605.

FRANK, J. D. Problem of controls in psychotherapy, as exemplified by the psychotherapy research project of the Phipps Psychiatric Clinic. In E. A. Rubinstein & M. B. Parloff (Eds.), *Research in psychotherapy.* Washington, D. C.: American Psychol. Ass., 1959. Pp. 10-26.

FRIESS, C., & NELSON, M. J. Psychoneurotics five years later. *Amer. J. med. Sci.,* 1942, *203,* 539-558.

GALLAGHER, J. J. Manifest anxiety changes concomitant with client-centered therapy. *J. consult. Psychol.,* 1953, *17,* 443-446.

GARDNER, G. GAIL. The psychotherapeutic relationship. *Psychol. Bull.,* 1964, *61,* 426-437.

GARFIELD, S. L., & KURZ, M. Evaluation of treatment and related procedures in 1216 cases referred to a mental hygiene clinic. *Psychiat. Quart.,* 1952, *26,* 414-424.

GOLDSTEIN, A. P. Patient's expectancies and non-specific therapy as a basis for (un)spontaneous remission. *J. clin. Psychol.,* 1960, *16,* 339-403.

GORDON, T., GRUMMON, D. L., ROGERS, C. R., & SEEMAN, J. Developing a program of research in psychotherapy. In Rogers, C. R., & Dymond, Rosalind F. (Eds.), *Psychotherapy and personality change.* Chicago: Univ. of Chicago Press, 1954. Pp. 12-34.

GROSSBERG, J. M. Behavior therapy: a review. *Psychol. Bull.*, 1964, *62*, 73-88.

GRUMMON, D. L. Design, procedures, and subjects for the first block. In C. R. Rogers & Rosalind F. Dymond (Eds.), *Psychotherapy and personality change*. Chicago: Univ. of Chicago Press, 1954. Pp. 35-52.

GRUMMON, D. L. Personality changes as a function of time in persons motivated for therapy. In Rogers, C. R., & Dymond, Rosalind F. (Eds.), *Psychotherapy and personality change*. Chicago: Univ. of Chicago Press, 1954. Pp. 238-255.

HACKER, F. J. Treatment motivation. *Bull. Menninger. Clin.*, 1962, *26*, 288-298.

HASTINGS, D. W. Follow-up results in psychiatric illness. *Amer. J. Psychiat.*, 1958, *114*, 1057-1066.

HATHAWAY, S. Some considerations relative to non-directive counseling as therapy. *J. clin. Psychol.*, 1948, *4*, 226-231.

HEINICKE, C. M., & GOLDMAN, A. Research on psychotherapy with children: a review and suggestions for further study. *Am. J. Orthopsychiat.*, 1960, *30*, 483-494.

HEWITT, L. E., & JENKINS, R. L. *Fundamental patterns of maladjustment*. (Springfield, Ill.: State of Illinois Publ., 1946.)

HELLER, K., & GOLDSTEIN, A. P. Client dependency and therapist expectancy as relationship maintaining variables in psychotherapy. *J. consult. Psychol.*, 1961, *25*, 371-375.

HOOD-WILLIAMS, J. The results of psychotherapy with children: A re-evaluation. *J. consult. Psychol.*, 1960, *24*, 84-88.

HUNT, J. McV. Toward an integrated program of research on psychotherapy. *J. consult. Psychol.*, 1952, *16*, 237-246.

IMBER, S. D., FRANK, J. D., NASH, E. H., STONE, A. R., & GLIEDMAN, L. H. Improvement and amount of therapeutic contact: An alternative to the use of no-treatment controls in psychotherapy. *J. consult. Psychol.*, 1957, *21*, 309-315.

JONES, MARY C. A laboratory study of fear: The case of Peter. *J. genet. Psychol.*, 1924, *31*, 308-315.

KAUFMAN, P. E. Changes in Minnesota Multiphasic Personality Inventory as a function of psychiatric therapy. *J. consult. Psychol.*, 1950, *14*, 458-464.

KELMAN, H. C., & PARLOFF, M. B. Inter-relations among three criteria of improvement in group therapy: comfort, effectiveness, and self-awareness. *J. abnorm. soc. Psychol.*, 1957, *54*, 281-288.

KIRTNER, W. L., & CARTWRIGHT, D. S. Success and failure in client-centered therapy as a function of client personality variables. *J. consult. Psychol.*, 1958, *22*, 259-264. (a)

KIRTNER, W. L., & CARTWRIGHT, D. S. Success and failure in client-centered therapy as a function of initial in-therapy behavior. *J. consult. Psychol.*, 1958, *22*, 329-333. (b)

KLINE, N. S. Criteria for psychiatric improvement. *Psychiat. Quart.*, 1957, *31*, 31-40.

KNIGHT, R. P. Evaluation of the results of psychoanalytic therapy. *Amer. J. Psychiat.*, 1941, *98*, 434-446.

KOGAN, L. S., HUNT, J. McV., & BARTELIME, P. A *follow-up study of the results of social casework.* New York: Family Assoc. of Amer., 1953.

KRASNER, L. Studies of the conditioning of verbal behavior. *Psychol. Bull.,* 1958, 55, 148-170.

KRASNER, L. The therapist as a social reinforcement machine. In H. H. Strupp & L. Luborsky (Eds.), *Research in psychotherapy.* Washington, D.C.: American Psychol. Assoc., 1962.

LANDIS, C. Statistical evaluation of psychotherapeutic methods. In L. E. Hinsie (Ed.), *Concepts and problems of psychotherapy.* New York: Columbia Univ. Press, 1937. Pp. 155-169.

LEHRMAN, L. J., SIRLUCK, HILDA, BLACK, B. J., & GLICK, SELMA J. Success and failure of treatment of children in the child guidance clinics of the Jewish Board of Guardians, New York City. *Jewish Bd. Guard. Res. Monogr.,* 1949, No. 1. Cited by E. E. Levitt, Results of psychotherapy with children. *J. consult. Psychol.,* 1957, 21, 189-196.

LEHRMAN, N. S. A state hospital population five years after admission: A yardstick for evaluative comparison of follow-up studies. *Psychiat. Quart.,* 1960, 34, 658-681.

LEVITT, E. E. The results of psychotherapy with children: an evaluation. *J. consult. Psychol.,* 1957, 21, 189-196. (a)

LEVITT, E. E. A comparison of "remainers" and "defectors" among child guidance patients. *J. consult. Psychol.,* 1957, 21, 316. (b)

LEVITT, E. E. A comparative judgmental study of "defection" from treatment at a child guidance clinic. *J. clin. Psychol.,* 1958, 14, 429-432.

LEVITT, E. E. Reply to Hood-Williams. *J. consult. Psychol.,* 1960, 24, 89-91.

LOEVINGER, J., & OSSORIO, A. Evaluation of therapy by self-report: a paradox. *J. abnorm. soc. Psychol.,* 1959, 58, 392-394.

LORD, E. Two sets of Rorschach records obtained before and after brief psychotherapy. *J. consult. Psychol.,* 1950. 14, 134-139.

LUBORSKY, L. A note on Eysenck's article: "The effects of psychotherapy: an evaluation." *Brit. J. Psychol.,* 1954, 45, 129-131.

LUBORSKY, L., & STRUPP, H. H. Research problems in psychotherapy: A three-year follow-up. In H. H. Strupp & L. Luborsky (Eds.), *Research in psychotherapy,* Washington, D.C.: American Psychol. Ass., 1962. Pp. 308-329.

LUFF, M. C., & GARROD, M. The after-results of psychotherapy in 500 adult cases. *Brit. med. J.,* 1935, 2, 54-59.

LUNDIN, R. W. *Personality: an experimental approach.* New York: Macmillan, 1961. Pp. 391-419.

MALMO, R. B., & SHAGASS, C. Physiologic study of symptom mechanisms in psychiatric patients under stress. *Psychosom. Med.,* 1949, 11, 25-29.

MALAMUD, D. I. Objective measurement of clinical status in psychopathological research. *Psychol. Bull.,* 1946, 43, 240-258.

McNEMAR, Q. *Psychological statistics.* New York: Wiley, 1949.

MEEHL, P. E. Psychotherapy. *Annu. Rev. Psychol.,* 1955, 6, 357-378.

MERENDA, P. F., & ROTHNEY, J. W. M. Evaluating the effects of counseling —8 years after. *J. counsel. Psychol.,* 1958, 5, 163-168.

METZNER, R. Learning theory and the therapy of neurosis. *Brit. J. Psychol.,* 1961, Monogr. Suppl. No. 33.

MICHAUX, W. W., & LORR, M. Psychotherapists' treatment goals. *J. counsel. Psychol.*, 1961, *8*, 250-254.

MODELL, A. H. Changes in human figure drawings by patients who recover from regressed states. *Amer. J. Orthopsychiat.*, 1951, *21*, 584-596.

MORTON, R. B. An experiment in brief psychotherapy. *Psychol. Monogr.*, 1955, *69*, No. 1 (Whole No. 386).

MOWRER, O. H. Changes in verbal behavior during psychotherapy. In O. H. Mowrer (Ed.), *Psychotherapy: theory and research.* New York: Ronald, 1953.

MUENCH, G. A. An evaluation of non-directive psychotherapy by means of the Rorschach and other tests. *App. Psychol. Monogr.*, 1947, *13*, 1-163.

MURRAY, E. J., AULD, F., JR. & WHITE, A. M. A psychotherapy case showing progress but no decrease in the discomfort relief quotient. *J. Consult. Psychol.*, 1954, *18*, 349-353.

PARLOFF, M. B. Therapist-patient relationships and outcome of psychotherapy. *J. consult. Psychol.*, 1961, *25*, 29-38.

PARLOFF, M. B., & RUBINSTEIN, E. A. Research problems in psychotherapy. In E. A. Rubinstein & M. B. Parloff (Eds.), *Research in psychotherapy.* Washington, D.C.: American Psychol. Ass., 1959. Pp. 276-293.

PASCAL, G. R., & ZAX, M. Psychotherapeutics: success or failure. *J. consult. Psychol.*, 1956, *20*, 325-331.

POWERS, E., & WITMER, HELEN *An experiment in the prevention of delinquency.* New York: Columbia Univ. Press, 1951.

QUAY, H. The effect of verbal reinforcement on the recall of early memories. *J. abnorm. soc. Psychol.*, 1959, *59*, 254-257.

RAYMOND, M. J. Case of fetishism treated by aversion therapy. *Brit. Med. J.*, 1956, *2*, 854-856.

REZNIKOFF, M., & TOOMEY, LAURA C. *Evaluation of changes associated with psychiatric treatment.* Springfield, Ill.: Charles C Thomas, 1959.

RIESS, B. F. The challenge of research for psychotherapy. *Amer. J. Psychother.*, 1960, *14*, 395-411.

ROGERS, C. R. *Client-centered therapy.* Boston: Houghton Mifflin, 1951.

ROGERS, C. R. Introduction. In C. R. Rogers & Rosalind F. Dymond (Eds.), *Psychotherapy and personality change.* Chicago: Univ. of Chicago Press, 1954. Pp. 3-11.

ROGERS, C. R., & DYMOND, ROSALIND F. *Psychotherapy and personality change.* Chicago: Univer. of Chicago Press, 1954.

ROSEN, J. N. *Psychoanalysis direct and indirect.* Doylestown, Pa.: Doylestown Foundation, 1964.

ROSENBAUM, M. Obstacles to research in psychotherapy. *Psychoanalysis & Psychoanalytic Rev.*, 1960, *47*, 97-105.

ROSENTHAL, D. Changes in some moral values following psychotherapy. *J. consult. Psychol.*, 1955, *19*, 431-436.

ROSENTHAL, D., & FRANK, J. D. Psychotherapy and the placebo effect. *Psychol. Bull.*, 1956, *53*, 294-302.

ROSENZWEIG, S. A transvaluation of psychotherapy: a reply to Hans Eysenck. *J. abnorm. soc. Psychol.*, 1954, *49*, 298-304.

ROSS, A. O., & LACEY, H. M. Characteristics of terminators and remainers in child guidance treatment. *J. consult. Psychol.*, 1961, *25*, 420-424.

ROTTER, J. B. Psychotherapy. *Annu. Rev. Psychol.*, 1960, *11*, 381-414.

SARGENT, HELEN D. Psychotherapy research project of the Menninger Clinic. II. Rationale. *Bull. Menninger Clin.*, 1956, *20*, 226-233.

SARGENT, HELEN D. Psychotherapy research project of the Menninger Clinic. III. Design. *Bull. Menninger Clin.*, 1956, *20*, 234-238.

SARGENT, HELEN D. Methodological problems of follow-up studies in psytherapy research. *Amer. J. Orthopsychiat.*, 1960, *30*, 495-508.

SASLOW, G., & PETERS, ANN D. A follow-up study of "untreated" patients with various behavior disorders. *Psychiat. Quart.*, 1956, *30*, 283-302.

SCHJELDERUP, H. Lasting effects of psychoanalytic treatment. *Psychiatry*, 1955, *18*, 109-133.

SEEMAN, J. Psychotherapy. *Annu. Rev. Psychol.*, 1961, *12*, 157-194.

SEEMAN, J. Psychotherapy and perceptual behavior. *J. clin. Psychol.*, 1962, *18*, 34-37.

SHAGASS, C., & MALMO, R. B. Psychodynamic themes and localized muscular tension during psychotherapy. *Psychosom. Med.*, 1954, *16*, 295-314.

SHLIEN, J. M., MOSAK, H. H., & DREIKURS, R. Effect of time limits: a comparison of two psychotherapies. *J. counsel. Psychol.*, 1962, *9*, 31-34.

STEVENSON, I. The challenge of results in psychotherapy. *Amer. J. Psychiat.*, 1959, *116*, 120-123.

STONE, A. R., FRANK, J. D., NASH, E. H., & IMBER, S. D. An intensive five-year follow-up study of treated psychiatric outpatients. *J. nerv. ment. Dis.*, 1961; *122*, 410-422.

STRUPP, H. H. The psychotherapist's contribution to the treatment process. *Behav. Sci.*, 1958, *3*, 34-67.

STRUPP, H. H. Psychotherapy. *Annu. Rev. Psychol.*, 1962, *13*, 445-478.

STRUPP, H. H. The therapist's contribution to the treatment process: Beginnings and vagaries of a research program. In H. H. Strupp & L. Luborsky (Eds.), *Research in psychotherapy*, Washington D.C.: American Psychol. Ass., 1962. Pp. 25-41.

STRUPP, H. H. The outcome problem in psychotherapy revisited. *Psychotherapy*, 1963, *1*, 1-13.

STRUPP, H. H. *A bibliography of research in psychotherapy*. Chapel Hill, N. C.: Psychotherapy Research Project, Dept. of Psychiatry, Univ. of North Carolina, 1964.

TEUBER, H. L. & POWERS, E. Evaluating therapy in a delinquency prevention program. *Res. Publ. Assn., Nerv. Ment. Dis.*, 1951, *31*, 138-147.

THETFORD, W. M. The measurement of physiological response to frustration before and after non-directive psychotherapy. *Amer. Psychol.*, 1948, *3*, 278.

THORNE, F. C. Rules of evidence in the evaluation of the effects of psychotherapy. *J. Clin. Psychol.*, 1952, *8*, 38-41.

TODD, W. B., & EWING, T. N. Changes in self-reference during counseling. *J. counsel. Psychol.*, 1961, *8*, 112-115.

TRUAX, C. B. Effective ingredients in psychotherapy: an approach to unraveling the patient-therapist interaction. *J. counsel. Psychol.*, 1963, *10*, 256-263.

VOTH, H. M., MELDIN, H. C., & ORTH, MARJORIE H. Situational variables in the assessment of psychotherapeutic results. *Bull. Menninger Clin.*, 1962, *25*, 73-81.

WATSON, R. I. Measuring the effectiveness of psychotherapy: Problems for investigation. *J. clin. Psychol.*, 1952, *8*, 60-64.

WATTERSON, D. J. Problems in evaluation of psychotherapy. *Bull. Menninger Clin.*, 1954, *18*, 232-241.

WEISS, R. L., KRASNER, L., & ULLMAN, L. P. Responsivity to verbal conditioning as a function of emotional atmosphere and pattern of reinforcement. *Psychol. Repts.*, 1960, *6*, 415-426.

WILDER, J. Facts and figures on psychotherapy. *J. clin. Psychopath.*, 1945, *7*, 311-347. Cited by R. DeCharms, J. Levy, & M. Wertheimer, A note on attempted evaluations of psychotherapy. *J. clin. Psychol.*, 1954, *10*, 233-235.

WILLIAMS, J. E. Changes in self and other perceptions following brief educational-vocational counseling. *J. counsel. Psychol.*, 1962, *9*, 18-30.

WIRT, R. D., & WIRT, ANNE L. Psychotherapeutic processes. *Annu. Rev. Psychol.*, 1963, *14*, 365-390.

WITMER, HELEN L., & KELLER, JANE. Outgrowing childhood problems: a study in the value of child guidance treatment. *Smith Coll. Stud. Soc. Wk.*, 1942, *13*, 74-90. Cited by E. E. Levitt, Results of psychotherapy with children. *J. consult. Psychol.*, 1957, *21*, 189-196.

WOLFE, J. The prognosis in unpsychoanalyzed recovery from neurosis. *Amer. J. Psychiat.*, 1961, *118*, 35-39.

WOLPE, J. *Psychotherapy by reciprocal inhibition.* Stanford, Calif.: Stanford Univ. Press, 1958.

WOLPE, J. Reciprocal in hibition as the main basis of psychotherapeutic effects. In H. J. Eysenck (Ed.), *Behavior therapy and the neuroses.* New York: Pergamon Press, 1960.

WOLPE, J., SALTER, A., & REYNA, L. J. *The conditioning therapies:* New York: Holt, Rinehart & Winston, 1964.

ZAX, M., & KLEIN, A. Measurement of personality and behavior changes following psychotherapy. *Psychol. Bull.*, 1960, *57*, 435-448.

D. An Annotated Bibliography of Models in Psychotherapy [9]

ACKERMAN, N. W. *The psychodynamics of family life.* New York: Basic Books, 1958.

"This book . . . presents a way of understanding health through the 'emotional give and take' of family relationships. It outlines a conceptual approach to emotional disturbance in the individual through analysis of the psychological content of his family experience." The interdependence of individual, family, and society is discussed in terms of Freudian theory and is illustrated with clinical therapeutic case material. 15-page bibliography. (H. P. David, *Psychol. Abstr.*, *33*, 600)

---

9. Messrs. D. Boutin and W. Link assisted with the gathering of these references.

ALEXANDER, F., & FRENCH, T. *Psychoanalytic therapy*. New York: Ronald Press, 1946.

The plan of treatment reported upon is based on a dynamic-diagnostic appraisal of the patient's personality and of the actual problems of his life situation, with stress upon a flexibility of therapeutic technique adapted to the patient's needs rather than a rigid psychoanalytic procedure. . . . In the final chapter the conclusion is offered that the principle of flexibility opens for psychoanalysis new possibilities of much greater social significance than those values available from the rigid classical psychoanalytic procedure. (M. H. Erickson, *Psychol. Abstr., 20*, 250)

ALLEN, F. H. Trends in therapy. IV. Participation therapy. *Amer. J. Orthopsychiat.*, 1939, 9, 737-742.

This is a discussion of the child's own participation in the therapeutic situation and the steps and stages many children go through as this experience comes to have meaning for them. Despite the difficulty of generalizing about a situation that is used so differently by children who have different needs and different capacities to utilize a relationship with another for their own development, there are three phases through which every child undergoing treatment will go: (1) the child's entering and becoming engaged in this relationship, (2) the use he can make of this experience for his own self-differentiation within this relationship, (3) the child's participation in bringing this experience to a close. Through all of this the therapist must start where the child is now and not become preoccupied with the child that was. (R. E. Perl, *Psychol. Abstr., 14*, 194)

ANDERSON, CAMILLA. *Beyond Freud*. New York: Harper, 1957.

"The answer is simple. No matter what the theory, *there is one fundamental technique which is used by all: the elimination of hostile or morally judgmental attitudes against the patient in treatment.* No matter what the patient says or does, the therapist treats it as a fact to be understood rather than one to be judged. To be sure, critical evaluation is fostered, but the moralistic approach is conspicuously absent. People become free to get well in no other atmosphere than in the nonjudgmental. This does not imply either an indulgent or a 'forgiving' attitude on the part of the therapist but rather one of critical objectivity free from blame or praise" (p. 245). The main thesis of the book is that when a person is in emotional bondage to his past, he cannot experience "the good life." The author attempts to create her own theory of behavior after examining the various schools of thought. In the first part, the biological and emotional factors shaping personality from birth to maturity are discussed. Part 2 reviews the stresses, anxieties, defenses, and symptoms connected with behavior problems. The final part includes the author's psychotherapeutic approach and a chapter on religion and psychiatry. (D. Prager, *Psychol. Abstr., 32*, 42)

ANSBACHER, H. L., & ANSBACHER, ROWENA R. (Eds.) *The individual psychology of Alfred Adler*. New York: Basic Books, 1956.

With the aim of making Adler's important but not too lucidly expressed ideas more readily available, two of his former students have undertaken to make this judicious selection from his writings, many of which appear here in English for the first time. The selections, appropriately annotated by the editors, make a systematic presentation of Adler's formulations of personality theory and development; the result is an important source book for students of psychology. (Booklist, 52, 422)

AXELRODE, J. Some indications for supportive therapy. *Amer. J. Orthopsychiat.*, 1940, *10*, 264-271.

Many cases judged "not amenable to treatment" show on closer examination only that the child was not amenable to interview therapy directed toward exploration of his problems. In many of these cases the feeling has grown that, regardless of symptoms shown, the child was actually suffering from a definite emotional deprivation, often accompanied by reality deprivations. Affect hunger can be viewed as a deficiency disease like rickets. The treatment is supportive therapy, a conscious attempt to mitigate the child's affect hunger through a strong emotional tie to the case worker, a deliberate giving of affection, not as a means of strengthening a therapy but as the therapy itself. Two cases are given to illustrate the use and possibilities of supportive therapy. (R. E. Perl, *Psychol. Abstr.*, *14*, 423)

AXLINE, VIRGINIA. *Play therapy.* New York: Houghton Mifflin, 1947.

This book presents a nondirective method of play therapy and the theory of personality structure upon which it is based. Materials suitable for nondirective play therapy and desirable characteristics of the playroom are suggested. Specific instances and illustrations of the method are given, both for group and individual therapy. Implications for education are considered. Excerpts from individual and group therapy records make up about half of the book. At the conclusion of each excerpt are given the reasons for the referral and a brief summary of the child's problem. This material is put at the end of the case material in order that the reader may formulate his own hypotheses as he reads and then check to see how revealing the play has been. (M. Mercer, *Psychol. Abstr.*, 22, 95)

AYLLON, T., & HAUGHTON, E. Control of the behavior of schizophrenic patients by food. *J. exp. anal. Behav.*, 1962, 5, 343-352.

Experiment I: 32 female patients, 7 of whom had displayed chronic feeding problems, were deprived of social reinforcement (sympathy, etc.) during meal time by keeping the nurses away from these patients during meal time. Thirty minutes were allowed the patients in gaining access to the dining room. ". . . patients were not told of the time limit. A nurse called the meal, opened the dining room, and at the end of 30 minutes closed the door and refused admittance to anyone. The development of normal eating occurred slowly. The patients with eating problems eventually ate 70 per cent of their meals *entirely unassisted!* Moreover, when the time allowable for gaining entrance to the dining room was decreased from 30 to 20 to 15 minutes (this occurred over a period of 12 weeks), even the problems Ss were observed to 'keep up with the new schedule.' For the sake of comparison, the (normal) schizophrenics were observed to eat 90 per cent of their meals."

Experiment II: ". . . six new problem feeders were added. . . . In addition to the procedures of experiment I, Ss were now required to drop a penny into the slot of a collection can to gain entrance to the dining room. All Ss learned the motor response required to obtain food reinforcement. . . . Up to this point little verbal interaction was observed among the patients. However, during the first two weeks of the experiment, Ss were observed to ask each other how to get pennies."

Experiment III: "Seven more patients who were problem eaters were included in this study . . . in addition to appearing at the dining room on time and dropping pennies into a slot, Ss were required, before 'paying for their meal,' to press a button situated on one end of a table . . . a button on the other side of the table and 7½ feet away had to be pressed at the same time. . . . Only one patient failed to develop the social response." (Quotations from Peter G. Kepros in *An operant analysis of psychotic behavior*. Seminar presentation, University of Utah, 1963.)

BACH, G. R. Dramatic play therapy with adult groups. *J. Psychol.*, 1950, 29, 225-246.

Motivation for fantasy release is a function of the intensity of the frustration; hence play activities have a high therapeutic value. The steps followed in Play Drama were: making a group decision, selection of characters, and stimulation of thematic role taking. The author puts forth three hypotheses as to results: (1) play drama helps to develop psychological interdependence between members of psychotherapy groups; (2) it facilitates relatively uninhibited communication of tabu feelings; (3) a symbolic learning process is instigated, resulting in greater objectivity in perception of the self role in living reality. Several protocols are presented. (R. W. Husband, *Psychol. Abstr.*, 24, 663-664)

BACH, G. R. *Intensive group psychotherapy*. New York: Ronald, 1954.

"This volume describes both the practice and the theory of intensive group psychotherapy, a relatively new and rapidly developing method of treating personality disorders. It is practical in describing clinical procedures, and yet it tries to come to terms with basic theoretical problems. Part I deals with clinical technique; Part II explores the nature of the therapeutic process that is fostered by group therapy participation; Part III examines the group dynamic forces that influence the therapeutic process in the individual." (From preface, page V, Bach, G. R., *Intensive group psychotherapy*. New York: Ronald, 1954, 15 page bibliography.)

BECKER, E. *Zen: A rational critique*. New York: Norton, 1961.

Following the stated purpose, "to show that Zen really is a denial of life, a negation of the Western ethic of individuation and autonomy," Zen's origins are traced from magical Taoism, Buddhism, and esoteric Eastern tradition. Dissection is accomplished by an examination of Zen values, cosmology, the role of the trance, and the conversion (i.e., psychotherapeutic) process. These are viewed against a background of Chinese "thought reform" and psychoanalysis. The conclusion is made that to function creatively within western tradition one needs to "accept the fact that neither corps of Zennists nor of psychoanalysts will or can create tomorrow's utopia." (C. W. Page, *Psychol. Abstr.*, 36, 516)

Boss, M. *Psychoanalysis and daseinsanalysis.* New York: Basic Books, 1963.
"Perhaps the most significant area in which Daseinsanalytic thinking differs from psychoanalytic thinking is in the conception of transference . . ." (p. 237). "The Daseinsanalyst admits 'transference love or hate' as the genuine interpersonal relationship to the analyst as which the analysand experiences them . . . the analyst permits him (the patient) to unfold more fully his real and essential being within a safe interpersonal relationship on the 'playground of the transference'" (p. 239).
The analysis of Dasein (existence), based upon Martin Heidegger's philosophy, is like psychoanalysis in its effort to be open to the experience of the patient, but it differs from psychoanalysis in that it does not accept a natural-science approach to psychology. Daseinsanalysis, too, rejects the concept "unconscious" as being "superfluous." Finally, Daseinsanalysis does not consider "transference" responses to be transferred from images developed in infantile experiences, but instead views the patient's feelings as belonging to "the genuine interpersonal relationship to the analyst." In Daseinsanalysis, acting out of "transference feelings" should be permitted and encouraged. (F. Auld, *Psychol. Abstr.*, 38, 115)

BUHLER, CHARLOTTE. *Values in psychotherapy.* New York: Free Press of Glencoe, 1962.
"Values permeate our development and personality to such a degree that they can never be left out of the picture." The book considers two problems: (1) "whether, why, and how the psychotherapist has to get involved with the value problems of his patients" and (2) "how the therapist's and the patient's self-development and self-understanding and the role that values play for them in human life must by necessity affect the process of therapy. . . . The basic theme of the book is a discussion of psychotherapy as value-discrimination, either by reduction of generalization or by 'new' seeing." (C. H. Miley, *Psychol. Abstr.*, 37, 679)

CAMMER, L. Conditioning and psychiatric theory. *Amer. J. Orthopsychiat.*, 1961, 31, 810-819.
In Russia the theoretical basis for psychiatric practice is organized around Pavlovian laws of conditioning. The purpose of this paper is to clarify and summarize its basic principles. (R. E. Perl, *Psychol. Abstr.*, 36, 812)

CARMICHAEL, B. Psychosynthesis. *J. clin. Psychopath.*, 1949, 10, 73-84.
The process of psychoanalysis should be considered as synthetic and constructive, as well as analytic and dissective. Furthermore, the process of synthesis in successful cases continues long after the analysis is terminated. Consequently, the author presents a written account of a very intelligent former patient who, some months after treatment, recorded these processes and changes as he experienced them both during and after the analysis. (G. A. Muench, *Psychol. Abstr.*, 24, 664)

CONN, J. H. The play-interview as an investigative and therapeutic procedure. *Nerv. Child.*, 1948, 7, 257-286.
The use of planned play situations as a therapeutic procedure is described through the presentation of detailed clinical reports. It is

felt that the play situation allows the child to participate actively in the discussion of his own problems, and to express his feelings, as an impartial and objective observer. (G. S. Speer, *Psychol. Abstr.*, 23, 216)

CORSINI, R. J. Immediate therapy; with special emphasis upon psychoanalysis and psychodrama. *Group Psychother.*, 1952, 4, 322-330.

In terms of time-economy of treatment, psychoanalysis is generally considered slow and expensive. On the other hand, "if psychodrama as a method of psychic cure is a method as good as any other, and since it appears to be faster, then at least from an economic point of view it is of greater social value than psychoanalysis." Psychodrama involves individual therapy in group situations, self-direction, and a peak of emotional effect "which would be within the subject's limit of tolerance but beyond the threshold of control." The author's principles of group therapy include rapid therapy because resistance tends to increase; precipitation of anxiety and refusal to reduce it; irradiation of solutions to various areas; release; and teleology in terms of goal direction. (V. Johnson, *Psychol. Abstr.*, 27, 746)

DEABLER, H. L. The psychotherapeutic use of the Thematic Apperception Test. *J. clin. Psychol.*, 1947, 3, 246-252.

A case study is presented showing how the TAT may be used therapeutically. The taking of the test may cause the client, either spontaneously or on request, to relate his stories to his own problems. When used for therapeutic purposes, it is suggested that the test be given early in the counseling contact as an icebreaker or, if initially the client talks readily, at a later time when the counseling process seems to be marking time. (L. B. Heathers, *Psychol. Abstr.*, 22, 41)

DEUTSCH, F., & MURPHY, W. F. *The clinical interview.* (2 vols.) New York: International University, 1955.

(Volume I) *Diagnosis.*

Out of the experience gained in training psychiatric residents in a large VA neuropsychiatric training center, a program is presented illustrating the use of "sector psychotherapy" on the Open Ward Service, and the "associative anamnesis technique" upon which it is based. The purpose is not to analyze the mass of interview material, but to "read between the lines" and detect the blending of the patient's unconscious fantasies with the manifest material and to communicate these to the patient. Besides three theoretical chapters there are 12 other chapters on as many disorders, each with a case presentation, preliminary discussion, the interview, a final discussion and follow-up. There is a final, integrating summary chapter. (W. H. Pronko, *Psychol. Abstr.*, 29, 374)

DOLLARD, J., & MILLER, N. E. *Personality and psyche therapy.* New York: McGraw-Hill, 1950.

A systematic analysis of neurosis and psychotherapy in terms of psychological principles and social conditions of learning, in eight parts: orientation; basic principles of learning; normal use of the mind in solving emotional problems; how neurosis is learned; new conditions of therapeutic learning; conflict; special aspects of therapy; and two applications to normal living. 186-item bibliography. (A. J. Sprow, *Psychol. Abstr.*, 25, 454-455)

DREIKURS, R. Techniques and dynamics of multiple psychotherapy. *Psychiat. Quart.*, 1950, *24*, 788-799.

All forms of psychotherapy where several therapists treat a single patient simultaneously may be considered multiple psychotherapy. The principle dynamics of multiple psychotherapy are similar to those of group psychotherapy. Negative transference and resistance are more easily handled in multiple psychotherapy. Chances of omissions or inaccurate conclusions are decreased in multiple psychotherapy. Discussion between therapists helps the patient gain an understanding of his own case. The period of reorientation is considerably shortened through multiple psychotherapy. Multiple therapy has particular value for training less experienced therapists. (D. Prager, *Psychol. Abstr.*, *26*, 287-288)

DREIKURS, R. Music therapy with psychotic children. *Psychiat. Quart.*, 1960, *34*, 722-734.

Two 5-year-olds and one 14-year old are presented as case illustrations. Music therapy brought results where other approaches failed. The music stimulated participation, increased attention span, and raised the child's frustration tolerance. External and internal tensions decreased as reality became less threatening. The demands for participation were so subtle that they were not resented or defied. Institutionalization was no longer mandatory unless the child was too destructive at home. Music therapy is still in the exploratory and experimental stages. (D. Prager, *Psychol. Abstr.*, *36*, 141)

ELLIS, A. Rationalism and its therapeutic applications. *Ann. Psychother.*, 1959, *1* (2), 55-64.

"The rationalist belief is that the so-called emotions or motivations of adult human beings who are raised in a civilized community largely consist of attitudes, perceptual biases, beliefs, assumptions, and ideas which are acquired by social learning and which therefore can be reviewed, questioned, challenged, reconstructed, and changed with sufficient effort and practice on the part of the emoting individual. . . . There are perhaps a dozen basic irrational beliefs which virtually all neurotics in our culture learn to accept . . . and which make it almost impossible for them to act effectively." (Quoted by S. Glasner, *Psychol. Abstr.*, *34*, 749)

ENNEIS, J. M. The hypnodramatic technique. *Group Psychother.*, 1950, *3*, 11-54.

Hypnotherapists have probably been making use of hypnodrama in abreaction and other procedures in which the patient places himself in certain situations and the therapist consciously or unconsciously takes the role of an auxiliary ego. In most instances, however, the patient is limited to verbal expression. In hypnodrama he is free to act, and is given auxiliary egos to help portray his drama. (V. Johnson, *Psychol. Abstr.*, *25*, 102)

EYSENCK, H. J. The effects of psychotherapy: an evaluation. *J. consult. Psychol.*, 1952, *16*, 319-324.

"A survey was made of reports on the improvement of neurotic patients after psychotherapy, and the results compared with the best available estimates of recovery without benefit of such therapy. The figures fail to support the hypothesis that psychotherapy facilitates recovery from neurotic disorder. In view of the many difficulties attending such actuarial comparisons, no further conclusions could be derived from the data, whose shortcomings highlight the necessity of properly planned and executed experimental studies into this important field." 40 references. (F. Costin, *Psychol. Abstr.*, 27, 607)

FEIBLEMAN, J. K. The stressed conditioning of psychotics. *J. Psychol.*, 1962, 53 (2), 295-299.

An extension of existing techniques in the treatment of certain types of psychoses is proposed. The therapy will consist of two separate phases. In the first stage, the delusional system is extinguished by means of noxious stimulation accompanying the interviews. In the second stage, a positive set of beliefs is instilled under the technique of stressed conditioning. Stressed conditioning is the imposition of beliefs at a deep level of analysis carried out under stress. (Author abstract, *Psychol. Abstr.*, 37, 139-140)

FEIFEL, H., & SCHWARTZ, A. D. Group psychotherapy with acutely disturbed psychotic patients. *J. consult. Psychol.*, 1953, 17, 113-121.

A description of how 20 group psychotherapy sessions of an "open-end type" were carried on by the authors with acutely disturbed schizophrenic patients. The main themes dominating the discussion are examined. Certain selected biographical factors were compared with patients not receiving the treatment. In general, the group psychotherapy patients showed more improvement, both in a quantitative as well as a qualitative sense, than did a similar group who did not receive group psychotherapy. Areas for further research are presented. (F Costin, *Psychol. Abstr.*, 28, 267)

FINE, R., DALY, D., & FINE, L. Psychodance: An experiment in psychotherapy and training. *Group Psychother.*, 1962, 15 (3), 203-223.

Psychodance is a form of psychotherapy felt to be effective with groups of both nonverbal and verbal patients. These movements emphasize both self-expressive and interpersonal contact operations. The authors present a theoretical background and offer several examples of this technique. (I. W. Kidorf, *Psychol. Abstr.*, 37, 817)

FISHER, V. E. *The meaning and practice of psychotherapy.* New York: Macmillan, 1950.

Part I presents a general orientation to the psychotherapeutic procedure, including the first consultation, psychological testing, securing the case history, and types of therapy. In Parts II, III, and IV are presented the various techniques and approaches which the author has found to be most effective in the treatment of disorders. Part II deals with psychotic and closely related disorders, Part III with psychoneurotic reactions, and Part IV with some maladjustive psychosocial reactions and tendencies. Case histories are used throughout, and 22 cases (one for each clinical syndrome covered) are fully presented in terms of treatment of the patients. 84 selected readings; 15-page glossary. (L. Solomon, *Psychol. Abstr.*, 25, 382)

FOULKES, S. H. Group therapy; a short survey and orientation with particular reference to group analysis. *Brit. J. med. Psychol.*, 1950, 23, 199-205.

Following a brief review of the development of group therapy, the

general procedure, conditions and theory of a psychoanalytical approach
to group therapy are presented. General areas of applicability are discussed. 27 references. (C. L. Winder, *Psychol. Abstr., 25,* 745)

FRANK, J. D. *Persuasion and healing: A comparative study of psychotherapy.*
Baltimore, Md.: Johns Hopkins University Press, 1961.

Social and personal factors are examined which are common to
various "systematic time-limited contacts between a person in distress
and someone who tries to reduce the distress by producing changes
in the sufferer's feelings, attitudes and behavior." These contacts include
individual and group psychotherapy, religious healing, thought reform
through revivalism, and brainwashing. The persuasive nature of psychotherapy is stressed, and descriptions of experimental studies of
persuasion are included. The author examines American psychotherapy
as it is influenced by American values and cultural traditions. (L. Katz,
Psychol. Abstr., 36, 344)

FRANKL, V. E. *The doctor and the soul; an introduction to logotherapy.*
(Translated by Richard and Clara Winston.) New York: Knopf, 1955.

Logotherapy "not only recognizes man's spirit but actually starts
from it," emphasizing spiritual values, "medical ministry," and the
quest for meaning in life. Originally published in Austria in 1952,
this volume includes papers on the psychology of the concentration
camp, anxiety, obsession, melancholia, and schizophrenia. Other papers
deal with General Existential Analysis, discussing life's meaning, suffering, work, and love. (H. P. David, *Psychol. Abstr., 30,* 410)

FREEMAN, M. J. Reinforcement therapy: a re-evaluation of the concept of
"insight" in psychotherapy. *Amer. J. Psychother.,* 1951, *5,* 32-37.

Successful therapy must lead not only to the formulation of more
adequate insights, but also to organismic reinforcements of these
insights. Diagrammatic reinforcement consists of using graphic demon-
strations of concepts or insights. The use of psychofilms, primarily as
a media for identification, is a second method of producing reinforcement and ego shifts in behavior. Situational reinforcement, as a third
technique, would utilize the laboratory method of synthetic situations
wherein behavior is directly observed, desensitized, and redirected.
(L. N. Solomon, *Psychol. Abstr., 25,* 746)

FREUD, S. *An outline of psychoanalysis.* New York: Norton, 1949.

Freud presents here "the doctrines of psychoanalysis . . . dog-
matically—in the most concise form and the most positive terms." Nine
brief chapters state the hypotheses relating the psychical apparatus
(Id, Ego, Superego), the instinctual forces (Libido and Aggressiveness,
or Eros and Death instincts), the developmental stages of the sexual
function, the mental qualities of the unconsciousness and the primary
processes. These concepts are shown at work in statements of the
principles of dream-interpretation and of therapeutic psychoanalytic
technique with the neurosis. Further theoretical considerations locate
the central roles of the Oedipus Complex, castration fears, sexual
renunciation, transference, and the cultural definition of ego-superego
factors. Freud offers these as working hypotheses by stating their
methodological assumptions, and by pointing up their gaps, limitations,
and obscurities. (J. Shor, *Psychol. Abstr., 23,* 371)

GARNER, H. H. A nascent somatic delusion treated psychotherapeutically by a confrontation technique. *J. clin. exp. Psychopath.*, 1959, *20*, 135-143.

The special treatment consists of a statement, command, or verbal expression by the therapist, followed by the request, "What do you think of what I told you?" Free association is the basic rule and interpretation of resistance is the outstanding activity of the therapist. (S. Kavruck, *Psychol. Abstr.*, *34*, 298)

GITELSON, M. The curative factors in psychoanalysis. Part I. *Int. J. Psychoanal.*, 1962, *43* (4-5), 194-205.

The patient-therapist relationship involved in the positive transference and in the transference neurosis is the main curative vehicle in psychoanalytical treatment; and its importance transcends that of development of insight by the patient. (G. Elias, *Psychol. Abstr.*, *37*, 816)

GOLDMAN, G. S. Reparative psychotherapy. In Rado, S., & Daniels, G. E. (Eds.), *Changing concepts of psychoanalytic medicine.* New York: Grune & Stratton, 1956.

This is òne of 20 articles published in this volume based on papers presented at the Decennial Celebration of the Columbia University Psychoanalytic Clinic in March 1955.

"Reparative psychotherapy differs from reconstructive psychoanalytic therapy in that the goals are less ambitious, the variety and extent of the patient population encompassed are far broader, and the methods are more elastic, eclectic and pragmatic. The demands upon the therapist as to judgment, skill and resourcefulness are probably greater" (pp. 112-113).

GROSSMAN, D. An experimental investigation of a psychotherapeutic technique. *J. consult. Psychol.*, 1952, *16*, 325-331.

Two matched groups of ten male subjects each were manipulated experimentally as follows: In one group the therapist recognized only "explicit feelings" (the "surface" group); in the other, the therapist recognized only "implicit feelings" (the "deep" group). The evidence indicated that greater emotional insight was achieved by the "deep" group. The author also presents this study in support of the "contention that psychotherapy can be studied objectively and experimentally." (F. Costin, *Psychol. Abstr.*, *27*, 608)

HERZOG-DÜREK, J. *Menschsein als Wagnis.* ("Being human as a venture") Stuttgart, Germany: Klett, 1960.

A discussion, with case presentations, of the psychotherapy of neuroses from the personalistic standpoint, emphasizing the holistic character of the encounters between persons. Such a viewpoint abandons natural scientific objectification for phenomenologically contemplative and illuminating method. As such, psychotherapy is "practice at being human." (E. W. Eng, *Psychol. Abstr.*, *36*, 342)

HES, J. P., & HANDLER, S. L. Multidimensional group psychotherapy. *Arch. gen. Psychiat.*, 1961, *5*, 70-75.

On a psychiatric ward patients and their relatives met in separate and combined groups. The combined meetings provided material for the patients' meetings. In the combined meetings patients and relatives first separate into subgroups. With approaching discharge communication between patients and relatives improved. Meetings of relatives

permitted the latter to ventilate their feelings towards the patients
and made for more constructive attitudes towards the sick family
members. Selection of patients for the groups by the leader and long-
term projects of this kind are suggested for the future. (L. W. Brandt,
Psychol. Abstr., *36*, 519)

HOBBS, N. Group-centered psychotherapy. In C. R. Rogers, *Client-centered
therapy*. Boston: Houghton Mifflin, 1951. Pp. 278-319.

The chapter describes the application of client-centered techniques
in group psychotherapy.

HOBBS, N. Sources of gain in psychotherapy. *Amer. Psychologist*, 1962, *17*
(10), 741-747.

Insight is not a cause of change but a possible result of change.
"It is not a source of therapeutic gain but one among a number of
possible consequences of gain." Five "major sources of gain, five kinds
of experiences that are the wellsprings of personality reorganization"
are specified. Psychotherapy is a unique life situation designed to maximize these sources of gain: (1) a sustaining experience of intimacy with
another human without getting hurt; (2) divesting verbal and other
symbols of their anxiety producing potential; (3) the transference
relationship; (4) client opportunities to practice decision-making, to
learn to be responsible for himself, to develop an improved self-con-
cept; and (5) insight which facilitates repression and symptom elimination, and involves cognitive structured modifications. (S. J. Cachman,
Psychol. Abstr., *37*, 680)

HORNEY, KAREN. *New ways in psychoanalysis*. New York: Norton, 1939.

The thesis is developed that neuroses are the result of the contradictory tendencies of protective habits (such as perfectionism, self-
inflation, dependency) which have been elaborated to guard a
threatened security. The implications of this point of view are compared with those of classical Freudianism. . . . (R. R. Willoughby,
Psychol. Abstr., *13*, 368)

Therapy, for Horney, employs the same tools as in classical analysis,
but to investigate present functions and their implications other than
genesis.

HORWITZ, SELMA. The spontaneous drama as a technique in group therapy.
Nerv. child., 1945, *4*, 252-273.

Two records are presented to demonstrate the value of the drama
as a technique and the effect of the handling of the material by the
therapist. Both cases reveal the far-reaching effects of the drama for
the children involved and also demonstrate the failure and success of
the technique in terms of its use by the therapist. Active handling
of the material by the therapist is effective, while passivity creates
danger and, in some cases, actual damage to the child. (G. S. Speer,
Psychol. Abstr., *20*, 100)

IKIN, ALICE G. *New concepts of healing: medical, psychological, and
religious*. New York: Association Press, 1956.

"An inquiry into the overlapping areas of the ministry, medicine,
and psychiatry in healing the sick in body, mind, or spirit. The
approach is from the religious point of view. First published in England and revised for American publications with appendixes of educa-

tional resources for education in pastoral psychology in the U.S., reports of healing in the U.S., and pertinent medical statements." (*Booklist*, 52, 374)

JACOBSON, E. *Progressive relaxation.* (2nd ed.) Chicago: University of Chicago Press, 1938.

The author presents in 21 chapters a clinical, practical and scientific discussion of the method of progressive relaxation whereby the subject is trained to reduce greatly or to eliminate residual muscular tensions. With the consequent reduction of excitatory impulses there is a reduction in the irritability of nerve centers. Suggestion is ruled out as an explanatory factor. Inhibitory processes may play a role. 44-page bibliography. (W. S. Hunter, *Psychol. Abstr.*, 12, 521)

JOHNSON, W. *People in quandaries.* New York: Harper, 1946.

Social and individual problems are approached through a study of language structure. It is pointed out that adequate behavior demands awareness of the fact that our words represent abstractions with many details omitted. "The fundamental thesis of this book is simply that science, clearly understood, can be used from moment to moment in everyday life, and that it provides a sound basis for warmly human efficient living." Concrete applications are pointed out, and exercises given. In an appendix, the methods used by the author in a series of studies of language are outlined. (R. B. Ammons, *Psychol. Abstr.*, 20, 392)

JUNG, C. G. *The practice of psychotherapy.* New York: Pantheon, 1954.

Part I includes nine papers . . . on general problems of psychotherapy published originally between 1930 and 1951. Part II includes one paper on abreaction, one on dream-analysis, and a translation of the book *Die Psychologie der Übertragung*, including its 167-item bibliography. (C. M. Loutit, *Psychol. Abstr.*, 28, 828)

KAREN, E. S., & BERTRAM, P. Techniques of primitive witchcraft in modern psychotherapy. *Acta psychother. psychosom.*, Basel, 1961, 9 (6), 393-400.

Many problems are unresponsive to conventional techniques. The techniques of primitive witch doctors can in specific cases prove effective for therapeutic transference. (G. Rubin-Rabson, *Psychol. Abstr.*, 37, 140-141)

KARPMAN, B. Objective psychotherapy. *J. clin. Psychol.*, 1949, 5, 189-342.

The author describes his "objective" psychotherapy, an analytically oriented approach which attempts to minimize interpersonal subjective factors in therapy. The therapy consists of frequent but very brief (5- to 10-minute) interviews, a series of written questions to which the patient responds in writing, periodic written summaries and interpretations by the therapist of the patient's material, suggested readings about which the patient writes, and written reports of the patient's dreams. The initial series of questions are concerned primarily with case history material; later questions are developed about the material the particular patient brings up. The data on a case are given in detail; the case record includes the therapist's written communications as well as the patient's. (L. B. Heathers, *Psychol. Abstr.*, 24, 151-152)

KELLEY, D. M. The use of general semantics and Korzybskian principles as an extensional method of group psychotherapy in traumatic neuroses. *J. nerv. ment. Dis.*, 1951, *114*, 189-220.

A group psychotherapeutic technique is discussed as it was evolved by the author and employed in the European theater during World War II. It is essentially an application of general semantics and explains the how and why of the patient's action and offers him specific remedies. Actual "lectures" reported verbatim and/or in summary form as well as an outline of same is included. (N. H. Pronko, *Psychol. Abstr.*, *26*, 230)

KELLY, G. A. *The psychology of personal constructs.* Vol. II. New York: Norton, 1955.

This volume is "concerned with the implications of the psychology of personal constructs in the field of clinical practice . . . here we have striven for extensive coverage of cook-book details . . . the role of the psychotherapist and some of his stand-by techniques, the cataloguing of experience and activity data, and a schedule of diagnostic procedures." (Quoted by H. P. Davis, *Psychol. Abstr.*, *30*, 399)

KLAPMAN, J. W. *Group psychotherapy: theory and practice.* New York: Grune & Stratton, 1946.

Part I (two chapters) deals with the historical background of group therapy and theorizes regarding the cultural origin of group relationships. Part II (three chapters) is concerned with the dynamics operating in group psychotherapy, especially the relationship of the group to the leader. Part III (eight chapters) describes various group techniques and various situations in which these techniques have been applied. There is an 8-page bibliography. (L. B. Heathers, *Psychol. Abstr.*, *20*, 293)

KORZYBSKI, A. *Science and sanity.* Lancaster, Pa.: Science Press, 1941.

"If man is ever to make full and effective use of his uniquely human nervous organization, he must give up identifying words with the objects for which they stand. . . . In a new introduction, the author reviews the recent progress of general semantics, points out the hurdles in its path, and offers current illustrations to support his view that not only the well-being of each individual but even the survival of democracy is contingent upon a radical revision of man's mode of thought. The inadequacy of Aristotelian intentional definition which leaves most terms 'over/under defined,' causes a distortion of values out of which grow fears, confusion, unhappiness, as well as lowered cultural and ethical standards. The non-Aristotelian method, grounded upon extensional definition, eliminates the needless tensions and blockages arising from uncertainty, frustration, etc., and so leads to a better integration between cortical and thalamic functions. . . ." (M. R. Sheehan, *Psychol. Abstr.*, *16*, 142)

KOTKOV, B. Technique and explanatory concepts of short term group psychotherapy. *J. clin. Psychopath.*, 1949, *10*, 304-316.

A technique of short term group therapy as used at the Boston Mental Hygiene Unit of the V. A. with selected patients is described. Both the mechanical and dynamic aspects of the therapeutic situation are explained, although the results of the procedure are to be reported in a later paper. The following aspects of the relationship are discussed:

selection of patients; reasons for referral; mechanics, objectives, composition and function of the group; and the role and function of the therapist. (G. A. Muench, *Psychol. Abstr.*, 25, 38)

KRONHAUSEN, E. W., & KRONHAUSEN, PHYLLIS E. Family milieu therapy: the non-institutional treatment of severe emotional disturbances. *Psychoanalysis*, 1957, 5, 45-62.

As a rule mental hospitals are not the proper place to treat emotional disturbances. The authors are married psychologists who treat emotionally disturbed patients in the family setting of their own home, receiving outside psychiatric supervision. Family milieu therapy emphasizes the impact of an emotionally hygienic home environment on the disturbed individual. It stresses the interaction processes in the nuclear family group as the primary therapeutic agent and considers specialized techniques only within this environmental concept. The authors make "great efforts to acquaint ourselves with the patients' parents, siblings, and other significant persons in his original environment in order to orient our interaction with him with this particular pattern in mind." With further refinement it should be possible to treat the majority of mental patients ouside of hospitals. (D. Prager, *Psychol. Abstr.* 33, 150)

LASSNER, R. Playwriting and acting as diagnostic-therapeutic techniques with delinquents. *J. clin. Psychol.*, 1947, 3, 349-356.

"In correctional institutions there is a great need for group treatment techniques. Playwriting and acting in a permissive atmosphere, with freedom of choice regarding plot and role, with subsequent group discussions, has been found useful in this respect. Improvement seen in three typical institutionalized boys, either brought about or precipitated by this technique, has been described to exemplify its applications and value." (L. B. Heathers, *Psychol. Abstr.*, 22, 568)

LAWLOR, G. W. Role therapy. *Sociatry*, 1947, 1, 51-55.

All people are called upon to play many different and often conflicting roles in everyday life. Difficulties arising can be minimized or alleviated by education in the nature of roles and by training in the playing of roles. Psychoanalysis is indicated only in those cases which cannot respond to role therapy, and even here role therapy can serve as a useful supplementary technique. (R. B. Ammons, *Psychol. Abstr.*, 21, 436-437)

LENNARD, H. L., & BERNSTEIN, A. *The anatomy of psychotherapy: Systems of communication and expectation.* New York: Columbia University Press, 1960.

"Concepts and methods developed by sociologists for the description and analysis of small group behavior are here applied to study the processes of interaction that occur during individual psychotherapy. The authors, using pre-selected categories of data analysis, dissect over 500 tape-recorded sessions from eight individual therapies." (*Amer. J. Pub. Health*)

"They consider therapy as a system of action, as an informal exchange system, as a system of role expectations, and finally they consider the interrelations between communication and expections for the therapist-patient duo." (F. J. Goldstein, *Psychol. Abstr.*, 34, 750)

LESLIE, ROBERT C. Pastoral group psychotherapy. *J. pastoral Care*, 1952, 6, 56-61.

The Christian church has had group activity from its beginning, and this may become more effective in meeting individual needs as groups are utilized for emotional release, modification of attitudes, and personal growth as laboratories of social living. To do this the group must have a democratic, permissive atmosphere, and yet be goal directed toward well understood and accepted purposes. (P. E. Johnson, *Psychol. Abstr.*, 27, 609)

LEVY, D. M. Release therapy in young children. *Psychiatry*, 1938, 1, 387-390.

Release therapy or abreaction therapy is a treatment limited entirely to procedures in the office, and to cases in which the child is the primary consideration rather than the mother or other members of the family. The object of the therapist is to create a situation by the use of play methods in which the anxiety of the child is given expression. This treatment may be called a "specific release therapy." "General release therapy" is utilized typically when symptoms have arisen in the child because of the excessive demands or prohibitions made on him at too early an age. The test of its value is in the results achieved. Two case histories illustrate the theory and technique of the therapy. The younger the child the sooner can results be achieved. (M. Grotjahn, *Psychol. Abstr.*, 13, 143)

LEVY, D. M. Trends in therapy. III. Release therapy. *Amer. J. Orthopsychiat.*, 1939, 9, 713-737.

The author cites 35 cases which he treated by release therapy. The criteria for selecting children for release therapy are these (1) the problem should be a definite symptom picture precipitated by a specific event; (2) the problem should not be of too long duration; (3) the child must be suffering from something that happened in the past and not from a difficult situation existing at the time of treatment. When a child is accepted for release therapy, it is assumed that the family relationships are normal or that the particular problem presented is not primarily related to the family situation at the time. The methodological principle of this therapy is the acting-out principle in play. The interpretive function of the therapist is reduced to a minimum and may be entirely absent in very young children. Three functions of release therapy in the playroom can be differentiated: (1) simple release of aggressive behavior or of infantile pleasures, (2) release of feelings in standard situations, (3) release of feelings in specific play situations set up to resemble a definite experience in the life of the patient. (R. E. Perl, *Psychol. Abstr.*, 14, 197)

LIFTON, R. J. *Thought reform and the psychology of totalism: A study of "brainwashing" in China.* New York: Norton, 1961.

"Psychiatric interviews with 25 western long-term sojourners in China and 15 native Chinese, all 40 of whom extruded or escaped during the Korean War, provide the data. . . . Thought reform is viewed by the Chinese Communists, Lifton points out, as an essentially humanitarian and rehabilitative program. . . . No evidence is presented by Lifton that they have a worked out scientific theory of behavior that

320 : *Topical Reference Lists*

guides their actions, that they claim or display any special acute observational sensitivity about people, or that any psychological research or researchers have been used in developing the practices. Like over-committed and compulsive practitioners the world over, the Communists are interested in the results accomplished . . . steps involving confessions and guilt . . . bring about a new 'self-role.' " (Reviewed by Robert Chin in Saving the self from jeopardy, *Contemp. Psychol.*, 1962, 7, 61-62)

LINDNER, R. M. Hypnoanalysis. In Harriman, P. L., *Encycl. Psychol.*, 1946, pp. 245-248.

Hypnoanalysis is a radically abbreviated form of deep psychotherapy in which the hypnotic method is used as an adjunct to, and in combination with, psychoanalysis. It has the advantages of speed, effectiveness, and wide application, but makes high demands on the therapist because of the unusually intense transference situation which develops. It appears applicable to all psychogenic disorders in which the patient presents a relatively intact ego. "It is the youngest of psychotherapeutic forms, and on the basis of performance to this date seems promising." (E. M. L. Burchard, *Psychol. Abstr.*, 21, 266)

LINDSLEY, O. R. Operant conditioning methods applied to research in chronic schizophrenia. *Psychiat. res. Rep.*, 1956, 5, 118-153.

The theoretical and historical background of the method of operant conditioning is first given. This is followed by a description of the modifications necessary in work thus far with 60 psychotic patients and 15 normal subjects. The advantages and disadvantages of this approach, in line with the results presented in overview, are set forth. Pp. 140-153 are given over to a discussion of this paper. (L. A. Pennington, *Psychol. Abstr.*, 31, 554)

LUCHINS, A. S. Restructuring social perceptions: a group psychotherapy technique. *J. consult. Psychol.*, 1950, 14, 446-451.

Male veterans diagnosed as psychotic were organized into small groups meeting from 3-5 times each week over a period of about six months. Six procedures of group discussion are described, some of them using playbacks of previously recorded sessions. The emphasis in therapy is placed upon patients learning more about their social roles. (N. Glaser, *Psychol. Abstr.*, 26, 104)

LYLE, J., & HOLLY, S. B. The therapeutic value of puppets. *Bull. Menninger Clinic*, 1941, 5, 223-226.

The therapeutic possibilities of puppets in a program of re-education of the mentally ill adult are briefly outlined, and some illustrative case material is given. (W. A. Varvel, *Psychol. Abstr.*, 16, 218)

McCANN, W. H., & ALMADA, A. A. Round-table psychotherapy: A technique in group psychotherapy. *J. consult. Psychol.*, 1950, 14, 421-435.

A specific kind of group therapy is described which has the possibility of reaching a larger number of functionally ill mental patients in state hospitals. The general characteristics and compositions of various groups of patients are presented as well as the procedure for conducting group sessions. A detailed transcription of recording taken of one session is included to show what takes place in this sort of therapy. The purpose is to help the patient develop reality testing in a social situation. (N. Glaser, *Psychol. Abstr.*, 26, 104)

MASSERMAN, J. H. (Ed.) *Science and psychoanalysis. Vol. II. Individual and familial dynamics.* New York: Grune & Stratton, 1959.

Papers and discussion from 1957-58 meetings of the Academy of Psychoanalysis. Part I, "Masochism," contains a review of theory and therapy by Leon Salzmann with extended commentary and discussion of the topic by 20 analysts. Part II, "Familial and Social Dynamics," contains: (a) a survey of trends in research and practice in analytic family therapy by Martin Grotjahn; (b) various papers on familial dynamics by Nathan Ackerman, Don Jackson, Stephen Fleck et al., John Speigel, and Alexander Gralnick; and (c) discussion by additional participants. (A. E. Wessman, *Psychol. Abstr.,* 34, 485)

MAY, R. Existential bases of psychotherapy. *Amer. J. Orthopsychiat.,* 1960, 30, 685-695.

Existential psychology examines the ontological characteristics in the human being: (a) every existing person is centered in self; (b) he has the character of self-affirmation, the need to preserve his centeredness; (c) he has the need and possibility of going out from his centeredness to participate in other beings; (d) the subjective side of centeredness is awareness; (e) the uniquely human form of awareness is self-consciousness; (f) anxiety, or the state of the human being in the struggle against what (external or internal) would destroy his being. (R. E. Perl, *Psychol. Abstr.,* 35, 670)

MEARES, A. *Shapes of sanity: A study in the therapeutic use of modelling in the waking and hypnotic state.* Springfield, Ill.: Charles C Thomas, 1959.

Psychotherapy relies almost exclusively on verbalizations. . . . This book is one of the few printed records in which psychotherapy is based on what patients have created nonverbally. Plastic production by patients is not a substitute for psychotherapy . . . (but) serves merely as an adjunct to psychotherapy in that it enables patients to express some of their conflicts in visible and tangible forms. . . . The use of plastic modelling, according to him, leads to a more rapid ventilation of the significant conflicts and thus reduces treatment time. (Reviewed by Adolf G. Woltmann in Silent analysan, *Contemp. Psychol.,* 1961, 6, 116-117)

METZNER, R. Learning theory and the therapy of neurosis. *Brit. J. Psychol. monogr. Suppl.,* 1961, 33, 29.

Three things have been attempted in this paper: (1) to bring together a number of recent studies of what is generally known as "conditioning" therapy, (2) to show how these therapies may be described and analyzed in the language used to describe certain "extinction" procedures in animal learning, and (3) to point out that many of the features of human neurosis and of psychotherapy may be profitably described and discussed in these terms. (C. T. Morgan, *Psychol. Abstr.,* 36, 519)

MITTLEMAN, B. Simultaneous treatment of both parents and their child. In Bychowski, G., & Despert, J. Louise (Eds.), *Specialized techniques in psychotherapy.* New York: Basic Books, 1952.

A case history is presented and the advantages and occasional necessity of the concurrent treatment of more than one family member are discussed and exemplified.

MORENO, J. L. *Psychodrama*. Vol. I. New York: Beacon House, 1946.

This is the first of three volumes covering the technique of psychodrama. Materials presented are taken from German and English papers previously difficult to obtain, psychodramatic protocols, and documents outlining the development of psychodrama from 1910-1945. Nine sections are entitled as follows: The Cradle of Psychodrama, The Therapeutic Theater, Creative Revolution, Principles of Spontaneity, Role Theory and Role Practice, Psychodrama, Psychomusic, Sociodrama, and Therapeutic Motion Pictures. Some case materials are presented. The discussion is couched in terms of the author's theoretical system. (G. A. Kimble, *Psychol. Abstr.*, *20*, 499)

MORENO, ZERKA T. The "reluctant therapist" and the "reluctant audience" technique in psychodrama. *Group Psychother.*, 1958, *11*, 278-282.

Technique of the reluctant therapist is discussed and illustrated by a case study. It points out the "negative tele" that the therapist may have for the patient and urges a positive patient-therapist tele early in the therapeutic situation. In the "reluctant audience" technique, no efforts should be spared to assist the patient in a reevaluation of his behavior; and restraint, rather than permissiveness should be offered, since mere permissiveness would inhibit growth and integration. (S. Kasman, Psychol. Abstr., *34*, 301)

MUNCIE, W. *Psychobiology and psychiatry*. St. Louis: Mosby, 1939.

This textbook, intended primarily for teaching purposes, constitutes a comprehensive presentation of the conceptions, teaching and working methods developed under the direction of Adolf Meyer at the Phipps Clinic of the Johns Hopkins Hospital. Part I, "Psychobiology—the Study of Normal Behavior," devotes a chapter to the "Historical and Philosophical Bases of Psychobiology," and three chapters to the "Student's Personality Study" in which the method of the study of normal behavior is taken up in systematic detail. Part II, "Abnormal Behavior-Pathology and Psychiatry," contains 11 chapters, answers various criticisms of psychobiological psychiatry, and then presents a detailed study of the various reaction types, specifically the pathergasias, holergasias, thymergasias, topical delusional states and para-reactions, perergasias, dysergasias, and anergasias. Part III, containing seven chapters, deals with the general problems of therapy, therapeutic aids, and the specific methods of treatment for the various reaction types. Part IV constitutes an "Historical Survey of the Concepts Underlying the Principal Reaction Sets (except the Organic Deficit States)." (M. H. Erickson, *Psychol. Abstr.*, *14*, 87)

PHILLIPS, E. L. *Psychotherapy: a modern theory and practice*. Englewood Cliffs, N.J.: Prentice-Hall, 1956.

A non-depth theory known as "interference theory" is developed to handle the breadth of problems confronting the clinician. This theory views behavior as the function of a perceiving-acting organism instead of a static layered unconscious mind. The author's difference in methodology centers around the ideographic-nomothetic controversy, his argument being that there is no difference between the methods of the clinician and that of the experimentalist. Implications and clinical applications of the theory are in terms of interference with the patient's behavior, his assumption system, etc. (N. H. Pronko, *Psychol. Abstr.,* *31,* 266)

POWELL, J. W. Group reading in mental hospitals. *Psychiat.,* 1950, *13,* 213-226.

The benefits of group reading are presented in this brief report of the author's "first year's work with reading-discussion groups of patients in mental hospitals." (N. H. Pronko, *Psychol. Abstr.,* 25, 39)

REICH, W. *Character analysis.* New York: Orgone Institute, 1945.

The bearing and attitude of the patient, his nonverbal experience behavior identifies to the observer his characterological approach, and with it his specific chaos of psychic contradictory content. In character analysis this information is used as a guiding thread to the world of the individual's past.

ROGERS, C. R. The necessary and sufficient conditions of therapeutic personality change. *J. consult. Psychol.,* 1957, *21,* 95-103.

"For constructive personality change to occur, it is necessary that these conditions exist and continue over a period of time: (1) Two persons are in psychological contact. (2) The first, whom we shall term the client, is in a state of incongruence, being vulnerable or anxious. (3) The second person, whom we shall term the therapist, is congruent or integrated in the relationship. (4) The therapist experiences unconditional positive regard for the client. (5) The therapist experiences an empathic understanding of the client's internal frame of reference and endeavors to communicate this experience to the client. (6) The communication to the client of the therapist's empathic understanding and unconditional regard is to a minimal degree achieved." (A. J. Bachrach, *Psychol. Abstr.,* 33, 88)

ROGERS, C. R. *On becoming a person.* Boston: Houghton Mifflin, 1961.

"Therapy seems to mean a getting back to basic sensory and visceral experience. Prior to therapy the person is prone to ask himself, often unwittingly, 'What do others think I should do in this situation?' . . . He is . . . acting *in terms of* the expectations . . . of others. During the process of therapy the individual comes to ask himself, . . . 'How do *I* experience this?' 'What does it mean to me?' . . . He comes to act on a basis of what may be termed realism—a realistic balancing of the satisfactions and dissatisfactions which any action will bring to himself" (pp. 103-104).

ROSEN, J. N. *Direct analysis.* New York: Grune & Stratton, 1953.

Nine papers depicting direct analysis (the psychoanalysis of psychotics) are presented. "Direct analysis is a psychologic technique having for its purpose the treatment and care of psychotic patients." The papers are: (1) Direct analysis: general principles, (2) A method of resolving acute catatonic excitement, (3) The treatment of schizophrenic psychosis by direct analytic therapy, (4) The perverse mother, (5) The survival function of schizophrenia, (6) The prognostic outlook with direct analysis, (7) Discussion of treatment techniques, (8) An initial interview, (9) Some observations on Bleuler's conception of dementia praecox. (S. Hutter, *Psychol. Abstr.,* 28, 270)

ROSS, H. D. Use of obscene words in psychotherapy. *Arch. gen. Psychiat.,* 1962, *6,* 123-131.

Sixty-three Californian psychiatrists replied to a questionnaire about the frequency of their and their patients' use of obscene words and the relationship between the two as well as their attitude toward the use of such words, its importance as expression of feelings, its association with various diagnostic categories and the psychiatrist's use of such words in everyday life. Obscene words are found to be useful in the expression of affects, particularly hostile ones. (L. W. Brandt, *Psychol. Abstr., 36*, 816)

ROTTER, J. B. *Social learning and clinical psychology.* New York: Prentice-Hall, 1954.

"The purpose of this book is to arrive at a systematic theory from which may be drawn specific principles for actual clinical practice, and to illustrate some of the more important applications of the theory to the practice." Social learning theory is applied specifically to the measurement of personality (personality diagnosis), and psychotherapy. In 12 chapters the following topics are discussed: the importance of theory in clinical psychology; criteria for a descriptive language in clinical psychology; major problems of clinical psychology; social learning as a framework of personality study; relationships among needs, values, goals, and reinforcement; relationship of social learning to other theoretical approaches; clinical measurement of personality; psychological therapy; environmental treatment of children. (F. Costin, *Psychol. Abstr., 29*, 373)

RUDOLF, G. DE M. Deconditioning and time-therapy. *J. ment. Sci.*, 1961, *107*, 1097-1101.

Severe anxiety symptoms in 35 soldier patients during severe air raids on Plymouth between October 1940 and May 1941 were definitely decreased for 16, and in no case was there any increase in objective signs of fear. No psychotherapy was used, and it is concluded that deconditioning to danger can produce improvement in the physical signs of fear. (W. L. Wilkins, *Psychol. Abstr., 36*, 815)

RUESCH, J. *Therapeutic communication.* New York: Norton, 1961.

". . . therapeutic communication remains a mixture of observable facts, reportable experiences, and nonreportable emotions. Art, craft, and science are combined to help the individual maintain his own identity and sanity against the pressures of mass communication and the collective state. . . . (It) is a skill practiced by professionals in order to help people overcome temporary stress, to get along with other people, to adjust to the unalterable, and to overcome psychological blocks which stand in the path of self-realization." The book is organized into seven parts. These are: "The framework," "The recognition of disturbed communicative behavior," "The doctor's therapeutic operations," "Long-term therapeutic goals," "Therapy with the disturbed individual," "The disturbed individual and his surroundings," and "Summary." (C. J. Adkins, *Psychol. Abstr. 37*, 141)

SALTER, A. Conditioned reflex therapy: the direct approach to the reconstruction of personality. (2nd ed.) New York: Putnam, 1961.

A reproduction, without change, of a book originally published in 1949. Psychotherapy, "based on Pavlovian principles, represents the most hopeful approach to the rapid and deep modification of human personality." (C. T. Morgan, *Psychol. Abstr.*, 36, 142)

SCHEIN, E. H. The Chinese indoctrination program for prisoners of war. *Psychiat.*, 1956, 19, 149-172.

Data, collected from interviews with 20 American soldiers repatriated from Communist Chinese prisons in 1953, are described in a composite picture. The experiences of these randomly chosen individuals were compared by three psychiatrists with the accounts of 300 other men. The prisoner-of-war experience, the indoctrination program and the reactions to the program are outlined, with reference to different reactions by various personality types. The effectiveness of the simultaneous use of several techniques is evaluated. They failed in general to change the beliefs of the prisoners but succeeded in eliciting and controlling behavior during imprisonment. Some recommendations are set forth for further understanding of brainwashing. C. T. Bever, *Psychol. Abstr.*, 31, 509)

SHRODES, CAROLINE. The dynamics of reading: Implications for bibliotherapy. *Etc.*, 1961, 18, 21-33.

Discusses interrelationship between the personality of the reader and the nature of his vicarious experience in bibliotherapy. Mention is made of semantic reactions, projection of fears and anxieties upon book characters, and provision of new frame of reference which permits the reader to understand and to alter reality. (R. F. Wagner, *Psychol. Abstr.*, 36, 141)

SKINNER, B. F. What is psychotic behavior? *Wash. Univ. Stud.*, 1956 (Aug.), 77-99.

The thesis is developed, by way of the author's theoretical position, that "psychotic behavior, like all behavior, is part of the world of observable events to which the powerful methods of natural science apply. . . ." A review is given of ongoing experiments with psychotic subjects and their rationale. (L. A. Pennington, *Psychol. Abstr.*, 32, 168)

SLAVSON, S. R. *Analytic group psychotherapy with children, adolescents, and adults.* New York: Columbia University Press, 1950.

The purpose of the author is to present "group psychotherapy in a strictly clinical setting and to base its practice on specific and accepted clinical concepts." Group therapy which he finds basically identical with individual psychotherapy and dynamic psychiatry may be divided into two general types: (1) Activity (where lack of restraint and lack of interpretation form the treatment process), and (2) Analytic (where the treatment is founded on transference and interpretation). This book is focused on the latter type. (G. A. Muench, *Psychol. Abstr.*, 25, 39)

SNOWDEN, E. N. Mass psychotherapy. *Lancet*, 1940, 239, 769-770.

Psychotherapy by explanation and reeducation "depends on the facts that in nearly all cases of anxiety or loss of function the cause of the condition is well known to the patient, or can be discovered by a little careful questioning, and that he has not associated the symptoms with the cause. He must be helped to see that the symptoms of anxiety are physiological and physical more often than . . . mental, and are a normal response to the circumstances in which they arise. . . . Once the patient realizes that the symptoms need not cause anxiety, and that the originating cause is in the past, the way is prepared for reeducation" in which the patient takes an active part. This method can be used as lectures to a class, supplemented with short personal interviews. "Mass psychotherapy of this kind has been tried over a period of 12 months with satisfactory results." (C. K. Trueblood, *Psychol. Abstr., 16,* 68)

SNYDER, W. U., & SNYDER, B. JUNE. *The psychotherapy relationship.* New York: Macmillan, 1961.

". . . within a framework of learning theory, [the therapist] will attempt to increase all behaviors which will increase drive toward or increase reward, or decrease punishment of the *desired* behavior, and he will punish all behavior which has the opposite effect" (p. 57). "If the assumption can be made that positive transference exists, i.e., that the relationship is positive, then it is logical to utilize the phenomenon of stimulus generalization in the cause of the therapeutic goal. If the client is favorably disposed toward the therapist, it is hoped he will be favorably disposed toward suggestions emanating from that source" (p. 60). "The therapist consciously uses teaching methods proudly. . . ." (Reviewed by Frederick R. Fosmire in Growth or regression in client-centered therapy. *Contemp. Psychol.,* 1962, *7,* 47-49.)

SOBEL, F. S. Remedial teaching as therapy. *Amer. J. Psychother.,* 1948, *2,* 615-623.

". . . children who are experiencing difficulty in school and who are not physically ill or mentally retarded are often in need of a therapeutically oriented remedial program. The program should combine good diagnostic and remedial techniques with a psychotherapeutic approach." Five salient steps in the program, following initial tentative diagnosis and plan, are briefly described. (E. M. L. Burchard, *Psychol. Abstr., 23,* 335)

SOLOMON, J. C. Active play therapy. *Amer. J. Orthopsychiat.,* 1938, *8,* 479-498.

The author proposes a modified methodology for the diagnosis and treatment of personality disturbances in children. In this procedure the therapist takes an active part in revealing unconscious conflicts by means of re-enacting life situations with the aid of dolls and other toys. "The author believes that active play therapy offers rapid diagnostic and therapeutic assistance in the emotional problems of childhood." (S. W. Bijou, *Psychol. Abstr., 13,* 111)

STECKEL, W. *Conditions of nervous anxiety and their treatment.* New York: Liveright, 1950.

Fear is an unpleasant emotion with a logical basis serving the instinct of self-preservation; anxiety is also an expression of self-preservation but is the product of repression. Anxiety is the reaction against the death instinct engendered by the suppression of the sex or self-preservative instinct. Anxiety, like all psychic diseases, can only be cured by psychic treatment. The psychotherapeutic method is as old as human history. The modern analytic movement, founded by Freud, is the best means for the treatment of nervous anxiety which is greater in our modern world and abnormal civilization. (R. J. Corsini, *Psychol. Abstr.*, 27, 63)

STRUPP, H. H. Psychotherapy. *Annu. Rev. Psychol.*, 1962, *13*, 445-478.

The review is organized in five divisions: New Books and Edited Works, Research Contributions, Theoretical Contributions, Special Applications and Techniques, and Trends. Encouragement is found in "the increasing effort to identify meaningful research questions, to apply greater caution in conceptual analysis, to plan more carefully before embarking on major research efforts." 77 references. (E. Y. Beeman, *Psychol. Abstr.*, 36, 815)

SULLIVAN, H. S. *The psychiatric interview.* New York: Norton, 1954.

Based on two lecture series given in 1944 and 1945, the book is a statement of the practical application of the author's views on personality theory to the technique of interviewing. The 10 chapters addressed to the psychiatrist, social worker, personnel manager, and counsellor contain: (1) basic concepts in the psychiatric interview; (2) the structuring of the interview situation; (3) some general technical considerations in interviewing; (4) the early stages of the interview; (5) the detailed inquiry: the theoretical setting; (6) the interview as a process; (7) the developmental history as a frame of reference in the detailed inquiry; (8) diagnostic signs and patterns of mental disorder, mild and severe; (9) the termination of the interview; (10) problems of communication in the interview. (E. Schwerin, *Psychol. Abstr.*, 29, 84)

TAUBER, L. E., & ISAACSON, L. E. Group-need therapy: An approach to group planning. *J. counsel. Psychol.*, 1961, 8, 260-262.

Interviews with 24 male group therapy patients in a Veterans Administration neuropsychiatric hospital elicited attitudes concerning vocational situations and aspects of group therapy. ". . . motivation for responsiveness in group therapy is to be fostered by utilizing the needs of the patient." These needs are to be determined by structured interview. (M. M. Reece *Psychol. Abstr.*, 36, 817)

THORNE, F. C. Directive psychotherapy; theory, practice, and social implications. *J. Clin. Psychol.*, 1953, 9, 267-280.

Since "psychological pressures produced by conflicting styles of life constitute a major cause of personal and group tensions," psychologists should utilize the scientific method to determine what are true, good, healthy values and should assume the responsibility for assisting patients to exchange their untrue, unhealthy life styles for healthy life styles. A scientific, eclectic, directive psychotherapy is better prepared than other forms of therapy for this responsibility. (L. B. Heathers, *Psychol. Abstr.*, 28, 247)

ULLMAN, L. P., KRASNER, L., & COLLINS, BEVERLY J. Modification of behavior through verbal conditioning: Effects in group therapy. *J. abnorm. soc. Psychol.*, 1961, 62, 128-132.

An hypothesis that seems to be gaining acceptance on the basis of experimental (as opposed to heretofore face) validity, is that the interpersonal relationship in therapy is not only able to modify the patient's behavior, but in a predictable and desirable direction. This hypothesis was cross-validated by using a group of patients in a Veterans Administration hospital, all in group therapy. The experimental condition, the independent variable, involved exposing S to a TAT-like situation outside of therapy. E responded differentially to the emotionally-toned words used by S: (a) by nodding and saying "hm-hm," (b) communicating to S via a machine that emitted a clicking sound and added on a counter, and (c) a "no reinforcement" group. Change in the patient's behavior, the dependent variable, was assessed by ratings on a scale to measure interpersonal relationships in group therapy. Significant improvement in the measure of interpersonal behavior in the group therapy was noted in condition only. (G. Frank, *Psychol. Abstr.*, *36*, 518)

WALKER, A. M., RABLEN, R. A., & ROGERS, C. R. Development of a scale to measure process changes in psychotherapy. *J. clin. Psychol.*, 1960, *16*, 79-85.

Change of process in psychotherapy described on the basis of the overall scale is conceived as a gradation from stasis and fixity to changingness and flow in such areas as one's relations to feelings and personal meanings, manner of experiencing, degree of incongruence, communication of self, construing of experience, relationship to problems, and manner of relating to others. In using this scale 24 unidentified samples were evaluated. Two judges working independently achieved a high degree of reliability in all comparisons. The results were interpreted as implying that this scale promises to tap a significant dimension of personality change. (V. J. Bieliauskas, *Psychol. Abstr.*, *16*, 138-139)

WATKINS, J. G. Poison pen therapy. *Amer. J. Psychother.* 1949, *3*, 410-418.

As soon as the dynamics of hostility begin to emerge in the therapeutic situation, the patient is encouraged to verbalize his feelings in letter form which has cathartic value. The letter is then used as a basis for discussion designed to clarify the expressed and implied feelings through which insight is established. (C. B. Greene, *Psychol. Abstr.*, *25*, 103-104)

WHITAKER, C. A., & MALONE, T. P. *The roots of psychotherapy*. New York: Blakiston Co., 1953.

This book is divided into three sections dealing respectively with the foundation, the process, and techniques of psychotherapy. The type of psychotherapy advocated by the authors is a brief, intensive therapy, the emphasis of which is the patient-therapist relationship. 63-item bibliography. (J. A. Stern, *Psychol. Abstr.*, *28*, 248)

WHORF, B. L. Language, thought, and reality. In Carrol, J. B. (Ed.), *Selected writings of B. L. Whorf*. New York: Wiley & Sons, 1956.

This volume includes nearly all of Whorf's writings on the hypothesis of linguistic relativity, i.e., "the structure of a human being's language influences the manner in which he understands reality and behaves with respect to it." Bibliography of Whorf and works related to him. (C. M. Loutit, *Physchol. Abstr.*, *30*, 639)

WOLBERG, L. R. Hypnosis and psychoanalytic therapy (hypnoanalysis). *Amer. J. Psychother.*, 1947, *1*, 412-435.

Hypnoanalysis is not a substitute for psychoanalysis but can be utilized in many cases to shorten the analytic process. It should always be used in connection with psychoanalysis and is most effective during periods of resistance. "As a general rule, patients who would respond to psychoanalysis will be most responsive to hypnoanalysis . . . character disorders, psychotics, and severe compulsion neurotics are usually resistive to treatment." Hypnoanalytic procedures are described and evaluated. 25 references. (E. M. L. Burchard, *Psychol. Abstr., 22,* 391-392)

WOLPE, J. *Psychotherapy by reciprocal inhibition.* Stanford, Calif: Stanford University Press, 1958.

By applying known laws of learning to the special problems of neurosis, a method of therapy is evolved which results in a ratio of "apparently cured" and "much improved" patients that is consistently in the region of 90%. Fundamental psychotherapeutic effects follow reciprocal inhibition of neurotic responses, this inhibition resulting directly from the substitution of assertive, relaxation, sexual, etc., responses for the previous neurotic responses. Specific techniques for forming new and antagonistic habits in the stimulus situation which formerly aroused neurotic habits are presented. 11-page bibliography. (L. N. Solomon, *Psychol. Abstr., 32,* 398)

ZIRKLE, G. A. Five-minute psychotherapy. *Amer. J. Psychiat.* 1961, *118,* 544-546.

Three matched groups of ten male patients were selected. Group I received five-minute therapeutic contacts daily over a six-week period. Group II received six 25-minute weekly sessions. Group III received no therapy. The groups were rated before and after therapy. Statistical analysis of the ratings showed Group I to have profited more from the therapy than the other two groups (P= .10), and Group II to have profited more than Group III. The data points to an advantage of five-minute therapy sessions.

AUTHOR INDEX

Starred page numbers refer to authors recorded in the Topical Reference List; non-starred page numbers refer to this text.

Abramson, J. H., 19, 285
Ackerman, N. W., 141, 285, 305°
Adler, P. T., 289°
Ainsworth, Mary D., 87, 287
Alexander, F., 306°
Allen, Bernadene V., 6, 287
Allen, F. H., 306°
Allen, K. Eileen, 289°, 291°
Allport, G. W., 294°, 298°
Almada, A. A., 320°
Amean, L., 296°
Anderson, Camilla, 306°
Ansbacher, H. L., 306°
Ansbacher, Rowena R., 306°
Arden, A. F., 139, 288
Armitage, S. G., 291°
Asmond, H., 293°
Assum, A. L., 298°
Astin, A. W., 298°
Auld, F., Jr., 298°, 303°
Aungst, L. F., 294°
Axelrode, J., 307°
Axline, Virginia, 307°
Ayllon, T., 289°, 290°, 291°, 307°
Azrin, N. H., 289°, 290°, 291°

Bach, G. R., 308°
Bachrach, A. J., 290°
Baer, D. M., 290
Bales, R. F., 262, 288, 298°
Bandura, A., 203, 207, 208, 268, 285, 290°, 298°
Barker, S. C., 5, 285
Barnett, C. D., 290°
Barrett, Beatrice H., 290°

Barron, F. B., 298°
Bartelime, P., 302°
Bateson, G., 141, 142, 285
Becker, E., 308°
Beckett, S., 11, 285
Bell, J. E., 141, 285
Bellin, H., 298°
Bennett, E. L., 267, 288
Berdie, R. F., 298°
Berg, I. A., 298°
Bergin, A. E., 273, 285, 298°
Berne, E., 141, 285
Bernstein, A., 13, 318°
Bernstein, B., 294°
Bernstein, L., 141, 285
Bertram, P., 316°
Bielinski, B., 294°
Bijou, S. W., 290°, 292°
Bindra, D., 298°
Bixler, R., 174, 285
Black, B. J., 302°
Black, J. D., 300°
Black, J. W., 294°
Blane, H. T., 293°
Block, J., 298°
Bordin, E. S., 298°
Borgatta, E. F., 298°
Boss, M., 309°
Bowers, J. W., 294°
Bradway, K., 297°
Brady, J. P., 290°, 298°
Braunstein, P., 296°
Brecher and Brecher, 274
Breger, L., 290°
Brill, N. Q., 299°

331

Stone, P. J., 262, 288
Storrow, H. A., 299°
Strupp, H. H., 302°, 304°, 327°
Sullivan, H. S., 11, 19, 38, 288, 327°
Swenson, E. W., 293°
Szasz, T. S., 140, 288

Tanber, L. E., 327°
Taylor, H. C., 297°
Teuber, H. L., 304°
Thetford, W. M., 304°
Thomas, H., 298°
Thomas, J., 5, 286, 291°
Thompson, C. W., 297°
Thompson, Diana F., 297°
Thompson, G. N., 294°
Thorne, F. C., 304°, 327°
Tiedemann, J. G., 295°
Tilton, J. R., 291°
Todd, W. B., 304°
Toomey, Laura C., 303°
Tougas, 65
Truax, C. B., 304°

Ullman, L. P., 292°, 294°, 305°, 327°

Valentine, M., 296°
Vogel, J. L., 299°
Voieers, W. D., 298°
Voth, H. M., 304°

Walker, A. M., 328°
Walters, R. H., 268, 285, 290°, 298°
Watkins, J. G., 328°
Watson, G., 17, 288

Watson, R. I., 305°
Watterson, D. J., 305°
Weakland, J. H., 141, 285, 286
Weingarten, E., 300°
Weiss, I. H., 298°
Weiss, R. L., 294°, 305°
Weitman, M., 6, 287
Whalen, Carol, 207, 285, 287
Whitaker, C. A., 328°
White, A. M., 303°
Whorf, B., 328°
Wiens, A. N., 6, 287
Wilder, J., 305°
Williams, C. D., 294°
Williams, J. E., 305°
Wirt, R. D., 305°
Witmer, Helen L., 303°, 305°
Wolberg, L. R., 328°
Wolf, M. M., 289°, 291°, 294°
Wolfe, J., 305°
Wolff, H. G., 290°
Wolff, W., 298°
Wolpe, J., 294°, 305°, 329°
Wortheimer, M., 299°
Wynne, L. C., 295°

Yates, A. J., 294°

Zalowitz, E., 295°
Zax, M., 303°, 305°
Zeller, W. W., 298°
Zimet, 208
Zimmerman, Elaine H., 294°
Zimmerman, J., 294°
Zirkle, G. A., 329°

SUBJECT INDEX